W9-CTW-447

DATE DUE

1996 Edition

CHILDREN'S BOOKS:
Awards & Prizes

Includes Prizes and Awards
for Young Adult Books

Compiled & Edited by
the Children's Book Council

The Children's Book Council, Inc.
568 Broadway, New York, NY 10012

Editor: Lisa V. Mahmoud
Designer: Carol Goldenberg

Copyright © 1969, 1971, 1973, 1975, 1977, 1979, 1981, 1986, 1992, 1996
by The Children's Book Council, Inc.
568 Broadway, New York, NY 10012
ISBN 0-933633-03-3
ISSN 0069-3472
Manufactured in the United States of America

Editor's Note &

The current edition of *Children's Books: Awards & Prizes,* the tenth since 1969, follows the format of the previous edition, published in 1992. It contains 213 awards and prizes, in four sections: United States Awards Selected by Adults; United States Awards Selected by Young Readers; Australian, Canadian, New Zealand, and United Kingdom Awards; and Selected International and Multinational awards. In response to readers' suggestions, the classified lists have been moved to the front of the book, thus making the alphabetical listing of awards more accessible. This is followed by a breakdown by section — the *de facto* table of contents, and several specialized lists by award type (nonfiction, young adult, etc.). The roster of Publications and Lists for Selecting U.S. Children's and Young Adult Books which debuted in the 1992 edition makes a return appearance at the end of the volume, followed by the title and person indices.

Some observations

Six awards, whose terminations were announced in the 1992 edition, have been removed from the present one. Nine more which have been discontinued in the interim (five of them publisher-sponsored contests) remain in this volume, for the record. Many of the ongoing award programs have continued to evolve and grow over the years — reorganizing, seeking new sponsorship, adjusting their focus, and adding new categories. The most popular new addition has been a category for nonfiction, followed by one for young adult books, revealing a welcome trend toward the publication of more high quality books in these long overlooked areas.

Twenty-eight new awards have been added to this edition. Most have been initiated since 1992 but a few are well-established and time-honored. The variety of the new award programs reflects the diversity of children's experiences in today's world and the effort on the part of publishers to mirror these experiences in books for young people. A concern for books with multicultural themes is evident as is a greater awareness of environmental issues. There are two new awards for poetry (thanks to the generosity of Lee Bennett Hopkins), one for folklore, one for fantasy, two which recognize the gay and lesbian experience, and two publisher-sponsored contests. Six new children's choice awards attest to the popularity of this format among administrators and children alike. For a bit of trivia, the single most popular book chosen by young readers during the last four years was *Shiloh* by Phyllis Reynolds Naylor, followed closely by Jerry Spinelli's *Maniac Magee*. Among Australian children, any book by Paul Jennings seems destined to be chosen as a favorite.

Many thanks

The difficulties inherent in assembling a volume of this nature are many and overcoming them is dependent upon the assistance of a great number of people. The rotating nature of award committees and chairpersons often makes them difficult to identify and locate but once found, they are extremely giving of their time and enthusiastic about sharing details of their programs. Many thanks go out to each and every one who mailed, phoned, faxed, or e-mailed updated information about their awards and prizes. Special thanks are also due Sandra Vince of Book Trust in London and Lyn Linning of the Children's Book Council of Australia for their invaluable fact-finding efforts in their respective countries.

Lisa V. Mahmoud
New York City
July, 1996

Alphabetical listing of all awards in this volume

Listing by section of all awards in this volume

PART I

United States Awards Selected by Adults

PART II

United States Awards Selected by Young Readers

PART III
Australian, Canadian, New Zealand, and United Kingdom (UK) Awards

AUSTRALIA

CANADA

Awards that are for, or specifically include, young adult literature

Awards that are for, or specifically include, nonfiction

Awards in which site, e. g., birthplace or residence of author, location of story, etc. is a factor

CANADA

Awards or competitions for manuscripts or other works that may subsequently be published

UNITED STATES AWARDS SELECTED BY ADULTS

UNITED KINGDOM (UK)

INTERNATIONAL AND MULTINATIONAL AWARDS

PART I ❧

United States Awards
Selected by Adults

Jane Addams Book Award ❧

Given annually in the fall since 1953 by the Women's International League for Peace and Freedom and the Jane Addams Peace Association (777 United Nations Plaza, New York, NY 10017) to the children's book of the year that "most effectively promotes peace, social justice, world community and the equality of the sexes and all races." A Picture Book Award *(PB)* was instituted in 1993. (Certificate)

1953
PEOPLE ARE IMPORTANT by Eva Knox Evans *(Golden)*
1954
STICK-IN-THE-MUD by Jean Ketchum *(Scott)*
1955
RAINBOW ROUND THE WORLD by Elizabeth Yates *(Bobbs)*
1956
STORY OF THE NEGRO by Arna Bontemps *(Knopf)*
1957
BLUE MYSTERY by Margot Benary-Isbert *(HBJ)*
1958
THE PERILOUS ROAD by William O. Steele *(HBJ)*
1959
No Award
1960
CHAMPIONS OF PEACE by Edith Patterson Meyer *(Little, Brown)*
1961
WHAT THEN, RAMAN? by Shirley L. Arora *(Follett)*
1962
THE ROAD TO AGRA by Aimee Sommerfelt *(Criterion)*
1963
THE MONKEY AND THE WILD, WILD WIND by Ryerson Johnson *(Abelard)*
1964
PROFILES IN COURAGE by John F. Kennedy *(Harper)*
1965
MEETING WITH A STRANGER by Duane Bradley *(Lippincott)*
1966
BERRIES GOODMAN by Emily Cheney Neville *(Harper)*
1967
QUEENIE PEAVY by Robert Burch *(Viking)*

1968
THE LITTLE FISHES by Erik Christian Haugaard *(Houghton)*
1969
THE ENDLESS STEPPE by Esther Hautzig *(Crowell)*
1970
THE CAY by Theodore Taylor *(Doubleday)* Note: The author of
the 1970 Award returned the Certificate to the donors in 1975.
See *Top of the News* (American Library Association, 50 E.
Huron St., Chicago, IL 60611), April 1975, pp. 284-8.
1971
JANE ADDAMS: PIONEER OF SOCIAL JUSTICE by Cornelia
Meigs *(Little, Brown)*
1972
THE TAMARACK TREE by Betty Underwood *(Houghton)*
1973
THE RIDDLE OF RACISM by S. Carl Hirsch *(Viking)*
1974
NILDA by Nicholasa Mohr *(Harper)*
1975
THE PRINCESS AND THE ADMIRAL by Charlotte Pomerantz
(Addison)
1976
PAUL ROBESON by Eloise Greenfield *(Crowell)*
1977
NEVER TO FORGET: THE JEWS OF THE HOLOCAUST by
Milton Meltzer *(Harper)*
1978
CHILD OF THE OWL by Laurence Yep *(Harper)*
1979
MANY SMOKES, MANY MOONS by Jamake Highwater
(Lippincott)
1980
THE ROAD FROM HOME: THE STORY OF AN
ARMENIAN GIRL by David Kherdian *(Greenwillow)*
1981
FIRST WOMAN IN CONGRESS: JEANNETTE RANKIN by
Florence White *(Messner)*
1982
A SPIRIT TO RIDE THE WHIRLWIND by Athena Lord
(Macmillan)
1983
HIROSHIMA NO PIKA by Toshi Maruki *(Lothrop)*
1984
RAIN OF FIRE by Marion Dane Bauer *(Clarion)*
1985
THE SHORT LIFE OF SOPHIE SCHOLL by Hermann Vinke
(Harper)

1986
AIN'T GONNA STUDY WAR NO MORE: THE STORY OF
AMERICA'S PEACE SEEKERS by Milton Meltzer *(Harper)*
1987
NOBODY WANTS A NUCLEAR WAR by Judith Vigna
(Whitman)
1988
WAITING FOR THE RAIN by Sheila Gordon *(Orchard)*
1989 (Joint winners)
ANTHONY BURNS: THE DEFEAT AND TRIUMPH OF A
FUGITIVE SLAVE by Virginia Hamilton *(Knopf)*
LOOKING OUT by Victoria Boutis *(Four Winds)*
1990
A LONG HARD JOURNEY: THE STORY OF THE
PULLMAN PORTER by Patricia C. and Frederick L. McKissack
(Walker)
1991
THE BIG BOOK FOR PEACE edited by Ann Durell and
Marilyn Sachs *(Dutton)*
1992
JOURNEY OF THE SPARROWS by Fran Leeper Bus with Daisy
Cubias *(Lodestar)*
1993
A TASTE OF SALT: A STORY OF MODERN HAITI by
Frances Temple *(Orchard)*
PB: AUNT HARRIET'S UNDERGROUND RAILROAD IN
THE SKY by Faith Ringgold *(Crown)*
1994
FREEDOM'S CHILDREN: YOUNG CIVIL RIGHTS
ACTIVISTS TELL THEIR OWN STORIES by Ellen Levine
(Putnam)
PB: THIS LAND IS MY LAND by George Littlechild *(Children's
Book Press)*
1995
KIDS AT WORK: LEWIS HINE AND THE CRUSADE
AGAINST CHILD LABOR by Russell Freedman *(Clarion)*
PB: SITTI'S SECRET by Naomi Shihab Nye, ill. by Nancy
Carpenter *(Four Winds)*

Aesop Prize ❧

The Aesop Prize is conferred annually by the Children's Folklore Section of the American Folklore Society (4350 N. Fairfax Dr., Suite 640, Arlington, VA 22203) on a work that best incorporates folklore in text and illustrations into a book for children or young adults. English language books published in the year of the award or the preceding year are eligible. The use of folklore should be central to the book's contents and illustrations and adequate folklore source information must be provided. The winner is announced at the Annual Meeting of the American Folklore Society in October. In addition, an annual roster of exceptional books from among prize nominees comprise the Aesop Accolade List (not included here due to space limitations). (Certificate)

1992
AESOP AND COMPANY: WITH SCENES FROM HIS LEGENDARY LIFE by Barbara Bader, ill. by Arthur Geisert *(Houghton)*
DAYS OF AWE: STORIES FOR ROSH HASHANAH AND YOM KIPPUR by Eric Kimmel, ill. by Erika Weihs *(Viking)*
1993
CUT FROM THE SAME CLOTH: AMERICAN WOMEN IN MYTH, LEGEND, AND TALL TALE by Robert D. San Souci, ill. by Brian Pinkney *(Philomel)*
LOVE FLUTE by Paul Goble *(Bradbury)*
1994
JOHN HENRY by Julius Lester, ill. by Jerry Pinkney *(Dial)*
1995
FAIR IS FAIR: WORLD FOLKTALES OF JUSTICE by Sharon Creeden *(August House)*

African Studies Association ❧
CHILDREN'S BOOK AWARD

Created by the Outreach Council of the African Studies Association (Emory University, Credit Union Bldg., Atlanta, GA 30322) to highlight the importance of the production of high-quality children's materials about Africa, this award is given annually to the author and illustrator of the best children's book about Africa published in the previous year. Books published in the U.S. for children in grades K-12 and foreign titles published by a U.S. publisher are eligible for nomination by their publishers.

The awards are presented during the annual conference of the African Studies Association, a non-profit corporation founded in 1957 and open to all persons and institutions interested in African affairs. (Plaque)

1992
THE ORIGIN OF LIFE ON EARTH: AN AFRICAN CREATION MYTH by David Anderson, ill. by Kathleen Atkins Wilson *(Sights Productions)*
1993
SUNDIATA, THE LION KING by David Wisniewski *(Clarion)*
1994
No award
1995
IT TAKES A VILLAGE by Jane Cowen-Fletcher *(Scholastic)*

American Booksellers Book of the Year (ABBY) Award ❧

The ABBY Award is voted annually by members of the American Booksellers Association (828 S. Broadway, Tarrytown, NY 10591-9884) to honor the books they most often recommended to customers during the previous year. A children's book category was created in 1993. The award is presented during the ABA convention. (Engraved Tiffany glass prism and $5000)

1993
OLD TURTLE by Douglas Wood *(Pfeifer Hamilton)*
1994
STELLALUNA by Janell Cannon *(Harcourt)*
1995
THE RAINBOW FISH by Marcus Pfister *(North-South)*
1996
GUESS HOW MUCH I LOVE YOU by Sam McBratney *(Candlewick)*

American Institute of Physics ❧
CHILDREN'S SCIENCE-WRITING AWARD

Works eligible for this award are books (and also articles and booklets) written in English or translated into English, dealing primarily with physics and astronomy, and directed at children from preschool ages up to fifteen years of age. The sponsor is the American Institute of Physics (One Physics Ellipse, College Park, MD 20740-3843). The award's purpose is to "recognize and stimulate distinguished writing and illustration that improves children's understanding and appreciation of physics and astronomy." ($3,000 to winner(s), a Windsor Chair, and testimonial; publisher also receives testimonial)

1988
SPLASH! ALL ABOUT BATHS by Susan Kovacs Buxbaum and Rita Golden Gelman, ill. by Maryann Cocca-Leffler *(Little, Brown)*

1989
MICROMYSTERIES: STORIES OF SCIENTIFIC DETECTION by Gail Kay Haines *(Putnam)*

1990
THE WAY THINGS WORK by David Macaulay *(Houghton)*

1991
AIRBORNE: THE SEARCH FOR THE SECRET OF FLIGHT by Richard Maurer *(Simon & Schuster)*

1992
ALMOST THE REAL THING by Gloria Skurzynski *(Bradbury)*

1993
STARGAZERS by Gail Gibbons *(Holiday House)*

1994
MAKE IT WORK! (Series) by Wendy Baker, Andrew Haslam, and Alexandra Parsons *(Macmillan)*

1995
THE THIRD PLANET: EXPLORING THE EARTH FROM SPACE by Sally Ride and Tam O'Shaughnessy *(Crown)*

1996
BOUNCING AND BENDING LIGHT: PHANTASTIC PHYSICAL PHENOMENA by Steve Tomecek, ill. by Arnie Ten *(W.H. Freeman)*

American Library Association Gay, Lesbian, and Bisexual Book Awards ❧

Established in 1971 by the ALA Social Responsibilities Round Table's (SRRT) Gay, Lesbian, and Bisexual Task Force (50 E. Huron St., Chicago, IL 60611), these awards are made annually to authors of books of exceptional merit published during the prior calendar year examining the lesbian, gay, and/or bisexual experience. Awards are given in two categories: literature and nonfiction. Children's and young adult books are eligible and are frequently nominated. Nominations may be made by any individual not affiliated with the publisher and must be accompanied by a brief statement of reasons for the nomination. The awards are presented at the ALA Annual Conference. We list only the years in which winners or finalists were children's or young adult titles. (Honorarium)

1995
Literature (Winner): AM I BLUE? COMING OUT FROM THE SILENCE ed. by Marion Dane Bauer *(HarperCollins)*
1996
Literature (Finalist): BABY BE-BOP by Francesca Lia Block *(HarperCollins)*
Nonfiction (Finalist): JOINING THE TRIBE: GROWING UP GAY & LESBIAN IN THE 90's by Linnea Due *(Anchor)*

Américas Award for Children's and Young Adult Literature ❧

In 1993, the Consortium of Latin American Studies Programs (CLASP) (Committee on Teaching and Outreach, c/o The Center for Latin America, University of Wisconsin, P.O. Box 413, Milwaukee, WI 53201) initiated an annual children's and young adult book award, with a commended list of finalists. The award is given each spring in recognition of a U.S. work of fiction, poetry, or folklore, from picture books to books for young adults, published in the previous year in English or Spanish which authentically and engagingly presents the experience of individuals in Latin America or the Caribbean, or of Latinos in the United States. By linking the Americas, the award seeks to reach beyond geographic borders and cultural boundaries to focus instead upon cultural heritages within the hemisphere. The award winners and other commended books (not listed here due to space limitations) are selected for their quality of story, cultural authenticity, and potential for classroom use. (Plaque and $200)

1993 VEJIGANTE MASQUERADER by Lulu Delacre *(Scholastic)*
1994
THE MERMAID'S TWIN SISTER: MORE STORIES FROM TRINIDAD by Lynn Joseph, ill. by Donna Perrone *(Clarion)*
1995
TONIGHT, BY SEA by Frances Temple *(Orchard)*

Avon/Flare Young Adult Novel Competition ❧

This biennial award for a manuscript by a writer between the ages of 13 and 18 has been discontinued. The competition was sponsored by Avon Books For Young Readers (1350 Avenue of the Americas, New York, NY 10019). ($2,500 publishing contract)

1983
DRAGON FALL by Lee J. Hindle *(Avon)*
1985
BUCK by Tamela Larimer *(Avon)*
1987
AT THE EDGE by Michael Behrens *(Avon)*
1989
FLUTE SONG MAGIC by Andrea Shettle *(Avon)*
1991
FACE-OFF by Stacy Drumtra *(Avon)*

Mildred L. Batchelder Award &

Established in 1966, this annual award honors the former Executive Director of the Association for Library Service to Children (ALSC), a division of the American Library Association (ALA). Announced during ALA's annual Midwinter Conference, a citation is awarded to an American publisher for a children's book (any trade book for children from pre-nursery through ninth grade) considered to be the most outstanding of those books originally published in a foreign language in a foreign country, and subsequently translated into English and published in the United States. As of 1979 the award has been given to a publisher for a book published in the preceding year. Before 1979, the award had been given to a book published two years previously. The award is made annually unless the award committee is of the opinion no book of that particular year is worthy of the award. As of the 1991 award, the selection committee may also designate Honor Book publishers. Donated and administered by Association for Library Service to Children of ALA (50 E. Huron St., Chicago, IL 60611). (Citation)

1968
THE LITTLE MAN by Erich Kästner, translated from German by James Kirkup *(Knopf)*
1969
DON'T TAKE TEDDY by Babbis Friis-Baastad, translated from Norwegian by Lise Sømme McKinnon *(Scribner)*
1970
WILDCAT UNDER GLASS by Alki Zei, translated from Greek by Edward Fenton *(Holt)*
1971
IN THE LAND OF UR, THE DISCOVERY OF ANCIENT MESOPOTAMIA by Hans Baumann, translated from German by Stella Humphries *(Pantheon)*
1972
FRIEDRICH by Hans Peter Richter, translated from German by Edite Kroll *(Holt)*
1973
PULGA by S. R. Van Iterson, translated from Dutch by Alexander and Alison Gode *(Morrow)*
1974
PETROS' WAR by Alki Zei, translated from Greek by Edward Fenton *(Dutton)*
1975
AN OLD TALE CARVED OUT OF STONE by A. Linevski, translated from Russian by Maria Polushkin *(Crown)*

1976
THE CAT AND MOUSE WHO SHARED A HOUSE by Ruth
Hürlimann, translated from German by Anthea Bell *(Walck)*
1977
THE LEOPARD by Cecil Bødker, translated from Danish by
Gunnar Poulsen *(Atheneum)*
1978
No Award
1979
KONRAD by Christine Nöstlinger, translated from German by
Anthea Bell *(Watts)* (Published 1977)
RABBIT ISLAND by Jörg Steiner, translated from German by
Ann Conrad Lammers *(HBJ)* (Published 1978)
1980
THE SOUND OF THE DRAGON'S FEET by Alki Zei,
translated from Greek by Edward Fenton *(Dutton)*
1981
THE WINTER WHEN TIME WAS FROZEN by Els Pelgrom,
translated from Dutch by Maryka and Raphael Rudnik *(Morrow)*
1982
THE BATTLE HORSE by Harry Kullman, translated from
Swedish by George Blecher and Lone Thygesen Blecher
(Bradbury)
1983
HIROSHIMA NO PIKA by Toshi Maruki, translated from
Japanese through Kurita-Bando Literary Agency *(Lothrop)*
1984
RONIA, THE ROBBER'S DAUGHTER by Astrid Lindgren,
translated from Swedish by Patricia Crampton *(Viking)*
1985
THE ISLAND ON BIRD STREET by Uri Orlev, translated from
Hebrew by Hillel Halkin *(Houghton)*
1986
ROSE BLANCHE by Christophe Gallaz and Robert Innocenti,
translated from Italian by Martha Coventry and Richard Craglia
(Creative Education)
1987
NO HERO FOR THE KAISER by Rudolf Frank, translated
from German by Patricia Crampton *(Lothrop)*
1988
IF YOU DIDN'T HAVE ME by Ulf Nilsson, translated from
Swedish by Lone Thygesen Blecher and George Blecher
(McElderry)
1989
CRUTCHES by Peter Härtling, translated from German by
Elizabeth D. Crawford *(Lothrop)*

1990
BUSTER'S WORLD by Bjarne Reuter, translated from Danish by
Anthea Bell *(Dutton)*
1991
A HAND FULL OF STARS by Rafik Schami, translated from
German by Rika Lesser *(Dutton)*
1992
THE MAN FROM THE OTHER SIDE by Uri Orlev, translated
from Hebrew by Hillel Halkin *(Houghton)*
1993
No Award
1994
THE APPRENTICE by Pilar Molina Llorente, translated from
Spanish by Robin Longshaw *(Farrar)*
1995
THE BOYS FROM ST. PETRI by Bjarne Reuter, translated from
Danish by Anthea Bell *(Dutton)*
1996
THE LADY WITH THE HAT by Uri Orlev, translated from
Hebrew by Hillel Halkin *(Houghton)*

Bay Area Book Reviewers Association Awards ❧

This San Francisco Bay Area awards program is designed to
honor outstanding contributions to books and literature by
writers living and working in the Bay Area. The award for
children's literature—the only category we list—was added in the
fourth year of the program, which is administered by the Bay
Area Book Reviewers Association (c/o Jonathan Sharp, Chandler
& Sharp, 11A Commercial Blvd., Novato, CA 94949). The year
sequence has been changed to reflect the year of the book's
publication. (Citation and $100)

1984
LIKE JAKE AND ME by Mavis Jukes *(Knopf)*
1985
THE HAPPIEST ENDING by Yoshiko Uchida *(McElderry)*
1986
FISH FRIDAY by Gayle Pearson *(Atheneum)*
1987
FRAN ELLEN'S HOUSE by Marilyn Sachs *(Dutton)*

1988
A GIRL FROM YAMHILL: A MEMOIR by Beverly Cleary
(Morrow)
1989
BERCHICK: MY MOTHER'S HORSE by Esther Silverstein
Blanc *(Volcano)*
1990
STARGONE JOHN by Ellen Kindt McKenzie *(Holt)*
1991
TREE OF CRANES by Allen Say *(Houghton)*
1992
DANNY AIN'T by Joe Cottonwood *(Scholastic)*
1993
BULL RUN by Paul Fleischman *(HarperCollins)*
1994
CATHERINE, CALLED BIRDY by Karen Cushman *(Clarion)*
1995
OFFICER BUCKLE AND GLORIA by Peggy Rathmann
(Putnam)

John and Patricia Beatty Award ᴥ

"The purpose of this annual award is to encourage the writing of
quality children's books highlighting California, its culture,
heritage and/or future." The late John and Patricia Beatty wrote
eleven novels together; separately, Patricia Beatty wrote many
other young peoples' books, some with California settings. She
was also a recipient of the Scott O'Dell Award for Historical
Fiction. She established the endowment for the Beatty Award in
1987. The administrator is the California Library Association
(717 K St., Suite 300, Sacramento, CA 95814). One important
standard for selecting the winner is that "the California setting
must be depicted authentically and must serve as an integral
focus for the book." (Plaque and $500)

1989
CHANG'S PAPER PONY by Eleanor Coerr *(Harper)*
1990
THE GREAT AMERICAN GOLD RUSH by Rhoda Blumberg
(Bradbury)
1991
BASEBALL IN APRIL AND OTHER STORIES by Gary Soto *(HBJ)*

1992
SIERRA by Diane Siebert, ill. by Wendell Minor *(HarperCollins)*
1993
CHILDREN OF THE DUST BOWL: THE TRUE STORY OF
THE SCHOOL AT WEEDPATCH CAMP by Jerry Stanley
(Crown)
1994
DRAGON'S GATE by Laurence Yep *(HarperCollins)*
1995
CAT RUNNING by Zilpha Keatley Snyder *(Delacorte)*

Irma S. and James H. Black Award for Excellence in Children's Literature

Presented annually since 1973 by the Bank Street College of
Education (610 W. 112th St., New York, NY 10025-1120), this
award goes to an outstanding picture book for young children—
"a book in which text and illustrations are inseparable, each
enhancing and enlarging on the other to produce a singular
whole." Formerly known as the Irma Simonton Black Award in
honor of a writer, editor, and founding member of the Bank
Street Writers Laboratory, James Black's name was added in
1992 in recognition of his ardent support of the award. Children
are the final judges of the winning book from a list of about 35
titles chosen by an adult group of writers, librarians and
educators. The award is presented at a May ceremony in New
York City. (Scroll and seal designed by Maurice Sendak)

1972
MOUSE TALES by Arnold Lobel *(Harper)*
1973
BEAR MOUSE by Bernice Freschet, ill. by Donald Carrick
(Scribner)
HARLEQUIN AND THE GIFT OF MANY COLORS by Remy
Charlip and Burton Supree *(Parent's Magazine Press)*
1974
SHE COMES BRINGING ME THAT LITTLE BABY GIRL by
Eloise Greenfield, ill. by John Steptoe *(Lippincott)*
1975
MORRIS'S DISAPPEARING BAG by Rosemary Wells *(Dial)*
THE MAGGIE B. by Irene Haas *(Atheneum)*

1976
THE EASTER EGG ARTISTS by Adrienne Adams *(Scribner)*
EVERYONE KNOWS WHAT A DRAGON LOOKS LIKE by
Jay Williams, ill. by Mercer Mayer *(Four Winds)*
1977
THE MYSTERIOUS TADPOLE by Steven Kellogg *(Dial)*
1978
FELIX IN THE ATTIC by Larry Bograd, ill. by Dirk Zimmer
(Harvey House)
1979
THE GARDEN OF ABDUL GASAZI by Chris Van Allsburg
(Houghton)
1980
GORKY RISES by William Steig *(Farrar)*
1981
THE STORIES JULIAN TELLS by Ann Cameron, ill. by Ann
Strugnell *(Macmillan)*
1982
MUSTARD by Charlotte Towner Graeber, ill. by Donna
Diamond *(Macmillan)*
1983
NO ONE IS GOING TO NASHVILLE by Mavis Jukes, ill. by
Lloyd Bloom *(Pantheon)*
1984
THE MYSTERIES OF HARRIS BURDICK by Chris Van
Allsburg *(Houghton)*
1985
CHLOE AND MAUDE by Sandra Boynton *(Little, Brown)*
1986
DR. CHANGE by Joanna Cole, ill. by Donald Carrick *(Morrow)*
1987
HEDKEDY PEG by Audrey Wood, ill. by Don Wood *(HBJ)*
1988
THE PORCUPINE MOUSE by Bonnie Pryor, ill. by Maryjane
Begin *(Morrow)*
1989
THE TALKING EGGS: A FOLKTALE FROM THE
AMERICAN SOUTH retold by Robert D. San Souci, ill. by
Jerry Pinkney *(Dial)*
1990
CHARLIE ANDERSON by Barbara Abercrombie, ill. by Mark
Graham *(McElderry)*
1991
THE ENCHANTED WOOD by Ruth Sanderson *(Little, Brown)*
1992
THE KING'S EQUAL by Katherine Paterson, ill. by Vladimir
Vagin *(HarperCollins)*

1993
THREE SACKS OF TRUTH by Eric Kimmel, ill. by Robert
Rayevsky *(Holiday House)*
1994
PINK AND SAY by Patricia Polacco *(Philomel)*
1995
WICKED JACK adapted by Connie Wooldridge, ill. by Will
Hillenbrand *(Holiday House)*

Boston Globe—Horn Book Awards ಎ

Awarded annually in the fall since 1967 by *The Boston Globe*
and *The Horn Book Magazine* (11 Beacon St., Suite 1000,
Boston, MA 02108). Through 1975, two awards were given—for
outstanding text and for outstanding illustration; in 1976 the
award categories were changed to and currently are Outstanding
Fiction or Poetry, Outstanding Nonfiction and Outstanding
Illustration. ($500 to the winner in each category)

1967
Text: THE LITTLE FISHES by Erik Christian Haugaard
(Houghton)
Illustration: LONDON BRIDGE IS FALLING DOWN! ill. by
Peter Spier *(Doubleday)*
1968
Text: THE SPRING RIDER by John Lawson *(Crowell)*
Illustration: TIKKI TIKKI TEMBO by Arlene Mosel, ill. by
Blair Lent *(Holt)*
1969
Text: A WIZARD OF EARTHSEA by Ursula K. Le Guin
(Parnassus/Houghton)
Illustration: THE ADVENTURES OF PADDY PORK by
John S. Goodall *(HBJ)*
1970
Text: THE INTRUDER by John Rowe Townsend *(Lippincott)*
Illustration: HI, CAT! by Ezra Jack Keats *(Macmillan)*
1971
Text: A ROOM MADE OF WINDOWS by Eleanor Cameron
(Atlantic-Little, Brown)
Illustration: IF I BUILT A VILLAGE by Kazue Mizumura
(Crowell)
1972
Text: TRISTAN AND ISEULT by Rosemary Sutcliff *(Dutton)*
Illustration: MR. GUMPY'S OUTING by John Burningham *(Holt)*

1973
Text: THE DARK IS RISING by Susan Cooper *(McElderry)*
Illustration: KING STORK by Trina Schart Hyman *(Little, Brown)*
1974
Text: M.C. HIGGINS, THE GREAT by Virginia Hamilton *(Macmillan)*
Illustration: JAMBO MEANS HELLO by Muriel Feelings, ill. by Tom Feelings *(Dial)*
1975
Text: TRANSPORT 7-41-R by T. Degens *(Viking)*
Illustration: ANNO'S ALPHABET by Mitsumasa Anno *(Crowell)*
1976
Fiction: UNLEAVING by Jill Paton Walsh *(Farrar)*
Nonfiction: VOYAGING TO CATHAY: AMERICANS IN THE CHINA TRADE by Alfred Tamarin and Shirley Glubok *(Viking)*
Illustration: THIRTEEN by Remy Charlip and Jerry Joyner *(Four Winds)*
1977
Fiction: CHILD OF THE OWL by Laurence Yep *(Harper)*
Nonfiction: CHANCE, LUCK AND DESTINY by Peter Dickinson *(Atlantic-Little, Brown)*
Illustration: GRANFA' GRIG HAD A PIG AND OTHER RHYMES WITHOUT REASON FROM MOTHER GOOSE by Wallace Tripp *(Little, Brown)*
1978
Fiction: THE WESTING GAME by Ellen Raskin *(Dutton)*
Nonfiction: MISCHLING, SECOND DEGREE: MY CHILDHOOD IN NAZI GERMANY by Ilse Koehn *(Greenwillow)*
Illustration: ANNO'S JOURNEY by Mitsumasa Anno *(Philomel)*
1979
Fiction: HUMBUG MOUNTAIN by Sid Fleischman *(Atlantic-Little, Brown)*
Nonfiction: THE ROAD FROM HOME: THE STORY OF AN ARMENIAN GIRL by David Kherdian *(Greenwillow)*
Illustration: THE SNOWMAN by Raymond Briggs *(Random)*
1980
Fiction: CONRAD'S WAR by Andrew Davies *(Crown)*
Nonfiction: BUILDING: THE FIGHT AGAINST GRAVITY by Mario Salvadori *(McElderry)*
Illustration: THE GARDEN OF ABDUL GASAZI by Chris Van Allsburg *(Houghton)*
1981
Fiction: THE LEAVING by Lynn Hall *(Scribner)*
Nonfiction: THE WEAVER'S GIFT by Kathryn Lasky *(Warne)*
Illustration: OUTSIDE OVER THERE by Maurice Sendak *(Harper)*

1982
Fiction: PLAYING BEATIE BOW by Ruth Park *(Atheneum)*
Nonfiction: UPON THE HEAD OF THE GOAT:
A CHILDHOOD IN HUNGARY 1939—1944 by Aranka Siegal
(Farrar)
Illustration: A VISIT TO WILLIAM BLAKE'S INN: POEMS
FOR INNOCENT AND EXPERIENCED TRAVELERS by
Nancy Willard, ill. by Alice and Martin Provensen *(HBJ)*
1983
Fiction: SWEET WHISPERS, BROTHER RUSH by Virginia
Hamilton *(Philomel)*
Nonfiction: BEHIND BARBED WIRE: THE IMPRISONMENT
OF JAPANESE AMERICANS DURING WORLD WAR II by
Daniel S. Davis *(Dutton)*
Illustration: A CHAIR FOR MY MOTHER by Vera B. Williams
(Greenwillow)
1984
Fiction: A LITTLE FEAR by Patricia Wrightson *(McElderry)*
Nonfiction: THE DOUBLE LIFE OF POCAHONTAS by Jean
Fritz *(Putnam)*
Illustration: JONAH AND THE GREAT FISH retold and ill. by
Warwick Hutton *(McElderry)*
1985
Fiction: THE MOVES MAKE THE MAN by Bruce Brooks
(Harper)
Nonfiction: COMMODORE PERRY IN THE LAND OF THE
SHOGUN by Rhoda Blumberg *(Lothrop)*
Illustration: MAMA DON'T ALLOW by Thacher Hurd *(Harper)*
Special Award: 1, 2, 3 by Tana Hoban *(Greenwillow)*
1986
Fiction: IN SUMMER LIGHT by Zibby Oneal *(Viking)*
Nonfiction: AUKS, ROCKS AND THE ODD DINOSAUR:
INSIDE STORIES FROM THE SMITHSONIAN'S MUSEUM
OF NATURAL HISTORY by Peggy Thomson *(Crowell)*
Illustration: THE PAPER CRANE by Molly Bang *(Greenwillow)*
1987
Fiction: RABBLE STARKEY by Lois Lowry *(Houghton)*
Nonfiction: PILGRIMS OF PLIMOTH by Marcia Sewall
(Atheneum)
Illustration: MUFARO'S BEAUTIFUL DAUGHTERS: AN
AFRICAN TALE by John Steptoe *(Lothrop)*
1988
Fiction: THE FRIENDSHIP by Mildred D. Taylor *(Dial)*
Nonfiction: ANTHONY BURNS: THE DEFEAT AND
TRIUMPH OF A FUGITIVE SLAVE by Virginia Hamilton
(Knopf)

Illustration: THE BOY OF THE THREE-YEAR NAP by Dianne Snyder, ill. by Allen Say *(Houghton)*

1989
Fiction: THE VILLAGE BY THE SEA by Paula Fox *(Orchard)*
Nonfiction: THE WAY THINGS WORK by David Macaulay *(Houghton)*
Illustration: SHY CHARLES by Rosemary Wells *(Dial)*

1990
Fiction: MANIAC MAGEE by Jerry Spinelli *(Little, Brown)*
Nonfiction: THE GREAT LITTLE MADISON by Jean Fritz *(Putnam)*
Illustration: LON PO PO: A RED RIDING HOOD STORY FROM CHINA translated and ill. by Ed Young *(Philomel)*
Special Award: VALENTINE & ORSON by Nancy Ekholm Burkert *(Farrar)*

1991
Fiction: THE TRUE CONFESSIONS OF CHARLOTTE DOYLE by Avi *(Orchard)*
Nonfiction: APPALACHIA: THE VOICES OF SLEEPING BIRDS by Cynthia Rylant, ill. by Barry Moser *(HBJ)*
Illustration: THE TALE OF THE MANDARIN DUCKS by Katherine Paterson, ill. by Leo and Diane Dillon *(Lodestar)*

1992
Fiction: MISSING MAY by Cynthia Rylant *(Orchard)*
Nonfiction: TALKING WITH ARTISTS, compiled and edited by Pat Cummings *(Bradbury)*
Illustration: SEVEN BLIND MICE by Ed Young *(Philomel)*

1993
Fiction: AJEEMAH AND HIS SON by James Berry *(HarperCollins)*
Nonfiction: SOJOURNER TRUTH: AIN'T I A WOMAN? by Patricia C. and Frederick L. McKissack *(Scholastic)*
Illustration: THE FORTUNE TELLERS by Lloyd Alexander, ill. by Trina Schart Hyman *(Dutton)*

1994
Fiction: SCOOTER by Vera B. Williams *(Greenwillow)*
Nonfiction: ELEANOR ROOSEVELT: A LIFE OF DISCOVERY by Russell Freedman *(Clarion)*
Illustration: GRANDFATHER'S JOURNEY by Allen Say *(Houghton)*

1995
Fiction: SOME OF THE KINDER PLANETS by Tim Wynne-Jones *(Orchard)*
Nonfiction: ABIGAIL ADAMS: WITNESS TO A REVOLUTION by Natalie S. Bober *(Atheneum)*
Illustration: JOHN HENRY by Julius Lester, ill. by Jerry Pinkney *(Dial)*

Elizabeth Burr Award ੨ঌ

This award has been presented annually since 1993 by the Children's Book Award Committee of the Wisconsin Library Association (4785 Hayes Rd., Madison, WI 53704) to a Wisconsin author or illustrator for a book of distinguished achievement published in the previous year. The award was named to honor Elizabeth Burr for her outstanding contributions to library service for children during her many years of professional service in Wisconsin. It is sponsored by the Worzalla Publishing Company of Stevens Point, Wisconsin, and is presented at the Wisconsin Library Association's annual conference. Each year, the committee also names one notable author for lifetime achievement and ten notable children's books published by Wisconsin authors or illustrators (not listed here due to space limitations). (Medallion)

1992
RED LEAF, YELLOW LEAF by Lois Ehlert *(Harcourt)*
Notable Author: Anne Pellowski
1993
WORDS OF STONE by Kevin Henkes *(Greenwillow)*
Notable Author: Virginia Kahl
1994
SHIZUKO'S DAUGHTER by Kyoko Mori *(Holt)*
Notable Author: David Kherdian
1995
CRANBERRIES: FRUIT OF THE BOGS by Diane L. Burns, ill. by Cheryl Walsh Bellville *(Carolrhoda)*
Notable Author: Nancy Ekholm Burkert

The John Burroughs List of Nature Books for Young Readers ੨ঌ

Established in 1988, this Young Readers List was named in honor of the Hudson River naturalist and essayist whose writings for children enabled nature study to blossom in classrooms all over America. Selected books contain perceptive and artistic accounts of direct experiences in the world of nature. The list seeks to encourage writers, artists, and publishers to produce books that invite young readers to explore nature for themselves.

The annual competition is sponsored by the John Burroughs Association (15 W. 77th St., New York, NY 10024). Authors, illustrators, photographers, and publishers are honored at an awards ceremony at New York's American Museum of Natural History in the spring. (Certificate)

1988
THE AMERICAN MARTEN by Denise Casey, photos by Tim W. Clark and others *(Putnam)*
THE BIG BEAST BOOK by Jerry Booth, ill. by Martha Weston *(Little, Brown)*
THE BIG ROCK by Bruce Hiscock *(Atheneum)*
DINOSAUR BONES by Aliki Brandenberg *(Crowell)*
FEET by Peter Parnall *(Macmillan)*
GLACIERS by Wendell V. Tangborn, ill. by Marc Simont *(Crowell)*
GREENS by Arnold Adoff, ill. by Betsy Lewin *(Lothrop)*
THE HOUSE OF A MOUSE by Aileen Fisher, ill. by Joan Sandin *(Harper)*
I WAS BORN IN A TREE AND RAISED BY BEES by Jim Arnosky *(Bradbury)*
THE LION FAMILY BOOK by Angelika Hofer, photos by Günter Ziesler *(Picture Book Studio)*
MOJAVE by Diane Siebert, ill. by Wendell Minor *(Harper)*
NATURE'S LIVING LIGHTS by Alvin and Virginia Silverstein, ill. by Pamela and Walter Carroll *(Little, Brown)*
NICKY, THE NATURE DETECTIVE by Ulf Svedberg, translated by Ingrid Selberg, ill. by Lena Anderson *(Farrar)*
THE PENGUIN FAMILY BOOK by Lauritz Somme and Sybille Kalas, translated by Patricia Crampton *(Picture Book Studio)*
PLANTING A RAINBOW by Lois Ehlert *(Harcourt)*
RAIN FOREST by Helen Cowcher *(Farrar)*
SAFARI by Caren Barzelay Stelson, photos by Kim A. Stelson *(Carolrhoda)*
SKETCHING OUTDOORS IN SUMMER by Jim Arnosky *(Lothrop)*
TRACKING WILD CHIMPANZEES by Joyce Powzyk *(Lothrop)*
A WALK ON THE GREAT BARRIER REEF by Caroline Arnold, photos by Arthur Arnold *(Carolrhoda)*
1989
ANIMALS, ANIMALS, compiled by Laura Whipple, ill. by Eric Carle *(Philomel)*
AT THE FROG POND by Tilde Michels, ill. by Reinhard Michl, translated by Nina Ignatowicz *(Lippincott)*
BEARMAN by Laurence Pringle, photos by Lynn Rogers *(Scribner)*
BOX TURTLE AT LONG POND by William T. George, ill. by Lindsay Barrett George *(Greenwillow)*
CURIOUS CREATURES IN PARTICULAR PLACES by Amy Goldman Koss *(Price, Stern, Sloan)*

EYES by Judith Worthy, ill. by Béba Hall *(Doubleday)*
HEARTLAND by Diane Siebert, ill. by Wendell Minor *(Crowell)*
IN THE FOREST by Jim Arnosky *(Lothrop)*
JOURNEY THROUGH A TROPICAL JUNGLE by Adrian
Forsyth *(Simon & Schuster)*
LILY PAD POND by Bianca Lavies *(Dutton)*
A LOOK THROUGH THE MOUSE HOLE by Heiderose and
Andreas Fischer-Nagel *(Carolrhoda)*
THE MOON COMES HOME by Mary Jo Salter, ill. by Stacey
Schuett *(Knopf)*
QUIET by Peter Parnall *(Morrow)*
RESCUE OF THE STRANDED WHALES by Kenneth Mallory
and Andrea Conley *(Simon & Schuster)*
WALTER WARTHOG by Betty Leslie-Melville *(Doubleday)*
WOODPECKER FOREST by Keizaburo Tejima *(Philomel)*
1990
CRINKLEROOT'S GUIDE TO WALKING IN WILD PLACES
by Jim Arnosky *(Bradbury)*
DINOSAUR DIG by Kathryn Lasky, ill. by Christopher G.
Knight *(Morrow)*
THE HIDDEN LIFE OF THE DESERT by Thomas Wiewandt
(Crown)
IF THE OWL CALLS AGAIN compiled by Myra Cohn
Livingston, ill. by Antonio Frasconi *(McElderry)*
AN OWL IN THE HOUSE by Bernd Heinrich, adapted by Alice
Calaprice *(Joy Street/Little Brown)*
URBAN ROOSTS by Barbara Bash *(Sierra Club/Little, Brown)*
THE WATER'S JOURNEY by Eleonore Schmid *(North-South)*
1991
BATMAN by Laurence Pringle, photos by Merlin D. Tuttle
(Scribner)
BROTHER EAGLE, SISTER SKY: A MESSAGE FROM CHIEF
SEATTLE ill. by Susan Jeffers *(Dial)*
CHAMELEONS, DRAGONS IN THE TREES by James Martin,
photos by Art Wolfe *(Crown)*
DAWN TO DUSK IN THE GALAPAGOS by Rita Golden
Gelman, photos by Tui De Roy, *(Little, Brown)*
THE HOIHO by Adele Vernon, photos by Dean Schneider *(Putnam)*
IN THE BEARS' FOREST by Bertil Petterson, translated by
Steven T. Murray *(R&S Books)*
NATURE BY DESIGN by Bruce Brooks *(Farrar)*
THE ROCK by Peter Parnall *(Macmillan)*
SIERRA by Diane Siebert, ill. by Wendell Minor *(HarperCollins)*
SUMMER by Ron Hirschl, photos by Thomas D. Mangelsen
(Cobblehill)
SWANFALL: JOURNEY OF THE TUNDRA SWANS by Tom
Horton, photos by David Harp *(Walker)*
TIGER WITH WINGS: THE GREAT HORNED OWL by
Barbara Juster Esbensen, ill. by Mary Barrett Brown *(Orchard)*

WALRUS ON LOCATION by Kathy Darling, photos by Tara
Darling *(Lothrop)*
WASPS AT HOME by Bianca Lavies *(Dutton)*
1992
THE CALL OF THE RUNNING TIDE: A PORTRAIT OF AN
ISLAND FAMILY by Nancy Price Graff, photos by Richard
Howard *(Little, Brown)*
COME BACK SALMON: HOW A GROUP OF DEDICATED
KIDS ADOPTED PIGEON CREEK AND BROUGHT IT BACK
TO LIFE by Molly Cone, photos by Sidnee Wheelwright *(Sierra
Club)*
ELEPHANTS CALLING by Katherine Payne *(Crown)*
JOHN MUIR, WILDERNESS PROTECTOR by Ginger
Wadsworth *(Lerner)*
NATURE SPY by Shelley Rotner and Ken Kreisler, photos by
Shelley Rotner *(Macmillan)*
THE NIGHT OF THE WHIPPOORWILL compiled by Nancy
Larrick, ill. by David Ray *(Philomel)*
ORPHAN: THE STORY OF A BABY WOODCHUCK by Faith
McNulty, ill. by Darby Morrell *(Scholastic)*
1993
AMONG THE ORANGUTANS: THE BIRUTÉ GALDIKAS
STORY by Evelyn Gallardo *(Chronicle)*
ASSATEAGUE ISLAND OF THE WILD PONIES by Andrea
Jack and Larry Points *(Macmillan)*
BACKYARD BIRDS by Jonathan Pine, ill. by Julie Zickefoose
(HarperCollins)
A BEACH FOR THE BIRDS by Bruce McMillan *(Houghton)*
THE BIG STORM by Bruce Hiscock *(Atheneum)*
CHARLES DARWIN: REVOLUTIONARY BIOLOGIST by J.
Edward Evans *(Lerner)*
COUNTING CRANES by Mary Beth Owens *(Little, Brown)*
EARTH KEEPERS by Joan Anderson, photos by George Ancona
(Harcourt)
 A GATHERING OF GARTER SNAKES by Bianca Lavies
(Dutton)
JACKAL WOMAN by Laurence Pringle, photos by Patricia D.
Moehlman *(Scribner)*
JUNGLE DAYS, JUNGLE NIGHTS by Martin and Tanis Jordan
(Kingfisher)
MAKING SENSE: ANIMAL PERCEPTION AND
COMMUNICATION by Bruce Brooks *(Farrar)*
MICROALIENS: DAZZLING JOURNEYS WITH AN
ELECTRON MICROSCOPE by Howard Tomb, photos by
Dennis Kunkel *(Farrar)*
OF THINGS NATURAL, WILD, AND FREE: A STORY
ABOUT ALDO LEOPOLD by Marybeth Lorbiecki, ill. by Kerry
Maguire *(Carolrhoda)*

PLAYFUL SLIDER: THE NORTH AMERICAN RIVER
OTTER by Barbara Juster Esbensen, ill. by Mary Barrett Brown
(Little, Brown)
TRACKS IN THE WILD by Betsy Bowen *(Little, Brown)*
1994
CITY DOG by Karla Kuskin *(Clarion)*
THE EAGLE AND THE RIVER by Charles Craighead, photos
by Thomas D. Mangelsen *(Macmillan)*
EVERGLADES: BUFFALO TIGER AND THE RIVER OF
GRASS by Peter Lourie *(Boyds Mills)*
GRIZZLIES IN THE WILD by Kennan Ward *(North Word
Press)*
SAND AND FOG: ADVENTURES IN SOUTHERN AFRICA by
Jim Brandenburg *(Walker)*
THE SEARCH FOR SEISMOSAURUS by J. Lynett Gillette, ill.
by Mark Hallett *(Dial)*
A SNAKE IN THE HOUSE by Faith McNulty, ill. by Ted Rand
(Scholastic)
TANO & BINTI: TWO CHIMPANZEES RETURN TO THE
WILD by Linda DaVolls, ill. by Andy DaVolls *(Clarion)*
WETLANDS by Ronald Rood, ill. by Marlene Hill Donnelly
(HarperCollins)
WILDLIFE RESCUE: THE WORK OF DR. KATHLEEN
RAMSAY by Jennifer Owings Dewey, photos by Don MacCarter
(Boyds Mills)
1995
BACKYARD SAFARIS: 52 YEAR-ROUND SCIENCE
ADVENTURES by Phyllis S. Busch, ill. by Wayne J. Trim
(Simon & Schuster)
THE DAY THE SKY SPLIT APART by Roy A. Gallant
(Atheneum)
EVERGLADES by Jean Craighead George, ill. by Wendell Minor
(HarperCollins)
IF YOU SHOULD HEAR A HONEY GUIDE by April Pulley
Sayre *(Houghton)*
IF YOU'RE NOT FROM THE PRAIRIE by David Bouchard, ill.
by Henry Ripplinger *(Atheneum)*
SKY TREE, ill. by Thomas Locker, Candace Christiansen,
collaborator *(HarperCollins)*
TREES by Jonathan Pine, ill. by Ken Joudrey *(HarperCollins)*
WORKING RIVER by Fred Powledge *(Farrar)*

Randolph Caldecott Medal 🖋

Donated by the Frederic G. Melcher family, the Caldecott Medal, named in honor of the nineteenth-century illustrator, has been awarded annually since 1938, under the supervision of the Association for Library Service to Children of the American Library Association (50 E. Huron St., Chicago, IL 60611), to the illustrator of the most distinguished picture book for children published in the U.S. during the preceding year. Announced in January, the award is limited to residents or citizens of the U.S. (Medal)

1938
ANIMALS OF THE BIBLE by Helen Dean Fish, ill. by Dorothy P. Lathrop *(Lippincott)*
HONOR BOOKS
FOUR AND TWENTY BLACKBIRDS by Helen Dean Fish, ill. by Robert Lawson *(Stokes)*
SEVEN SIMEONS by Boris Artzybasheff *(Viking)*
1939
MEI LI by Thomas Handforth *(Doubleday)*
HONOR BOOKS
ANDY AND THE LION by James Daugherty *(Viking)*
BARKIS by Clare Newberry *(Harper)*
THE FOREST POOL by Laura Adams Armer *(Longmans)*
SNOW WHITE AND THE SEVEN DWARFS by Wanda Gág *(Coward)*
WEE GILLIS by Munro Leaf, ill. by Robert Lawson *(Viking)*
1940
ABRAHAM LINCOLN by Ingri and Edgar Parin d'Aulaire *(Doubleday)*
HONOR BOOKS
THE AGELESS STORY by Lauren Ford *(Dodd)*
COCK-A-DOODLE DOO by Berta and Elmer Hader *(Macmillan)*
MADELINE by Ludwig Bemelmans *(Viking)*
1941
THEY WERE STRONG AND GOOD by Robert Lawson *(Viking)*
HONOR BOOK
APRIL'S KITTENS by Claire Newberry *(Harper)*
1942
MAKE WAY FOR DUCKLINGS by Robert McCloskey *(Viking)*
HONOR BOOKS
AN AMERICAN ABC by Maud and Miska Petersham *(Macmillan)*
IN MY MOTHER'S HOUSE by Ann Nolan Clark, ill. by Velino Herrera *(Viking)*

NOTHING AT ALL by Wanda Gág *(Coward)*
PADDLE-TO-THE-SEA by Holling C. Holling *(Houghton)*

1943
THE LITTLE HOUSE by Virginia Lee Burton *(Houghton)*
HONOR BOOKS
DASH AND DART by Mary and Conrad Buff *(Viking)*
MARSHMALLOW by Clare Newberry *(Harper)*

1944
MANY MOONS by James Thurber, ill. by Louis Slobodkin *(HBJ)*
HONOR BOOKS
A CHILD'S GOOD NIGHT BOOK by Margaret Wise Brown,
ill. by Jean Charlot *(Scott)*
GOOD LUCK HORSE by Chin-Yi Chan, ill. by Plao Chan
(Whittlesey)
THE MIGHTY HUNTER by Berta and Elmer Hader
(Macmillan)
PIERRE PIGEON by Lee Kingman, ill. by Arnold E. Bare
(Houghton)
SMALL RAIN: VERSES FROM THE BIBLE selected by Jessie
Orton Jones, ill. by Elizabeth Orton Jones *(Viking)*

1945
PRAYER FOR A CHILD by Rachel Field, ill. by Elizabeth Orton
Jones *(Macmillan)*
HONOR BOOKS
THE CHRISTMAS ANNA ANGEL by Ruth Sawyer, ill. by Kate
Seredy *(Viking)*
IN THE FOREST by Marie Hall Ets *(Viking)*
MOTHER GOOSE ill. by Tasha Tudor *(Walck)*
YONIE WONDERNOSE by Marguerite de Angeli *(Doubleday)*

1946
THE ROOSTER CROWS (traditional Mother Goose) ill. by
Maud and Miska Petersham *(Macmillan)*
HONOR BOOKS
LITTLE LOST LAMB by Golden MacDonald, ill. by Leonard
Weisgard *(Doubleday)*
MY MOTHER IS THE MOST BEAUTIFUL WOMAN IN THE
WORLD by Becky Reyher, ill. by Ruth C. Gannett *(Lothrop)*
SING MOTHER GOOSE by Opal Wheeler, ill. by Marjorie
Torrey *(Dutton)*
YOU CAN WRITE CHINESE by Kurt Wiese *(Viking)*

1947
THE LITTLE ISLAND by Golden MacDonald, ill. by Leonard
Weisgard *(Doubleday)*
HONOR BOOKS
BOATS ON THE RIVER by Marjorie Flack, ill. by Jay Hyde
Barnum *(Viking)*
PEDRO, THE ANGEL OF OLVERA STREET by Leo Politi
(Scribner)

RAIN DROP SPLASH by Alvin Tresselt, ill. by Leonard Weisgard *(Lothrop)*

SING IN PRAISE: A COLLECTION OF THE BEST LOVED HYMNS by Opal Wheeler, ill. by Marjorie Torrey *(Dutton)*

TIMOTHY TURTLE by Al Graham, ill. by Tony Palazzo *(Welch)*

1948

WHITE SNOW, BRIGHT SNOW by Alvin Tresselt, ill. by Roger Duvoisin *(Lothrop)*

HONOR BOOKS

BAMBINO THE CLOWN by George Schreiber *(Viking)*

McELLIGOT'S POOL by Dr. Seuss *(Random)*

ROGER AND THE FOX by Lavinia Davis, ill. by Hildegard Woodward *(Doubleday)*

SONG OF ROBIN HOOD edited by Anne Malcolmson, ill. by Virginia Lee Burton *(Houghton)*

STONE SOUP by Marcia Brown *(Scribner)*

1949

THE BIG SNOW by Berta and Elmer Hader *(Macmillan)*

HONOR BOOKS

ALL AROUND THE TOWN by Phyllis McGinley, ill. by Helen Stone *(Lippincott)*

BLUEBERRIES FOR SAL by Robert McCloskey *(Viking)*

FISH IN THE AIR by Kurt Wiese *(Viking)*

JUANITA by Leo Politi *(Scribner)*

1950

SONG OF THE SWALLOWS by Leo Politi *(Scribner)*

HONOR BOOKS

AMERICA'S ETHAN ALLEN by Stewart Holbrook, ill. by Lynd Ward *(Houghton)*

BARTHOLOMEW AND THE OOBLECK by Dr. Seuss *(Random)*

THE HAPPY DAY by Ruth Krauss, ill. by Marc Simont *(Harper)*

HENRY FISHERMAN by Marcia Brown *(Scribner)*

THE WILD BIRTHDAY CAKE by Lavinia Davis, ill. by Hildegard Woodward *(Doubleday)*

1951

THE EGG TREE by Katherine Milhous *(Scribner)*

HONOR BOOKS

DICK WHITTINGTON AND HIS CAT by Marcia Brown *(Scribner)*

IF I RAN THE ZOO by Dr. Seuss *(Random)*

THE MOST WONDERFUL DOLL IN THE WORLD by Phyllis McGinley, ill. by Helen Stone *(Lippincott)*

T-BONE, THE BABY SITTER by Clare Newberry *(Harper)*

THE TWO REDS by Will, ill. by Nicolas *(HBJ)*

1952

FINDERS KEEPERS by Will, ill. by Nicolas *(HBJ)*

HONOR BOOKS
ALL FALLING DOWN by Gene Zion, ill. by Margaret Bloy
Graham *(Harper)*
BEAR PARTY by William Pène du Bois *(Viking)*
FEATHER MOUNTAIN by Elizabeth Olds *(Houghton)*
MR. T. W. ANTHONY WOO by Marie Hall Ets *(Viking)*
SKIPPER JOHN'S COOK by Marcia Brown *(Scribner)*
1953
THE BIGGEST BEAR by Lynd Ward *(Houghton)*
HONOR BOOKS
APE IN A CAPE by Fritz Eichenberg *(HBJ)*
FIVE LITTLE MONKEYS by Juliet Kepes *(Houghton)*
ONE MORNING IN MAINE by Robert McCloskey *(Viking)*
PUSS IN BOOTS by Charles Perrault, ill. by Marcia Brown
(Scribner)
THE STORM BOOK by Charlotte Zolotow, ill. by Margaret
Bloy Graham *(Harper)*
1954
MADELINE'S RESCUE by Ludwig Bemelmans *(Viking)*
HONOR BOOKS
A VERY SPECIAL HOUSE by Ruth Krauss, ill. by Maurice
Sendak *(Harper)*
GREEN EYES by A. Birnbaum *(Capitol)*
JOURNEY CAKE, HO! by Ruth Sawyer, ill. by Robert
McCloskey *(Viking)*
THE STEADFAST TIN SOLDIER by Hans Christian Andersen,
ill. by Marcia Brown *(Scribner)*
WHEN WILL THE WORLD BE MINE? by Miriam Schlein, ill.
by Jean Charlot *(Scott)*
1955
CINDERELLA, OR THE LITTLE GLASS SLIPPER by Charles
Perrault, ill. by Marcia Brown *(Scribner)*
HONOR BOOKS
BOOK OF NURSERY AND MOTHER GOOSE RHYMES ill.
by Marguerite de Angeli *(Doubleday)*
THE THANKSGIVING STORY by Alice Dalgliesh, ill. by Helen
Sewell *(Scribner)*
WHEEL ON THE CHIMNEY by Margaret Wise Brown, ill. by
Tibor Gergely *(Lippincott)*
1956
FROG WENT A-COURTIN' retold by John Langstaff, ill. by
Feodor Rojankovsky *(HBJ)*
HONOR BOOKS
CROW BOY by Taro Yashima *(Viking)*
PLAY WITH ME by Marie Hall Ets *(Viking)*
1957
A TREE IS NICE by Janice May Udry, ill. by Marc Simont
(Harper)

HONOR BOOKS
ANATOLE by Eve Titus, ill. by Paul Galdone *(McGraw-Hill)*
GILLESPIE AND THE GUARDS by Benjamin Elkin, ill. by
James Daugherty *(Viking)*
LION by William Pène du Bois *(Viking)*
MR. PENNY'S RACE HORSE by Marie Hall Ets *(Viking)*
1 IS ONE by Tasha Tudor *(Walck)*
1958
TIME OF WONDER by Robert McCloskey *(Viking)*
HONOR BOOKS
ANATOLE AND THE CAT by Eve Titus, ill. by Paul Galdone
(McGraw-Hill)
FLY HIGH, FLY LOW by Don Freeman *(Viking)*
1959
CHANTICLEER AND THE FOX adapted from Chaucer, ill. by
Barbara Cooney *(Crowell)*
HONOR BOOKS
THE HOUSE THAT JACK BUILT by Antonio Frasconi *(HBJ)*
UMBRELLA by Taro Yashima *(Viking)*
WHAT DO YOU SAY, DEAR? A BOOK OF MANNERS FOR
ALL OCCASIONS by Sesyle Joslin, ill. by Maurice Sendak
(Scott)
1960
NINE DAYS TO CHRISTMAS by Marie Hall Ets and Aurora
Labastida, ill. by Marie Hall Ets *(Viking)*
HONOR BOOKS
HOUSES FROM THE SEA by Alice E. Goudey, ill. by Adrienne
Adams *(Scribner)*
THE MOON JUMPERS by Janice May Udry, ill. by Maurice
Sendak *(Harper)*
1961
BABOUSHKA AND THE THREE KINGS by Ruth Robbins, ill.
by Nicholas Sidjakov *(Parnassus)*
HONOR BOOK
INCH BY INCH by Leo Lionni *(Astor-Honor)*
1962
ONCE A MOUSE... by Marcia Brown *(Scribner)*
HONOR BOOKS
THE DAY WE SAW THE SUN COME UP by Alice E. Goudey,
ill. by Adrienne Adams *(Scribner)*
THE FOX WENT OUT ON A CHILLY NIGHT ill. by Peter
Spier *(Doubleday)*
LITTLE BEAR'S VISIT by Else Holmelund Minarik, ill. by
Maurice Sendak *(Harper)*
1963
THE SNOWY DAY by Ezra Jack Keats *(Viking)*
HONOR BOOKS
MR. RABBIT AND THE LOVELY PRESENT by Charlotte
Zolotow, ill. by Maurice Sendak *(Harper)*

HONOR BOOKS
THE SUN IS A GOLDEN EARRING by Natalia M. Belting, ill. by Bernarda Bryson (Holt)
1964
WHERE THE WILD THINGS ARE by Maurice Sendak (Harper)
HONOR BOOKS
ALL IN THE MORNING EARLY by Sorche Nic Leodhas, ill. by Evaline Ness (Holt)
MOTHER GOOSE AND NURSERY RHYMES ill. by Philip Reed (Atheneum)
SWIMMY by Leo Lionni (Pantheon)
1965
MAY I BRING A FRIEND? by Beatrice Schenk de Regniers, ill. by Beni Montresor (Atheneum)
HONOR BOOKS
A POCKETFUL OF CRICKET by Rebecca Caudill, ill. by Evaline Ness (Holt)
RAIN MAKES APPLESAUCE by Julian Scheer, ill. by Marvin Bileck (Holiday House)
THE WAVE by Margaret Hodges, ill. by Blair Lent (Houghton)
1966
ALWAYS ROOM FOR ONE MORE by Sorche Nic Leodhas, ill. by Nonny Hogrogian (Holt)
HONOR BOOKS
HIDE AND SEEK FOG by Alvin Tresselt, ill. by Roger Duvoisin (Lothrop)
JUST ME by Marie Hall Ets (Viking)
TOM TIT TOT by Evaline Ness (Scribner)
1967
SAM, BANGS & MOONSHINE by Evaline Ness (Holt)
HONOR BOOK
ONE WIDE RIVER TO CROSS by Barbara Emberley, ill. by Ed Emberley (Prentice-Hall)
1968
DRUMMER HOFF by Barbara Emberley, ill. by Ed Emberley (Prentice-Hall)
HONOR BOOKS
THE EMPEROR AND THE KITE by Jane Yolen, ill. by Ed Young (World)
FREDERICK by Leo Lionni (Pantheon)
SEASHORE STORY by Taro Yashima (Viking)
1969
THE FOOL OF THE WORLD AND THE FLYING SHIP retold by Arthur Ransome, ill. by Uri Shulevitz (Farrar)
HONOR BOOK
WHY THE SUN AND THE MOON LIVE IN THE SKY by Elphinstone Dayrell, ill. by Blair Lent (Houghton)

1970
SYLVESTER AND THE MAGIC PEBBLE by William Steig
(Windmill/Simon & Schuster)
HONOR BOOKS
ALEXANDER AND THE WIND-UP MOUSE by Leo Lionni
(Pantheon)
GOGGLES by Ezra Jack Keats *(Macmillan)*
THE JUDGE by Harve Zemach, ill. by Margot Zemach *(Farrar)*
POP CORN & MA GOODNESS by Edna Mitchell Preston, ill.
by Robert Andrew Parker *(Viking)*
THY FRIEND, OBADIAH by Brinton Turkle *(Viking)*
1971
A STORY—A STORY by Gail E. Haley *(Atheneum)*
HONOR BOOKS
THE ANGRY MOON by William Sleator, ill. by Blair Lent
(Atlantic-Little, Brown)
FROG AND TOAD ARE FRIENDS by Arnold Lobel *(Harper)*
IN THE NIGHT KITCHEN by Maurice Sendak *(Harper)*
1972
ONE FINE DAY by Nonny Hogrogian *(Macmillan)*
HONOR BOOKS
HILDILID'S NIGHT by Cheli Durán Ryan, ill. by Arnold Lobel
(Macmillan)
IF ALL THE SEAS WERE ONE SEA by Janina Domanska
(Macmillan)
MOJA MEANS ONE by Muriel Feelings, ill. by Tom Feelings
(Dial)
1973
THE FUNNY LITTLE WOMAN retold by Arlene Mosel, ill. by
Blair Lent *(Dutton)*
HONOR BOOKS
ANANSI THE SPIDER adapted and ill. by Gerald McDermott
(Holt)
HOSIE'S ALPHABET by Hosea, Tobias and Lisa Baskin, ill. by
Leonard Baskin *(Viking)*
SNOW-WHITE AND THE SEVEN DWARFS ill. by Nancy
Eckholm Burkert *(Farrar)*
WHEN CLAY SINGS by Byrd Baylor, ill. by Tom Bahti *(Scribner)*
1974
DUFFY AND THE DEVIL retold by Harve Zemach, ill. by
Margot Zemach *(Farrar)*
HONOR BOOKS
CATHEDRAL by David Macaulay *(Houghton)*
THREE JOVIAL HUNTSMEN by Susan Jeffers *(Bradbury)*
1975
ARROW TO THE SUN by Gerald McDermott *(Viking)*
HONOR BOOK
JAMBO MEANS HELLO by Muriel Feelings, ill. by Tom
Feelings *(Dial)*

1976
WHY MOSQUITOES BUZZ IN PEOPLE'S EARS retold by
Verna Aardema, ill. by Leo and Diane Dillon *(Dial)*
HONOR BOOKS
THE DESERT IS THEIRS by Byrd Baylor, ill. by Peter Parnall
(Scribner)
STREGA NONA retold and ill. by Tomie dePaola *(Prentice)*
1977
ASHANTI TO ZULU: AFRICAN TRADITIONS by Margaret
Musgrove, ill. by Leo and Diane Dillon *(Dial)*
HONOR BOOKS
THE AMAZING BONE by William Steig *(Farrar)*
THE CONTEST retold and ill. by Nonny Hogrogian
(Greenwillow)
FISH FOR SUPPER by M. B. Goffstein *(Dial)*
THE GOLEM by Beverly Brodsky McDermott *(Lippincott)*
HAWK, I'M YOUR BROTHER by Byrd Baylor, ill. by Peter
Parnall *(Scribner)*
1978
NOAH'S ARK ill. by Peter Spier *(Doubleday)*
HONOR BOOKS
CASTLE by David Macaulay *(Houghton)*
IT COULD ALWAYS BE WORSE: A YIDDISH FOLKTALE
retold and ill. by Margot Zemach *(Farrar)*
1979
THE GIRL WHO LOVED WILD HORSES by Paul Goble *(Bradbury)*
HONOR BOOKS
FREIGHT TRAIN by Donald Crews *(Greenwillow)*
THE WAY TO START A DAY by Byrd Baylor, ill. by Peter
Parnall *(Scribner)*
1980
OX-CART MAN by Donald Hall, ill. by Barbara Cooney
(Viking)
HONOR BOOKS
BEN'S TRUMPET by Rachel Isadora *(Greenwillow)*
THE GARDEN OF ABDUL GASAZI by Chris Van Allsburg
(Houghton)
THE TREASURE by Uri Shulevitz *(Farrar)*
1981
FABLES by Arnold Lobel *(Harper)*
HONOR BOOKS
THE BREMEN-TOWN MUSICIANS retold and ill. by Ilse
Plume *(Doubleday)*
THE GREY LADY AND THE STRAWBERRY SNATCHER by
Molly Bang *(Four Winds)*
MICE TWICE by Joseph Low *(McElderry)*
TRUCK by Donald Crews *(Greenwillow)*
1982
JUMANJI by Chris Van Allsburg *(Houghton)*

ON MARKET STREET words by Arnold Lobel, ill. by Anita Lobel *(Greenwillow)*
OUTSIDE OVER THERE by Maurice Sendak *(Harper)*
A VISIT TO WILLIAM BLAKE'S INN: POEMS FOR INNOCENT AND EXPERIENCED TRAVELERS by Nancy Willard, ill. by Alice and Martin Provensen *(HBJ)*
WHERE THE BUFFALOES BEGIN by Olaf Baker, ill. by Stephen Gammell *(Warne)*

1983
SHADOW by Blaise Cendrars, ill. by Marcia Brown *(Scribner)*
HONOR BOOKS
A CHAIR FOR MY MOTHER by Vera B. Williams *(Greenwillow)*
WHEN I WAS YOUNG IN THE MOUNTAINS by Cynthia Rylant, ill. by Diane Goode *(Dutton)*

1984
THE GLORIOUS FLIGHT: ACROSS THE CHANNEL WITH LOUIS BLÉRIOT by Alice and Martin Provensen *(Viking)*
HONOR BOOKS
LITTLE RED RIDING HOOD retold and ill. by Trina Schart Hyman *(Holiday House)*
TEN, NINE, EIGHT by Molly Bang *(Greenwillow)*

1985
SAINT GEORGE AND THE DRAGON retold by Margaret Hodges, ill. by Trina Schart Hyman *(Little, Brown)*
HONOR BOOKS
HANSEL AND GRETEL retold by Rika Lesser, ill. by Paul O. Zelinsky *(Dodd)*
HAVE YOU SEEN MY DUCKLING? by Nancy Tafuri *(Greenwillow)*
THE STORY OF JUMPING MOUSE retold and ill. by John Steptoe *(Lothrop)*

1986
THE POLAR EXPRESS by Chris Van Allsburg *(Houghton)*
HONOR BOOKS
KING BIDGOOD'S IN THE BATHTUB by Audrey Wood, ill. by Don Wood *(HBJ)*
THE RELATIVES CAME by Cynthia Rylant, ill. by Stephen Gammell *(Bradbury)*

1987
HEY, AL by Arthur Yorinks, ill. by Richard Egielski *(Farrar)*
HONOR BOOKS
ALPHABATICS by Suse MacDonald *(Bradbury)*
RUMPELSTILTSKIN by Paul O. Zelinsky *(Dutton)*
THE VILLAGE OF ROUND AND SQUARE HOUSES by Ann Grifalconi *(Little, Brown)*

1988
OWL MOON by Jane Yolen, ill. by John Schoenherr *(Philomel)*

HONOR BOOK
MUFARO'S BEAUTIFUL DAUGHTERS: AN AFRICAN TALE
by John Steptoe *(Lothrop)*

1989
SONG AND DANCE MAN by Karen Ackerman, ill. by Stephen
Gammell *(Knopf)*
HONOR BOOKS
THE BOY OF THE THREE-YEAR NAP by Dianne Snyder, ill.
by Allen Say *(Houghton)*
FREE FALL by David Wiesner *(Lothrop)*
GOLDILOCKS AND THE THREE BEARS by James Marshall
(Dial)
MIRANDY AND BROTHER WIND by Patricia C. McKissack,
ill. by Jerry Pinkney *(Knopf)*

1990
LON PO PO: A RED-RIDING HOOD STORY FROM CHINA
translated and ill. by Ed Young *(Philomel)*
HONOR BOOKS
BILL PEET: AN AUTOBIOGRAPHY by Bill Peet *(Houghton)*
COLOR ZOO by Lois Ehlert *(Lippincott)*
HERSHEL AND THE HANUKKAH GOBLINS by Eric Kimmel,
ill. by Trina Schart Hyman *(Holiday House)*
THE TALKING EGGS: A FOLKTALE FROM THE
AMERICAN SOUTH retold by Robert D. San Souci, ill. by
Jerry Pinkney *(Dial)*

1991
BLACK AND WHITE by David Macaulay *(Houghton)*
HONOR BOOKS
"MORE MORE MORE," SAID THE BABY: 3 LOVE STORIES
by Vera B. Williams *(Greenwillow)*
PUSS IN BOOTS by Charles Perrault, translated by Malcolm
Arthur, ill. by Fred Marcellino *(Farrar)*

1992
TUESDAY by David Wiesner *(Clarion)*
HONOR BOOK
TAR BEACH by Faith Ringgold *(Crown)*

1993
MIRETTE ON THE HIGH WIRE by Emily Arnold McCully
(Putnam)
HONOR BOOKS
SEVEN BLIND MICE by Ed Young *(Philomel)*
THE STINKY CHEESE MAN AND OTHER FAIRLY STUPID
TALES by Jon Scieszka, ill. by Lane Smith *(Viking)*
WORKING COTTON by Sherley Anne Williams, ill. by Carole
Byard *(Harcourt)*

1994
GRANDFATHER'S JOURNEY by Allen Say *(Houghton)*
HONOR BOOKS
IN THE SMALL, SMALL POND by Denise Fleming *(Holt)*

OWEN by Kevin Henkes *(Greenwillow)*
PEPPE THE LAMPLIGHTER by Elisa Bartone, ill. by Ted Lewin *(Lothrop)*
RAVEN: A TRICKSTER TALE FROM THE PACIFIC NORTHWEST by Gerald McDermott *(Harcourt)*
YO! YES? by Chris Raschka *(Orchard)*
1995
SMOKY NIGHT by Eve Bunting, ill. by David Diaz *(Harcourt)*
HONOR BOOKS
JOHN HENRY by Julius Lester, ill. by Jerry Pinkney *(Dial)*
SWAMP ANGEL by Anne Isaacs, ill. by Paul O. Zelinsky *(Dutton)*
TIME FLIES by Eric Rohmann *(Crown)*
1996
OFFICER BUCKLE AND GLORIA by Peggy Rathmann *(Putnam)*
HONOR BOOKS
ALPHABET CITY by Stephen T. Johnson *(Viking)*
THE FAITHFUL FRIEND by Robert D. Sans Souci, ill. by Brian Pinkney *(Simon & Schuster)*
TOPS AND BOTTOMS by Janet Stevens *(Harcourt)*
ZIN! ZIN! ZIN! A VIOLIN by Lloyd Moss, ill. by Marjorie Priceman *(Simon & Schuster)*

Catholic Book Awards 🙚
CHILDREN'S AND YOUTH BOOK CATEGORIES

The Catholic Press Association of the United States and Canada (3555 Veterans Memorial Hwy., Unit O. Ronkonkoma, NY 11779), a professional trade association for publishers of Catholic newspapers, magazines, newsletters, books, and other media, sponsors an annual awards program that includes books for children up to age 12 and youths, ages 12 and older. The awards honor the best Catholic books of the year, the contents of which must reflect "sound Christian and psychological values." No awards were presented in these categories from 1987 through 1992. (Certificate)

1984
Children
THE STORY OF BROTHER FRANCIS by Lene Mayer-Skumanz *(Ave Maria)*
Youth
NO STRANGERS TO VIOLENCE, NO STRANGERS TO LOVE by Boniface Hanley *(Ave Maria)*

1985
Children
STRINGS AND THINGS: POEMS AND OTHER MESSAGES
FOR CHILDREN by Christy Kenneally *(Paulist)*
Youth
MOTHER TERESA OF CALCUTTA by David Michelinie and
Roy M. Gasnick *(Franciscan Communications Office/Marvel
Comics/Paulist)*
1986
Children
BACK-BACK AND THE LIMA BEAR by Thomas L. Weck
(Winston-Derek)
Youth
HANG TOUGHF by Matthew Lancaster *(Paulist)*
1987-1992
No awards
1993
Children
ME AT FOUR by Mary Irene Flanagan *(Winston)*
Youth
ST. JOAN OF ARC by Margaret and Matt Bunson *(Winston)*
1994
Children
BEDTIME PARABLES, VOL. 1, by Bill Dodds *(Our Sunday
Visitor)*
Youth
JESUS FORGIVES MY SIN by Mary Terese Donze *(Ligouri)*
1995
Children
A CHILD'S FIRST CATHOLIC DICTIONARY by Richard W.
Dyches, ill. by Thomas Mustachio *(Ave Maria)*
Youth
ONE-OF-A-KIND FRIEND by Ethel Pochocki *(St. Anthony
Messenger)*

Children's Book Award
CHILD STUDY CHILDREN'S BOOK COMMITTEE
AT BANK STREET COLLEGE

Given each year by The Child Study Children's Book Committee
(Bank Street College of Education, 610 West 112th St., New York,
NY 10025) to honor a book for children or young people that
deals realistically and in a positive way with problems in their
world. In the listing below, the year cited is the year of the

book's publication. (This award was once known as the Child Study Association/Wel-Met Children's Book Award.) (Scroll and honorarium)
    See also Flora Stieglitz Straus Award.

1943
KEYSTONE KIDS by John R. Tunis *(HBJ)*
1944
THE HOUSE by Marjorie Allee *(Houghton)*
1945
THE MOVED-OUTERS by Florence Crannell Means *(Houghton)*
1946
HEART OF DANGER by Howard Pease *(Doubleday)*
1947
JUDY'S JOURNEY by Lois Lenski *(Lippincott)*
1948
THE BIG WAVE by Pearl Buck *(John Day)*
1949
PAUL TIBER: FORESTER by Maria Gleit *(Scribner)*
1950
THE UNITED NATIONS AND YOUTH by Eleanor Roosevelt and Helen Ferris *(Doubleday)*
1951
No Award
1952
JAREB by Miriam Powell *(Crowell)*
TWENTY AND TEN by Claire Huchet Bishop *(Viking)*
1953
IN A MIRROR by Mary Stolz *(Harper)*
1954
HIGH ROAD HOME by William Corbin *(Coward)*
THE ORDEAL OF THE YOUNG HUNTER by Jonreed Lauritzen *(Little, Brown)*
1955
CROW BOY by Taro Yashima *(Viking)*
PLAIN GIRL by Virginia Sorensen *(HBJ)*
1956
THE HOUSE OF SIXTY FATHERS by Meindert DeJong *(Harper)*
1957
SHADOW ACROSS THE CAMPUS by Helen Roney Sattler *(Dodd)*
1958
SOUTH TOWN by Lorenz Graham *(Follett)*
1959
JENNIFER by Zoa Sherburne *(Morrow)*

1960
JANINE by Robin McKown *(Messner)*
1961
THE GIRL FROM PUERTO RICO by Hila Colman *(Morrow)*
THE ROAD TO AGRA by Aimee Sommerfelt *(Criterion)*
1962
THE TROUBLE WITH TERRY by Joan M. Lexau *(Dial)*
1963
THE PEACEABLE KINGDOM by Betty Schechter *(Houghton)*
THE ROCK AND THE WILLOW by Mildred Lee *(Lothrop)*
1964
THE HIGH PASTURE by Ruth Harnden *(Houghton)*
1965
THE EMPTY SCHOOLHOUSE by Natalie Savage Carlson
(Harper)
1966
QUEENIE PEAVY by Robert Burch *(Viking)*
Special Citation: CURIOUS GEORGE GOES TO THE
HOSPITAL by Margaret and H. A. Rey *(Houghton)*
1967
THE CONTENDER by Robert Lipsyte *(Harper)*
1968
WHAT IT'S ALL ABOUT by Vadim Frolov *(Doubleday)*
Special Citation: WHERE IS DADDY? THE STORY OF A
DIVORCE by Beth Goff *(Beacon)*
1969
THE EMPTY MOAT by Margaretha Shemin *(Coward)*
1970
MIGRANT GIRL by Carli Laklan *(McGraw-Hill)*
ROCK STAR by James Lincoln Collier *(Four Winds)*
1971
JOHN HENRY McCOY by Lillie D. Chaffin *(Macmillan)*
Special Citation: THE PAIR OF SHOES by Aline Glasgow *(Dial)*
1972
A SOUND OF CHARIOTS by Mollie Hunter *(Harper)*
1973
A TASTE OF BLACKBERRIES by Doris Buchanan Smith
(Crowell)
1974
LUKE WAS THERE by Eleanor Clymer *(Holt)*
1975
THE GARDEN IS DOING FINE by Carol Farley *(Atheneum)*
1976
SOMEBODY ELSE'S CHILD by Roberta Silman *(Warne)*
1977
THE PINBALLS by Betsy Byars *(Harper)*

1978
THE DEVIL IN VIENNA by Doris Orgel *(Dial)*
1979
THE WHIPMAN IS WATCHING by T. A. Dyer *(Houghton)*
1980
A BOAT TO NOWHERE by Maureen Crane Wartski
(Westminster)
1981
A SPIRIT TO RIDE THE WHIRLWIND by Athena Lord
(Macmillan)
1982
HOMESICK: MY OWN STORY by Jean Fritz *(Putnam)*
1983
THE SIGN OF THE BEAVER by Elizabeth George Speare
(Houghton)
THE SOLOMON SYSTEM by Phyllis Reynolds Naylor
(Atheneum)
1984
ONE-EYED CAT by Paula Fox *(Bradbury)*
1985
WITH WESTIE AND THE TIN MAN by C. S. Adler
(Macmillan)
Special Citation: AIN'T GONNA STUDY WAR NO MORE:
THE STORY OF AMERICA'S PEACE SEEKERS by Milton
Meltzer *(Harper)*
1986
JOURNEY TO JO'BURG: A SOUTH AFRICAN STORY by
Beverley Naidoo *(Lippincott)*
1987
RABBLE STARKEY by Lois Lowry *(Houghton)*
1988
DECEMBER STILLNESS by Mary Downing Hahn *(Clarion)*
THE MOST BEAUTIFUL PLACE IN THE WORLD by Ann
Cameron *(Knopf)*
1989
SHADES OF GRAY by Carolyn Reeder *(Macmillan)*
1990
SECRET CITY, U. S. A. by Felice Holman *(Scribner)*
1991
SHADOW BOY by Susan E. Kirby *(Orchard)*
1992
BLUE SKIN OF THE SEA by Graham Salisbury *(Delacorte)*
1993
MAKE LEMONADE by Virginia Euwer Wolff *(Holt)*
1994
EARTHSHINE by Theresa Nelson *(Orchard)*

1995
THE WATSONS GO TO BIRMINGHAM—1963 by Christopher
Paul Curtis *(Delacorte)*
MUSIC FROM A PLACE CALLED HALF MOON by Jerrie
Oughton *(Houghton)*

Children's Book Council Honors Program 🙖

Irregularly, and customarily at conferences sponsored by the
Children's Book Council (568 Broadway, New York, NY
10012), the Council Honors Program salutes individuals for
sustained contributions to children. The first program cited three
people: J. Larry Brown for Child Advocacy, Fred Rogers ('Mister
Rogers') for Communications, and the author noted below for
Books and Literature. The second program cited two authors "for
a body of work that has examined significant social issues in
outstanding books for young readers." The listing below includes
honorees for literature only. (Citation)

1985 Beverly Cleary

1988 Milton Meltzer
Mildred D. Taylor

Christopher Awards 🙖
CHILDREN'S BOOK CATEGORY

Established in 1949, the award is given by The Christophers (12
E. 48th St., New York, NY 10017) to works "of professional
excellence that affirm the highest values of the human spirit."
Awards are given to books, motion pictures, and television
specials. Books for young people were first honored as of the
1970 program. (Bronze medallion that incorporates the
Christopher motto, "It is better to light one candle than to curse
the darkness.")

1970

Ages 4-8

ALEXANDER AND THE WIND-UP MOUSE by Leo Lionni *(Pantheon)*

Ages 8-12

TUCKER'S COUNTRYSIDE by George Selden *(Farrar)*

Teen-age

BROTHER, CAN YOU SPARE A DIME? by Milton Meltzer *(Knopf)*

ESCAPE FROM NOWHERE by Jeannette Eyerly *(Lippincott)*

1971

Ages 4-8

THE ERIE CANAL by Peter Spier *(Doubleday)*

Ages 8-12

A MOMENT OF SILENCE by Pierre Janssen *(Atheneum)*

THE CHANGELING by Zilpha Keatley Snyder *(Atheneum)*

Teen-age

THE GUARDIANS by John Christopher *(Macmillan)*

SEA AND EARTH: THE LIFE OF RACHEL CARSON by Philip Sterling *(Crowell)*

All Ages

UNICEF BOOK OF CHILDREN'S LEGENDS, UNICEF BOOK OF CHILDREN'S POEMS, UNICEF BOOK OF CHILDREN'S PRAYERS and UNICEF BOOK OF CHILDREN'S SONGS by William I. Kaufman *(Stackpole)*

1972

Ages 4-8

EMMET OTTER'S JUG-BAND CHRISTMAS by Russell Hoban *(Parents)*

ON THE DAY PETER STUYVESANT SAILED INTO TOWN by Arnold Lobel *(Harper)*

Ages 8-12

ANNIE AND THE OLD ONE by Miska Miles *(Atlantic-Little, Brown)*

POCAHONTAS AND THE STRANGERS by Clyde Robert Bulla *(Crowell)*

Teen-age

THE HEADLESS CUPID by Zilpha Keatley Snyder *(Atheneum)*

THE RIGHTS OF THE PEOPLE — THE MAJOR DECISIONS OF THE WARREN COURT by Elaine and Walter Goodman *(Farrar)*

1973

Ages 4-8

THE ADVENTURES OF OBADIAH by Brinton Turkle *(Viking)*

Ages 8-12

THE BOOK OF GIANT STORIES by David L. Harrison *(McGraw-Hill)*

TRACKING THE UNEARTHLY CREATURES OF MARSH AND POND by Howard G. Smith *(Abingdon)*

Teen-age
FREAKY FRIDAY by Mary Rodgers *(Harper)*
VANISHING WINGS by Griffing Bancroft *(Watts)*
Young Adult
THIS STAR SHALL ABIDE by Sylvia Louise Engdahl
(Atheneum)
All Ages
DOMINIC by William Steig *(Farrar)*
1974
Pre-School
IT'S RAINING SAID JOHN TWAINING by N.M. Bodecker
(McElderry)
I'LL PROTECT YOU FROM THE JUNGLE BEASTS by
Martha Alexander *(Dial)*
GORILLA, GORILLA by Carol Fenner *(Random)*
Ages 8-12
THE WOLF by Michael Fox *(Coward)*
Ages 12 up
GUESTS IN THE PROMISED LAND by Kristin Hunter
(Scribner)
THE RIGHT TO KNOW—CENSORSHIP IN AMERICA by
Robert A. Liston *(Watts)*
1975
Pre-school
DAWN by Uri Shulevitz *(Farrar)*
Ages 4-8
MY GRANDSON LEW by Charlotte Zolotow *(Harper)*
Ages 8-12
FIRST SNOW by Helen Coutant *(Knopf)*
SAVE THE MUSTANGS by Ann E. Weiss *(Messner)*
Ages 12 up
A BILLION FOR BORIS by Mary Rodgers *(Harper)*
1976
Picture book
ANNO'S ALPHABET by Mitsumasa Anno *(Crowell)*
Ages 7-11
HOW THE WITCH GOT ALF by Cora Annett *(Watts)*
Ages 9-12
TUCK EVERLASTING by Natalie Babbitt *(Farrar)*
Ages 12 up
BERT BREEN'S BARN by Walter D. Edmonds *(Little, Brown)*
Nonfiction
PYRAMID by David Macaulay *(Houghton)*
1977
Picture book
WILLY BEAR by Mildred Kantrowitz *(Parents)*
Ages 6-8
FROG AND TOAD ALL YEAR by Arnold Lobel *(Harper)*

Ages 9-12
THE CHAMPION OF MERRIMACK COUNTY by Roger W. Drury *(Little, Brown)*
Ages 9 up
HURRY, HURRY, MARY DEAR! AND OTHER NONSENSE POEMS by N.M. Bodecker *(McElderry)*
Ages 12 up
DEAR BILL, REMEMBER ME? AND OTHER STORIES by Norma Fox Mazer *(Delacorte)*
1978
Picture book
NOAH'S ARK by Peter Spier *(Doubleday)*
Ages 6-9
THE SEEING STICK by Jane Yolen *(Crowell)*
Ages 12 up
COME TO THE EDGE by Julia Cunningham *(Pantheon)*
WHERE'S YOUR HEAD? PSYCHOLOGY FOR TEENAGERS by Dale Carlson *(Atheneum)*
All Ages
THE WHEEL OF KING ASOKA by Ashok Davar *(Follett)*
1979
Picture book
PANDA CAKE by Rosalie Seidler *(Parents)*
Ages 7-9
CHESTER CHIPMUNK'S THANKSGIVING by Barbara Williams *(Dutton)*
Ages 9-12
THE GREAT GILLY HOPKINS by Katherine Paterson *(Crowell)*
Young Adult
GENTLEHANDS by M.E. Kerr *(Harper)*
1980
Ages 5-8
FREDERICK'S ALLIGATOR by Esther Allen Peterson *(Crown)*
Ages 9-12
WHAT HAPPENED IN HAMELIN by Gloria Skurzynski *(Four Winds)*
Ages 12 up
ALL TOGETHER NOW by Sue Ellen Bridgers *(Knopf)*
All Ages
THE NEW YORK KID'S BOOK edited by Catherine Edmonds et al. *(Doubleday)*
1981
Picture book
PEOPLE by Peter Spier *(Doubleday)*
Ages 8-12
ALL TIMES, ALL PEOPLE: A WORLD HISTORY OF SLAVERY by Milton Meltzer *(Harper)*
SON FOR A DAY by Corrine Gerson *(Atheneum)*

Ages 12 up
ENCOUNTER BY EASTON by Avi *(Pantheon)*
THE HARDEST LESSON: PERSONAL ACCOUNTS OF A
SCHOOL DESEGREGATION CRISIS by Pamela Bullard and
Judith Stoia *(Little, Brown)*

1982
Picture book
MY MOM TRAVELS A LOT by Caroline Feller Bauer, ill. by
Nancy Winslow Parker *(Warne)*
Ages 6-9
EVEN IF I DID SOMETHING AWFUL by Barbara Shook
Hazen *(Atheneum)*
Ages 10-14
A GIFT OF MIRRORVAX by Malcolm Macloud *(Atheneum)*
Young Adult
THE ISLANDERS by John Rowe Townsend *(Lippincott)*

1983
Ages 4-7
WE CAN'T SLEEP by James Stevenson *(Greenwillow)*
Ages 8-12
HOMESICK: MY OWN STORY by Jean Fritz *(Putnam)*
Ages 12 up
A FORMAL FEELING by Zibby Oneal *(Viking)*
All Ages
DRAWING FROM NATURE by Jim Arnosky *(Lothrop)*

1984
Picture book
POSY by Charlotte Pomerantz *(Greenwillow)*
Ages 8-10
DEAR MR. HENSHAW by Beverly Cleary *(Morrow)*
Ages 10-12
THE SIGN OF THE BEAVER by Elizabeth George Speare
(Houghton)
Ages 12 up
THE NUCLEAR ARMS RACE—CAN WE SURVIVE IT? by
Ann E. Weiss *(Houghton)*

1985
Picture book
PICNIC by Emily Arnold McCully *(Harper)*
Ages 6-8
HOW MY PARENTS LEARNED TO EAT by Ina R. Friedman,
ill. by Allen Say *(Houghton)*
Ages 8-10
SECRETS OF A SMALL BROTHER by Richard J. Margolis
(Macmillan)
Ages 10 up
ONE-EYED CAT by Paula Fox *(Bradbury)*

All Ages
IMAGINE THAT!!! EXPLORING MAKE BELIEVE by Joyce Strauss *(Human Sciences)*

1986
Ages 4-8
THE PATCHWORK QUILT by Valerie Flournoy, ill. by Jerry Pinkney *(Dial)*
Ages 8-10
SARAH, PLAIN AND TALL by Patricia MacLachlan *(Harper)*
Ages 8 up
PROMISE NOT TO TELL by Carolyn Polese, ill. by Jennifer Barrett *(Human Sciences)*
Ages 10-12
UNDERDOG by Marilyn Sachs *(Doubleday)*
Young Adult
THE MOUNT RUSHMORE STORY by Judith St. George *(Putnam)*

1987
Ages 4-6
DUNCAN AND DOLORES by Barbara Samuels *(Bradbury)*
Ages 6-8
THE PURPLE COAT by Amy Hest, ill. by Amy Schwartz *(Four Winds)*
Ages 8-12
BORROWED SUMMER by Marion Walker Doren *(Harper)*
Young Adult
CLASS DISMISSED II by Mel Glenn *(Clarion)*

1988
Picture Book
HECKEDY PEG by Audrey Wood, ill. by Don Wood *(HBJ)*
Ages 6-8
HUMPHREY'S BEAR by Jan Wahl, ill. by William Joyce *(Holt)*
Ages 9-12
THE GOLD CADILLAC by Mildred D. Taylor *(Dial)*
Ages 12 up
INTO A STRANGE LAND: UNACCOMPANIED REFUGEE YOUTH IN AMERICA by Brent Ashabranner and Melissa Ashabranner *(Dodd)*

1989
Ages 5-7
THE GOOD-BYE BOOK by Judith Viorst, ill. by Kay Chorao *(Macmillan)*
Ages 7-10
FAMILY FARM by Thomas Locker *(Dial)*
Ages 10-14
LIES, DECEPTION AND TRUTH by Ann E. Weiss *(Houghton)*

Young Adult
LOOKING THE TIGER IN THE EYE: CONFRONTING THE
NUCLEAR THREAT by Carl B. Feldbaum and Ronald J. Bee
(Harper)

1990
Ages 4-7
KEEPING A CHRISTMAS SECRET by Phyllis Reynolds Naylor,
ill. by Lena Shiffman *(Atheneum)*
Ages 8-11
WILLIAM AND GRANDPA by Alice Schertle, ill. by Lydia
Dabcovich *(Lothrop)*
Ages 10-12
CAN THE WHALES BE SAVED? by Philip Whitfield *(Viking)*
Young Adult
SO MUCH TO TELL YOU by John Marsden *(Joy Street/Little,
Brown)*

1991
Ages 9-12
MISSISSIPPI BRIDGE by Mildred D. Taylor, ill. by Max
Ginsburg *(Dial)*
All Ages
PAUL REVERE'S RIDE by Henry Wadsworth Longfellow, ill.
by Ted Rand *(Dutton)*

1992
Ages 4-6
SOMEBODY LOVES YOU, MR. HATCH by Eileen Spinelli, ill.
by Paul Yalowitz *(Bradbury)*
Ages 6-8
STEPHEN'S FEAST by Jean Richardson, ill. by Alice Englander
(Little, Brown)
Ages 8-10
THE GOLD COIN by Alma Flor Ada, translated by Bernice
Randall, ill. by Neil Waldman *(Atheneum)*
Ages 10 up
THE STAR FISHER by Laurence Yep *(Morrow)*
All ages
WHERE DOES GOD LIVE? QUESTIONS AND ANSWERS
FOR PARENTS AND CHILDREN by Marc Gellman and
Thomas Hartman, ill. by William Zdinak *(Triumph)*

1993
Ages 5-8
THE RAINBOW FISH by Marcus Pfister, translated by J. Alison
James *(North-South)*
Ages 6-8
ROSIE AND THE YELLOW RIBBON by Paula DePaolo, ill. by
Janet Wolf *(Little, Brown)*
Ages 8-12
LETTERS FROM RIFKA by Karen Hesse *(Holt)*

Ages 12 up
MISSISSIPPI CHALLENGE by Mildred Pitts Walter *(Bradbury)*
1994
Ages 5-8
THE CRYSTAL BALL by Gerda Marie Scheidl, ill. by Nathalie
Duroussy, translated by Rosemary Lanning *(North-South)*
Ages 10 up
IT'S OUR WORLD, TOO! STORIES OF YOUNG PEOPLE
WHO ARE MAKING A DIFFERENCE by Phillip Hoose *(Joy
Street/Little, Brown)*
Young Adult
ANNE FRANK, BEYOND THE DIARY: A PHOTOGRAPHIC
REMEMBRANCE by Rian Verhoeven and Ruud van der Rol,
translated by Tony Langham and Plym Peters *(Viking)*
1995
Ages 4-6
I'LL SEE YOU WHEN THE MOON IS FULL by Susi Gregg
Fowler, ill. by Jim Fowler *(Greenwillow)*
Ages 6-8
PRIZE IN THE SNOW by Bill Easterling, ill. by Mary Beth
Owens *(Little, Brown)*
Ages 8-12
THE LEDGERBOOK OF THOMAS BLUE EAGLE by Jewel H.
Grutman and Gay Matthaei, ill. by Adam Cvijanovic
(Thomasson-Grant)
Ages 12 up
TAKING HOLD: MY JOURNEY INTO BLINDNESS by Sally
Hobart Alexander *(Macmillan)*
1996
Ages 6-9
THE CHRISTMAS MIRACLE OF JONATHAN TOOMEY by
Susan Wojciechowski, ill. by P.J. Lynch *(Candlewick)*
Ages 10-12
BEEN TO YESTERDAYS: POEMS OF A LIFE by Lee Bennett
Hopkins, ill. by Charlene Rendeiro *(Wordsong/Boyds Mills)*
Ages 12-14
MOTHER JONES: ONE WOMAN'S FIGHT FOR LABOR by
Betsy Harvey Kraft *(Clarion)*
Young Adult
PARALLEL JOURNEYS by Eleanor Ayer with Helen Waterford
and Alfons Heck *(Atheneum)*

Colorado Book Awards 🍂

Formerly known as the Colorado Book Authors Competition, this award program is sponsored by the Colorado Center for the Book (P.O. Box 360, Denver, CO 80201). Books written by Colorado residents are honored in five categories, including Children's *(C)* and Young Adult *(YA)*, the categories we list. In 1995 the award year was changed to reflect the year of the award presentation rather than the year of the book's publication. (Honored at annual awards banquet; $500 cash prize)

1991
C: SAND DUNE PONY by Franklin Folsom *(Roberts Rinehart)*
1992
C/YA: EAGLES: HUNTERS OF THE SKY by Ann C. Cooper *(Roberts Rinehart)*
1993
C: WAY OUT WEST LIVES A COYOTE NAMED FRANK by Jillian Lund *(Dutton)*
YA: BEARDANCE by Will Hobbs *(Atheneum)*
1995
C: GOOSE AND THE MOUNTAIN LION by Marian Harris *(Northland)*
YA: THE MERLIN EFFECT by Tom Barron *(Philomel)*

Commonwealth Club of California Book Awards 🍂
CHILDREN'S BOOK CATEGORIES

This annual awards program honors books "with exceptional literary merit" in several categories. As of the program for books published in 1990, there have been two children's book categories: fiction or nonfiction for children up to 10, and also for children ages 11-16. Authors must have been legal residents of California at the time the manuscript was submitted for publication. In the listing below, the year cited is the year of a book's publication. The sponsor is Commonwealth Club of California (595 Market St., San Francisco, CA 94105). (For children's books, silver medals)

1939
BRIGHT HERITAGE by Mary Virginia Powers *(Longmans)*

1940
BLUE WILLOW by Doris Gates *(Viking)*

1942
LONG ADVENTURE: THE STORY OF WINSTON CHURCHILL by Hildegarde Hawthorne *(Appleton)*

1943
SPURS FOR ANTONIA by Katherine Wigmore Eyre *(Oxford)*

1944
THUNDERBOLT HOUSE by Howard Pease *(Doubleday)*

1945
THE SINGING CAVE by Margaret Leighton *(Houghton)*

1946
TOWARDS OREGON by E. H. Staffelbach *(Macrae)*

1947
SANCHO OF THE LONG, LONG HORNS by Allen R. Bosworth *(Doubleday)*

1948
SEABIRD by Holling C. Holling *(Houghton)*

1949
AT THE PALACE GATES by Helen Rand Parrish *(Viking)*

1950
TOMAS AND THE RED HEADED ANGEL by Marion Garthwaite *(Messner)*

1951
SANDRA AND THE RIGHT PRINCE by Mildred N. Anderson *(Oxford)*

1952
WAPITI THE ELK by Rutherford Montgomery *(Little, Brown)*

1953
ROARING RIVER by Bill Brown *(Coward)*

1954
EPICS OF EVEREST by Leonard Wibberley *(Farrar)*

1955
WESTWARD THE EAGLE by Frederick A. Lane *(Holt)*

1956
SPOOK THE MUSTANG by Harlan Thompson *(Doubleday)*

1957
DAVID AND THE PHOENIX by Edward Ormondroyd *(Follett)*

1958
FIRST SCIENTIST OF ALASKA: WILLIAM HEALY DALL by Edward A. Herron *(Messner)*

1959
THIS IS THE DESERT by Phillip H. Ault *(Dodd)*
1960
HAWAII, THE ALOHA STATE by Helen Bauer *(Doubleday)*
1961
THE GRAY SEA RAIDERS by Gordon D. Shirreffs *(Chilton)*
1962
FIRST WOMAN AMBULANCE SURGEON: EMILY
BARRINGER by Iris Noble *(Messner)*
1963
THE KEYS AND THE CANDLE by Maryhale Woolsey
(Abingdon)
1964
THE SPELL IS CAST by Eleanor Cameron *(Atlantic-Little, Brown)*
1965
CAMPION TOWERS by John and Patricia Beatty *(Macmillan)*
1966
CHANCY AND THE GRAND RASCAL by Sid Fleischman
(Atlantic-Little, Brown)
1967
SILENT SHIP, SILENT SEA by Robb White *(Doubleday)*
1968
QUEST FOR FREEDOM by Paul Rink *(Messner)*
1969
THE CAY by Theodore Taylor *(Doubleday)*
1970
JONAH AND THE GREAT FISH by Clyde Robert Bulla
(Crowell)
1971
ANNIE AND THE OLD ONE by Miska Miles *(Atlantic-Little, Brown)*
1972
SAMURAI OF GOLD HILL by Yoshiko Uchida *(Scribner)*
1973
No Award
1974
THE PAPER PARTY by Don Freeman *(Viking)*
1975
COYOTES, LAST ANIMALS ON EARTH? by Harold E.
Thomas *(Lothrop)*
1976
THE BOY WHO SANG THE BIRDS by John Weston *(Scribner)*
1977
A SHEPHERD WATCHES, A SHEPHERD SINGS by Louis
Irigaray and Theodore Taylor *(Doubleday)*

1978
NORTH OF DANGER by Dale Fife *(Dutton)*
1979
THE FOOL AND THE DANCING BEAR by Pamela Stearns
(Atlantic-Little, Brown)
1980
FLIGHT OF THE SPARROW by Julia Cunningham *(Pantheon)*
THE HALF-A-MOON INN by Paul Fleischman *(Harper)*
1981
A JAR OF DREAMS by Yoshiko Uchida *(McElderry)*
1982
JAKE AND HONEYBUNCH GO TO HEAVEN by Margot
Zemach *(Farrar)*
1983
DEAR MR. HENSHAW by Beverly Cleary *(Morrow)*
1984
MONKEY PUZZLE AND OTHER POEMS by Myra Cohn
Livingston *(McElderry)*
1985
THE WILLOW MAIDEN by Meghan Collins *(Dial)*
1986
THE SECRET OF THE MOUNTAIN by Esther Linfield
(Greenwillow)
1987
NELL'S QUILT by Susan Terris *(Farrar)*
1988
STEP INTO THE NIGHT by Joanne Ryder *(Four Winds)*
1989
No Award
1990
Up to 10: BABUSHKA'S DOLL by Patricia Polacco *(Simon &*
Schuster)
11-16: THE FABULOUS FIFTY by Morton Grosser *(Atheneum)*
1991
Up to 10: FLY AWAY HOME by Eve Bunting *(Clarion)*
11-16: JAYHAWKER by Patricia Beatty *(Morrow)*
1992
Up to 10: A BOWL OF MISCHIEF by Ellen Kindt McKenzie
(Holt)
CHICKEN SUNDAY by Patricia Polacco *(Philomel)*
11-16: EARTHQUAKE AT DAWN by Kristiana Gregory
(Harcourt)
1993
Up to 10: GRANDFATHER'S JOURNEY by Allen Say
(Houghton)
11-16: DRAGON'S GATE by Laurence Yep *(HarperCollins)*
BULL RUN by Paul Fleischman *(HarperCollins)*

1994
Up to 10: SMOKY NIGHT by Eve Bunting *(Harcourt)*
11-16: CATHERINE, CALLED BIRDY by Karen Cushman
(Clarion)
1995
Up to 10: THE FAITHFUL FRIEND by Robert D. San Souci
(Four Winds)
11 to 16: A TIME FOR DANCING by Davida Wills Hurwin
(Little Brown)
CANTO FAMILIAR by Gary Soto *(Harcourt)*

Marguerite de Angeli Contest🦋

This contest was designed to encourage the writing of fiction for
and about children in the same spirit as the works of Marguerite
De Angeli (1889-1987), author and illustrator of twenty-eight
works and winner of numerous awards. Sponsored by Bantam
Doubleday Dell Books for Young Readers (1540 Broadway, New
York, NY 10036), the prize of a book contract for a hardcover
and a paperback edition, including an advance and royalties, is
awarded annually to a work of fiction suitable for readers 7 to
10 years of age that concerns the diversity of the American
experience, either contemporary or historical. The contest is open
to U.S. and Canadian writers who have not previously published
a novel for middle-grade readers. ($1,500 in cash and a $3,500
advance against royalties)

1992
JACKSON JONES AND THE PUDDLE OF THORNS by Mary
Quattlebaum *(Delacorte, 1994)*
1993
SETH AND SAMONA by Joanne Hyppolite *(Delacorte, 1995)*
1994
No prizewinner
1995
BEASTLE *(tentative title)* by Vicki Winslow Wolfinger

Delacorte Press Prize
for a First Young Adult Novel

This annual contest is open to American and Canadian writers who have not previously published a young adult novel. Submissions must have contemporary settings and be suitable for readers ages 12 to 18. The sponsor is Delacorte Press (Department BFYR, 1540 Broadway, New York, NY 10036). ($1,500 cash prize, and $6,000 advance against royalties for hardcover edition published by Delacorte Press and paperback edition published by Dell)

See also Marguerite de Angeli Contest.

1983
CENTER LINE by Joyce Sweeney *(Delacorte)*
1984
WALK THROUGH COLD FIRE by Cin Forshay-Lunsford *(Delacorte)*
1985
THE IMPACT ZONE by Ray Maloney *(Delacorte)*
1986
No prizewinner
1987
CAL CAMERON BY DAY, SPIDER-MAN BY NIGHT by A. E. Cannon *(Delacorte)*
1988
OZZY ON THE OUTSIDE by R. E. Allen *(Delacorte)*
1989
HANK by James Sauer *(Delacorte)*
1990
LIZARD by Dennis Covington *(Delacorte)*
1991
SQUASHED by Joan Bauer *(Delacorte)*
1992
LIFE BELTS by Jane Hosie-Bounar *(Delacorte)*
1993
No prizewinner
1994
UNDER THE MERMAID ANGEL by Martha A. Moore *(Delacorte)*
1995
No prizewinner

Dutton Children's Books
Picture Book Competition 🙐

This competition, which aimed to encourage new and talented children's book illustrators, has been discontinued. It was open to students and recent graduates of art schools, design institutes, or university programs whose work had not previously been published. The sponsor was E. P. Dutton Children's Books (375 Hudson St., New York, NY 10014) which had an option to publish any prizewinner and offered an advance and royalties in addition to the prize money. (Cash prize)

1986
MINERVA LOUISE by Janet Morgan Stoeke *(Dutton)*
1988
Winner was Annette Le Blanc; entry not published
1990
No winners

Margaret A. Edwards Award 🙐

Named for a youth services librarian who worked at the Enoch Pratt Free Library in Baltimore, MD, and wrote *The Fair Garden and the Swarm of Beasts: The Library and the Young Adult*, this award is sponsored by the Young Adult Library Services Association of the American Library Association (50 East Huron St., Chicago, IL 60611) in cooperation with *School Library Journal*, the donor of the stipend. Formerly the Young Adult Author Achievement Award, the award is for a living writer whose "book or books, over a period of time, have been accepted by young people as an authentic voice that continues to illuminate their experiences and emotions, giving insight into their lives." ($1,000 and citation)

1988   S. E. Hinton
1990   Richard Peck
1991   Robert Cormier
1992   Lois Duncan
1993   M.E. Kerr
1994   Walter Dean Myers
1995   Judy Blume

Empire State Award for Excellence in Literature for Young People ❧

This award is for a body of work "which represents excellence in children's or young adult literature and has made a significant contribution to literature for young people." Recipients must be residents of New York State. The sponsor is the Youth Services Section of the New York Library Association (252 Hudson Ave., Albany, NY 12210). (Medallion)

1990 Maurice Sendak
1991 Madeleine L'Engle
1992 Leo and Diane Dillon
1993 Russell Freedman
1994 Paula Fox
1995 Ed Young

Joan Fassler Memorial Book Award ❧

Sponsored by the Association for the Care of Children's Health (7910 Woodmont Ave., Suite 300, Bethesda, MD 20814-3015), a multidisciplinary nonprofit membership organization of professionals and parents working together "to ensure that all aspects of children's health care are family-centered, psychosocially sound, and developmentally appropriate," this award is named for the late Joan Fassler, a child psychologist and children's trade book author. It is for a book that makes an "outstanding contribution to children's literature dealing with hospitalization, disease, disabling conditions, death, and dying." ($1,000 and plaque)

1989
SAYING GOODBYE TO GRANDMA by Jane Resh Thomas, ill. by Marcia Sewall *(Clarion)*
1990
HOW IT FEELS TO FIGHT FOR YOUR LIFE by Jill Krementz *(Joy Street/Little, Brown)*

1991
THE CANADA GEESE QUILT by Natalie Kinsey-Warnock
(Cobblehill)
1992
COLT by Nancy Springer (Dial)
1993
I WILL SING LIFE: VOICES FROM THE HOLE IN THE
WALL CAMP GANG compiled by Larry Berger and Dahlia
Lithwick (Little, Brown)
1994
HERO OF LESSER CAUSES by Julie Johnston (Joy Street/Little,
Brown)
1995
LAURIE TELLS by Linda Lowery (Carolrhoda)
STAYING FAT FOR SARAH BYRNES by Chris Crutcher
(Greenwillow)

Carolyn W. Field Award ࠭

This award is named for the former Coordinator of Children's
Services at the Free Library of Philadelphia who has been
designated by her state a "Distinguished Daughter of
Pennsylvania." Sponsored by the Youth Services Division of the
Pennsylvania Library Association (1919 N. Front St., Harrisburg,
PA 17102), the award is given annually to a Pennsylvania author
or illustrator for a distinguished children's book published in the
preceding year. In the listing below, when there is more than one
by-line, the name of the award recipient is followed by an
asterisk. (Medal)

1984
SOME THINGS GO TOGETHER by Charlotte Zolotow, ill. by
Karen Gundersheimer* (Crowell)
1985
SAINT GEORGE AND THE DRAGON retold by Margaret
Hodges*, ill. by Trina Schart Hyman (Little, Brown)
1986
THE NEW BABY by Fred Rogers (Putnam)
1987
THE ILLYRIAN ADVENTURE by Lloyd Alexander (Dutton)
1988
LITTLE TREE by e. e. cummings, ill. by Deborah Kogan Ray*
(Crown)

1989
CATWINGS by Ursula LeGuin, ill. by S.D. Schindler* *(Orchard)*
1990
BOX TURTLE AT LONG POND by William T. George*, ill.
by Lindsay Barrett George* *(Greenwillow)*
1991
MANIAC MAGEE by Jerry Spinelli *(Little, Brown)*
1992
I AM REGINA by Sally Keehn *(Philomel)*
1993
THE GREAT PUMPKIN SWITCH by Megan McDonald*, ill.
by Ted Lewin *(Orchard)*
1994
DREAMPLACE by George Ella Lyon, ill. by Peter Catalanotto*
(Orchard)
1995
HOW TO MAKE AN APPLE PIE AND SEE THE WORLD by
Marjorie Priceman *(Knopf)*

Friends of American Writers Awards 🕊️

JUVENILE BOOK AWARD

Presented annually in the spring since 1960 by Friends of
American Writers/Chicago, Young People's Literature
Commission (c/o Kay O'Connor, Chairman, Juvenile Literature
Awards Committee, 15237 W. Redwood Ln., Libertyville, IL
60048) the award was given to a single title through 1972. In
1973, the awards program expanded; first-place juvenile writing
award winners are listed below. (An award for illustration was
also presented from 1973-1977 and in 1979 and 1980 and those
awards are listed.) The awards are for books published in the
year preceding the award presentation. The winner must be a
native or a resident, for at least five years, of one of thirteen
Midwestern states or one of those states must be the locale of the
winning book. (Various stipends)

1960
FIRST BOY ON THE MOON by Clifford B. Hicks *(Holt)*
1961
SEQUOYAH, YOUNG CHEROKEE GUIDE by Dorothea J.
Snow *(Bobbs)*

1962
HOSTAGE TO ALEXANDER by Mary Evans Andrews
(McKay)
1963
CATHIE AND THE PADDY BOY by Nora Tully MacAlvay
(Viking)
1964
I JESSIE by Ruth Painter Randall *(Little, Brown)*
1965
THE FAR-OFF LAND by Rebecca Caudill *(Viking)*
1966-1968
No Awards
1969
JUD by Charles Raymond *(Houghton)*
1970
TRAILBLAZER: NEGRO NURSE IN THE AMERICAN RED
CROSS by Jean Maddern Pitrone *(HBJ)*
1971
TOUCH OF LIGHT by Anne Neimark *(HBJ)*
1972
WAR WORK by Zibby Oneal *(Viking)*
1973
THE WINTER CAT by Howard Knotts *(Harper)*
Illustration: AUTHORIZED AUTUMN CHARTS OF THE
UPPER RED CANOE RIVER COUNTRY by Peter Zachary
Cohen, ill. by Tomie dePaola *(Atheneum)*
1974
SIX DAYS FROM SUNDAY by Betty Biesterveld *(Rand
McNally)*
Illustration: THE LONG HUNGRY NIGHT by Elizabeth C.
Foster and Slim Williams, ill. by Glo Coalson *(Atheneum)*
1975
THE TARTAR'S SWORD by Eric Kimmel *(Coward)*
Illustration: KONGA AND KUMBA by Alice Shick, ill. by
Joseph Cellini *(Dial)*
1976
FIRST STEP by Anne Snyder *(Holt)*
Illustration: THE DEVIL DID IT by Susan Jeschke *(Holt)*
1977
TOBY, GRANNY & GEORGE by Robbie Branscum
(Doubleday)
Illustration: LITTLE FOX GOES TO THE END OF THE
WORLD by Ann Tompert, ill. by John Wallner *(Crown)*
1978
THE DREAM RUNNER by Audree Distad *(Harper)*
1979
A CLEARING IN THE FOREST by Gloria Whelan *(Putnam)*

HARVEY, THE BEER CAN KING by Jamie Gilson
Illustration: ON THE FOREST EDGE by Carol Lerner *(Morrow)*
1980
BETWEEN DARK AND DAYLIGHT by Crystal Thrasher
(McElderry)
Illustration: THE KING AT THE DOOR by Brock Cole *(Doubleday)*
1981
THE SNOWBIRD by Patricia Calvert *(Scribner)*
1982
BEYOND TWO RIVERS by David Kherdian *(Greenwillow)*
1983
THE LAND I LOST: ADVENTURES OF A BOY IN
VIETNAM by Huynh Quang Nhuong *(Harper)*
1984
RASPBERRY ONE by Charles Ferry *(Houghton)*
1985
RODEO SUMMER by Judie Gulley *(Houghton)*
1986
WHERE THE PIRATES ARE by Tom Townsend *(Eakin)*
1987
ROVER AND COO COO by John Hay *(Green Tiger)*
1988
ISLAND OF PERIL by Raboo Rodgers *(Houghton)*
1989
THE SECRET FRIENDSHIP by Virginia Brosseit
(Winston-Derek)
1990
DYING SUN by Gary L. Blackwood *(Atheneum)*
1991
BOY IN THE MOON by Ron Koertge *(Joy Street/Little, Brown)*
NIGHT OWLS by Sharon P. Denslow, ill. by Jill Kastner
(Bradbury)
1992
CHILDREN OF THE FIRE by Harriette Gillem Robinet
(Atheneum)
A PLACE TO CLAIM AS HOME by Patricia C. Willis *(Clarion)*
1993
FINDING MY VOICE by Marie G. Lee *(Houghton)*
THE DEER STAND by A.M. Monson *(Lothrop)*
1994
FROM MISS IDA'S PORCH by Sandra Belton, ill. by Floyd
Cooper *(Four Winds)*
ANNE IS ELEGANT by Marie Louise Cuneo *(HarperCollins)*
1995
A SHARE OF FREEDOM by June Rae Wood *(Putnam)*
CIRCUS OF THE WOLVES by Jack Bushnell, ill. by Robert
Andrew Parker *(Lothrop)*

Friends of Children and Literature (FOCAL) Award ða

The Friends of Children and Literature (FOCAL) is a support group of the Central Library, Los Angeles Public Library (630 W. 5th St., Los Angeles, CA 90071). Its annual award is for the author or illustrator of a creative book that has enriched a child's appreciation for and knowledge of California. There are no restrictions as to the publication years of books considered for the award. (Hand-crafted puppet of a main character in the honored book; puppet holds a calligraphed scroll, with title, etc.; duplicate of puppet is presented to Central Library)

1980
PEDRO, THE ANGEL OF OLVERA STREET by Leo Politi
(Scribner)
1981
ISLAND OF THE BLUE DOLPHINS by Scott O'Dell
(Houghton)
1982
BLUE WILLOW by Doris Gates (Viking)
1983
BY THE GREAT HORN SPOON by Sid Fleischman (Atlantic-Little, Brown)
1984
DRAGONWINGS by Laurence Yep (Harper)
1985
JULIA AND THE HAND OF GOD by Eleanor Cameron
(Dutton)
1986
A JAR OF DREAMS by Yoshiko Uchida (McElderry)
1987
DEAR MR. HENSHAW by Beverly Cleary (Morrow)
1988
FAREWELL TO MANZANAR by Jeanne Wakatsuki Houston
(Houghton)
1989
A ROOM MADE OF WINDOWS by Eleanor Cameron
(Atlantic-Little, Brown)
1990
COME THE MORNING by Mark Jonathan Harris (Bradbury)
1991
THE GREAT AMERICAN GOLD RUSH by Rhoda Blumberg
(Bradbury)

1992
CHILD OF THE OWL by Laurence Yep *(HarperCollins)*
1993
CHILDREN OF THE DUST BOWL: THE TRUE STORY OF
THE SCHOOL AT WEEDPATCH CAMP by Jerry Stanley
(Crown)
1994
FRIDA MARIA: A STORY OF THE OLD SOUTHWEST by
Deborah Nourse Lattimore *(Harcourt)*
1995
EARTHSHINE by Theresa Nelson *(Orchard)*

Golden Kite Awards ❧

Sponsored and administered by the Society of Children's Book
Writers and Illustrators (SCBWI) (22736 Vanowen St., Suite 106,
West Hills, CA 91307), these awards are presented annually to
those members of SCBWI whose books "best exhibit excellence in
writing or illustration and genuinely appeal to the interests and
concerns of children." Originally an award for fiction *(F)* only, a
nonfiction *(NF)* category was added in 1977, and a picture-
illustration *(PI)* category in 1982. Beginning in 1996, a fourth
award will be presented for picture book text. The year date in
our listing is the publication year. (Statuette)

1973
SUMMER OF MY GERMAN SOLDIER by Bette Greene *(Dial)*
1974
THE GIRL WHO CRIED FLOWERS by Jane Yolen *(Crowell)*
1975
THE GARDEN IS DOING FINE by Carol Farley *(Atheneum)*
1976
ONE MORE FLIGHT by Eve Bunting *(Warne)*
1977
F: THE GIRL WHO HAD NO NAME by Berniece Rabe
(Dutton)
NF: PEEPER, FIRST VOICE OF SPRING by Robert McClung
(Morrow)
1978
F: AND YOU GIVE ME A PAIN, ELAINE by Stella Pevsner
(Clarion)
NF: HOW I CAME TO BE A WRITER by Phyllis Reynolds
Naylor *(Atheneum)*

1979
F: THE MAGIC OF THE GLITS by C. S. Adler *(Macmillan)*
NF: RUNAWAY TEENS by Arnold Madison *(Elsevier/Nelson)*
1980
F: ARTHUR, FOR THE VERY FIRST TIME by Patricia
MacLachlan *(Harper)*
NF: THE LIVES OF SPIDERS by Dorothy Hinshaw Patent
(Holiday House)
1981
F: LITTLE LITTLE by M.E. Kerr *(Harper)*
NF: BLISSYMBOLICS by Elizabeth Helfman *(Lodestar)*
1982
F: RALPH S. MOUSE by Beverly Cleary *(Morrow)*
NF: CHIMNEY SWEEPS by James Cross Giblin *(Crowell)*
PI: GIORGIO'S VILLAGE by Tomie dePaola *(Putnam)*
1983
F: THE TEMPERING by Gloria Skurzynski *(Clarion)*
NF: THE ILLUSTRATED DINOSAUR DICTIONARY by Helen
Roney Sattler *(Lothrop)*
PI: LITTLE RED RIDING HOOD by Trina Schart Hyman
(Holiday House)
1984
F: TANCY by Belinda Hurmence *(Clarion)*
NF: WALLS: DEFENSES THROUGHOUT HISTORY by James
Cross Giblin *(Little, Brown)*
PI: THE NAPPING HOUSE by Audrey Wood, ill. by Don
Wood *(HBJ)*
1985
F: SARAH, PLAIN AND TALL by Patricia MacLachlan *(Harper)*
NF: COMMODORE PERRY IN THE LAND OF THE
SHOGUN by Rhoda Blumberg *(Lothrop)*
PI: THE DONKEY'S DREAM by Barbara Helen Berger
(Philomel)
1986
F: AFTER THE DANCING DAYS by Margaret I. Rostkowski
(Harper)
NF: POVERTY IN AMERICA by Milton Meltzer *(Morrow)*
PI: ALPHABATICS by Suse MacDonald *(Bradbury)*
1987
F: RABBLE STARKEY by Lois Lowry *(Houghton)*
NF: THE INCREDIBLE JOURNEY OF LEWIS AND CLARK
by Rhoda Blumberg *(Lothrop)*
PI: THE DEVIL & MOTHER CRUMP by Valerie Scho Carey,
ill. by Arnold Lobel *(Harper)*
1988
F: BORROWED CHILDREN by George Ella Lyon *(Orchard)*
NF: LET THERE BE LIGHT: A BOOK ABOUT WINDOWS by
James Cross Giblin *(Crowell)*

PI: FOREST OF DREAMS by Rosemary Wells, ill. by Susan Jeffers *(Dial)*

1989

F: JENNY OF THE TETONS by Kristiana Gregory *(Gulliver/HBJ)*

NF: PANAMA CANAL: GATEWAY TO THE WORLD by Judith St. George *(Putnam)*

PI: TOM THUMB by Richard Jesse Watson *(HBJ)*

1990

F: THE TRUE CONFESSIONS OF CHARLOTTE DOYLE by Avi *(Orchard)*

NF: THE BOY'S WAR: CONFEDERATE AND UNION SOLDIERS TALK ABOUT THE CIVIL WAR by Jim Murphy *(Clarion)*

PI: HOME PLACE by Crescent Dragonwagon, ill. by Jerry Pinkney *(Macmillan)*

1991

F: THE RAINCATCHERS by Jean Thesman *(Houghton)*

NF: THE WRIGHT BROTHERS: HOW THEY INVENTED THE AIRPLANE by Russell Freedman *(Holiday House)*

PI: MAMA, DO YOU LOVE ME? by Barbara M. Joosse, ill. by Barbara Lavallee *(Chronicle)*

1992

F: LETTERS FROM A SLAVE GIRL by Mary E. Lyons *(Scribner)*

NF: THE LONG ROAD TO GETTYSBURG by Jim Murphy *(Clarion)*

PI: CHICKEN SUNDAY by Patricia Polacco *(Philomel)*

1993

F: MAKE LEMONADE by Virginia Euwer Wolff *(Holt)*

NF: ELEANOR ROOSEVELT: A LIFE OF DISCOVERY by Russell Freedman *(Clarion)*

PI: BY THE LIGHT OF THE HALLOWEEN MOON by Caroline Stutson, ill. by Kevin Hawkes *(Lothrop)*

1994

F: CATHERINE, CALLED BIRDY by Karen Cushman *(Clarion)*

NF: KIDS AT WORK: LEWIS HINE AND THE CRUSADE AGAINST CHILD LABOR by Russell Freedman *(Clarion)*

PI: BIG FAT HEN by Keith Baker *(Harcourt)*

1995

F: THE WATSONS GO TO BIRMINGHAM—1963 by Christopher Paul Curtis *(Delacorte)*

NF: ABIGAIL ADAMS: WITNESS TO A REVOLUTION by Natalie S. Bober *(Atheneum)*

PI: FAIRY WINGS by Lauren Mills, ill. by Dennis Nolan and Lauren Mills *(Little, Brown)*

Eva L. Gordon Award for Children's Science Literature 🐚

This award is named for the late Eva L. Gordon, author, reviewer and professor of children's science literature at Cornell University. It honors the body of work of an author or illustrator whose science trade books exemplify "high standards of accuracy, readability, sensitivity to interrelationships, timeliness and joyousness while they extend either directly or subtly an invitation to the child to become involved." The sponsor is the American Nature Study Society (ANSS) (Contact: Janet S. Naher-Snowden, Chair, Eva L. Gordon Award Selection Cte., 541 Tamiami Trail, Akron, OH 44303). (Certificate)

1964   Millicent Selsam
1965   Edwin Way Teale
1966   Robert M. McClung
1967-1969   No Awards
1970   Jean Craighead George
1971   Verne Rockcastle
1972-1973   No Awards
1974   Phyllis S. Busch
1975   Jeanne Bendick
1976   Helen Ross Russell
1977   Herman and Nina Schneider
1978   George Mason
       Dorothy Shuttlesworth
1979   Ross Hutchins
1980   Glenn O. Blough
1981   Herbert Zim
1982   Peter Parnall
1983   Laurence Pringle
1984   Seymour Simon
1985   Vicki Cobb
1986   Dorothy Hinshaw Patent
1987   Patricia Lauber
1988   Franklyn M. Branley
1989   Ada and Frank Graham
1990   Joanna Cole
1991   Jim Arnosky
1992   Byrd Baylor
1993   Augusta Goldin
1994   Eric Carle
1995   Joanne Ryder

Lee Bennett Hopkins Poetry Award ❧

Presented by the Children's Literature Council of Pennsylvania (226 E. Emaus St., Middletown, PA 17057) this annual award celebrates the importance of poetry for children. It recognizes the work of an American poet or compiler and is given for a volume of poetry, either a single poem, an original collection, or an anthology published during the preceding year. The award is made possible by the generosity of its namesake whose hope is that poetry will continue "to flow freely in our children's lives." (Replica of award seal featuring art by Jessie Wilcox Smith and $500 donated by Mr. Hopkins)

1993
SING TO THE SUN by Ashley Bryan *(HarperCollins)*
1994
SPIRIT WALKER by Nancy Wood *(Doubleday)*
1995
BEAST FEAST! by Douglas Florian *(Harcourt)*
1996
DANCE WITH ME by Barbara Juster Esbensen *(HarperCollins)*

Jefferson Cup Award ❧

This annual award is named for the famous Virginian and third President of the United States, Thomas Jefferson, whose personal library provided the nucleus for the Library of Congress, Washington, DC. The award, administered by the Children's and Young Adult Round Table of the Virginia Library Association (669 S. Washington St., Alexandria, VA 22314) is for a distinguished book for young people in the fields of American history, biography or historical fiction, and published in the preceding year. (Silver-plated inscribed Jefferson Cup and $500 honorarium)

1983
THE JEWISH AMERICANS: A HISTORY IN THEIR OWN WORDS, 1650-1950 by Milton Meltzer *(Crowell)*
1984
WHO SPEAKS FOR WOLF? by Paula Underwood Spencer *(Tribe of Two Press)*

1985
IN THE YEAR OF THE BOAR AND JACKIE ROBINSON by
Bette Bao Lord *(Harper)*
1986
SARAH, PLAIN AND TALL by Patricia MacLachlan *(Harper)*
1987
AFTER THE DANCING DAYS by Margaret I. Rostkowski
(Harper)
1988
LINCOLN: A PHOTOBIOGRAPHY by Russell Freedman
(Clarion)
1989
ANTHONY BURNS: THE DEFEAT AND TRIUMPH OF A
FUGITIVE SLAVE by Virginia Hamilton *(Knopf)*
1990
SHADES OF GRAY by Carolyn Reeder *(Macmillan)*
1991
FRANKLIN DELANO ROOSEVELT by Russell Freedman
(Clarion)
1992
THE WRIGHT BROTHERS: HOW THEY INVENTED THE
AIRPLANE by Russell Freedman *(Holiday House)*
1993
CHILDREN OF THE DUST BOWL: THE TRUE STORY OF
THE SCHOOL AT WEEDPATCH CAMP by Jerry Stanley
(Crown)
1994
ACROSS AMERICA ON AN EMIGRANT TRAIN by Jim
Murphy *(Clarion)*
1995
PINK AND SAY by Patricia Polacco *(Philomel)*
Outstanding Series: AFRICAN AMERICAN ARTISTS AND
ARTISANS by Mary E. Lyons *(Simon & Schuster)*

Ezra Jack Keats
New Writer Award ❧

Administered by the Early Childhood Resources and Information
Center of the New York Public Library (66 Leroy St., New
York, NY 10014), and funded by the Ezra Jack Keats
Foundation, this award is for a promising new writer of not
more than six published children's picture books "that reflect the
tradition of Ezra Jack Keats" (1916-1983), a Caldecott Medal

winner whose books often featured multicultural settings and portrayed strong family relationships and universal qualities of childhood. Honorees need not have illustrated the book(s) nominated for the award; books must appeal to children ages 9 and under. The award is now given at two-year intervals. (Medallion and honorarium)

1986
THE PATCHWORK QUILT by Valerie Flournoy, ill. by Jerry Pinkney *(Dial)*
1987
JAMAICA'S FIND by Juanita Havill, ill. by Anne Sibley O'Brien *(Houghton)*
1989
ANNA'S SPECIAL PRESENT by Yoriko Tsutsui, ill. by Akiko Hayashi *(Viking)*
1991
TELL ME A STORY, MAMA by Angela Johnson, ill. by David Soman *(Orchard)*
1993
TAR BEACH by Faith Ringgold *(Crown)*
1995
TAXI, TAXI by Cari Best, ill. by Dale Gottlieb *(Little, Brown)*

Keene State College Children's Literature Festival Award

The award is for an author and/or illustrator who has made outstanding contributions over a period of years and whose "work shows variety and diversity while maintaining the highest standards in literature for children." (Keene State College Children's Literature Festival, 229 Main Street, Keene, NH 03431) (Honorarium and engraved Paul Revere bowl)

1986   Maurice Sendak
1987   Katherine Paterson
1988   Leo and Diane Dillon
1989   Barbara Cooney
1990   Betsy Byars
1991   Trina Schart Hyman
1992   Eric Carle
1993   Natalie Babbitt
1994   Patricia C. McKissack
1995   Jane Yolen

Kerlan Award 🐾

Established in 1975 by the Twenty-Fifth Kerlan Anniversary
Committee of the University of Minnesota (The Kerlan
Collection, 109 Walter Library, 117 Pleasant St., S.E.,
Minneapolis, MN 55455), the award is given "in recognition of
singular attainments in the creation of children's literature and in
appreciation for generous donation of unique resources to the
Kerlan Collection for the study of children's literature." (Plaque)

1975 Marie Hall Ets
Elizabeth Coatsworth
Marguerite Henry
1976 Roger Duvoisin
1977 Wanda Gág
1978 Carol Ryrie Brink
1979 Margot Zemach
1980 Glen Rounds
1981 Tomie dePaola
1982 Jean Craighead George
1983 Katherine Paterson
1984 Margaret Wise Brown (Also honored were Brown's editors
and illustrators, represented by Clement Hurd, illustrator
of Brown's GOODNIGHT MOON.)
1985 Eleanor Cameron
1986 Charlotte Zolotow
1987 Charles Mikolaycak
1988 Jane Yolen
1989 Gail E. Haley
1990 Madeleine L'Engle
1991 Leonard Everett Fisher
1992 Barbara Cooney
1993 Mary Stolz
1994 Myra Cohn Livingston
1995 Phyllis Reynolds Naylor
Margot Tomes
1996 Marion Dane Bauer
Paul Galdone

Coretta Scott King Awards

This award was designed "to commemorate and foster the life, works and dreams" of Dr. Martin Luther King, Jr., and to honor his wife Coretta Scott King "for her courage and determination to continue the work for peace and world brotherhood." The award is given annually to a black author *(A)* and, since 1974, to a black illustrator *(I)*, whose books, published in the preceding year, are outstanding, inspirational and educational contributions to literature for children and young people. The awards are administered by the Social Responsibilities Round Table, with the cooperation of the Association for Library Service to Children, of the American Library Association (50 E. Huron St., Chicago, IL 60611). (Citation, honorarium and an encyclopedia)

1970
MARTIN LUTHER KING, JR.: MAN OF PEACE by Lillie Patterson *(Garrard)*
1971
BLACK TROUBADOR: LANGSTON HUGHES by Charlemae Rollins *(Rand McNally)*
1972
17 BLACK ARTISTS by Elton C. Fax *(Dodd)*
1973
I NEVER HAD IT MADE by Jackie Robinson as told to Alfred Duckett *(Putnam)*
1974
A: RAY CHARLES by Sharon Bell Mathis *(Crowell)*
I: the same title, ill. by George Ford
1975
A: THE LEGEND OF AFRICANA by Dorothy Robinson *(Johnson)*
I: the same title, ill. by Herbert Temple
1976
A: DUEY'S TALE by Pearl Bailey *(HBJ)*
I: No Award
1977
A: THE STORY OF STEVIE WONDER by James Haskins *(Lothrop)*
I: No Award
1978
A: AFRICA DREAM by Eloise Greenfield *(Day/Crowell)*
I: the same title, ill. by Carole Byard
1979
A: ESCAPE TO FREEDOM by Ossie Davis *(Viking)*

I: SOMETHING ON MY MIND by Nikki Grimes, ill. by Tom Feelings *(Dial)*

1980
A: THE YOUNG LANDLORDS by Walter Dean Myers *(Viking)*
I: CORNROWS by Camille Yarbrough, ill. by Carole Byard *(Coward)*

1981
A: THIS LIFE by Sidney Poitier *(Knopf)*
I: BEAT THE STORY-DRUM, PUM-PUM by Ashley Bryan *(Atheneum)*

1982
A: LET THE CIRCLE BE UNBROKEN by Mildred D. Taylor *(Dial)*
I: MOTHER CROCODILE: AN UNCLE AMADOU TALE FROM SENEGAL adapted by Rosa Guy, ill. by John Steptoe *(Delacorte)*

1983
A: SWEET WHISPERS, BROTHER RUSH by Virginia Hamilton *(Philomel)*
I: BLACK CHILD by Peter Mugabane *(Knopf)*

1984
A: EVERETT ANDERSON'S GOOD-BYE by Lucille Clifton *(Holt)*
I: MY MAMA NEEDS ME by Mildred Pitts Walter, ill. by Pat Cummings *(Lothrop)*

1985
A: MOTOWN AND DIDI by Walter Dean Myers *(Viking)*
I: No Award

1986
A: THE PEOPLE COULD FLY: AMERICAN BLACK FOLKTALES by Virginia Hamilton *(Knopf)*
I: THE PATCHWORK QUILT by Valerie Flournoy, ill. by Jerry Pinkney *(Dial)*

1987
A: JUSTIN AND THE BEST BISCUITS IN THE WORLD by Mildred Pitts Walter *(Lothrop)*
I: HALF A MOON AND ONE WHOLE STAR by Crescent Dragonwagon, ill. by Jerry Pinkney *(Macmillan)*

1988
A: THE FRIENDSHIP by Mildred D. Taylor *(Dial)*
I: MUFARO'S BEAUTIFUL DAUGHTERS: AN AFRICAN TALE by John Steptoe *(Lothrop)*

1989
A: FALLEN ANGELS by Walter Dean Myers *(Scholastic)*
I: MIRANDY AND BROTHER WIND by Patricia C. McKissack, ill. by Jerry Pinkney *(Knopf)*

1990
A: A LONG HARD JOURNEY: THE STORY OF THE
PULLMAN PORTER by Patricia C. and Fredrick L. McKissack
(Walker)
I: NATHANIEL TALKING by Eloise Greenfield, ill. by Jan
Spivey Gilchrist (Black Butterfly)
1991
A: THE ROAD TO MEMPHIS by Mildred D. Taylor (Dial)
I: AÏDA told by Leontyne Price, ill. by Leo and Diane Dillon
(Gulliver/HBJ)
1992
A: NOW IS YOUR TIME!: THE AFRICAN AMERICAN
STRUGGLE FOR FREEDOM by Walter Dean Myers
(HarperCollins)
I: TAR BEACH by Faith Ringgold (Crown)
1993
A: THE DARK THIRTY: SOUTHERN TALES OF THE
SUPERNATURAL by Patricia C. McKissack (Knopf)
I: THE ORIGIN OF LIFE ON EARTH: AN AFRICAN
CREATION MYTH by David Anderson, ill. by Kathleen Atkins
Wilson (Sights Productions)
1994
A: TONING THE SWEEP by Angela Johnson (Orchard)
I: SOUL LOOKS BACK IN WONDER by Tom Feelings (Dial)
1995
A: CHRISTMAS IN THE BIG HOUSE, CHRISTMAS IN THE
QUARTERS by Patricia C. and Fredrick L. McKissack
(Scholastic)
I: THE CREATION by James Weldon Johnson, ill. by James E.
Ransome (Holiday)
1996
A: HER STORIES: AFRICAN AMERICAN FOLKTALES,
FAIRY TALES, AND TRUE TALES by Virginia Hamilton, ill.
by Leo and Diane Dillon (Blue Sky/Scholastic)
I: THE MIDDLE PASSAGE: WHITE SHIPS BLACK CARGO by
Tom Feelings (Dial)

Knickerbocker Award
for Juvenile Literature &

Named for a group of 19th century authors who wished to
nurture a national literature, this award honors a living author
currently residing in New York State whose body of work is of
superior quality and supports the educational needs of students.
Its sponsor is the School Library Media Section of the New York

Library Association (252 Hudson Ave., Albany, NY 12210). (Tiffany sculpture)

1991   Jean Craighead George
1992   Jean Fritz
1993   Russell Freedman
1994   Seymour Simon
1995   Robert Kimmel Smith
1996   Joseph Bruchac

Lambda Literary Awards 🙶
CHILDREN'S/YOUNG ADULT LITERATURE CATEGORY

Sponsored by *Lambda Book Report* (1625 Connecticut Ave., NW, Washington, DC 20009), the "Lammies" have been given annually since 1989 to recognize excellence in gay and lesbian literature. The awards have a three-tier selection process: a list of nominees is assembled from ballots sent in by readers; the books are narrowed down to five finalists in each category by a committee that includes gay and lesbian book professionals, members of the lesbian and gay press, and the staff of the *Lambda Book Report;* and finally, a single winner is selected in each category by a broad cross-section of the entire lesbian and gay literary community (nearly 100 in 1995). Years listed below are those of the books' publication; awards are presented the following year at a gala banquet during the American Booksellers Association annual convention. (Trophy)

1989
LOSING UNCLE TIM by MaryKate Jordan *(Albert Whitman)*
1990
DADDY'S ROOMMATE by Michael Willhoite *(Alyson)*
1991
THE DUKE WHO OUTLAWED JELLYBEANS AND OTHER STORIES by Johnny Valentine *(Alyson Wonderland)*
1992
WHEN HEROES DIE by Penny Raife Durant *(Atheneum)*
1993
THE CAT CAME BACK by Hilary Mullins *(Naiad Press)*
1994
AM I BLUE? COMING OUT FROM THE SILENCE ed. by Marion Dane Bauer *(HarperCollins)*
1995
FROM THE NOTEBOOKS OF MELANIN SUN by Jacqueline Woodson *(Blue Sky/Scholastic)*

Anne Spencer Lindbergh Prize in Children's Literature ❧

This prize will be given annually, beginning in December 1996, to the children's fantasy novel judged to be the best published during the year. It was established in honor of Anne Spencer Lindbergh, daughter of Charles and Anne Morrow Lindbergh, a writer of juvenile fantasy novels that take ordinary children and put them into extraordinary situations. She passed away in 1993 at the age of 53. Books published during 1995 or 1996 are eligible for the first prize, with those published in subsequent years eligible on a current-year basis. Nominees are sought from publishers (3 copies of each book and a $25.00 application fee per title) and will be judged by a panel of writers, editors, librarians, and children's literature specialists. The deadline for submissions is November 1st. The prize is administered by the Charles A. and Anne Morrow Lindbergh Foundation (708 S. 3rd St., Suite 110, Minneapolis, MN 55415-1141). ($5,000)

Judy Lopez Memorial Award ❧

Sponsored by the Women's National Book Association/Los Angeles Chapter (P. O. Box 7034, Beverly Hills, CA 90212-0034), this award honors the memory of one if its founding members, who was active in the publishing and bookselling professions, and who had a strong interest in literacy development. Eligible titles are "works of literary excellence for nine to twelve year olds, written by a citizen or resident of the United States." We list the award year; winners were published in the preceding year. (Medal and honorarium)

1986
PRAIRIE SONGS by Pam Conrad *(Harper)*
1987
COME A STRANGER by Cynthia Voigt *(Atheneum)*
1988
M. E. AND MORTON by Sylvia Cassedy *(Crowell)*
1989
THE TROUBLE WITH GRAMARY by Betty Levin
(Greenwillow)
1990
THE WINTER ROOM by Gary Paulsen *(Orchard)*

1991
THE TRUE CONFESSIONS OF CHARLOTTE DOYLE by Avi
(Orchard)
1992
YEAR OF IMPOSSIBLE GOODBYES by Sook Nyul Choi
(Houghton)
1993
BLUE SKIN OF THE SEA by Graham Salisbury *(Delacorte)*
1994
THE BOGGART by Susan Cooper *(McElderry)*
1995
MY BROTHER, MY SISTER, AND I by Yoko Kawashima
Watkins *(Bradbury)*

Lupine Award ?❧

Sponsored by the Children's and Young Adult's Services Section
of the Maine Library Association (Local Government Center,
Community Drive, Augusta, ME 04330), this award honors a
living author or illustrator who is a Maine resident, or who has
created a work whose focus is Maine as shown through
characterization, plot, or setting. Anyone can nominate a book
for consideration—titles must be appropriate for readers and
listeners up to 17 years of age, published within the calendar
year preceding the award presentation, and must be in print. The
award takes its name from the glorious landscape depicted in
Barbara Cooney's *Miss Rumphius*. The award year is that of the
book's publication. (Plate with picture of lupine; honoree selects
a library as recipient of gift copy of book; award seals for
winning books)

1989
BRICKYARD SUMMER by Paul Janeczko *(Orchard)*
1990
HATTIE AND THE WILD WAVES by Barbara Cooney
(Viking)
1991
ROSEBUD AND RED FLANNEL by Ethel Pochocki, ill. by
Marh Beth Owens *(Holt)*
1992
SING TO THE SUN by Ashley Bryan *(HarperCollins)*
1993
WILD FOX by Cherie Mason, ill. by Jo Ellen McAllister
Stammen *(Downeast)*

1994
PRIZE IN THE SNOW by Bill Easterling, ill. by Mary Beth
Owens *(Little, Brown)*
1995
A YEAR ON MONHEGAN ISLAND by Julia Dean *(Ticknor &
Fields)*

David McCord
Children's Literature Citation ❧

Sponsored by Framingham State College (Curriculum Library,
Framingham State College, Framingham, MA 01701) and the
Nobscot Reading Council of the International Reading
Association, this award is for "significant contribution to
excellence" in the field of children's books. It honors David
McCord, first recipient of the National Council of Teachers of
English Award for Excellence in Poetry for Children, and
recipient of Harvard's first honorary degree of Doctor of Humane
Letters. It was originally presented as part of notable anniversary
observances of both its sponsors, and is designed to single out
authors or illustrators whose work continues David McCord's
traditions. (Engraved Jefferson cup, citation, and honorarium)

1986   Tomie dePaola
1987   Steven Kellogg
1988   Jean Fritz
1989   Peter Spier
1990   Barbara Cooney
1991   Rosemary Wells
1992   Jerry Pinkney
1993   Jan Brett
1994   Joanna Cole
1995   Eric Carle

Milkweed Prize for Children's Literature ᑌ

Inaugurated in 1993 to spark an interest in writing books for children in the middle grades (ages 8-14), this prize includes publication by Milkweed Editions (430 First Ave., N., Suite 400, Minneapolis, MN 55401-1743) and a $2,000 cash prize over and above any advances, royalties, or other payment agreed upon in the contractual arrangement negotiated at the time of acceptance. Prior to 1996, manuscripts were solicited specifically for the contest, but for the 1996 and subsequent contests, the prize will be awarded to the best manuscript accepted for publication during the calendar year by a writer not previously published by Milkweed. Manuscripts should consist of a novel or biography of high literary quality that embodies humane values and contributes to cultural understanding. Guidelines for submission are available upon request from the publisher.

1994
A BRIDE FOR ANNA'S PAPA by Isabel Marvin *(Milkweed)*
1995
THE SUMMER OF THE BONEPILE MONSTER by Aileen Kilgore Henderson *(Milkweed)*
1996
BEHIND THE BEDROOM WALL by Laura E. Williams *(Milkweed)*

Minnesota Book Awards ᑌ
CHILDREN'S BOOK CATEGORIES

"The Minnesota Book Awards recognizes, promotes, and celebrates the rich variety of resident authors and illustrators who contribute to the state's quality of life. The intention of this awards program is to strengthen the linkages among the Minnesota community of the book between authors and illustrators, publishers, the mass media, booksellers, librarians, and other educators, and readers. In this awards program, identification of winners is subordinate to these greater aims." Awards are given in several categories; books suitable for young readers may be honored in other categories *(noted +)*, as well. The award "year" for the program changed in 1991. Awards are currently presented in the spring to books published in the preceding calendar year. The sponsors are the Minnesota Center

for the Book (2324 University Ave. West, Suite 116, St. Paul
MN 55414) working with the Office of Library Development and
Services and other partners. (Certificate)

1988
Younger children: THE STAR MAIDEN: AN OJIBWAY TALE
by Barbara Juster Esbensen *(Little, Brown)*
Older children: HATCHET by Gary Paulsen *(Bradbury)*
1989
Children: GOING THE MOOSE WAY HOME by Jim Latimer
(Scribner)
Book arts +: THE ARCTIC WOLF: LIVING WITH THE
PACK by L. David Mech *(Voyageur)*
1991 (see introductory note)
Younger children: HOW THE GUINEA FOWL GOT HER
SPOTS: A SWAHILI TALE retold and ill. by Barbara Knutson
(Carolrhoda)
Older children: WOODSONG by Gary Paulsen *(Bradbury)*
Science fiction & fantasy +: DEALING WITH DRAGONS by
Patricia C. Wrede *(Jane Yolen/HBJ)*
1992
Younger children (Author): OLD TURTLE by Douglas Wood
(Pfeifer-Hamilton)
Younger children (Illustrator): THE SALAMANDER ROOM by
Anne Mazer, ill. by Steve Johnson *(Knopf)*
Fantasy & science fiction: ELSEWHERE by Will Shetterley
(Harcourt)
1993
Younger children (Author): DREAMCATCHER by Audrey
Osofsky *(Orchard)*
Younger children (Illustrator): OLD BLACK FLY by Jim
Aylesworth, ill. by Stephen Gammell *(Holt)*
Older children: WHAT'S YOUR STORY: A YOUNG PERSON'S
GUIDE TO WRITING FICTION by Marion Dane Bauer
(Clarion)
1994
Younger Children (Author): SUNGURA AND LEOPARD: A
SWAHILI TRICKSTER TALE by Barbara Knutson *(Little,
Brown)*
Younger children (Illustrator): TRACKS IN THE WILD by Betsy
Bowen *(Little, Brown)*
Children's nonfiction: TO THE TOP OF THE WORLD:
ADVENTURES WITH ARCTIC WOLVES by Jim Brandenburg
(Walker)
Older children's fiction: REVOLUTIONS OF THE HEART by
Marsha Qualey *(Houghton)*
Fantasy & science fiction +: RING OF SWORDS by Eleanor
Arnason *(TOR)*

1995
Younger children (Author): EVE AND SMITHY: AN IOWA
TALE by Michelle Edwards *(Lothrop)*
Younger children (Illustrator): IMANI IN THE BELLY by
Deborah M. Newton Chocolate, ill. by Alex Boies *(BridgeWater)*
Children's nonfiction: SOVIETREK: A JOURNEY BY BICYCLE
ACROSS RUSSIA by Dan Buettner *(Lerner)*
Older children's fiction: AM I BLUE? COMING OUT FROM
THE SILENCE ed. by Marion Dane Bauer *(HarperCollins)*
Fantasy & science fiction +: A COLLEGE OF MAGICS by
Caroline Stevermer *(TOR)*

1996
Younger children (Author): DADDY PLAYED MUSIC FOR
THE COWS by Maryann N. Weidt *(Lothrop)*
Younger children (Illustrator): ELLIS ISLAND: DOORWAY TO
FREEDOM by Steven Kroll, ill. by Karen Ritz *(Holiday House)*
Children's nonfiction: BOOKWORKS: MAKING BOOKS BY
HAND by Gwenyth Swain with Minnesota Center for Book Arts
(Carolrhoda)
Young adult fiction: HOMETOWN by Marsha Qualey
(Houghton)

Mountains and Plains Booksellers Association Awards ❧

CHILDREN'S/YOUNG ADULT
BOOK CATEGORY

The Mountains and Plains Booksellers Association (805 LaPorte
Ave., Fort Collins, CO 80521) gives awards at its annual Author
Banquet to "regional" books and/or authors in four categories,
including an award for a book for young readers.

1990
BEARSTONE by Will Hobbs *(Atheneum)*

1991
CANYONS by Gary Paulsen *(Delacorte)*

1992-1993
No Awards

1994
I AM LAVINA CUMMING by Susan Lowell *(Milkweed)*

1995
DAILY LIFE IN A COVERED WAGON by Paul Erickson
(Breslich & Foss/Preservation Press)

National Council of Teachers of English Award for Excellence in Poetry for Children ❧

Sponsored by the National Council of Teachers of English (1111 Kenyon Rd., Urbana, IL 61801), the award was given annually 1977-1982 to a living American poet in recognition of an aggregate body of work for children ages 3-13. Currently, the award is presented every three years. (Citation and medallion design of seal for dust jacket use)

1977   David McCord
1978   Aileen Fisher
1979   Karla Kuskin
1980   Myra Cohn Livingston
1981   Eve Merriam
1982   John Ciardi
1985   Lilian Moore
1988   Arnold Adoff
1991   Valerie Worth
1994   Barbara Esbensen

National Jewish Book Awards ❧
CHILDREN'S BOOK CATEGORIES

Sponsored by the JWB Jewish Book Council (15 E. 26th St., New York, NY 10010), this awards program is designed to promote American Jewish literary creativity and an appreciation of Jewish literature. The awards program includes several categories. Since 1952 a Children's Literature award has been given to the writer of a specific book or to an author for a cumulative contribution to Jewish juvenile literature. Beginning in 1983, an award for an Illustrated Children's Book *(I)* has been given when warranted. (Certificate and $750)

1952
ALL-OF-A-KIND FAMILY by Sydney Taylor *(Follett)*
1953
STAR LIGHT STORIES *(Bloch)* and STORIES OF KING DAVID *(Jewish Publication Society)* by Lillian S. Freehof

1954
THE JEWISH PEOPLE: BOOK THREE by Deborah Pessin
(United Synagogue Commission)
1955
KING SOLOMON'S NAVY by Nora Benjamin Kubie *(Harper)*
1956
Sadie Rose Weilerstein
1957
Elma E. Levinger
1958
JEWISH JUNIOR ENCYCLOPEDIA by Naomi Ben Asher and
Hayim Leaf *(Shengold)*
1959
BORDER HAWK: AUGUST BONDI by Lloyd Alexander
(Farrar)
1960
KEYS TO A MAGIC DOOR: ISAAC LEIB PERETZ by Sylvia
Rothchild *(Farrar)*
1961
DISCOVERING ISRAEL by Regina Tor *(Random)*
1962
TEN AND A KID by Sadie Rose Weilerstein *(Doubleday)*
1963
RETURN TO FREEDOM by Josephine Kamm *(Abelard)*
1964
A BOY OF OLD PRAGUE by Sulamith Ish-Kishor *(Pantheon)*
1965
WORLDS LOST AND FOUND by Dov Peretz Elkins and Azriel
Eisenberg *(Abelard)*
1966
THE DREYFUS AFFAIR by Betty Schechter *(Houghton)*
1967
THE STORY OF ISRAEL by Meyer Levin *(Putnam)*
1968-1969
No Awards
1970
MARTIN BUBER: WISDOM IN OUR TIME by Charlie May
Simon *(Dutton)*
THE STORY OF MASADA retold by Gerald Gottlieb *(Random)*
1971
JOURNEY TO AMERICA by Sonia Levitin *(Atheneum)*
1972
THE MASTER OF MIRACLE: A NEW NOVEL OF THE
GOLEM by Sulamith Ish-Kishor *(Harper)*
1973
THE UPSTAIRS ROOM by Johanna Reiss *(Crowell)*

1974
UNCLE MISHA'S PARTISANS by Yuri Suhl *(Four Winds)*
1975
THE HOLOCAUST: A HISTORY OF COURAGE AND
RESISTANCE by Bea Stadtler *(Behrman House)*
1976
HAYM SALOMON: LIBERTY'S SON by Shirley Milgrim
(Jewish Publication Society)
1977
RIFKA GROWS UP by Chaya M. Burstein *(Bonim
Books/Hebrew Publishing Co.)*
1978
NEVER TO FORGET: THE JEWS OF THE HOLOCAUST by
Milton Meltzer *(Harper)*
1979
JOSHUA: FIGHTER FOR BAR KOCHBA by Irene Narell
(Akiba Press)
1980
DITA SAXOVA by Arnost Lustig *(Harper)*
1981
A RUSSIAN FAREWELL by Leonard Everett Fisher *(Four
Winds)*
1982
THE NIGHT JOURNEY by Kathryn Lasky *(Warne)*
1983
KING OF THE SEVENTH GRADE by Barbara Cohen
(Lothrop)
I: YUSSEL'S PRAYER: A YOM KIPPUR STORY by Barbara
Cohen, ill. by Michael Deraney *(Lothrop)*
1984
THE JEWISH KIDS CATALOG by Chaya M. Burstein *(Jewish
Publication Society)*
1985
GOOD IF IT GOES by Gary Provost and Gail Levine-Freidus
(Bradbury)
I: MRS. MOSKOWITZ AND THE SABBATH CANDLESTICKS
by Amy Schwartz *(Jewish Publication Society)*
1986
IN KINDLING FLAME: THE STORY OF HANNAH SENESH,
1921-1944 by Linda Atkinson *(Lothrop)*
I: BROTHERS retold by Florence B. Freedman, ill. by Robert
Andrew Parker *(Harper)*
1987
MONDAY IN ODESSA by Eileen Bluestone Sherman *(Jewish
Publication Society)*
I: POEMS FOR JEWISH HOLIDAYS selected by Myra Cohn
Livingston, ill. by Lloyd Bloom *(Holiday House)*

1988
THE RETURN by Sonia Levitin *(Atheneum)*
I: EXODUS adapted from the Bible by Miriam Chaikin, ill. by Charles Mikolaycak *(Holiday House)*
1989
THE DEVIL'S ARITHMETIC by Jane Yolen *(Viking)*
I: JUST ENOUGH IS PLENTY: A HANUKKAH TALE by Barbara Diamond Goldin, ill. by Seymour Chwast *(Viking)*
1990
NUMBER THE STARS by Lois Lowry *(Houghton)*
I: BERCHICK: MY MOTHER'S HORSE by Esther Silverstein Blanc, ill. by Tennessee Dixon *(Volcano)*
1991
BECOMING GERSHONA by Nava Semel *(Viking)*
I: HANUKKAH! by Roni Schotter, ill. by Marylin Hafner *(Joy Street/Little, Brown)*
1992
THE MAN FROM THE OTHER SIDE by Uri Orlev, translated by Hillel Halkin *(Houghton)*
I: CHICKEN MAN by Michelle Edwards *(Lothrop)*
1993
LETTERS FROM RIFKA by Karen Hesse *(Holt)*
I: ELIJAH'S ANGEL by Michael J. Rosen, ill. by Aminah Brenda Lynn Robinson *(Harcourt)*
1994
GOLDEN WINDOWS AND OTHER STORIES OF JERUSALEM by Adele Geras *(HarperCollins)*
I: THE ALWAYS PRAYER SHAWL by Sheldon Oberman, ill. by Ted Lewin *(Boyds Mills)*
1995
UNDER THE DOMIN TREE by Gila Almagor, translated by Hillel Schenker *(Simon & Schuster)*

National Parenting Publications Awards (NAPPA) ❧

Formerly the California Children's Book, Video, and Software Awards, the NAPPA program is now presented on a national level and has been expanded to include music and toys. Sponsored by 36 regional parenting magazines reaching more than 4 million readers, the NAPPA awards seek to enrich the educational and entertainment experiences of children by honoring the best quality in children's media. (Contact: L.A.

Parent Magazine, 443 E. Irving Dr., Burbank, CA 91504.) We
list the book awards. (Honored titles featured in the holiday
issues of participating magazines)

1990
Baby/Toddler
FOLLOW ME! by Nancy Tafuri *(Greenwillow)*
HO FOR A HAT by William Jay Smith, ill. by Lynn Munsinger
(Joy Street/Little, Brown)
I WENT WALKING by Sue Williams, ill. by Julie Vivas *(HBJ)*
"MY FIRST LOOK AT" Series *(Random)*
Picture Book
AÏDA told by Leontyne Price, ill. by Leo and Diane Dillon *(HBJ)*
GUESS WHAT? by Mem Fox, ill. by Vivienne Goodman
(Gulliver/HBJ)
THE TUNNEL by Anthony Browne *(Knopf)*
THE VERY QUIET CRICKET by Eric Carle *(Philomel)*
Nonfiction
THE BIG BOOK FOR PEACE edited by Ann Durell and
Marilyn Sachs *(Dutton)*
"EYEWITNESS JUNIORS" Series *(Knopf)*
FAMILIES: A CELEBRATION OF DIVERSITY,
COMMITMENT, AND LOVE by Aylette Jenness *(Houghton)*
SPRING FLEECE: A DAY OF SHEEPSHEARING by Catherine
Paladino *(Joy Street/Little, Brown)*
1991
Baby/Toddler
COLOR FARM by Lois Ehlert *(Lippincott)*
"FINGER MAGIC BOOKS" Series *(Schneider)*
HATCH, EGG, HATCH! by Shen Roddie *(Little, Brown)*
TEN LITTLE RABBITS by Virginia Grossman, ill. by Sylvia
Long *(Chronicle)*
Picture Book
BORREGUITA AND THE COYOTE by Verna Aardema, ill. by
Petra Mathers *(Knopf)*
MAMA, DO YOU LOVE ME? by Barbara M. Joosse, ill. by
Barbara Lavalle *(Chronicle)*
THE SALAMANDER ROOM by Anne Mazer, ill. by Steve
Johnson *(Knopf)*
TAR BEACH by Faith Ringgold *(Crown)*
Early Elementary
BROTHER EAGLE, SISTER SKY: A MESSAGE FROM CHIEF
SEATTLE by Susan Jeffers *(Dial)*
FLY AWAY HOME by Eve Bunting, ill. by Ronald Himler
(Clarion)
THE JOLLY CHRISTMAS POSTMAN by Janet and Allan
Ahlberg *(Little, Brown)*
TO RIDE A BUTTERFLY edited by Nancy Larrick and Wendy
Lamb *(Bantam/Doubleday/Dell)*

Nonfiction
THE BUCK STOPS HERE by Alice Provensen *(HarperCollins)*
CHILDREN OF PROMISE: AFRICAN-AMERICAN
LITERATURE AND ART FOR YOUNG PEOPLE edited
by Charles Sullivan *(Abrams)*
THE RANDOM HOUSE CHILDREN'S ENCYCLOPEDIA
(Random)
A YOUNG PAINTER: THE LIFE AND PAINTINGS OF
WANG YANI—CHINA'S EXTRAORDINARY YOUNG
ARTIST by Zheng Zhensun and Alice Low *(Scholastic)*
1992
Preschool/Toddler
JINGLE BUGS by David A. Carter *(Simon & Schuster)*
PEEK-A-BOO FAMILY by Diana Laufer *(Price, Stern, Sloan)*
PHONE BOOK by Anne Carter, ill. by Jan Pieńkowski *(Price, Stern, Sloan)*
"TWELVE LITTLE GOLDEN BOOKS BY FAVORITE
AUTHORS AND ARTISTS PAST AND PRESENT" boxed set
(Western)
Picture Book
THE FIELD BEYOND THE OUTFIELD by Mark Teague
(Scholastic)
LI'L SIS AND UNCLE WILLIE by Gwen Everett, ill. by
William H. Johnson *(Rizzoli)*
THE RAG COAT by Lauren Mills *(Little, Brown)*
SEVEN BLIND MICE by Ed Young *(Philomel)*
Fable, Poetry, and Song
HOW THE STARS FELL INTO THE SKY: A NAVAJO
LEGEND by Jerrie Oughton, ill. by Lisa Desimini *(Houghton)*
SONGS OF THE WILD WEST arranged by Dan Fox
(Metropolitan Museum of Art/Simon & Schuster)
TALKING LIKE THE RAIN: A FIRST BOOK OF POEMS
selected by X.J. Kennedy and Dorothy M. Kennedy, ill. by Jane
Dyer *(Little, Brown)*
1993
Preschool/Toddler
GO AWAY, BIG GREEN MONSTER! by Ed Emberley *(Little, Brown)*
NO DODOS: A COUNTING BOOK OF ENDANGERED
ANIMALS by Amanda Wallwork *(Scholastic)*
OINK, OINK, by Arthur Geisert *(Houghton)*
TODAY IS MONDAY by Eric Carle *(Philomel)*
Picture Book
THE EYES OF GRAY WOLF by Jonathan London, ill. by Jon
Van Zale *(Chronicle)*
GRANDFATHER'S JOURNEY by Allen Say *(Houghton)*
ONE HUNDRED HUNGRY ANTS by Elinor J. Pinczes, ill. by
Bonnie MacKain *(Houghton)*

THIS LAND IS MY LAND by George Littlechild *(Children's Book Press)*
Folklore, Poetry, and Song
THE DRAGON'S PEARL by Julie Lawson, ill. by Paul Morin *(Clarion)*
FROM SEA TO SHINING SEA selected by Amy Cohn, ill. by Molly Bang, et al. *(Scholastic)*
MERMAID TALES FROM AROUND THE WORLD retold by Mary Pope Osborne, ill. by Troy Howell *(Scholastic)*
POEMS FOR THE VERY YOUNG edited by Michael Rosen, ill. by Bob Graham *(Kingfisher)*
Nonfiction
ALVIN AILEY by Andrea Davis Pinkney, ill. by Brian Pinkey *(Hyperion)*
FRIDA KAHLO by Robyn M. Turner *(Little, Brown)*
MOMMY LAID AN EGG by Babette Cole *(Chronicle)*
WHALING DAYS by Carol Carrick, ill. by David Frampton *(Clarion)*

1994
Preschool/Toddler
BARNYARD DANCE! by Sandra Boynton *(Workman)*
BIG FAT HEN by Keith Baker *(Harcourt)*
"DOLL'S HOUSE BOARD BOOKS" Series by Andrew Bale *(Little, Brown)*
Picture Book
HARVEY POTTER'S BALLOON FARM by Jerdine Nolan *(Lothrop)*
OREGON'S JOURNEY by Louis Joos *(BridgeWater)*
TIME TO WAKE UP by Marisabina Russo *(Greenwillow)*
Folklore, Poetry, and Song
BABA YAGA AND VASILISA THE BRAVE by Marianna Mayer *(Morrow)*
BEAST FEAST! by Douglas Florian *(Harcourt)*
SCARED SILLY! A BOOK FOR THE BRAVE by Marc Brown *(Little, Brown)*
Nonfiction
EXPLORING SPACE, Voyages of Discovery Series *(Scholastic)*
ONE VERY SMALL SQUARE: NIGHTTIME IN MY BACKYARD by Donald M. Silver *(Scientific American)*
THE MAGIC SCHOOL BUS IN THE TIME OF THE DINOSAURS by Joanna Cole, ill. by Bruce Degen *(Scholastic)*

1995
Preschool
AMAZING ANIMALS by Ingrid and Dieter Schubert *(Front Street)*
NANTA'S LION: A SEARCH-AND-FIND ADVENTURE by Suse MacDonald *(Morrow)*
TEN FLASHING FIREFLIES by Philemon Sturges, ill. by Anna Vojtech *(North-South)*

Picture Books
HOME LOVELY by Lynne Rae Perkins *(Greenwillow)*
THE IGUANA BROTHERS: A TALE OF TWO LIZARDS by
Tony Johnston, ill. by Mark Teague *(Scholastic)*
TOPS AND BOTTOMS by Janet Stevens *(Harcourt)*
Nonfiction
GARDENING WIZARDRY FOR KIDS by L. Patricia Kite, ill.
by Yvette Santiago Banek *(Barron's)*
THE NATIONAL CIVIL RIGHTS MUSEUM CELEBRATES
EVERYDAY PEOPE by Alice F. Duncan, ill. by J. Gerald Smith
(BridgeWater)
TREES AND FORESTS, THE WORLD OF THEATER,
EXPLORING ENERGY, THE ART OF SCULPTURE, Voyages
of Discovery Series *(Scholastic)*
Folklore, Poetry, and Song
COYOTE: A TRICKSTER TALE FROM THE SOUTHWEST
by Gerald McDermott *(Harcourt)*
HOW NOW, BROWN COW? by Alice Schertle, ill. by Amanda
Schaffer *(Harcourt)*
MY FIRST BOOK OF PROVERBS/MY PRIMER LIBRO DE
DICHOS by Ralfka Gonzalez and Ana Ruiz *(Children's Book
Press)*

New England Book Awards 🐛
CHILDREN'S BOOK CATEGORY

This annual awards program is designed "to focus attention on
the lifetime achievements of New England's outstanding
community of writers, book illustrators, and book publishers."
Achievement in children's literature is one of the areas honored.
The sponsor and administrator is the New England Booksellers
Association (847 Massachusetts Ave., Cambridge, MA 02139),
which solicits nominations for the awards from its over 500
bookstore members. (Announcement, ceremony, and gift)

1990   Jan Brett
1991   Barbara Cooney
1992   Katherine Paterson
1993   William Steig
1994   Ashley Bryan
1995   Natalie Babbitt
1996   Steven Kellogg

New Voices/New World Minority Fiction Contest ⫧

This contest for writers from ethnic minority backgrounds for a first children's book was discontinued after the 1993 award. The winners received a $5,000 cash award and a contract for publication. In addition, the Joy Street Books imprint was discontinued the same year. All former Joy Street titles have been absorbed into the Little, Brown Children's Books backlist.

1990
DUMPLING SOUP by Jama Kim Rattigan, ill. by Lillian Hsu-Flanders *(Joy Street/ Little, Brown)* (1993 title)
1993
AUNT MATTIE'S PRESENT by Deborah Connor Coker, ill. by Brenda Joysmith *(Little, Brown)* (1998 title-tentative)

New York Academy of Sciences ⫧
CHILDREN'S SCIENCE BOOK AWARDS

The New York Academy of Sciences (2 East 63rd St., New York, NY 10021) has presented awards for children's books "to encourage the writing of more high-quality books about science for children" and to "bring the importance of science to the attention of children and to adults who work with children, thus helping to promote a greater understanding of the role science plays in today's world." First given to one book, in the second year of the program awards were given in two categories, Younger *(Y)* and Older *(0)*. As the program matured, illustrators were included as honorees if the author was not the illustrator. The program also included Special Awards for, for example, an outstanding series, outstanding photography, body of work, etc., as well as excellent Honorable Mention lists of titles highly regarded by the distinguished panel of judges reviewing submissions. Our listing is of the presentation year. The program was temporarily discontinued after the 1990 presentations; the New York Academy of Sciences plans to continue it in due course. (Citations, and also honoraria, shared between authors and illustrators when the award is for both)

1972
THE STARS AND SERENDIPITY by Robert Richardson
(Pantheon)

1973
Y: CITY LEAVES, CITY TREES by Edward Gallob *(Scribner)*
0: READING THE PAST by Leonard Cottrell *(Crowell-Collier)*

1974
Y: THE WEB IN THE GRASS by Bernice Freschet *(Scribner)*
0: A NATURAL HISTORY OF GIRAFFES by Dorcas
MacClintock and Ugo Mochi *(Scribner)*

1975
Y: SEE WHAT I AM by Roger Duvoisin *(Lothrop)*
0: HUNTERS OF THE WHALE by Ruth Kirk and Richard D.
Daugherty *(Morrow)*

1976
Y: EMPEROR PENGUIN by Jean-Claude Deguine *(Stephen
Greene)*
0: DOCTOR IN THE ZOO by Bruce Buchenholz *(Viking)*

1977
Y: CORN IS MAIZE by Aliki *(Crowell)*
0: WATCHING THE WILD APES by Bettyann Kevles *(Dutton)*

1978
Y: WILD MOUSE by Irene Brady *(Scribner)*
0: GRAINS by Elizabeth Burton Brown *(Prentice-Hall)*

1979
Y: THE SMALLEST LIFE AROUND US by Lucia Anderson, ill.
by Leigh Grant *(Crown)*
0: LASER LIGHT by Herman Schneider, ill. by Radu Vero
(McGraw-Hill)

1980
Y: A SPACE STORY by Karla Kuskin, ill. by Marc Simont
(Harper)
0: BUILDING: THE FIGHT AGAINST GRAVITY by Mario
Salvadori, ill. by Saralinda Hooker and Christopher Ragus
(McElderry)

1981
Y: BET YOU CAN'T! by Vicki Cobb and Kathy Darling, ill. by
Martha Weston *(Lothrop)*
0: MOVING HEAVY THINGS by Jan Adkins *(Houghton)*

1982
Y: MESSING AROUND WITH WATER PUMPS AND
SIPHONS by Bernie Zubrowski, ill. by Steve Lindblom *(Little,
Brown)*

1983
Y: THE SNAIL'S SPELL by Joanne Ryder, ill. by Lynne Cherry
(Warne)
0: THE BROOKLYN BRIDGE: THEY SAID IT COULDN'T BE
BUILT by Judith St. George *(Putnam)*

1984
Y: OAK & COMPANY by Richard Mabey, ill. by Clare Roberts
(Greenwillow)
0: VOLCANO WEATHER by Henry Stommel and Elizabeth
Stommel *(Seven Seas)*
1985
Y: THE SECRET LANGUAGE OF SNOW by Terry Tempest
Williams and Ted Major, ill. by Jennifer Dewey *(Sierra
Club/Pantheon)*
0: THE DAYWATCHERS by Peter Parnall *(Macmillan)*
1986
Y: THE BIG STRETCH by Ada and Frank Graham, ill. by
Richard Rosenblum *(Knopf)*
0: BREAKTHROUGH: THE TRUE STORY OF PENICILLIN
by Francine Jacobs *(Dodd)*
1987
Y: WHEN SHEEP CANNOT SLEEP: THE COUNTING BOOK
by Satoshi Kitamura *(Farrar)*
0: THE EVOLUTION BOOK by Sara Stein, photog. by Rona
Beame *(Workmen)*
1988
Y: ICEBERGS AND GLACIERS by Seymour Simon *(Morrow)*
0: EXPLORING THE NIGHT SKY by Terence Dickinson, ill.
by John Bianchi *(Camden)*
1989
No presentations
1990
Y: THE SIERRA CLUB WAYFINDING BOOK by Vicki
McVey, ill. by Martha Weston *(Sierra Club/Little Brown)*
0: DIGGING DINOSAURS by John R. Horner and James
Gorman, ill. by Donna Braginetz and Kris Ellingsen *(Workman)*

New York Times Best Illustrated Children's Books of the Year ❧

Sponsored by *The New York Times* (229 W. 43rd St., New
York, NY 10036), this annual selection of best illustrated
children's books of the year by a panel of three judges was
initiated in 1952. (Certificate)

1952
THE ANIMAL FAIR by Alice and Martin Provensen *(Golden)*
BEASTS AND NONSENSE by Marie Hall Ets *(Viking)*

THE DOGCATCHER'S DOG by Andre Dugo *(Holt)*
FIVE LITTLE MONKEYS by Juliet Kepes *(Houghton)*
THE HAPPY PLACE by Ludwig Bemelmans *(Little, Brown)*
A HOLE IS TO DIG by Ruth Krauss, ill. by Maurice Sendak
(Harper)
THE MAGIC CURRANT BUN by John Symonds, ill. by André
Francois *(Lippincott)*

1953

FAST IS NOT A LADYBUG by Miriam Schlein, ill. by Leonard
Kessler *(Scott)*
FLORINA AND THE WILD BIRD by Selina Chonz, ill. by Alois
Carigiet *(Walck)*
THE GOLDEN BIBLE FOR CHILDREN: THE NEW
TESTAMENT edited by Elsa Jane Werner, ill. by Alice and
Martin Provensen *(Golden)*
GREEN EYES by A. Birnbaum *(Golden)*
A HERO BY MISTAKE by Anita Brenner, ill. by Jean Charlot
(Scott)
LUCKY BLACKY by Eunice Lackey, ill. by Winifred Greene
(Watts)
MADELINE'S RESCUE by Ludwig Bemelmans *(Viking)*
MOTHER GOOSE RIDDLE RHYMES by Joseph Low *(HBJ)*
PITSCHI by Hans Fischer *(HBJ)*
WHO GAVE US? by Madeleine Gekiere *(Pantheon)*

1954

ANDY SAYS BONJOUR by Pat Diska, ill. by Chris Jenkyns
(Vanguard)
THE ANIMAL FROLIC by 12th century Japanese artist,
probably Toba Sojo *(Putnam)*
CIRCUS RUCKUS by Will, ill. by Nicolas *(HBJ)*
THE HAPPY LION by Louise Fatio, ill. by Roger Duvoisin
(McGraw-Hill)
HEAVY IS A HIPPOPOTAMUS by Miriam Schlein, ill. by
Leonard Kessler *(Scott)*
I'LL BE YOU AND YOU BE ME by Ruth Krauss, ill. by
Maurice Sendak *(Harper)*
JENNY'S BIRTHDAY BOOK by Esther Averill *(Harper)*
A KISS IS ROUND by Blossom Budney, ill. by Vladimir Bobri
(Lothrop)
THE SUN LOOKS DOWN by Miriam Schlein, ill. by Abner
Graboff *(Abelard)*
THE WET WORLD by Norma Simon, ill. by Jane Miller
(Lippincott)

1955

BEASTS FROM A BRUSH by Juliet Kepes *(Pantheon)*
CHAGA by Will, ill. by Nicolas *(HBJ)*
THE HAPPY LION IN AFRICA by Louise Fatio, ill. by Roger
Duvoisin *(McGraw-Hill)*

A LITTLE HOUSE OF YOUR OWN by Beatrice Schenk de Regniers, ill. by Irene Haas *(HBJ)*
PARSLEY by Ludwig Bemelmans *(Harper)*
RUMPLESTILTSKIN by Jan B. Balet *(Rand McNally)*
SEE AND SAY by Antonio Frasconi *(HBJ)*
SWITCH ON THE NIGHT by Ray Bradbury, ill. by Madeleine Gekiere *(Pantheon)*
THE THREE KINGS OF SABA by Alf Evers, ill. by Helen Sewell *(Lippincott)*
UNCLE BEN'S WHALE by Walter D. Edmonds, ill. by William Gropper *(Dodd)*
1956
BABAR'S FAIR by Laurent De Brunhoff *(Random)*
CROCODILE TEARS by André Francois *(Universe)*
I KNOW A LOT OF THINGS by Ann Rand, ill. by Paul Rand *(HBJ)*
I WANT TO PAINT MY BATHROOM BLUE by Ruth Krauss, ill. by Maurice Sendak *(Harper)*
I WILL TELL YOU OF A TOWN by Alistair Reid, ill. by Walter Lorraine *(Houghton)*
JONAH THE FISHERMAN by Reiner Zimnik *(Pantheon)*
LITTLE BIG-FEATHER by Joseph Longstretch, ill. by Helen Borten *(Abelard)*
THE LITTLE ELEPHANT by Ylla *(Harper)*
REALLY SPRING by Gene Zion, ill. by Margaret Bloy Graham *(Harper)*
WAS IT A GOOD TRADE? by Beatrice Schenk de Regniers, ill. by Irene Haas *(HBJ)*
1957
BIG RED BUS by Ethel Kessler, ill. by Leonard Kessler *(Doubleday)*
THE BIRTHDAY PARTY by Ruth Krauss, ill. by Maurice Sendak *(Harper)*
CURIOUS GEORGE GETS A MEDAL by H.A. Rey *(Houghton)*
DEAR GARBAGE MAN by Gene Zion, ill. by Margaret Bloy Graham *(Harper)*
FAINT GEORGE by Robert E. Barry *(Houghton)*
THE FISHERMAN AND HIS WIFE by the Brothers Grimm, ill. by Madeleine Gekiere *(Pantheon)*
THE FRIENDLY BEASTS by Laura Baker, ill. by Nicholas Sidjakov *(Parnassus)*
THE RED BALLOON by Albert Lamorisse *(Doubleday)*
SPARKLE AND SPIN by Ann Rand, ill. by Paul Rand *(HBJ)*
THE UNHAPPY HIPPOPOTAMUS by Nancy Moore, ill. by Edward Leight *(Vanguard)*
1958
ALL ABOARD by Mary Britton Miller, ill. by Bill Sokol *(Pantheon)*
CHOUCHOU by Francoise *(Scribner)*
THE DADDY DAYS by Norma Simon, ill. by Abner Graboff *(Abelard)*

A FRIEND IS SOMEONE WHO LIKES YOU by Joan Walsh Anglund *(HBJ)*

THE GIANT GOLDEN BOOK OF ANIMALS by Anne Terry White, ill. by W. Suschitzky *(Golden)*

THE HOUSE THAT JACK BUILT by Antonio Frasconi *(HBJ)*

HOW TO HIDE A HIPPOPOTAMUS by Volney Croswell *(Dodd)*

THE MAGIC FEATHER DUSTER by Will, ill. by Nicolas Mordvinoff *(HBJ)*

ROLAND by Nelly Stephane, ill. by André Francois *(HBJ)*

WHAT DO YOU SAY, DEAR? A BOOK OF MANNERS FOR ALL OCCASIONS by Sesyle Joslin, ill. by Maurice Sendak *(Scott)*

1959

ANIMAL BABIES by Arthur Gregor, ill. by Ylla *(Harper)*

FATHER BEAR COMES HOME by Else Holmelund Minarik, ill. by Maurice Sendak *(Harper)*

THE FIRST NOEL by Alice and Martin Provensen *(Golden)*

FULL OF WONDER by Ann Kirn *(World)*

THE GIRL IN THE WHITE HAT by W.T. Cummings *(McGraw-Hill)*

KASIMIR'S JOURNEY by Monroe Stearns, ill. by Marlene Reidel *(Lippincott)*

LITTLE BLUE AND LITTLE YELLOW by Leo Lionni *(Astor-Honor)*

PABLO PAINTS A PICTURE by Warren Miller, ill. by Edward Sorel *(Little, Brown)*

THE REASON FOR THE PELICAN by John Ciardi, ill. by Madeleine Gekiere *(Lippincott)*

THIS IS LONDON by Miroslav Sasek *(Macmillan)*

1960

A B C by Bruno Munari *(World)*

THE ADVENTURES OF ULYSSES by Jacque le Marchand, ill. by André Francois *(Criterion)*

BABOUSHKA AND THE THREE KINGS by Ruth Robbins, ill. by Nicholas Sidjakov *(Parnassus)*

INCH BY INCH by Leo Lionni *(Astor-Honor)*

OPEN HOUSE FOR BUTTERFLIES by Ruth Krauss, ill. by Maurice Sendak *(Harper)*

SCRAPPY THE PUP by John Ciardi, ill. by Jane Miller *(Lippincott)*

THE SHADOW BOOK by Beatrice Schenk de Regniers, ill. by Isabel Gordon *(HBJ)*

THIS IS NEW YORK by Miroslav Sasek *(Macmillan)*

26 WAYS TO BE SOMEBODY ELSE by Devorah Boxer *(Pantheon)*

TWO LITTLE BIRDS AND THREE by Juliet Kepes *(Houghton)*

1961

THE BIG BOOK OF ANIMAL STORIES edited by Margaret Green, ill. by Janusz Grabianski *(Watts)*

DEAR RAT by Julia Cunningham, ill. by Walter Lorraine *(Houghton)*

THE HAPPY HUNTER by Roger Duvoisin *(Lothrop)*

LISTEN—THE BIRDS by Mary Britton Miller, ill. by Evaline Ness *(Pantheon)*

MY TIME OF YEAR by Katherine Dow, ill. by Walter Erhard *(Walck)*

ONCE A MOUSE...by Marcia Brown *(Scribner)*

SANDPIPERS by Edith Thacher Hurd, ill. by Lucienne Bloch *(Crowell)*

THE SNOW AND THE SUN by Antonio Frasconi *(HBJ)*

UMBRELLAS, HATS, AND WHEELS by Ann Rand, ill. by Jerome Snyder *(HBJ)*

THE WING ON A FLEA by Ed Emberley *(Little, Brown)*

1962

BOOKS! by Murray McCain, ill. by John Alcorn *(Simon & Schuster)*

THE EMPEROR AND THE DRUMMER BOY by Ruth Robbins, ill. by Nicholas Sidjakov *(Parnassus)*

GENNARINO by Nicola Simbari *(Lippincott)*

THE ISLAND OF FISH IN THE TREES by Eva-Lis Wuorio, ill. by Edward Ardizzone *(World)*

KAY-KAY COMES HOME by Nicholas Samstag, ill. by Ben Shahn *(Astor-Honor)*

LITTLE OWL by Reiner Zimnik, ill. by Hanne Axmann *(Atheneum)*

THE PRINCESSES by Sally P. Johnson, ill. by Beni Montresor *(Harper)*

THE SINGING HILL by Meindert DeJong, ill. by Maurice Sendak *(Harper)*

THE TALE OF A WOOD by Henry B. Kane *(Knopf)*

THE THREE ROBBERS by Tomi Ungerer *(Atheneum)*

1963

THE GREAT PICTURE ROBBERY by Leon Harris, ill. by Joseph Schindelman *(Atheneum)*

GWENDOLYN AND THE WEATHERCOCK by Nancy Sherman, ill. by Edward Sorel *(Golden)*

A HOLIDAY FOR MISTER MUSTER by Arnold Lobel *(Harper)*

HURLY BURLY AND THE KNIGHTS by Milton Rugoff, ill. by Emanuele Luzzati *(Platt & Munk)*

JOHN J. PLENTY AND FIDDLER DAN by John Ciardi, ill. by Madeleine Gekiere *(Lippincott)*

KAREN'S CURIOSITY by Alice and Martin Provensen *(Golden)*

ONCE UPON A TOTEM by Christie Harris, ill. by John Frazer Mills *(Atheneum)*

PLUNKETY PLUNK by Peter J. Lippman *(Farrar)*

SWIMMY by Leo Lionni *(Pantheon)*

WHERE THE WILD THINGS ARE by Maurice Sendak *(Harper)*

1964

THE BAT-POET by Randall Jarrell, ill. by Maurice Sendak (*Macmillan*)

CASEY AT THE BAT by E. L. Thayer, ill. by Leonard Everett Fisher (*Watts*)

THE CHARGE OF THE LIGHT BRIGADE by Alfred Lord Tennyson, ill. by Alice and Martin Provensen (*Golden*)

EXACTLY ALIKE by Evaline Ness (*Scribner*)

THE GIRAFFE OF KING CHARLES X by Miche Wynants (*McGraw-Hill*)

THE HAPPY OWLS by Celestino Piatti (*Atheneum*)

I'LL SHOW YOU CATS by C.N. Bonsall, ill. by Ylla (*Harper*)

THE LIFE OF A QUEEN by Colette Portal (*Braziller*)

RAIN MAKES APPLESAUCE by Julian Scheer, ill. by Marvin Bileck (*Holiday House*)

THE WAVE by Margaret Hodges, ill. by Blair Lent (*Houghton*)

1965

ALBERIC THE WISE AND OTHER JOURNEYS by Norton Juster, ill. by Domenico Gnoli (*Pantheon*)

THE ANIMAL FAMILY by Randall Jarrell, ill. by Maurice Sendak (*Pantheon*)

A DOUBLE DISCOVERY by Evaline Ness (*Scribner*)

HIDE AND SEEK FOG by Alvin Tresselt, ill. by Roger Duvoisin (*Lothrop*)

KANGAROO & KANGAROO by K. Braun, ill. by Jim McMullan (*Doubleday*)

PLEASE SHARE THAT PEANUT! by Sesyle Joslin, ill. by Simms Taback (*HBJ*)

PUNCH & JUDY by Ed Emberley (*Little, Brown*)

SVEN'S BRIDGE by Anita Lobel (*Harper*)

1966

ANANSE THE SPIDER by Peggy Appiah, ill. by Peggy Wilson (*Pantheon*)

ANIMAL ABC by Celestino Piatti (*Atheneum*)

A BOY WENT OUT TO GATHER PEARS by Felix Hoffmann (*HBJ*)

THE JAZZ MAN by Mary H. Weik, ill. by Ann Grifalconi (*Atheneum*)

THE MAGIC FLUTE by Stephen Spender, ill. by Beni Montresor (*Putnam*)

THE MONSTER DEN by John Ciardi, ill. by Edward Gorey (*Lippincott*)

NOTHING EVER HAPPENS ON MY BLOCK by Ellen Raskin (*Atheneum*)

SHAW'S FORTUNE by Edwin Tunis (*World*)

WONDERFUL TIME by Phyllis McGinley, ill. by John Alcorn (*Lippincott*)

ZLATEH THE GOAT AND OTHER STORIES by Isaac Bashevis Singer, ill. by Maurice Sendak (*Harper*)

1967
ANIMALS OF MANY LANDS by Hanns Reich *(Hill & Wang)*
BRIAN WILDSMITH'S BIRDS by Brian Wildsmith *(Watts)*
A DOG'S BOOK OF BUGS by Elizabeth Griffin, ill. by Peter Parnall *(Atheneum)*
FABLES OF AESOP by Sir Roger L'Estrange, ill. by Alexander Calder *(Dover)*
FREDERICK by Leo Lionni *(Pantheon)*
THE HONEYBEES by Franklin Russell, ill. by Collette Portal *(Knopf)*
HUBERT by Wendy Stang and Susan Richards, ill. by Robert L. Anderson *(Quist)*
KNEE-DEEP IN THUNDER by Sheila Moon, ill. by Peter Parnall *(Atheneum)*
SEASHORE STORY by Taro Yashima *(Viking)*
1968
HARRIET AND THE PROMISED LAND by Jacob Lawrence *(Windmill/Simon & Schuster)*
A KISS FOR LITTLE BEAR by Else Holmelund Minarik, ill. by Maurice Sendak *(Harper)*
MALACHI MUDGE by Edward Cecil, ill. by Peter Parnall *(McGraw-Hill)*
MISTER CORBETT'S GHOST by Leon Garfield, ill. by Alan E. Cober *(Pantheon)*
THE REAL TIN FLOWER by Aliki Barnstone, ill. by Paul Giovanopoulos *(Crowell-Collier)*
THE SECRET JOURNEY OF HUGO THE BRAT by François Ruy-Vidal, ill. by Nicole Claveloux *(Quist)*
SPECTACLES by Ellen Raskin *(Atheneum)*
STORY NUMBER 1 by Eugene Ionesco, ill. by Etienne Delessert *(Quist)*
TALKING WITHOUT WORDS by Marie Hall Ets *(Viking)*
THE VERY OBLIGING FLOWERS by Claude Roy, ill. by Alain LeFoll *(Grove)*
1969
ARM IN ARM by Remy Charlip *(Four Winds)*
BANG BANG YOU'RE DEAD by Louise Fitzhugh and Sandra Scoppetone, ill. by Louise Fitzhugh *(Harper)*
BIRDS by Juliet Kepes *(Walker)*
THE CIRCUS IN THE MIST by Bruno Munari *(World)*
THE DONG WITH A LUMINOUS NOSE by Edward Lear, ill. by Edward Gorey *(Scott)*
FREE AS A FROG by Elizabeth Hodges, ill. by Paul Giovanopoulos *(Addison)*
LIGHT PRINCESS by George MacDonald, ill. by Maurice Sendak *(Farrar)*
SARA'S GRANNY AND THE GROODLE by Joan Gill, ill. by Seymour Chwast *(Doubleday)*
WHAT IS IT FOR? by Henry Humphrey *(Simon & Schuster)*
WINTER'S EVE by Natalia M. Belting, ill. by Alan E. Cober *(Holt)*

1970
ALALA by Guy Monreal, ill. by Nicole Claveloux *(Quist)*
FINDING A POEM by Eve Merriam, ill. by Seymour Chwast
(Atheneum)
THE GNU AND THE GURU GO BEHIND THE BEYOND by
Peggy Clifford, ill. by Eric von Schmidt *(Houghton)*
HELP, HELP, THE GLOBOLINKS by Gian-Carlo Menotti,
adapted by Leigh Dean, ill. by Milton Glaser *(McGraw-Hill)*
IN THE NIGHT KITCHEN by Maurice Sendak *(Harper)*
LIFT EVERY VOICE AND SING by James Weldon Johnson
and J. Rosamond, ill. by Mozelle Thompson *(Hawthorn)*
MATILDA WHO TOLD LIES AND WAS BURNED TO
DEATH by Hillaire Belloc, ill. by Steven Kellogg *(Dial)*
TIMOTHY'S HORSE by Vladimir Mayakovsky, adapted by Guy
Daniels, ill. by Flavio Constantini *(Pantheon)*
TOPSY-TURVIES: PICTURES TO STRETCH THE
IMAGINATION by Mitsumasa Anno *(Weatherhill)*
YOU ARE RI-DI-CU-LOUS by André Francois *(Pantheon)*
1971
AMOS & BORIS by William Steig *(Farrar)*
BEAR CIRCUS by William Pène du Bois *(Viking)*
THE BEAST OF MONSIEUR RACINE by Tomi Ungerer
(Farrar)
CHANGES, CHANGES by Pat Hutchins *(Macmillan)*
LOOK AGAIN! by Tana Hoban *(Macmillan)*
LOOK WHAT I CAN DO by José Aruego *(Scribner)*
THE MAGIC TEARS by Jack Sendak, ill. by Mitchell Miller
(Harper)
MR. GUMPY'S OUTING by John Burningham *(Holt)*
ONE DANCING DRUM by Gail Kredenser and Stanley Mack,
ill. by Stanley Mack *(Phillips)*
THE SHRINKING OF TREEHORN by Florence Parry Heide,
ill. by Edward Gorey *(Holiday House)*
1972
BEHIND THE WHEEL by Edward Koren *(Holt)*
COUNT AND SEE by Tana Hoban *(Macmillan)*
GEORGE AND MARTHA by James Marshall *(Houghton)*
HOSIE'S ALPHABET by Hosea, Tobias and Lisa Baskin, ill. by
Leonard Baskin *(Viking)*
JUST SO STORIES by Rudyard Kipling, ill. by Etienne Delessert
(Doubleday)
A LITTLE SCHUBERT by M.B. Goffstein *(Harper)*
MISS JASTER'S GARDEN by N.M. Bodecker *(Golden)*
MOUSE CAFÉ by Patricia Coombs *(Lothrop)*
SIMON BOOM GIVES A WEDDING by Yuri Suhl, ill. by
Margot Zemach *(Four Winds)*
WHERE'S AL? by Byron Barton *(Seabury)*
1973
CATHEDRAL by David Macaulay *(Houghton)*

THE EMPEROR'S NEW CLOTHES by Hans Christian Andersen, ill. by Monika Laimgruber *(Addison)*
HECTOR PENGUIN by Louise Fatio, ill. by Roger Duvoisin *(McGraw-Hill)*
THE JUNIPER TREE AND OTHER TALES FROM GRIMM ill. by Maurice Sendak *(Farrar)*
KING GRISLY-BEARD ill. by Maurice Sendak *(Farrar)*
NUMBER 24 by Guy Billout *(Quist)*
A PRAIRIE BOY'S WINTER by William Kurelek *(Houghton)*
THE SILVER PONY by Lynd Ward *(Houghton)*
TIM'S LAST VOYAGE by Edward Ardizzone *(Walck)*

1974

THE GIRL WHO CRIED FLOWERS by Jane Yolen, ill. by David Palladini *(Crowell)*
A HOME by Lennart Rudstrom, ill. by Carl Larsson *(Putnam)*
LUMBERJACK by William Kurelek *(Houghton)*
THE MAN WHO TOOK THE INDOORS OUT by Arnold Lobel *(Harper)*
MISS SUZY'S BIRTHDAY by Miriam Young, ill. by Arnold Lobel *(Parents)*
ROSIE AND MICHAEL by Judith Viorst, ill. by Lorna Tomei *(Atheneum)*
A STORYBOOK by Tomi Ungerer *(Watts)*
THERE WAS AN OLD WOMAN by Steven Kellogg *(Four Winds)*

1975

ANNO'S ALPHABET by Mitsumasa Anno *(Crowell)*
A BOOK OF A-MAZE-MENTS by Jean Seisser and France de Ranchin *(Quist)*
MR. MICHAEL MOUSE UNFOLDS HIS TALE by Walter Crane *(Merrimack)*
THE PIG-TALE by Lewis Carroll, ill. by Leonard B. Lubin *(Little, Brown)*
THERE'S A SOUND IN THE SEA...A CHILD'S EYE VIEW OF THE WHALE collected by Tamar Griggs *(Scrimshaw)*
THIRTEEN by Remy Charlip and Jerry Joyner *(Four Winds)*
THE TUTTI-FRUTTI CASE by Harry Allard, ill. by James Marshall *(Prentice-Hall)*

1976

AS RIGHT AS RIGHT CAN BE by Anne Rose, ill. by Arnold Lobel *(Dial)*
ASHANTI TO ZULU: AFRICAN TRADITIONS by Margaret Musgrove, ill. by Leo and Diane Dillon *(Dial)*
THE BEAR AND THE FLY by Paula Winter *(Crown)*
EVERYONE KNOWS WHAT A DRAGON LOOKS LIKE by Jay Williams, ill. by Mercer Mayer *(Four Winds)*
FLY BY NIGHT by Randall Jarrell, ill. by Maurice Sendak *(Farrar)*
LITTLE THOUGH I BE by Joseph Low *(McGraw-Hill)*

MERRY EVER AFTER by Joe Lasker *(Viking)*

THE MOTHER GOOSE BOOK by Alice and Martin Provensen *(Random)*

A NEAR THING FOR CAPTAIN NAJORK by Russell Hoban, ill. by Quentin Blake *(Atheneum)*

1977

THE CHURCH MICE ADRIFT by Graham Oakley *(Atheneum)*

COME AWAY FROM THE WATER, SHIRLEY by John Burningham *(Crowell)*

IT COULD ALWAYS BE WORSE: A YIDDISH FOLK TALE retold and ill. by Margot Zemach *(Farrar)*

JACK AND THE WONDER BEANS by James Still, ill. by Margot Tomes *(Putnam)*

MERRY MERRY, FIBruary by Doris Orgel, ill. by Arnold Lobel *(Parents)*

MY VILLAGE, STURBRIDGE by Gary Bowen, wood engravings designed by Gary Bowen and engraved by Randy Miller *(Farrar)*

NOAH'S ARK by Peter Spier *(Doubleday)*

THE SURPRISE PICNIC by John S. Goodall *(McElderry)*

WHEN THE WIND BLEW by Margaret Wise Brown, ill. by Geoffrey Hayes *(Harper)*

1978

CLOUDY WITH A CHANCE OF MEATBALLS by Judith Barrett, ill. by Ron Barrett *(Atheneum)*

THE FORBIDDEN FOREST by William Pène du Bois *(Harper)*

THE GREAT SONG BOOK edited by Timothy John, music editor Peter Hankey, ill. by Tomi Ungerer *(Doubleday/Benn)*

HANUKAH MONEY by Sholem Aleichem, ill. by Uri Shulevitz *(Greenwillow)*

THE LEGEND OF SCARFACE: A BLACKFEET INDIAN TALE by Robert D. San Souci, ill. by Daniel San Souci *(Doubleday)*

THE NUTCRACKERS AND THE SUGAR-TONGS by Edward Lear, ill. by Marcia Sewall *(Atlantic-Little, Brown)*

ODETTE: A BIRD IN PARIS by Kay Fender, ill. by Phillipe Dumas *(Prentice-Hall)*

A PEACEABLE KINGDOM: THE SHAKER ABECEDARIUS, ill. by Alice and Martin Provensen *(Viking)*

THERE ONCE WAS A WOMAN WHO MARRIED A MAN by Norma Farber, ill. by Lydia Dabcovich *(Addison)*

THIS LITTLE PIG-A-WIG AND OTHER RHYMES ABOUT PIGS chosen by Lenore Blegvad, ill. by Erik Blegvad *(McElderry)*

1979

BY CAMEL OR BY CAR: A LOOK AT TRANSPORTATION by Guy Billout *(Prentice-Hall)*

THE GARDEN OF ABDUL GASAZI by Chris Van Allsburg *(Houghton)*

HAPPY BIRTHDAY OLIVER! by Pierre Le-Tan *(Random)*

KING KRAKUS AND THE DRAGON by Janina Domanska *(Greenwillow)*

THE LONG DIVE by Mr. and Mrs. Smith *(Atheneum/Cape)*

NATURAL HISTORY by M.B. Goffstein *(Farrar)*

OX-CART MAN by Donald Hall, ill. by Barbara Cooney *(Viking)*

THE TALE OF FANCY NANCY: A SPANISH FOLK TALE adapted by Marion Koenig, ill. by Klaus Ensikat *(Chatto/Merrimack)*

TILLY'S HOUSE by Faith Jaques *(McElderry)*

THE TREASURE by Uri Shulevitz *(Farrar)*

1980

AN ARTIST by M.B. Goffstein *(Harper)*

A CHILD'S CHRISTMAS IN WALES by Dylan Thomas, ill. by Edward Ardizzone *(Godine)*

GORKY RISES by William Steig *(Farrar)*

THE HEADLESS HORSEMAN RIDES TONIGHT: MORE POEMS TO TROUBLE YOUR SLEEP by Jack Prelutsky, ill. by Arnold Lobel *(Greenwillow)*

HOWARD by James Stevenson *(Greenwillow)*

THE LUCKY YAK by Annetta Lawson, ill. by Allen Say *(Parnassus)*

MR. MILLER THE DOG by Helme Heine *(McElderry)*

STONE & STEEL: A BOOK ABOUT ENGINEERING by Guy Billout *(Prentice-Hall)*

UNBUILDING by David Macaulay *(Houghton)*

THE WONDERFUL TRAVELS AND ADVENTURES OF BARON MÜNCHHAUSEN by Peter Nickl, ill. by Binette Schroeder *(Chatto/Merrimack)*

1981

THE CRANE WIFE retold by Sumiko Yagawa, ill. by Suekichi Akaba *(Morrow)*

FLIGHT: A PANORAMA OF AVIATION by Melvin B. Zisfein, ill. by Robert Andrew Parker *(Pantheon)*

JUMANJI by Chris Van Allsburg *(Houghton)*

THE MAID AND THE MOUSE AND THE ODD-SHAPED HOUSE: A STORY IN RHYME by Paul O. Zelinsky *(Dodd)*

ON MARKET STREET by Arnold Lobel, ill. by Anita Lobel *(Greenwillow)*

MY MOM TRAVELS A LOT by Caroline Feller Bauer, ill. by Nancy Winslow Parker *(Warne)*

THE NOSE TREE adapted and ill. by Warwick Hutton *(McElderry)*

OUTSIDE OVER THERE by Maurice Sendak *(Harper)*

THE STORY OF MRS. BRUBECK: AND HOW SHE LOOKED FOR TROUBLE AND WHERE SHE FOUND HIM by Lore Segal, ill. by Marcia Sewall *(Pantheon)*

WHERE THE BUFFALOES BEGIN by Olaf Baker, ill. by Stephen Gammell *(Warne)*

1982
ANNO'S BRITAIN by Mitsumasa Anno *(Philomel)*
BEN'S DREAM by Chris Van Allsburg *(Houghton)*
THE GIFT OF THE MAGI by O. Henry, lettering by Michael Neugebauer, ill. by Lisbeth Zwerger *(Picture Book Studio)*
MY UNCLE by Jenny Thorne *(McElderry)*
PADDY GOES TRAVELING by John S. Goodall *(McElderry)*
RAINBOWS ARE MADE: POEMS BY CARL SANDBURG edited by Lee Bennett Hopkins, ill. by Fritz Eichenberg *(HBJ)*
SMILE, ERNEST AND CELESTINE by Gabrielle Vincent *(Greenwillow)*
SQUID AND SPIDER: A LOOK AT THE ANIMAL KINGDOM by Guy Billout *(Prentice-Hall)*
THE STRANGE APPEARANCE OF HOWARD CRANEBILL, JR. by Henrik Drescher *(Lothrop)*
THE TINY VISITOR by Oscar de Mejo *(Pantheon)*
1983
THE FAVERSHAMS by Roy Gerrard *(Farrar)*
LEONARD BASKIN'S MINIATURE NATURAL HISTORY: FIRST SERIES by Leonard Baskin *(Pantheon)*
LITTLE RED CAP retold and ill. by Lisbeth Zwerger *(Morrow)*
ROUND TRIP by Ann Jonas *(Greenwillow)*
SIMON'S BOOK by Henrik Drescher *(Lothrop)*
TOOLS by Ken Robbins *(Four Winds)*
TWELVE CATS FOR CHRISTMAS by Martin Leman *(Pelham/ Merrimack)*
UP A TREE by Ed Young *(Harper)*
THE WRECK OF THE ZEPHYR by Chris Van Allsburg *(Houghton)*
1984
ANIMAL ALPHABET by Bert Kitchen *(Dial)*
BABUSHKA retold and ill. by Charles Mikolaycak *(Holiday House)*
IF THERE WERE DREAMS TO SELL compiled by Barbara Lalicki, ill. by Margot Tomes *(Lothrop)*
JONAH AND THE GREAT FISH retold and ill. by Warwick Hutton *(McElderry)*
THE MYSTERIES OF HARRIS BURDICK by Chris Van Allsburg *(Houghton)*
THE NAPPING HOUSE by Audrey Wood, ill. by Don Wood *(HBJ)*
THE NUTCRACKER by E.T.A. Hoffman, ill. by Maurice Sendak *(Crown)*
SAINT GEORGE AND THE DRAGON retold by Margaret Hodges, ill. by Trina Schart Hyman *(Little, Brown)*
SIR CEDRIC by Roy Gerrard *(Farrar)*
WHERE THE RIVER BEGINS by Thomas Locker *(Dial)*
1985
GORILLA by Anthony Browne *(Knopf)*

GRANPA by John Burningham *(Crown)*
HAZEL'S AMAZING MOTHER by Rosemary Wells *(Dial)*
THE INSIDE-OUTSIDE BOOK OF NEW YORK CITY by
Roxie Munro *(Dodd)*
THE LEGEND OF ROSEPETAL by Clemens Brentano, ill. by
Lisbeth Zwerger *(Picture Book Studio)*
THE NIGHTINGALE by Hans Christian Andersen, ill. by Demi
(HBJ)
THE PEOPLE COULD FLY: AMERICAN BLACK FOLKTALES
by Virginia Hamilton, ill. by Leo and Diane Dillon *(Knopf)*
THE POLAR EXPRESS by Chris Van Allsburg *(Houghton))*
THE RELATIVES CAME by Cynthia Rylant, ill. by Stephen
Gammell *(Bradbury)*
THE STORY OF MRS. LOVEWRIGHT AND PURRLESS HER
CAT by Lore Segal, ill. by Paul O. Zelinksy *(Knopf)*
1986
BRAVE IRENE by William Steig *(Farrar)*
CHERRIES AND CHERRY PITS by Vera B. Williams
(Greenwillow)
FLYING by Donald Crews *(Greenwillow)*
MOLLY'S NEW WASHING MACHINE by Laura Geringer, ill.
by Petra Mathers *(Harper)*
ONE MORNING by Canna Funakoshi, ill. by Yohji Izawa
(Picture Book Studio)
THE OWL SCATTERER by Howard Norman, ill. by Michael
McCurdy *(Atlantic-Little, Brown)*
PIGS FROM A TO Z by Arthur Geisert *(Houghton)*
REMBRANDT TAKES A WALK by Mark Strand, ill. by Red
Grooms *(Clarkson Potter)*
THE STRANGER by Chris Van Allsburg *(Houghton)*
THE UGLY DUCKLING by Hans Christian Andersen, ill. by
Robert Van Nutt *(Knopf)*
1987
THE CREMATION OF SAM McGEE by Robert W. Service, ill.
by Ted Harrison *(Greenwillow)*
FOX'S DREAM by Tejima *(Philomel)*
HALLOWEEN ABC by Eve Merriam, ill. by Lane Smith
(Macmillan)
HANDTALK BIRTHDAY by Remy Charlip and Mary Beth
Miller, photog. by George Ancona *(Four Winds)*
IN COAL COUNTRY by Judith Hendershot, ill. by Thomas B.
Allen *(Knopf)*
JUMP AGAIN! MORE ADVENTURES OF BRER RABBIT by
Joel Chandler Harris, adapted by Van Dyke Parks, ill. by Barry
Moser *(HBJ)*
THE MOUNTAINS OF TIBET by Mordicai Gerstein *(Harper)*
RAINBOW RHINO by Peter Sís *(Knopf)*
17 KINGS AND 42 ELEPHANTS by Margaret Mahy, ill. by
Patricia MacCarthy *(Dial)*

THE YELLOW UMBRELLA by Henrik Drescher *(Bradbury)*

1988

CATS ARE CATS compiled by Nancy Larrick, ill. by Ed Young *(Philomel)*

FIRE CAME TO THE EARTH PEOPLE by Susan L. Roth *(St. Martin's)*

I WANT TO BE AN ASTRONAUT by Byron Barton *(Crowell)*

LOOK! LOOK! LOOK! by Tana Hoban *(Greenwillow)*

A RIVER DREAM by Allen Say *(Houghton)*

SHAKA: KING OF THE ZULUS by Diane Stanley and Peter Vennema, ill. by Diane Stanley *(Morrow)*

SIR FRANCIS DRAKE: HIS DARING DEEDS by Roy Gerrard *(Farrar)*

STRINGBEAN'S TRIP TO THE SHINING SEA by Vera B. Williams, ill. by Vera B. Williams and Jennifer Williams *(Greenwillow)*

SWAN SKY by Tejima *(Philomel)*

THEODOR AND MR. BALBINI by Petra Mathers *(Harper)*

1989

THE DANCING SKELETON by Cynthia C. DeFelice, ill. by Robert Andrew Parker *(Macmillan)*

DOES GOD HAVE A BIG TOE? STORIES ABOUT STORIES IN THE BIBLE by Marc Gellman, ill. by Oscar de Mejo *(Harper)*

THE HEARTACHES OF A FRENCH CAT by Barbara McClintock *(Godine)*

HOW PIZZA CAME TO QUEENS by Dayal Kaur Khalsa *(Clarkson Potter)*

NICHOLAS CRICKET by Joyce Maxner, ill. by William Joyce *(Harper)*

OLSON'S MEAT PIES by Peter Cohen, ill. by Olof Landstrom *(R & S)*

PEACOCK PIE: A BOOK OF RHYMES by Walter de la Mare, ill. by Louise Brierley *(Holt)*

THESEUS AND THE MINOTAUR by Warwick Hutton *(McElderry)*

TURTLE IN JULY by Marilyn Singer, ill. by Jerry Pinkney *(Macmillan)*

WHALES by Seymour Simon, ill. with photogs. *(Crowell)*

1990

BEACH BALL by Peter Sís *(Greenwillow)*

BENEATH A BLUE UMBRELLA by Jack Prelutsky, ill. by Garth Williams *(Greenwillow)*

A CHRISTMAS CAROL by Charles Dickens, ill. by Roberto Innocenti *(Stewart, Tabori & Chang)*

THE DANCING PALM TREE: AND OTHER NIGERIAN FOLKTALES by Barbara K. Walker, ill. by Helen Siegl *(Texas Tech)*

FISH EYES: A BOOK YOU CAN COUNT ON by Lois Ehlert *(HBJ)*

THE FOOL AND THE FISH: A TALE FROM RUSSIA by Alexander Nikolayevich Afanasyev, retold by Lenny Hort, ill. by Gennady Spirin *(Dial)*

I'M FLYING! by Alan Wade, ill. by Petra Mathers *(Knopf)*

ONE GORILLA: A COUNTING BOOK by Atsuko Morozumi *(Farrar)*

THE TALE OF THE MANDARIN DUCKS by Katherine Paterson, ill. by Leo and Diane Dillon *(Lodestar)*

WAR BOY: A COUNTRY CHILDHOOD by Michael Foreman *(Arcade)*

1991

ANOTHER CELEBRATED DANCING BEAR by Gladys Scheffrin-Falk, ill. by Barbara Garrison *(Scribner)*

DIEGO by Jonah Winter, ill. by Jeanette Winter *(Knopf)*

FOLLOW THE DREAM by Peter Sis *(Knopf)*

LITTLE RED RIDING HOOD by Charles Perrault, ill. by Beni Montresor *(Doubleday)*

THE MARVELOUS JOURNEY THROUGH THE NIGHT by Helme Heine *(Farrar)*

OLD MOTHER HUBBARD AND HER WONDERFUL DOG by James Marshall *(Farrar)*

OOH-LA-LA: (MAX IN LOVE) by Maira Kalman *(Viking)*

PUNCH IN NEW YORK by Alice Provensen *(Viking)*

TAR BEACH by Faith Ringgold *(Crown)*

WHAT CAN RABBIT HEAR? by Lucy Cousins *(Tambourine)*

1992

BOODIL MY DOG by Pija Lindenbaum *(Holt)*

THE CATARACT OF LODORE by Robert Southey, ill. by David Catrow *(Holt)*

THE FORTUNE-TELLERS by Lloyd Alexander, ill. by Trina Schart Hyman *(Dutton)*

LI'L SIS AND UNCLE WILLIE by Gwen Everett, ill. by William H. Johnson *(Rizzoli)*

MARTHA SPEAKS by Susan Meddaugh *(Houghton)*

MIRETTE ON THE HIGH WIRE by Emily Arnold McCully *(Putnam)*

OSCAR DE MEJO'S ABC by Oscar de Mejo *(HarperCollins)*

THE STINKY CHEESE MAN AND OTHER FAIRLY STUPID TALES by Jon Scieszka, ill. by Lane Smith *(Viking)*

WHERE DOES IT GO? by Margaret Miller *(Greenwillow)*

WHY THE SKY IS FAR AWAY: A NIGERIAN FOLK TALE retold by Mary-Joan Gerson, ill. by Carla Golembe *(Joy Street/Little, Brown)*

1993

THE BRACELET by Yoshiko Uchida, ill. by Joanna Yardley *(Philomel)*

GRANDFATHER'S JOURNEY by Allen Say *(Houghton)*

GULLIVER'S ADVENTURES IN LILLIPUT by Jonathan Swift, retold by Ann Keay Beneduce, ill. by Gennady Spirin *(Philomel)*

HARVEY SLUMFENBURGER'S CHRISTMAS PRESENT by John Burningham *(Candlewick)*
HOW DOGS REALLY WORK! by Alan Snow *(Little, Brown)*
HUE BOY by Rita Phillips Mitchell, ill. by Caroline Binch *(Dial)*
MAN-OF-WAR: STEPHEN BIESTY'S CROSS SECTIONS by Richard Platt, ill. by Stephen Biesty *(Dorling Kindersley)*
A NUMBER OF ANIMALS by Christopher Wormell *(Creative Editions)*
THE PERILOUS PIT by Orel Odinov Protopopescu, ill. by Jacqueline Chwast *(Green Tiger)*
A SMALL TALL TALE FROM THE FAR FAR NORTH by Peter Sís *(Knopf)*

1994

THE BOY AND THE CLOTH OF DREAMS by Jenny Koralek, ill. by James Mayhew *(Candlewick)*
THE BOY WHO ATE AROUND by Henrik Drescher *(Hyperion)*
HOW GEORGIE RADBOURN SAVED BASEBALL by David Shannon *(Scholastic)*
MY HOUSE by Lisa Desimini *(Holt)*
SHIP OF DREAMS by Dean Morrissey *(Mill Pond/Abrams)*
THE SUNDAY OUTING by Gloria Jean Pinkney, ill. by Jerry Pinkney *(Dial)*
SWAMP ANGEL by Anne Isaacs, ill. by Paul O. Zelinsky *(Dutton)*
A TEENY TINY BABY by Amy Schwartz *(Orchard)*
THE THREE GOLDEN KEYS by Peter Sís *(Doubleday)*
THE WAVE OF THE SEA-WOLF by David Wisniewski *(Clarion)*

1995

ALPHABET CITY by Stephen T. Johnson *(Viking)*
BUZ by Richard Egielski *(HarperCollins)*
DOGS EVERHWHERE by Cor Hazelaar *(Knopf)*
KASHTANKA by Anton Chekhov, adapted from a new translation by Ronald Meyer, ill. by Gennady Spirin *(Harcourt)*
MY MAMA HAD A DANCING HEART by Libba Moore Gray, ill. by Raúl Colón *(Orchard)*
SHE'S WEARING A DEAD BIRD ON HER HEAD! by Kathryn Lasky, ill. by David Catrow *(Hyperion)*
SOMEPLACE ELSE by Carol P. Saul, ill. by Barry Root *(Simon & Schuster)*
WHEN THE WHIPPOORWILL CALLS by Candice F. Ransom, ill. by Kimberly Bulcken Root *(Tambourine)*
WHY THE SUN & MOON LIVE IN THE SKY by Niki Daly *(Lothrop)*
ZIN! ZIN! ZIN! A VIOLIN by Lloyd Moss, ill. by Marjorie Priceman *(Simon & Schuster)*

John Newbery Medal 🖎

Donated by the Frederic G. Melcher family, the Newbery Medal has been awarded annually since 1922 under the supervision of the Association for Library Service to Children of the American Library Association (50 E. Huron St., Chicago, IL 60611) to the author of the most distinguished contribution to literature for children published in the U.S. during the preceding year. Announced in January, the award is limited to residents or citizens of the U.S. (Medal)

1922
THE STORY OF MANKIND by Hendrik Willem van Loon *(Liveright)*
HONOR BOOKS
CEDRIC THE FORESTER by Bernard Marshall *(Appleton)*
THE GOLDEN FLEECE AND THE HEROES WHO LIVED BEFORE ACHILLES by Padraic Colum *(Macmillan)*
THE GREAT QUEST by Charles Hawes *(Little, Brown)*
THE OLD TOBACCO SHOP by William Bowen *(Macmillan)*
WINDY HILL by Cornelia Meigs *(Macmillan)*
1923
THE VOYAGES OF DOCTOR DOLITTLE by Hugh Lofting *(Lippincott)*
HONOR BOOK
No Record
1924
THE DARK FRIGATE by Charles Hawes *(Atlantic-Little, Brown)*
HONOR BOOK
No Record
1925
TALES FROM SILVER LANDS by Charles Finger *(Doubleday)*
HONOR BOOKS
DREAM COACH by Anne Parrish *(Macmillan)*
NICHOLAS by Anne Carroll Moore *(Putnam)*
1926
SHEN OF THE SEA by Arthur Bowie Chrisman *(Dutton)*
HONOR BOOK
VOYAGERS by Padraic Colum *(Macmillan)*
1927
SMOKY, THE COWHORSE by Will James *(Scribner)*
HONOR BOOK
No Record
1928
GAYNECK, THE STORY OF A PIGEON by Dhan Gopal Mukerji *(Dutton)*

HONOR BOOKS
DOWNRIGHT DENCEY by Caroline Snedeker *(Doubleday)*
THE WONDER SMITH AND HIS SON by Ella Young
(Longmans)

1929
THE TRUMPETER OF KRAKOW by Eric P. Kelly *(Macmillan)*
HONOR BOOKS
THE BOY WHO WAS by Grace Hallock *(Dutton)*
CLEARING WEATHER by Cornelia Meigs *(Little, Brown)*
MILLIONS OF CATS by Wanda Gág *(Coward)*
PIGTAIL OF AH LEE BEN LOO by John Bennett *(Longmans)*
RUNAWAY PAPOOSE by Grace Moon *(Doubleday)*
TOD OF THE FENS by Elinor Whitney *(Macmillan)*

1930
HITTY, HER FIRST HUNDRED YEARS by Rachel Field
(Macmillan)
HONOR BOOKS
DAUGHTER OF THE SEINE by Jeanette Eaton *(Harper)*
JUMPING-OFF PLACE by Marian Hurd McNeely *(Longmans)*
LITTLE BLACKNOSE by Hildegarde Swift *(HBJ)*
PRAN OF ALBANIA by Elizabeth Miller *(Doubleday)*
TANGLE-COATED HORSE AND OTHER TALES by Ella
Young *(Longmans)*
VAINO by Julia Davis Adams *(Dutton)*

1931
THE CAT WHO WENT TO HEAVEN by Elizabeth
Coatsworth *(Macmillan)*
HONOR BOOKS
THE DARK STAR OF ITZA by Alida Malkus *(HBJ)*
FLOATING ISLAND by Anne Parrish *(Harper)*
GARRAM THE HUNTER by Herbert Best *(Doubleday)*
MEGGY MACINTOSH by Elizabeth Janet Gray *(Doubleday)*
MOUNTAINS ARE FREE by Julia Davis Adams *(Dutton)*
OOD-LE-UK THE WANDERER by Alice Lide and Margaret
Johansen *(Little, Brown)*
QUEER PERSON by Ralph Hubbard *(Doubleday)*
SPICE AND THE DEVIL'S CAKE by Agnes Hewes *(Knopf)*

1932
WATERLESS MOUNTAIN by Laura Adams Armer *(Longmans)*
HONOR BOOKS
BOY OF THE SOUTH SEAS by Eunice Tietjens *(Coward)*
CALICO BUSH by Rachel Field *(Macmillan)*
THE FAIRY CIRCUS by Dorothy P. Lathrop *(Macmillan)*
JANE'S ISLAND by Marjorie Allee *(Houghton)*
OUT OF THE FLAME by Eloise Lownsbery *(Longmans)*
TRUCE OF THE WOLF AND OTHER TALES OF OLD
ITALY by Mary Gould Davis *(HBJ)*

1933
YOUNG FU OF THE UPPER YANGTZE by Elizabeth Lewis
(Winston)
HONOR BOOKS
CHILDREN OF THE SOIL by Nora Burglon *(Doubleday)*
THE RAILROAD TO FREEDOM by Hildegarde Swift *(HBJ)*
SWIFT RIVERS by Cornelia Meigs *(Little, Brown)*
1934
INVINCIBLE LOUISA by Cornelia Meigs *(Little, Brown)*
HONOR BOOKS
ABC BUNNY by Wanda Gág *(Coward)*
APPRENTICE OF FLORENCE by Anne Kyle *(Houghton)*
BIG TREE OF BUNLAHY by Padraic Colum *(Macmillan)*
THE FORGOTTEN DAUGHTER by Caroline Snedeker
(Doubleday)
GLORY OF THE SEAS by Agnes Hewes *(Knopf)*
NEW LAND by Sarah Schmidt *(McBride)*
SWORDS OF STEEL by Elsie Singmaster *(Houghton)*
WINGED GIRL OF KNOSSOS by Erik Berry *(Appleton)*
1935
DOBRY by Monica Shannon *(Viking)*
HONOR BOOKS
DAVY CROCKETT by Constance Rourke *(HBJ)*
DAY ON SKATES by Hilda Van Stockum *(Harper)*
PAGEANT OF CHINESE HISTORY by Elizabeth Seeger
(Longmans)

1936
CADDIE WOODLAWN by Carol Ryrie Brink *(Macmillan)*
HONOR BOOKS
ALL SAIL SET by Armstrong Sperry *(Winston)*
THE GOOD MASTER by Kate Seredy *(Viking)*
HONK, THE MOOSE by Phil Stong *(Dodd)*
YOUNG WALTER SCOTT by Elizabeth Janet Gray *(Viking)*
1937
ROLLER SKATES by Ruth Sawyer *(Viking)*
HONOR BOOKS
AUDUBON by Constance Rourke *(HBJ)*
THE CODFISH MUSKET by Agnes Hewes *(Doubleday)*
GOLDEN BASKET by Ludwig Bemelmans *(Viking)*
PHEBE FAIRCHILD: HER BOOK by Lois Lenski *(Stokes)*
WHISTLER'S VAN by Idwal Jones *(Viking)*
WINTERBOUND by Margery Bianco *(Viking)*
1938
THE WHITE STAG by Kate Seredy *(Viking)*
HONOR BOOKS
BRIGHT ISLAND by Mabel Robinson *(Random)*
ON THE BANKS OF PLUM CREEK by Laura Ingalls Wilder
(Harper)

PECOS BILL by James Cloyd Bowman *(Little, Brown)*
1939
THIMBLE SUMMER by Elizabeth Enright *(Rinehart)*
HONOR BOOKS
HELLO THE BOAT! by Phyllis Crawford *(Holt)*
LEADER BY DESTINY: GEORGE WASHINGTON, MAN
AND PATRIOT by Jeanette Eaton *(HBJ)*
MR. POPPER'S PENGUINS by Richard and Florence Atwater
(Little, Brown)
NINO by Valenti Angelo *(Viking)*
PENN by Elizabeth Janet Gray *(Viking)*
1940
DANIEL BOONE by James Daugherty *(Viking)*
HONOR BOOKS
BOY WITH A PACK by Stephen W. Meader *(HBJ)*
BY THE SHORES OF SILVER LAKE by Laura Ingalls Wilder
(Harper)
RUNNER OF THE MOUNTAIN TOPS by Mabel Robinson
(Random)
THE SINGING TREE by Kate Seredy *(Viking)*
1941
CALL IT COURAGE by Armstrong Sperry *(Macmillan)*
HONOR BOOKS
BLUE WILLOW by Doris Gates *(Viking)*
THE LONG WINTER by Laura Ingalls Wilder *(Harper)*
NANSEN by Anna Gertrude Hall *(Viking)*
YOUNG MAC OF FORT VANCOUVER by Mary Jane Carr
(Crowell)
1942
THE MATCHLOCK GUN by Walter D. Edmonds *(Dodd)*
HONOR BOOKS
DOWN RYTON WATER by Eva Roe Gaggin *(Viking)*
GEORGE WASHINGTON'S WORLD by Genevieve Foster
(Scribner)
INDIAN CAPTIVE: THE STORY OF MARY JEMISON by
Lois Lenski *(Lippincott)*
LITTLE TOWN ON THE PRAIRIE by Laura Ingalls Wilder
(Harper)
1943
ADAM OF THE ROAD by Elizabeth Janet Gray *(Viking)*
HONOR BOOKS
HAVE YOU SEEN TOM THUMB? by Mabel Leigh Hunt
(Lippincott)
THE MIDDLE MOFFAT by Eleanor Estes *(HBJ)*
1944
JOHNNY TREMAIN by Esther Forbes *(Houghton)*
HONOR BOOKS
FOG MAGIC by Julia Sauer *(Viking)*
MOUNTAIN BORN by Elizabath Yates *(Coward)*

RUFUS M. by Eleanor Estes *(HBJ)*
THESE HAPPY GOLDEN YEARS by Laura Ingalls Wilder *(Harper)*
1945
RABBIT HILL by Robert Lawson *(Viking)*
HONOR BOOKS
ABRAHAM LINCOLN'S WORLD by Genevieve Foster *(Scribner)*
THE HUNDRED DRESSES by Eleanor Estes *(HBJ)*
LONE JOURNEY: THE LIFE OF ROGER WILLIAMS by Jeanette Eaton *(HBJ)*
THE SILVER PENCIL by Alice Dalgliesh *(Scribner)*
1946
STRAWBERRY GIRL by Lois Lenski *(Lippincott)*
HONOR BOOKS
BHIMSA, THE DANCING BEAR by Christine Weston *(Scribner)*
JUSTIN MORGAN HAD A HORSE by Marguerite Henry *(Rand McNally)*
THE MOVED-OUTERS by Florence Crannell Means *(Houghton)*
NEW FOUND WORLD by Katherine Shippen *(Viking)*
1947
MISS HICKORY by Carolyn Sherwin Bailey *(Viking)*
HONOR BOOKS
THE AVION MY UNCLE FLEW by Cyrus Fisher *(Appleton)*
BIG TREE by Mary and Conrad Buff *(Viking)*
THE HEAVENLY TENANTS by William Maxwell *(Harper)*
THE HIDDEN TREASURE OF GLASTON by Eleanore Jewett *(Viking)*
WONDERFUL YEAR by Nancy Barnes *(Messner)*
1948
THE TWENTY-ONE BALLOONS by William Pène du Bois *(Viking)*
HONOR BOOKS
THE COW-TAIL SWITCH, AND OTHER WEST AFRICAN STORIES by Harold Courlander *(Holt)*
LI LUN, LAD OF COURAGE by Carolyn Treffinger *(Abingdon)*
MISTY OF CHINCOTEAGUE by Marguerite Henry *(Rand McNally)*
PANCAKES—PARIS by Claire Huchet Bishop *(Viking)*
THE QUAINT AND CURIOUS QUEST OF JOHNNY LONGFOOT by Catherine Besterman *(Bobbs)*
1949
KING OF THE WIND by Marguerite Henry *(Rand McNally)*
HONOR BOOKS
DAUGHTER OF THE MOUNTAINS by Louise Rankin *(Viking)*
MY FATHER'S DRAGON by Ruth S. Gannett *(Random)*
SEABIRD by Holling C. Holling *(Houghton)*

STORY OF THE NEGRO by Arna Bontemps *(Knopf)*

1950
THE DOOR IN THE WALL by Marguerite de Angeli
(Doubleday)

HONOR BOOKS
THE BLUE CAT OF CASTLE TOWN by Catherine Coblentz
(Longmans)
GEORGE WASHINGTON by Genevieve Foster *(Scribner)*
KILDEE HOUSE by Rutherford Montgomery *(Doubleday)*
SONG OF THE PINES by Walter and Marion Havighurst
(Winston)
TREE OF FREEDOM by Rebecca Caudill *(Viking)*

1951
AMOS FORTUNE, FREE MAN by Elizabeth Yates *(Dutton)*

HONOR BOOKS
ABRAHAM LINCOLN, FRIEND OF THE PEOPLE by Clara
Ingram Judson *(Follett)*
BETTER KNOWN AS JOHNNY APPLESEED by Mabel Leigh
Hunt *(Lippincott)*
GANDHI, FIGHTER WITHOUT A SWORD by Jeanette Eaton
(Morrow)
THE STORY OF APPLEBY CAPPLE by Anne Parrish *(Harper)*

1952
GINGER PYE by Eleanor Estes *(HBJ)*

HONOR BOOKS
AMERICANS BEFORE COLUMBUS by Elizabeth Baity *(Viking)*
THE APPLE AND THE ARROW by Mary and Conrad Buff
(Houghton)
THE DEFENDER by Nicholas Kalashnikoff *(Scribner)*
THE LIGHT AT TERN ROCKS by Julia Sauer *(Viking)*
MINN OF THE MISSISSIPPI by Holling C. Holling *(Houghton)*

1953
SECRET OF THE ANDES by Ann Nolan Clark *(Viking)*

HONOR BOOKS
THE BEARS ON HEMLOCK MOUNTAIN by Alice Dalgliesh
(Scribner)
BIRTHDAYS OF FREEDOM, VOL. 1 by Genevieve Foster
(Scribner)
CHARLOTTE'S WEB by E.B. White *(Harper)*
MOCCASIN TRAIL by Eloise McGraw *(Coward)*
RED SAILS TO CAPRI by Ann Weil *(Viking)*

1954
...AND NOW MIGUEL by Joseph Krumgold *(Crowell)*

HONOR BOOKS
ALL ALONE by Claire Huchet Bishop *(Viking)*
HURRY HOME CANDY by Meindert DeJong *(Harper)*
MAGIC MAIZE by Mary and Conrad Buff *(Houghton)*
SHADRACH by Meindert DeJong *(Harper)*

THEODORE ROOSEVELT, FIGHTING PATRIOT by Clara Ingram Judson *(Follett)*

1955

THE WHEEL ON THE SCHOOL by Meindert DeJong *(Harper)*

HONOR BOOKS

BANNER IN THE SKY by James Ullman *(Lippincott)*

COURAGE OF SARAH NOBLE by Alice Dalgliesh *(Scribner)*

1956

CARRY ON, MR. BOWDITCH by Jean Lee Latham *(Houghton)*

HONOR BOOKS

THE GOLDEN NAME DAY by Jennie Lindquist *(Harper)*

MEN, MICROSCOPES, AND LIVING THINGS by Katherine Shippen *(Viking)*

THE SECRET RIVER by Marjorie Kinnan Rawlings *(Scribner)*

1957

MIRACLES ON MAPLE HILL by Virginia Sorensen *(HBJ)*

HONOR BOOKS

BLACK FOX OF LORNE by Marguerite de Angeli *(Doubleday)*

THE CORN GROWS RIPE by Dorothy Rhoads *(Viking)*

THE HOUSE OF SIXTY FATHERS by Meindert DeJong *(Harper)*

MR. JUSTICE HOLMES by Clara Ingram Judson *(Follett)*

OLD YELLER by Fred Gipson *(Harper)*

1958

RIFLES FOR WATIE by Harold Keith *(Crowell)*

HONOR BOOKS

GONE-AWAY LAKE by Elizabeth Enright *(HBJ)*

THE GREAT WHEEL by Robert Lawson *(Viking)*

THE HORSECATCHER by Mari Sandoz *(Westminster)*

TOM PAINE, FREEDOM'S APOSTLE by Leo Gurko *(Crowell)*

1959

THE WITCH OF BLACKBIRD POND by Elizabeth George Speare *(Houghton)*

HONOR BOOKS

ALONG CAME A DOG by Meindert DeJong *(Harper)*

CHUCARO: WILD PONY OF THE PAMPA by Francis Kalnay *(HBJ)*

THE FAMILY UNDER THE BRIDGE by Natalie Savage Carlson *(Harper)*

THE PERILOUS ROAD by William O. Steele *(HBJ)*

1960

ONION JOHN by Joseph Krumgold *(Crowell)*

HONOR BOOKS

AMERICA IS BORN by Gerald W. Johnson *(Morrow)*

THE GAMMAGE CUP by Carol Kendall *(HBJ)*

MY SIDE OF THE MOUNTAIN by Jean Craighead George *(Dutton)*

1961
ISLAND OF THE BLUE DOLPHINS by Scott O'Dell
(Houghton)
HONOR BOOKS
AMERICA MOVES FORWARD by Gerald W. Johnson
(Morrow)
THE CRICKET IN TIMES SQUARE by George Selden (Farrar)
OLD RAMON by Jack Schaefer (Houghton)
1962
THE BRONZE BOW by Elizabeth George Speare (Houghton)
HONOR BOOKS
BELLING THE TIGER by Mary Stolz (Harper)
FRONTIER LIVING by Edwin Tunis (World)
THE GOLDEN GOBLET by Eloise McGraw (Coward)
1963
A WRINKLE IN TIME by Madeleine L'Engle (Farrar)
HONOR BOOKS
MEN OF ATHENS by Olivia Coolidge (Houghton)
THISTLE AND THYME by Sorche Nic Leodhas (Holt)
1964
IT'S LIKE THIS, CAT by Emily Cheney Neville (Harper)
HONOR BOOKS
THE LONER by Ester Wier (McKay)
RASCAL by Sterling North (Dutton)
1965
SHADOW OF A BULL by Maia Wojciechowska (Atheneum)
HONOR BOOKS
ACROSS FIVE APRILS by Irene Hunt (Follett)
1966
I, JUAN DE PAREJA by Elizabeth Borten de Treviño (Farrar)
HONOR BOOKS
THE ANIMAL FAMILY by Randall Jarrell (Pantheon)
THE BLACK CAULDRON by Lloyd Alexander (Holt)
THE NOONDAY FRIENDS by Mary Stolz (Harper)
1967
UP A ROAD SLOWLY by Irene Hunt (Follett)
HONOR BOOKS
THE JAZZ MAN by Mary H. Weik (Atheneum)
THE KING'S FIFTH by Scott O'Dell (Houghton)
ZLATEH THE GOAT AND OTHER STORIES by Isaac
Bashevis Singer (Harper)
1968
FROM THE MIXED-UP FILES OF MRS. BASIL E.
FRANKWEILER by E.L. Konigsburg (Atheneum)
HONOR BOOKS
THE BLACK PEARL by Scott O'Dell (Houghton)
THE EGYPT GAME by Zilpha Keatley Snyder (Atheneum)
THE FEARSOME INN by Isaac Bashevis Singer (Scribner)

JENNIFER, HECATE, MACBETH, WILLIAM McKINLEY, AND ME, ELIZABETH by E.L. Konigsburg *(Atheneum)*
1969
THE HIGH KING by Lloyd Alexander *(Holt)*
HONOR BOOKS
TO BE A SLAVE by Julius Lester *(Dial)*
WHEN SHLEMIEL WENT TO WARSAW & OTHER STORIES by Isaac Bashevis Singer *(Farrar)*
1970
SOUNDER by William H. Armstrong *(Harper)*
HONOR BOOKS
JOURNEY OUTSIDE by Mary Q. Steele *(Viking)*
THE MANY WAYS OF SEEING: AN INTRODUCTION TO THE PLEASURES OF ART by Janet Gaylord Moore *(World)*
OUR EDDIE by Sulamith Ish-Kishor *(Pantheon)*
1971
SUMMER OF THE SWANS by Betsy Byars *(Viking)*
HONOR BOOKS
ENCHANTRESS FROM THE STARS by Sylvia Louise Engdahl *(Atheneum)*
KNEE-KNOCK RISE by Natalie Babbitt *(Farrar)*
SING DOWN THE MOON by Scott O'Dell *(Houghton)*
1972
MRS. FRISBY AND THE RATS OF NIMH by Robert C. O'Brien *(Atheneum)*
HONOR BOOKS
ANNIE AND THE OLD ONE by Miska Miles *(Atlantic-Little, Brown)*
THE HEADLESS CUPID by Zilpha Keatley Snyder *(Atheneum)*
INCIDENT AT HAWK'S HILL by Allan W. Eckert *(Little, Brown)*
THE PLANET OF JUNIOR BROWN by Virginia Hamilton *(Macmillan)*
THE TOMBS OF ATUAN by Ursula K. Le Guin *(Atheneum)*
1973
JULIE OF THE WOLVES by Jean Craighead George *(Harper)*
HONOR BOOKS
FROG AND TOAD TOGETHER by Arnold Lobel *(Harper)*
THE UPSTAIRS ROOM by Johanna Reiss *(Crowell)*
THE WITCHES OF WORM by Zilpha Keatley Snyder *(Atheneum)*
1974
THE SLAVE DANCER by Paula Fox *(Bradbury)*
HONOR BOOK
THE DARK IS RISING by Susan Cooper *(McElderry)*
1975
M. C. HIGGINS, THE GREAT by Virginia Hamilton *(Macmillan)*

HONOR BOOKS
FIGGS & PHANTOMS by Ellen Raskin *(Dutton)*
MY BROTHER SAM IS DEAD by James Lincoln Collier and Christopher Collier *(Four Winds)*
THE PERILOUS GARD by Elizabeth Marie Pope *(Houghton)*
PHILIP HALL LIKES ME, I RECKON MAYBE by Bette Greene *(Dial)*
1976
THE GREY KING by Susan Cooper *(McElderry)*
HONOR BOOKS
DRAGONWINGS by Laurence Yep *(Harper)*
THE HUNDRED PENNY BOX by Sharon Bell Mathis *(Viking)*
1977
ROLL OF THUNDER, HEAR MY CRY by Mildred D. Taylor *(Dial)*
HONOR BOOKS
ABEL'S ISLAND by William Steig *(Farrar)*
A STRING IN THE HARP by Nancy Bond *(McElderry)*
1978
BRIDGE TO TERABITHIA by Katherine Paterson *(Crowell)*
HONOR BOOKS
ANPAO: AN AMERICAN INDIAN ODYSSEY by Jamake Highwater *(Lippincott)*
RAMONA AND HER FATHER by Beverly Cleary *(Morrow)*
1979
THE WESTING GAME by Ellen Raskin *(Dutton)*
HONOR BOOKS
THE GREAT GILLY HOPKINS by Katherine Paterson *(Crowell)*
1980
A GATHERING OF DAYS: A NEW ENGLAND GIRL'S JOURNAL, 1830-32 by Joan W. Blos *(Scribner)*
HONOR BOOK
THE ROAD FROM HOME: THE STORY OF AN ARMENIAN GIRL by David Kherdian *(Greenwillow)*
1981
JACOB HAVE I LOVED by Katherine Paterson *(Crowell)*
HONOR BOOKS
THE FLEDGLING by Jane Langton *(Harper)*
A RING OF ENDLESS LIGHT by Madeleine L'Engle *(Farrar)*
1982
A VISIT TO WILLIAM BLAKE'S INN: POEMS FOR INNOCENT AND EXPERIENCED TRAVELERS by Nancy Willard *(HBJ)*
HONOR BOOKS
RAMONA QUIMBY, AGE 8 by Beverly Cleary *(Morrow)*
UPON THE HEAD OF THE GOAT: A CHILDHOOD IN HUNGARY, 1939-1944 by Aranka Siegal *(Farrar)*

1983
DICEY'S SONG by Cynthia Voigt *(Atheneum)*
HONOR BOOKS
THE BLUE SWORD by Robin McKinley *(Greenwillow)*
DOCTOR DE SOTO by William Steig *(Farrar)*
GRAVEN IMAGES by Paul Fleischman *(Harper)*
HOMESICK: MY OWN STORY by Jean Fritz *(Putnam)*
SWEET WHISPERS, BROTHER RUSH by Virginia Hamilton
(Philomel)

1984
DEAR MR. HENSHAW by Beverly Cleary *(Morrow)*
HONOR BOOKS
THE SIGN OF THE BEAVER by Elizabeth George Speare
(Houghton)
A SOLITARY BLUE by Cynthia Voigt *(Atheneum)*
SUGARING TIME by Kathryn Lasky *(Macmillan)*
THE WISH GIVER by Bill Brittain *(Harper)*

1985
THE HERO AND THE CROWN by Robin McKinley
(Greenwillow)
HONOR BOOKS
LIKE JAKE AND ME by Mavis Jukes *(Knopf)*
THE MOVES MAKE THE MAN by Bruce Brooks *(Harper)*
ONE-EYED CAT by Paula Fox *(Bradbury)*

1986
SARAH, PLAIN AND TALL by Patricia MacLachlan *(Harper)*
HONOR BOOKS
COMMODORE PERRY IN THE LAND OF THE SHOGUN by
Rhoda Blumberg *(Lothrop)*
DOGSONG by Gary Paulsen *(Bradbury)*

1987
THE WHIPPING BOY by Sid Fleischman *(Greenwillow)*
HONOR BOOKS
A FINE WHITE DUST by Cynthia Rylant *(Bradbury)*
ON MY HONOR by Marion Dane Bauer *(Clarion)*
VOLCANO: THE ERUPTION AND HEALING OF MOUNT
ST. HELENS by Patricia Lauber *(Bradbury)*

1988
LINCOLN: A PHOTOBIOGRAPHY by Russell Freedman
(Clarion)
HONOR BOOKS
AFTER THE RAIN by Norma Fox Mazer *(Morrow)*
HATCHET by Gary Paulsen *(Bradbury)*

1989
JOYFUL NOISE: POEMS FOR TWO VOICES by Paul
Fleischman *(Harper)*
HONOR BOOKS
IN THE BEGINNING: CREATION STORIES FROM
AROUND THE WORLD by Virginia Hamilton *(HBJ)*

SCORPIONS by Walter Dean Myers *(Harper)*
1990
NUMBER THE STARS by Lois Lowry *(Houghton)*
HONOR BOOKS
AFTERNOON OF THE ELVES by Janet Taylor Lisle *(Orchard)*
SHABANU: DAUGHTER OF THE WIND by Suzanne Fisher Staples *(Knopf)*
THE WINTER ROOM by Gary Paulsen *(Orchard)*
1991
MANIAC MAGEE by Jerry Spinelli *(Little, Brown)*
HONOR BOOK
THE TRUE CONFESSIONS OF CHARLOTTE DOYLE by Avi *(Orchard)*
1992
SHILOH by Phyllis Reynolds Naylor *(Atheneum)*
HONOR BOOKS
NOTHING BUT THE TRUTH: A DOCUMENTARY NOVEL by Avi *(Orchard)*
THE WRIGHT BROTHERS: HOW THEY INVENTED THE AIRPLANE by Russell Freedman *(Holiday House)*
1993
MISSING MAY by Cynthia Rylant *(Orchard)*
HONOR BOOKS
THE DARK THIRTY: SOUTHERN TALES OF THE SUPERNATURAL by Patricia C. McKissack, ill. by Brian Pinkney *(Knopf)*
SOMEWHERE IN THE DARKNESS by Walter Dean Myers *(Scholastic)*
WHAT HEARTS by Bruce Brooks *(HarperCollins)*
1994
THE GIVER by Lois Lowry *(Houghton)*
HONOR BOOKS
CRAZY LADY! by Jane Leslie Conley *(HarperCollins)*
DRAGON'S GATE by Laurence Yep *(HarperCollins)*
ELEANOR ROOSEVELT: A LIFE OF DISCOVERY by Russell Freedman *(Clarion)*
1995
WALK TWO MOONS by Sharon Creech *(HarperCollins)*
HONOR BOOKS
CATHERINE, CALLED BIRDY by Karen Cushman *(Clarion)*
THE EAR, THE EYE AND THE ARM by Nancy Farmer *(Orchard)*
1996
THE MIDWIFE'S APPRENTICE by Karen Cushman *(Clarion)*
HONOR BOOKS
THE GREAT FIRE by Jim Murphy *(Scholastic)*
THE WATSONS GO TO BIRMINGHAM—1963 by Christopher Paul Curtis *(Delacorte)*
WHAT JAMIE SAW by Carolyn Coman *(Front Street)*
YOLANDA'S GENIUS by Carol Fenner *(McElderry)*

North Carolina Literary and Historical Association Awards ❧

AMERICAN ASSOCIATION OF UNIVERSITY WOMEN (AAUW) AWARD IN JUVENILE LITERATURE, NORTH CAROLINA DIVISION, AAUW

Given annually in November through the North Carolina Literary and Historical Association (109 E. Jones St., Raleigh, NC 27611). Author must have maintained legal or physical residence in state for three years. (Cup)

1953
PEANUT by Ruth and Latrobe Carroll *(Walck)*
1954
PENNY ROSE by Mebane Holloman Burgwyn *(Walck)*
1955
DIGBY, THE ONLY DOG by Ruth and Latrobe Carroll *(Walck)*
1956
FIDDLER'S FANCY by Julia Montgomery Street *(Follett)*
1957
TAFFY OF TORPEDO JUNCTION by Nell Wise Wechter *(Blair)*
1958
THE SECRET CIRCLE by Ina B. Forbus *(Viking)*
1959
CAPTAIN GHOST by Thelma Harrington Bell *(Viking)*
1960
STONEWALL JACKSON by Jonathan Daniels *(Random)*
1961
BEAVER BUSINESS: AN ALMANAC by Glen Rounds *(Prentice-Hall)*
1962
RIFLES AT RAMSOUR'S MILL by Manly Wade Wellman *(Washburn)*
1963
DULCIE'S WHALE by Julia Montgomery Street *(Bobbs)*
1964
THE BAT-POET by Randall Jarrell *(Macmillan)*
1965
THE FORGOTTEN DOOR by Alexander Key *(Westminster)*
1966
NORTH CAROLINA PARADE by Julia Montgomery Street and Richard Walser *(University of North Carolina)*

1967
THE SNAKE TREE by Glen Rounds *(World)*
1968
A BIOGRAPHY OF THOMAS WOLFE by Neal F. Austin
(Roger Beacham)
1969
BUGLES AT THE BORDER by Mary Gillett *(Blair)*
1970
THE CRACKAJACK PONY by Mebane Holoman Burgwyn
(Lippincott)
1971
PURRO AND THE PRATTLEBERRIES by Suzanne Newton
(Westminster)
1972
No Award
1973
THE PEOPLE OF NORTH CAROLINA by Barbara M.
Parramore *(Sadlier)*
1974
C/O ARNOLD'S CORNERS by Suzanne Newton *(Westminster)*
1975
THE MAGIC MEADOW by Alexander Key *(Westminster)*
1976
MR. YOWDER AND THE LION ROAR CAPSULES by Glen
Rounds *(Holiday House)*
1977
THE CITY ROSE by Ruth White Miller *(McGraw-Hill)*
1978
WHAT ARE YOU UP TO, WILLIAM THOMAS? by Suzanne
Newton *(Westminster)*
1979
REUBELLA AND THE OLD FOCUS HOME by Suzanne
Newton *(Westminster)*
1980
SAFE AS THE GRAVE by Caroline B. Cooney *(Coward)*
1981
No Award
1982
M. V. SEXTON by Suzanne Newton *(Viking)*
1983
WILD APPALOOSA by Glen Rounds *(Holiday House)*
1984
TANCY by Belinda Hurmence *(Clarion)*
1985
THE SUMMER THAT LASTED FOREVER by Catherine
Petroski *(Houghton)*

1986
GOLDEN GIRL by Nancy Tilly *(Farrar)*
1987
PERMANENT CONNECTIONS by Sue Ellen Bridgers *(Harper)*
1988
EATING CROW by Lila Hopkins *(Watts)*
1989
THE NIGHTWALKER by Belinda Hurmence *(Clarion)*
1990
TALKING TURKEY by Lila Hopkins *(Watts)*
1991
WHERE ARE YOU WHEN I NEED YOU? by Suzanne Newton
(Viking)
1992
WINGS by Bill Brittain *(HarperCollins)*
1993
THE DREAM OF THE STONE by Christina Askounis *(Farrar)*
1994
ASHPET: AN APPALACHIAN TALE by Joanne Compton
(Holiday House)
1995
SODY SALLYRATUS by Joanne Compton *(Holiday House)*

Scott O'Dell Award for Historical Fiction ❧

Originated and donated by Scott O'Dell (1898-1989), author of
several honored children's books and recipient in 1972 of the
Hans Christian Andersen Award of the International Board on
Books for Young People (IBBY) for the body of his work, this
award is for a distinguished work of historical fiction. The
winning titles must be published in English for children or young
adults by a U.S. publisher, and be set in the New World, i.e.,
North, Central, or South America. The award was established in
1981, but not given until the selection committee determined
there was an appropriate recipient. Administration and selection
are by an Advisory Board chaired by Zena Sutherland (1700 E.
56th St., Chicago, IL 60637). ($5,000)

1984
THE SIGN OF THE BEAVER by Elizabeth George Speare
(Houghton)

1985
THE FIGHTING GROUND by Avi *(Lippincott)*
1986
SARAH, PLAIN AND TALL by Patricia MacLachlan *(Harper)*
1987
STREAMS TO THE RIVER, RIVER TO THE SEA by Scott
O'Dell *(Houghton)*
Note: The award committee, with Scott O'Dell's agreement,
selected the Children's Book Council as the recipient of the cash
award.
1988
CHARLEY SKEDADDLE by Patricia Beatty *(Morrow)*
1989
THE HONORABLE PRISON by Lyll Becerra de Jenkins
(Lodestar)
1990
SHADES OF GRAY by Carolyn Reeder *(Macmillan)*
1991
A TIME OF TROUBLES by Pieter van Raven *(Scribner)*
1992
STEPPING ON THE CRACKS by Mary Downing Hahn
(Clarion)
1993
MORNING GIRL by Michael Dorris *(Hyperion)*
1994
BULL RUN by Paul Fleischman *(HarperCollins)*
1995
UNDER THE BLOOD-RED SUN by Graham Salisbury
(Delacorte)
1996
THE BOMB by Theodore Taylor *(Harcourt)*

Ohioana Book Awards 🍂
JUVENILE (OR YOUNG ADULT) BOOK CATEGORY

Awarded annually by the Ohioana Library Association (Suite
1105, 65 S. Front St., Columbus, OH 43215-0334) to an Ohio
author who has written an outstanding book published in the
preceding year or for the body of work of an Ohio author.
Author must have been born in Ohio or lived there a minimum
of five years. (Medal)

1943
BIBI: THE BAKER'S HORSE by Anna Bird Stewart *(Lippincott)*
1944
BAYOU SUZETTE by Lois Lenski *(Stokes)*
1945
ONE GOD: THE WAYS WE WORSHIP HIM by Florence Mary Fitch *(Lothrop)*
1946
THE WHITE DEER by James Thurber *(HBJ)*
1947
THE SNOW OWL'S SECRET by Harriet Torrey Evatt *(Bobbs)*
1948
LI LUN, LAD OF COURAGE by Carolyn Treffinger *(Abingdon)*
1949
BLUEBERRIES FOR SAL by Robert McCloskey *(Viking)*
1950
SONG OF THE PINES by Walter and Marion Havighurst *(Winston)*
1951-1953
No Awards
1954
TINKER'S TIM AND THE WITCHES by Bertha C. Anderson *(Little, Brown)*
1955
PREHISTORIC ANIMALS by William E. Scheele *(World)*
1956
THE FABULOUS FIREWORK FAMILY by James Flora *(HBJ)*
1957
KNIGHT'S CASTLE by Edward McMaken Eager *(HBJ)*
1958
TIME OF WONDER by Robert McCloskey *(Viking)*
1959
AMERICA'S OWN MARK TWAIN by Jeanette Eaton *(Morrow)*
1960
THE GAMMAGE CUP by Carol Kendall *(HBJ)*
1961
OLD RAMON by Jack Schaefer *(Houghton)*
1962
SHIPS, SHOALS AND AMPHORAS by Suzanne de Borhegyi *(Holt)*
1963
SEVEN-DAY MAGIC by Edward McMaken Eager *(HBJ)*
1964-1966
No Awards
1967
WALK A NARROW BRIDGE by Dale Fife *(Coward)*

1968
FOCUS THE BRIGHT LAND by Elisabeth Hamilton Friermood
(Doubleday)
1969
THE HOUSE OF DIES DREAR by Virginia Hamilton
(Macmillan)
1970
THE NORMAN ROCKWELL STORYBOOK by Jan Wahl
(Windmill/Simon & Schuster)
1971
OHIO by Marion Renick *(Coward)*
1972
WINDS by Mary O'Neill *(Doubleday)*
1973-1975
No Awards
1976
WITCH OF THE CUMBERLANDS by Mary Jo Stephens
(Houghton)
1977
DEEP IN THE FOREST by Brinton Turkle *(Dutton)*
ISLAND TIME by Brinton Turkle *(Lippincott)*
1978
POOR TOM'S GHOST by Jane Louise Curry *(McElderry)*
1979
ZOAR BLUE by Janet Hickman *(Macmillan)*
1980
Body of work of Andre Norton
1981
THE LIBERATION OF TANSY WARNER by Stephanie S.
Tolan *(Scribner)*
1982
ANOTHER HEAVEN, ANOTHER EARTH by H. M. Hoover
(Viking)
1983
No Award
1984
Body of work of Virginia Hamilton
1985 -1986
No Awards
1987
THE LOTUS CUP by Jane Louise Curry *(McElderry)*
1988
Body of work of Joseph Slate
1989
THE TSAR & THE AMAZING COW by J. Patrick Lewis *(Dial)*

1990
BUT I'LL BE BACK AGAIN: AN ALBUM by Cynthia Rylant
(Orchard)
1991
Lifetime career medal to Virginia Hamilton
Body of work of Mildred D. Taylor
WITH A NAME LIKE LULU, WHO NEEDS MORE
TROUBLE? by Tricia Springstubb *(Delacorte)*
1992
Body of work of Virginia Hamilton
APPALACHIA: THE VOICES OF SLEEPING BIRDS by Cynthia
Rylant *(Harcourt)*
1993
Body of work of Cynthia Rylant
THE FALCON'S WING by Dawna Lisa Buchanan *(Orchard)*
1994
Body of work of Natalie Babbitt
IN THE SMALL, SMALL POND by Denise Fleming *(Holt)*
1995
Body of work of Bonnie Pryor
JERICHO by Janet Hickman *(Greenwillow)*

Oklahoma Book Awards ❧
CHILDREN'S AND YOUNG ADULT CATEGORY

Sponsored by the Oklahoma Center for the Book (200 Northeast
18th St., Oklahoma City, OK 73105), this awards program has
five categories, including one for Children's and Young Adult
books, comprising fiction, nonfiction or poetry. "Books
considered for this award must have an Oklahoma-based theme
or have been written by an author who resides or has resided in
Oklahoma." (Medallion and citation)

1990
TYRANNOSAURUS REX AND ITS KIN: THE MESOZOIC
MONSTERS by Helen Roney Sattler *(Lothrop)*
1991
A CAPITAL FOR THE NATION by Stan Hoig *(Cobblehill)*
1992
HILLBACK TO BOGGY by Jess and Bonnie Speer *(Reliance)*
1993
RED DIRT JESSIE by Anna Myers *(Walker)*

1994
CHEROKEE SUMMER by Diane Hoyt-Goldsmith *(Holiday House)*

1995
THE CHOCTAW CODE by Brent Ashabranner and Russell G. Davis *(Cobblehill)*

1996
GRAVEYARD GIRL by Anna Myers *(Walker)*

Orbis Pictus Award for Outstanding Nonfiction for Children

Commemorating the work of "that brave old man, Johannes Amos Commenius, the fame of whose worth has been trumpeted as far as more than three languages could carry it," and whose book *Orbis Pictus (The World in Pictures)* is historically considered to be the first work created exclusively for children, this award honors distinction in nonfiction for children. An undertaking of and administered by the Orbis Pictus Committee of the National Council of Teachers of English (1111 W. Kenyon Rd., Urbana, IL 61801-1096), the committee considers "accuracy, organization, design, writing style, and usefulness for classroom teaching in grades K-8" in selecting the winner, up to five Honor Books, and a longer annual listing of "Outstanding Nonfiction Choices for Children." Our listing is of the award presentation year; winners were published in the previous year. (Plaque)

1990
THE GREAT LITTLE MADISON by Jean Fritz *(Putnam)*

1991
FRANKLIN DELANO ROOSEVELT by Russell Freedman *(Clarion)*

1992
FLIGHT: THE JOURNEY OF CHARLES LINDBERGH by Robert Burleigh *(Philomel)*

1993
CHILDREN OF THE DUST BOWL: THE TRUE STORY OF THE SCHOOL AT WEEDPATCH CAMP by Jerry Stanley *(Crown)*

1994
ACROSS AMERICA ON AN EMIGRANT TRAIN by Jim Murphy *(Clarion)*

1995
SAFARI BENEATH THE SEA: THE WONDER WORLD OF
THE NORTH PACIFIC COAST by Diane Swanson *(Sierra Club)*
1996
THE GREAT FIRE by Jim Murphy *(Scholastic)*

Outstanding Pennsylvania Author Award ❧

The purpose of this award "is to recognize a Pennsylvania author
who has made outstanding contributions in the field of
literature." The author must be from Pennsylvania originally, or
must currently live in Pennsylvania, or write about the state.
Books for readers from the first school years through high school
are considered. The sponsor is Pennsylvania School Librarians
Association (2422 Riverview Ave., Bloomsburg, PA 17815)
(Certificate)

1975   Marguerite De Angeli
1976   Lloyd Alexander
1977   Margaret Hodges
1978   Jean Fritz
1979   Carolyn Haywood
1980   Walter Farley
1981   Harriet May Savitz
1982   James A. Michener
1983   Robin Brancato
1984   Muriel Feelings
1985   Barbara Robinson
1986   Barbara Brenner
1987   Lucille Wallower
1988   Fred Rogers
1989   Marc Brown
1990   Carolyn Meyer
1991   Aliki
1992   Jerry Spinelli
1993   Paula Danziger
1994   Lois Lowry
1995   Robin Moore
1996   No Award

Parenting's Reading Magic Awards 🕮

Parenting (301 Howard St., San Francisco, CA 94105), a magazine with a circulation of about 1.1 million, presents awards for excellence in children's literature. "From lists compiled for Parenting by a panel of noted experts in the field of children's books," Parenting selects ten best books and—a most appealing feature of this award program—recognizes over 40 other titles for excellence. "The list of winners includes a wide range of titles, which are characterized by age: first books, up to age 5; picture books, ages 4 to 8; first readers, ages 5 to 8; middle readers, ages 9 to 12; and nonfiction books, which vary in age." This feature is published in the December/January issues of Parenting. (Certificate)

1988
THE BOY OF THE THREE-YEAR NAP retold by Dianne Snyder, ill. by Allen Say (Houghton)
A CARIBOU ALPHABET by Mary Beth Owens (Dog Ear Press)
CATWINGS by Ursula K. LeGuin, ill. by S. D. Schindler (Orchard)
DEAR MILI by Wilhelm Grimm, translated by Ralph Manheim, ill. by Maurice Sendak (Farrar)
A GIRL FROM YAMHILL: A MEMOIR by Beverly Cleary (Morrow)
HENRY by Nina Bawden (Lothrop)
MORE TALES OF UNCLE REMUS: FURTHER ADVENTURES OF BRER RABBIT, HIS FRIENDS, ENEMIES, AND OTHERS retold by Julius Lester, ill. by Jerry Pinkney (Dial)
THE THREE AND MANY WISHES OF JASON REID by Hazel J. Hutchins (Viking)
TOM AND PIPPO (series) by Helen Oxenbury (Aladdin)
WHERE THE FOREST MEETS THE SEA by Jeannie Baker (Greenwillow)

1989
BILL PEET: AN AUTOBIOGRAPHY by Bill Peet (Houghton)
EATING THE ALPHABET: FRUITS AND VEGETABLES FROM A TO Z by Lois Ehlert (HBJ)
INSPIRATIONS: STORIES ABOUT WOMEN ARTISTS by Leslie Sills (Whitman)
MOUSE PAINT by Ellen Stoll Walsh (HBJ)
THE PUP GREW UP! by Samuel Marshak, translated by Richard Pevear, ill. by Vladimir Radunsky (Holt)
QUENTIN BLAKE'S ABC by Quentin Blake (Knopf)
THE RAINBOW PEOPLE by Laurence Yep (Harper)

VALENTINE & ORSON by Nancy Ekholm Burkert *(Farrar)*
WE'RE GOING ON A BEAR HUNT retold by Michael Rosen, ill. by Helen Oxenbury *(McElderry)*
YOUNG LIONS by Toshi Yoshida *(Philomel)*
1990
BASEBALL IN APRIL AND OTHER STORIES by Gary Soto *(HBJ)*
THE BUCK STOPS HERE by Alice Provensen *(HarperCollins)*
COUSINS by Virginia Hamilton *(Philomel)*
EL CHINO by Allen Say *(Houghton)*
GOOD QUEEN BESS by Diane Stanley and Peter Vennema, ill. by Diane Stanley *(Four Winds)*
PUSS IN BOOTS by Charles Perrault, translated by Malcolm Arthur, ill. by Fred Marcellino *(Farrar)*
SHREK! by William Steig *(Farrar)*
TEHANU by Ursula K. LeGuin *(Atheneum)*
THE WHEELS ON THE BUS by Paul O. Zelinsky *(Dutton)*
WHITE PEAK FARM by Berlie Doherty *(Orchard)*
1991
AKI AND THE FOX by Akiko Hayashi *(Doubleday)*
CLOWNING AROUND by Cathryn Falwell *(Orchard)*
DOG; CAT; DUCK; *and* BEAR by Juan Wijngaard *(Crown)*
HOW THE OX STAR FELL FROM HEAVEN retold and ill. by Lily Toy Hong *(Whitman)*
PUNCH IN NEW YORK by Alice Provensen *(Viking)*
STARS COME OUT WITHIN by Jean Little *(Viking)*
STRIDER by Beverly Cleary *(Morrow)*
TUESDAY by David Wiesner *(Clarion)*
A WAVE IN HER POCKET by Lynn Joseph, ill. by Brian Pinkney *(Clarion)*
THE WRIGHT BROTHERS: HOW THEY INVENTED THE AIRPLANE by Russell Freedman *(Holiday House)*
1992
BARD OF AVON: THE STORY OF WILLIAM SHAKESPEARE by Diane Stanley and Peter Vennema, ill. by Diane Stanley *(Morrow)*
BENTLEY & EGG by William Joyce *(HarperCollins)*
CIRCUS by Lois Ehlert *(HarperCollins)*
DRYLONGSO by Virginia Hamilton, ill. by Jerry Pinkney *(Harcourt)*
FARMER DUCK by Martin Waddell, ill. by Helen Oxenbury *(Candlewick)*
I SAW ESAU edited by Iona and Peter Opie, ill. by Maurice Sendak *(Candlewick)*
AN INDIAN WINTER by Russell Freedman, ill. by Karl Bodmer *(Holiday House)*
MISSING MAY by Cynthia Rylant *(Orchard)*
SEVEN BLIND MICE by Ed Young *(Philomel)*

SUKEY AND THE MERMAID by Robert D. San Souci, ill. by
Brian Pinkney *(Four Winds)*

1993

BROWN ANGELS by Walter Dean Myers *(HarperCollins)*
ELEANOR ROOSEVELT: A LIFE OF DISCOVERY by Russell
Freedman *(Clarion)*
FREEDOM'S CHILDREN: YOUNG CIVIL RIGHTS
ACTIVISTS TELL THEIR OWN STORIES by Ellen Levine
(Putnam)
GRANDFATHER'S JOURNEY by Allen Say *(Houghton)*
THE GREAT MIGRATION by Jacob Lawrence *(HarperCollins)*
HUE BOY by Rita Phillips Mitchell, ill. by Caroline Binch *(Dial)*
MAKE LEMONADE by Virginia Euwer Wolff *(Holt)*
MATTHEW AND THE SEA SINGER by Jill Paton Walsh, ill.
by Alan Marks *(Farrar)*
SCOOTER by Vera B. Williams *(Greenwillow)*
WE ARE ALL IN THE DUMPS WITH JACK AND GUY by
Maurice Sendak *(HarperCollins)*

1994

BIG BANG BOING by Douglas Florian *(Harcourt)*
CATHERINE, CALLED BIRDY by Karen Cushman *(Clarion)*
JULIE by Jean Craighead George, ill. by Wendell Minor
(HarperCollins)
THE MAESTRO PLAYS by Bill Martin, Jr., ill. by Vladimir
Radunsky *(Holt)*
THE MENNYMS by Sylvia Waugh *(Greenwillow)*
MY BROTHER, MY SISTER, AND I by Yoko Kawashima
Watkins *(Bradbury)*
MY PAINTED HOUSE, MY FRIENDLY CHICKEN, AND ME
by Maya Angelou, photos by Margaret Courtney-Clarke *(Potter)*
SO MUCH by Trish Cooke, ill. by Helen Oxenbury
(Candlewick)
SWAMP ANGEL by Anne Isaacs, ill. by Paul O Zelinsky
(Dutton)
ZEKE PIPPIN by William Steig *(HarperCollins)*

1995

BINYA'S BLUE UMBRELLA by Ruskin Bond, ill. by Vera
Rosenberry *(Boyds Mills)*
EARTH by Ken Robbins *(Holt)*
A FENCE AWAY FROM FREEDOM by Ellen Levine *(Putnam)*
THE GREAT FIRE by Jim Murphy *(Scholastic)*
HER STORIES: AFRICAN AMERICAN FOLKTALES, FAIRY
TALES, AND TRUE TALES by Virginia Hamilton, ill. by Leo
and Diane Dillon *(Blue Sky/Scholastic)*
HEY, PIPSQUEAK! by Kate McMullan, ill. by Jim McMullan
(HarperCollins)
THE HOLE STORY by Eve Merriam, designed and ill. by Ivan
Chermayeff *(Simon & Schuster)*

LULLABIES, LYRICS AND GALLOWS SONGS by Christian Morgenstern, translated by Anthea Bell, ill. by Lisbeth Zwerger *(North-South)*
NAVAJO by Shonto Begay *(Scholastic)*
SOME OF THE KINDER PLANETS by Tim Wynne-Jones *(Orchard)*

PEN/Norma Klein Award 🎗

This award commemorates Norma Klein (1938-1989), author of more than thirty novels for teenagers and adults. Presented biennially, the prize recognizes "an emerging voice of literary merit among American writers of children's fiction...new authors whose books, for elementary school to adult readers, demonstrate the adventuresome and innovative spirit that characterizes the best children's literature and Norma Klein's own work (but need not resemble her novels stylistically)." The award is administered by PEN American Center (568 Broadway, New York, NY 10012), whose Children's Book Committee Norma Klein co-chaired. PEN International is a world association of writers with centers in Europe, Asia, Africa, Australia, and the Americas. ($3,000)

1991
Cynthia Grant, author of PHOENIX RISING *(Atheneum)* and other novels
1993
Graham Salisbury, author of BLUE SKIN OF THE SEA *(Dell)*
1995
Angela Johnson, author of HUMMING WHISPERS *(Orchard)*

Phoenix Award 🎗

This award, originated and sponsored by the Children's Literature Association (P.O. Box 138, Battle Creek, MI 49016), an organization encouraging the study of children's literature, is for "a book for children published twenty years earlier which did not win a major award at the time of its publication but which, from the perspective of time, is deemed worthy of special recognition for its literary quality." Only titles originally published in English are considered. The winners' first publishers appear in our listing; a book's U. S. publisher is also listed if the winner was first published abroad. (Statue)

1985
THE MARK OF THE HORSE LORD by Rosemary Sutcliff
(UK: Oxford, 1965; US: Walck, 1965)
1986
QUEENIE PEAVY by Robert Burch *(Viking, 1966)*
1987
SMITH by Leon Garfield *(UK: Constable, 1967; US: Pantheon, 1967)*
1988
THE RIDER AND HIS HORSE by Erik Christian Haugaard
(Houghton, 1968)
1989
THE NIGHT WATCHMEN by Helen Cresswell *(UK: Faber, 1969; US: Macmillan, 1969)*
1990
ENCHANTRESS FROM THE STARS by Sylvia Louise Engdahl
(Atheneum, 1970)
1991
A LONG WAY FROM VERONA by Jane Gardam *(UK: Hamish Hamilton, 1971; US: Macmillan, 1971)*
1992
A SOUND OF CHARIOTS by Mollie Hunter *(UK: Hamish Hamilton, 1972; US: Harper, 1972)*
1993
CARRIE'S WAR by Nina Bawden *(UK: Gollancz, 1973; US: Lippincott, 1973)*
1994
OF NIGHTINGALES THAT WEEP by Katherine Paterson *(US: Crowell, 1974)*
1995
DRAGONWINGS by Laurence Yep *(US: Harper, 1975)*
1996
THE STONE BOOK by Alan Garner *(UK: Collins, 1976)*

Please Touch Museum Book Award 🐛

This annual award is designed to recognize the publication of books that are particularly imaginative and effective in exploring concepts such as numbers, shapes, senses, or feelings. During its first ten years the award was limited to books for children ages 3 and younger. Beginning in 1995, a 4-7 age category was added. The award is sponsored by the Please Touch Museum for Children (210 N. 21st St., Philadelphia, PA 19103). (Medal)

1985
WHAT'S INSIDE? by Duanne Daughtry *(Knopf)*
1986
IS IT LARGER? IS IT SMALLER? by Tana Hoban
(Greenwillow)
1987
WHO'S COUNTING? by Nancy Tafuri *(Greenwillow)*
1988
CLAUDE AND SUN by Matt Novak *(Bradbury)*
1989
WHO'S SICK TODAY? by Lynne Cherry *(Dutton)*
1990
DINOSAURS, DINOSAURS by Byron Barton *(Crowell)*
1991
MAISY GOES TO BED by Lucy Cousins *(Little, Brown)*
1992
IN THE TALL, TALL GRASS by Denise Fleming *(Holt)*
1993
FIDDLE-I-FEE by Melissa Sweet *(Little, Brown)*
1994
ARNOLD ALWAYS ANSWERS by Deborah Kotter *(Doubleday)*
1995
Ages 3 & younger: HIPPITY HOP, FROG ON TOP by Natasha
Wing *(Simon & Schuster)*
Ages 4-7: PRIZE IN THE SNOW by Bill Easterling *(Little,
Brown)*

Edgar Allan Poe Awards ?

BEST JUVENILE AND YOUNG ADULT NOVEL CATEGORIES

The Mystery Writers of America (17 E. 47th St., New York, NY
10017) honors the best work in the mystery, crime, suspense,
and intrigue fields in several media each year. An award for "Best
Juvenile Novel" was added to the program in 1962, "Best Young
Adult Novel" in 1989. In our listing, we use the codes *"J"* and
"Y/A" as of 1989. The event at which the awards are presented
is called the "Edgars," the mystery world's equivalent of
Hollywood's "Oscars." (Ceramic bust of Poe)

1962
THE MYSTERY OF THE HAUNTED POOL by Phyllis A.
Whitney *(Westminster)*

1963
THE PHANTOM OF WALKAWAY HILL by Edward Fenton
(Doubleday)
1964
CUTLASS ISLAND by Scott Corbett *(Atlantic-Little, Brown)*
1965
THE MYSTERY OF THE HIDDEN HAND by Phyllis A.
Whitney *(Westminster)*
1966
THE MYSTERY AT CRANE'S LANDING by Marcella Thum
(Dodd)
1967
THE MYSTERY OF 22 EAST by Leon Ware *(Westminster)*
1968
SINBAD AND ME by Kin Platt *(Chilton)*
1969
SIGNPOST TO TERROR by Gretchen Sprague *(Dodd)*
1970
THE HOUSE OF DIES DREAR by Virginia Hamilton
(Macmillan)
1971
DANGER AT BLACK DYKE by Winifred Finlay *(Phillips)*
1972
THE INTRUDER by John Rowe Townsend *(Lippincott)*
1973
NIGHT FALL by Joan Aiken *(Holt)*
1974
DEATHWATCH by Robb White *(Doubleday)*
1975
THE LONG BLACK COAT by Jay Bennett *(Delacorte)*
1976
THE DANGLING WITNESS by Jay Bennett *(Delacorte)*
1977
Z FOR ZACHARIAH by Robert C. O'Brien *(Atheneum)*
1978
ARE YOU IN THE HOUSE ALONE? by Richard Peck *(Viking)*
1979
ALONE IN WOLF HOLLOW by Dana Brookins *(Clarion)*
1980
THE KIDNAPPING OF CHRISTINA LATTIMORE by Joan
Lowery Nixon *(HBJ)*
1981
THE SEANCE by Joan Lowery Nixon *(HBJ)*
1982
TAKING TERRI MUELLER by Norma Fox Mazer *(Avon)*

1983
THE MURDER OF HOUND DOG BATES by Robbie
Branscum *(Viking)*
1984
THE CALLENDER PAPERS by Cynthia Voigt *(Atheneum)*
1985
NIGHT CRY by Phyllis Reynolds Naylor *(Atheneum)*
1986
THE SANDMAN'S EYES by Patricia Windsor *(Delacorte)*
1987
THE OTHER SIDE OF DARK by Joan Lowery Nixon
(Delacorte)
1988
LUCY FOREVER AND MISS ROSETREE, SHRINKS by Susan
Shreve *(Holt)*
1989
J: MEGAN'S ISLAND by Willo Davis Roberts *(Atheneum)*
Y/A: INCIDENT AT LORING GROVES by Sonia Levitin *(Dial)*
1990
J: No Award
Y/A: SHOW ME THE EVIDENCE by Alane Ferguson
(Bradbury)
1991
J: STONEWORDS: A GHOST STORY by Pam Conrad
(HarperCollins)
Y/A: MOTE by Chap Reaver *(Delacorte)*
1992
J: WANTED...MUD BLOSSOM by Betsy Byars *(Delacorte)*
Y/A: THE WEIRDO by Theodore Taylor *(Harcourt)*
1993
J: COFFIN ON A CASE! by Eve Bunting *(HarperCollins)*
Y/A: A LITTLE BIT DEAD by Chap Reaver *(Delacorte)*
1994
J: THE TWIN IN THE TAVERN by Barbara Brooks Wallace
(Atheneum)
Y/A: THE NAME OF THE GAME WAS MURDER by Joan
Lowery Nixon *(Delacorte)*
1995
J: THE ABSOLUTELY TRUE STORY...HOW I VISITED
YELLOWSTONE PARK WITH THE TERRIBLE RUBES by
Willo Davis Roberts *(Atheneum)*
Y/A: TOUGHING IT by Nancy Springer *(Harcourt)*
1996
J: LOOKING FOR JAMIE BRIDGER by Nancy Springer *(Dial)*
Y/A: PROPHECY ROCK by Rob MacGregor *(Simon &*
Schuster)

Redbook Children's Picturebook Awards 🐚

Redbook, a monthly magazine with over four million readers, many of them young mothers, selected "the 10 best new picturebooks for kids" that appeared as a fully annotated and illustrated list in its December issues. In its first years, the list was separated into various categories; subsequently *Redbook*'s judges selected "ten winners." The program was discontinued after the 1991 awards due to editorial changes at the magazine. (*Redbook*, 224 West 57th St., New York, NY 10019). (Certificate)

1984
Hardcover
I KNOW A LADY by Charlotte Zolotow, ill. by James Stevenson (*Greenwillow*)
I'M COMING TO GET YOU by Tony Ross (*Dial*)
THE MYSTERIES OF HARRIS BURDICK by Chris Van Allsburg (*Houghton*)
YELLOW & PINK by William Steig (*Farrar*)
Paperback
THE EMPEROR'S NEW CLOTHES by Hans Christian Andersen, retold and ill. by Nadine Bernard Westcott (*Atlantic*)
MOON MAN by Tomi Ungerer (*Harper*)
WHERE THE WILD THINGS ARE by Maurice Sendak (*Harper*)
Pop-ups
THE CAR by Ray Marshall and John Bradley (*Viking*)
LEONARDO DA VINCI by Alice and Martin Provensen (*Viking*)
SAILING SHIPS by Ron van der Meer and Alan McGowan (*Viking*)
1985
Hardcover
ANNIE AND THE WILD ANIMALS by Jan Brett (*Houghton*)
IN OUR HOUSE by Anne Rockwell (*Crowell*)
THE POLAR EXPRESS by Chris Van Allsburg (*Houghton*)
SOLOMON THE RUSTY NAIL by William Steig (*Farrar*)
THERE WAS AN OLD WOMAN by Stephen Wyllie, ill. by Maureen Roffey (*Harper*)
WATCH THE STARS COME OUT by Riki Levinson, ill. by Diane Goode (*Dutton*)
Paperback
FREIGHT TRAIN by Donald Crews (*Puffin*)
IN THE NIGHT KITCHEN by Maurice Sendak (*Harper*)
MISS RUMPHIUS by Barbara Cooney (*Puffin*)

WILLIAM'S DOLL by Charlotte Zolotow, ill. by William Pène du Bois *(Harper)*

1986

Hardcover

ABIYOYO: BASED ON A SOUTH AFRICAN LULLABY AND FOLK STORY by Pete Seeger, ill. by Michael Hays *(Macmillan)*

BRAVE IRENE by William Steig *(Farrar)*

THE LITTLE BOOKMOBILE: COLORS, NUMBERS, AND SHAPES, ON WHEELS by Suzanne Green, ill. by Daisuke Yokoi *(Doubleday)*

RUMPELSTILTSKIN by Paul O. Zelinsky *(Dutton)*

A TOURNAMENT OF KNIGHTS by Joe Lasker *(Crowell)*

A YEAR OF BEASTS by Ashley Wolff *(Dutton)*

Paperback

ANNO'S COUNTING BOOK by Mitsumasa Anno *(Harper)*

THE GUINEA PIG ABC by Kate Duke *(Dutton)*

THE SNOWMAN by Raymond Briggs *(Random)*

WHAT DO YOU SAY, DEAR? A BOOK OF MANNERS FOR ALL OCCASIONS by Sesyle Joslin, ill. by Maurice Sendak *(Harper)*

1987

Hardcover

CREATURES OF THE DESERT WORLD *and* STRANGE ANIMALS OF THE SEA *(National Geographic)*

HIGHER ON THE DOOR by James Stevenson *(Greenwillow)*

HUMPHREY'S BEAR by Jan Wahl, ill. by William Joyce *(Holt)*

JUMP AGAIN! MORE ADVENTURES OF BRER RABBIT by Joel Chandler Harris, adapted by Van Dyke Parks, ill. by Barry Moser *(HBJ)*

THE LOATHSOME DRAGON retold by David Wiesner and Kim Kahng, ill. by David Wiesner *(Putnam)*

THE MIDNIGHT FARM by Reeve Lindbergh, ill. by Susan Jeffers *(Dial)*

MONKEY'S CRAZY HOTEL by Stephen Wyllie, ill. by Maureen Roffey *(Harper)*

THE MONSTER BED by Jeanne Willis, ill. by Susan Varley *(Lothrop)*

A PLACE FOR BEN by Jeanne Titherington *(Greenwillow)*

Paperback

THE WILD SWANS by Hans Christian Andersen, retold by Amy Ehrlich, ill. by Susan Jeffers *(Dial)*

1988

ANIMALS SHOWING OFF *and* CREATURES OF LONG AGO: DINOSAURS *(National Geographic)*

BLOSSOM COMES HOME by James Herriot, ill. by Ruth Brown *(St. Martin's)*

COMPANY'S COMING by Arthur Yorinks, ill. by David Small *(Crown)*

THE ENCHANTER'S DAUGHTER by Antonia Barber, ill. by Errol Le Cain *(Farrar)*
HOW MANY BUGS IN A BOX? by David A. Carter *(Simon & Schuster)*
THE INCREDIBLE PAINTING OF FELIX CLOUSSEAU by Jon Agee *(Farrar)*
JUNGLEWALK by Nancy Tafuri *(Greenwillow)*
THE SCAREBIRD by Sid Fleischman, ill. by Peter Sís *(Greenwillow)*
SPINKY SULKS by William Steig *(Farrar)*
TAIL FEATHERS FROM MOTHER GOOSE: THE OPIE RHYME BOOK compiled by Peter and Iona Opie *(Little, Brown)*

1989
ANIMALS ANIMALS compiled by Laura Whipple, ill. by Eric Carle *(Philomel)*
ANNABEL'S HOUSE by Norman Messenger *(Orchard)*
A CHILD'S GARDEN OF VERSES by Robert Louis Stevenson, various illustrators *(Chronicle)*
FRIEND OR FROG by Marjorie Priceman *(Houghton)*
THE LITTLE MERMAID by Hans Christian Andersen, ill. by Katie Thamer Treherne *(HBJ)*
MOUSE PAINT by Ellen Stoll Walsh *(HBJ)*
MY FIRST COOKBOOK by Angela Wilkes, photog. by David Johnson *(Knopf)*
NIGHT NOISES by Mem Fox, ill. by Terry Denton *(Gulliver/HBJ)*
SKIP TO MY LOU adapted and ill. by Nadine Bernard Westcott *(Joy Street/Little, Brown)*
TENREC'S TWIGS by Bert Kitchen *(Philomel)*

1990
AESOP'S FABLES compiled by Russell Ash and Bernard Higton, various illustrators *(Chronicle)*
BENJAMIN'S BARN by Reeve Lindbergh, ill. by Susan Jeffers *(Dial)*
CHARLIE ANDERSON by Barbara Abercrombie, ill. by Mark Graham *(McElderry)*
FEATHERS FOR LUNCH by Lois Ehlert *(HBJ)*
MANY MOONS by James Thurber, ill. by Marc Simont *(HBJ)*
TEAMMATES by Peter Golenbock, ill. by Paul Bacon *(HBJ)*
TRAIN SONG by Diane Siebert, ill. by Mike Wimmer *(Crowell)*
THE UGLY DUCKLING retold and ill. by Troy Howell *(Putnam)*
THE VERY QUIET CRICKET by Eric Carle *(Philomel)*
THE WHEELS ON THE BUS adapted and ill. by Paul O. Zelinsky *(Dutton)*

1991
A IS FOR ANIMALS by David Pelham *(Simon & Schuster)*
BORREGUITA AND THE COYOTE by Verna Aardema, ill. by Petra Mathers *(Knopf)*

THE FISH WHO COULD WISH by John Bush, ill. by Korky Paul *(Kane/Miller)*
IN THE TALL, TALL GRASS by Denise Fleming *(Holt)*
THE MINPINS by Roald Dahl *(Viking)*
POLAR BEAR, POLAR BEAR by Bill Martin Jr., ill. by Eric Carle *(Holt)*
SEE HOW THEY GROW: FROG/PUPPY/KITTEN/DUCK photographed by Jane Burton, Kim Taylor and Barrie Watts *(Lodestar)*
THE STORY OF CHRISTMAS: WORDS FROM THE GOSPELS OF MATTHEW AND LUKE by Jane Ray *(Dial)*
TEN LITTLE RABBITS by Virginia Grossman, ill. by Sylvia Long *(Chronicle)*
WHITE IS THE MOON by Valerie Greeley *(Macmillan)*

Marion Vannett Ridgway Awards ❧

To encourage new talent, this award is given for an author's or illustrator's first picture book for children published initially in the United States during the previous year. The award honors Marion Vannett Ridgway, a children's book author/artist and a pioneer New York representative for artists and writers. In addition to a First Prize, Honor Book awards are presented (not listed here due to space limitations). Special recognition is also given annually for a Photo Book. (Contact: Elizabeth Park, Administrator, Marion Vannett Ridgway Awards, P.O. Box 45432, Madison, WI 53744) (First Prize: $500)

1993
NEWF by Marie Killilea, ill. by Ian Schoenherr *(winner) (Philomel)*
Photo Book: THE SACRED HARVEST by Gordon Regguinti, photos by Dale Kakkak *(Lerner)*

1994
WINTER FOX by Jennifer Brutschy, ill. by Allen Garns *(Knopf)*
Photo book: COME WITH ME TO AFRICA by Gregory Scott Kreikemeier *(Western)*

1995
CASEY OVER THERE by Staton Rabin, ill. by Greg Shed *(Harcourt)*
Photo Book: EAGLE DRUM by Robert Crum *(FourWinds)*

1996
HEART OF A TIGER by Marcia Diane Arnold *(Dial)*
Photo Book: WHAT'S YOUR NAME? FROM ARIEL TO ZOE by Eve Sanders, photos by Marilyn Sanders *(Holiday House)*

Tomás Rivera Mexican-American Children's Book Award ❧

The Southwest Texas State University School of Education (601 University Dr., San Marcos, TX 78666-4613) has established an annual award to encourage authors, illustrators, and publishers to produce books that authentically reflect the lives of Mexican-American children and young adults in the American Southwest. It is named for author and educator Tomás Rivera who grew up as a migrant farm worker and, at the time of his death in 1984, was chancellor of the University of California at Riverside. Fiction or nonfiction works written by U.S. authors and published during the previous year are eligible for nomination. Portrayals of Mexican-Americans should be accurate, engaging, and rich in characterization, while avoiding stereotypes, with text and illustrations of the highest quality. A regional committee will determine the finalists and a national committee will chose the winner. The first award will be presented in the Fall of 1996. (Certificate and cash award)

Carl Sandburg Literary Arts Awards ❧
CHILDREN'S LITERATURE CATEGORY

This annual awards program, named for the famous Illinois poet and biographer, includes a children's literature category. The recipients are authors who are natives of or live in the six-county Chicago metropolitan area. The award is sponsored by the Friends of the Chicago Public Library (Harold Washington Library Center, 400 South State St. 9S-7, Chicago, IL 60605) (Medal and $1,000)

1980
CUTE IS A FOUR-LETTER WORD by Stella Pevsner *(Clarion)*
1981
DO BANANAS CHEW GUM? by Jamie Gilson *(Lothrop)*
1982
BEHIND THE SCENES AT THE HORSE HOSPITAL by Fern Brown *(Whitman)*
1983
WAIT, SKATES! by Mildred Johnson *(Children's Press)*

1984
PITCHER PLANTS, THE ELEGANT INSECT TRAPS by Carol Lerner *(Morrow)*
1985
THE SEARCH FOR GRISSI by Mary Frances Shura *(Dodd)*
1986
THATCHER PAYNE-IN-THE-NECK by Betty Bates *(Holiday House)*
1987
ELI'S GHOST by Betsy Hearne *(McElderry)*
1988
THE GOATS by Brock Cole *(Farrar)*
1989
A CIRCLE UNBROKEN by Sollace Hotze *(Clarion)*
1990
THE HOUSE ON WALENSKA STREET by Charlotte Herman *(Dutton)*
1991
THE BRIDGE DANCERS by Carol Saller *(Carolrhoda)*
1992
KNEE HOLES by Jerome Brooks *(Orchard)*
1993
LIFE'S A FUNNY PROPOSITION, HORATIO by Barbara Garland Polikoff *(Puffin)*
1994
CATHERINE, CALLED BIRDY by Karen Cushman *(Clarion)*
1995
SHADOW CATCHER: THE LIFE AND WORK OF EDWARD SHERRIFF CURTIS by Laurie Lawlor *(Walker)*

School Library Media Specialists of Southeastern New York Rip Van Winkle Award

This annual award is given to an author or illustrator living in a seven- county region of Southeastern New York State for a body of work that is an outstanding contribution to children's and/or young adult literature. It is sponsored by School Library Media Specialists of Southeastern New York, an affiliate of the School Library Media Section, New York Library Association. As the administration of this program changes annually, there is not a continuing address to contact for additional information. (Engraved silver bowl)

1980   Eleanor Clymer
1981   Jean Craighead George
1982   Leonard Kessler
1983   Susan Beth Pfeffer
1984   Jean Fritz
1985   Paul Galdone
1986   Alice and Martin Provensen
1987   Charlotte Zolotow
1988   Judie Angell
1989   Scott O'Dell
1990   Susan Jeffers
1991   Lilian Moore
1992   Nancy Willard
1993   Vicki Cobb
1994   John Peterson
1995   Todd Strasser
1996   Betty Miles

Skipping Stones Book Awards ❧

This award program was created to honor authors and publishers promoting multicultural awareness and ecological stewardship in visionary ways. Its sponsor, *Skipping Stones* (P.O. Box 3939, Eugene, OR 97402-0939) is a nonprofit, multicultural magazine for childrens aged 7 to 15 which encourages cooperation, creativity, and a celebration of cultural and ecological richness. Awards are made in two categories: *Multicultural* and *Nature & Ecology*. The annual awardees are selected by a multicultural group of readers including students, teachers, librarians, and *Skipping Stones* staff. (Winners are announced on Earth Day each April and reviewed in the Spring issue of the magazine.)

1994
Multicultural
FLYING WITH THE EAGLE, RACING THE GREAT BEAR: STORIES FROM NATIVE NORTH AMERICA by Joseph Bruchac *(BridgeWater)*
HALMONI AND THE PICNIC by Sook Nyul Choi *(Houghton)*
KIDS EXPLORE AMERICA'S HISPANIC HERITAGE by Westridge Young Writers Workshop *(John Muir)*
LI'L SIS AND UNCLE WILLIE by Gwen Everett *(Rizzoli)*
SOFIE AND THE HEARTMENDER by Marie Olofsdotter *(Free Spirit)*

Nature & Ecology
COME BACK, SALMON: HOW A GROUP OF DEDICATED
KIDS ADOPTED PIGEON CREEK AND BROUGHT IT BACK
TO LIFE by Molly Cone *(Sierra Club)*
ECO-ART! EARTH-FRIENDLY ART & CRAFT
EXPERIENCES FOR 3-TO-9-YEAR-OLDS by Laurie Carlson
(Williamson)
RESCUE MISSION: PLANET EARTH by Children of the World
(Kingfisher)
UN PASEO POR EL BOSQUE LLUVIOSO/A WALK IN THE
RAINFOREST by Kristin Joy Pratt *(Dawn)*
1995
Multicultural
THE GIRL WHO MARRIED THE MOON: TALES FROM
NATIVE NORTH AMERICA by Joseph Bruchac and Gayle
Ross *(BridgeWater)*
THE RED COMB by Fernando Picó *(BridgeWater)*
RESPECTING OUR DIFFERENCES: A GUIDE TO GETTING
ALONG IN A CHANGING WORLD by Lynn Duvall *(Free
Spirit)*
TALES ALIVE! TEN MULTICULTURAL FOLKTALES WITH
ACTIVITIES by Susan Milord *(Williamson)*
TELL THEM WE REMEMBER: THE STORY OF THE
HOLOCAUST by Susan D. Bachrach *(Little, Brown)*
Nature & Ecology
THE DESERT IS MY MOTHER/EL DESIERTO ES MI
MADRE by Pat Mora *(Arte Público)*
WHO WOULD WANT THOSE APPLES ANYWAY? by Laura
and Pam Griscom *(Share)*
1996
Multicultural
THE CHRISTMAS MENORAHS: HOW A TOWN FOUGHT
HATE by Janice Cohn *(Whitman)*
THE GOLDEN GOOSE KING: A TALE TOLD BY THE
BUDDHA by Judith Ernst *(Parvardigar Press)*
THE KIDS' MULTICULTURAL COOKBOOK by Deanna F.
Cook *(Williamson)*
ON THE DAY WE HAD TO RUN! by Sybella Wilkes
(Millbrook)
ON THE WINGS OF PEACE by various authors, coordinated
by Sheila Hamanaka *(Clarion)*
PEPITA TALKS TWICE: PEPITA HABLA DOS VECES by
Ofelia Duman Lachtman *(Piñata Books)*
THE STREETS ARE FREE by Kurusa *(Annick)*
THE TANGERINE TREE by Rigina Hanson *(Clarion)*
TREASURES 3: STORIES AND ART BY STUDENTS IN
JAPAN AND OREGON ed. by Chris Weber, Japanese stories
translated by Wayne Lammers and Clinton D. Morrison
(Oregon Students Writing and Art Foundation)

Nature & Ecology
ALL THE KING'S ANIMALS: THE RETURN OF
ENDANGERED WILDLIFE TO SWAZILAND by Cristina
Kessler *(Boyds Mills)*
THE CASE OF THE MUMMIFIED PIGS AND OTHER
MYSTERIES IN NATURE by Susan E. Quinlan *(Boyds Mills)*
SWEET MAGNOLIA by Virginia Kroll *(Charlesbridge)*

Society of Midland Authors Book Awards ﹌

CHILDREN'S FICTION & NONFICTION CATEGORIES

Beginning in 1961, the Society of Midland Authors (P.O. Box
10419, Chicago, IL 60610-0419) presented an annual award
named in honor of the distinguished writer and Laura Ingalls
Wilder Medalist, Clara Ingram Judson. That award was for an
outstanding children's book of the year written by a native or
resident of the Midwest. This awards program continued through
1970. Thereafter, the Society presented an award for children's
books from time to time. Currently, the Society sponsors an
awards program that includes children's fiction *(F)* and nonfiction
(NF) categories. The authors and/or subject matter of books
receiving the awards have a connection with the twelve-state
American Midland. A Midland author is one who now resides in
the Midland, who grew up there, or whose book has a Midland
setting. (Plaque and $300)

1961
GAUDENZIA: PRIDE OF THE PALIO by Marguerite Henry
(Rand)
1962
THE DRAGON TREE by Val Gendron *(McKay)*
1963
TO LIGHT A SINGLE CANDLE by Beverly Butler *(Dodd)*
1964
GEORGE SHANNON: YOUNG EXPLORER WITH LEWIS
AND CLARK by Virginia S. Eifert *(Dodd)*
1965
ACROSS FIVE APRILS by Irene Hunt *(Follett)*
1966
A CERTAIN SMALL SHEPHERD by Rebecca Caudill *(Holt)*

1967
THE LIVING COMMUNITY: A VENTURE INTO ECOLOGY
by S. Carl Hirsch *(Viking)*
1968
THE COUNT WHO WISHED HE WERE A PEASANT by
Morris Philipson *(Pantheon)*
1969
THE ILLINOIS RIVER by James Ayars *(Holt)*
1970
WIZARD OF THE DOME: R. BUCKMINSTER FULLER by
Sidney Rosen *(Little, Brown)*
1971-1975
No Awards
1976
HE AND SHE by S. Carl Hirsch *(Lippincott)*
1977
OUR SNOWMAN HAD OLIVE EYES by Charlotte Herman
(Dutton)
1978
AND YOU GIVE ME A PAIN, ELAINE by Stella Pevsner
(Clarion)
THE ORPHANS by Berniece Rabe *(Dutton)*
1979-1981
No Awards
1982
MOON AND ME by Hadley Irwin *(McElderry)*
1983
JOEL: GROWING UP A FARM MAN by Patricia and Jack
Demuth *(Dodd)*
1984
LOVE IN A DIFFERENT KEY by Marjorie Franco *(Houghton)*
1985
F: TRACKER by Gary Paulsen *(Bradbury)*
NF: WAITING TO WALTZ: A CHILDHOOD by Cynthia
Rylant *(Bradbury)*
1986
PRAIRIE SONGS by Pam Conrad *(Harper)*
1987
MRS. PORTREE'S PONY by Lynn Hall *(Scribner)*
1988
F: VIEW FROM THE PIGHOUSE ROOF by Violet Olsen
(Atheneum)
NF: MAGGIE BY MY SIDE by Beverly Butler *(Dodd)*
1989
F: SONG AND DANCE MAN by Karen Ackerman *(Knopf)*
NF: A series of books about dinosaurs by Janet Riehecky *(Child's
World)*

1990
No Awards
1991
F: ROBODAD by Alden R. Carter *(Putnam)*
NF: WOODSONG by Gary Paulsen *(Bradbury)*
1992
F: A PLACE TO CLAIM AS HOME by Patricia Willis *(Clarion)*
NF: THE HEROINE OF THE TITANIC by Joan W. Blos
(Morrow)
1993
F: THE ORIGINAL FREDDIE ACKERMAN by Hadley Irwin
(McElderry)
NF: ROSA PARKS: MOTHER TO A MOVEMENT by Rosa
Parks with James Haskins *(Dial)*
1994
F: NIGHT OF THE FULL MOON by Gloria Whelan *(Knopf)*
NF: MANY THOUSAND GONE: AFRICAN AMERICANS
FROM SLAVERY TO FREEDOM by Virginia Hamilton
(Knopf)
1995
F: JERICHO by Janet Hickman *(Greenwillow)*
NF: HEARING US OUT: VOICES FROM THE GAY AND
LESBIAN COMMUNITY by Roger Sutton *(Little, Brown)*

Southern California Council on Literature for Children and Young People Awards 🙶

The Southern California Council on Literature for Children and Young People (P.O. Box 5249, North Hollywood, CA 91616) gives awards to authors and illustrators living in Southern California. Areas in which awards are given vary from year to year. The listing below includes only the awards relating to literature. The program also includes an award for services on behalf of children and literature, now called the Dorothy C. McKenzie Award, in honor of SCCLCYP's founder. Specific books listed were published in the year before the award year. (Plaque)

1961
Notable book: ISLAND OF THE BLUE DOLPHINS by Scott
O'Dell *(Houghton)*
Significant contribution in the field of illustration: MOY MOY
by Leo Politi *(Scribner)*

Comprehensive contribution of lasting value: Conrad and Mary Buff, Lucille and Holling C. Holling

1962

Notable book: LEGEND OF BILLY BLUESAGE by Jonreed Lauritzen *(Little, Brown)*

A significant contribution in the field of illustration: COME AGAIN, PELICAN by Don Freeman *(Viking)*

Distinguished contribution to the field of children's literature: Clyde Robert Bulla

1963

Notable book: FROM THE EAGLE'S WING by Hildegard Hoyt Swift *(Morrow)*

Distinguished contribution to the field of children's literature: W.W. and Irene Robinson

1964

Notable book: BY THE GREAT HORN SPOON by Sid Fleischman *(Atlantic-Little, Brown)*

Significant contribution in the field of illustration: WILD WINGS OVER THE MARSHES by Lucielle N. and William D. Stratton, ill. by Bernard Garbutt *(Golden Gate)*

Distinguished contribution to the fields of illustration and writing: Taro Yashima

1965

Notable book: A DAWN IN THE TREES: THOMAS JEFFERSON, THE YEARS 1776 TO 1789 by Leonard Wibberley *(Farrar)*

Distinguished contribution to the field of children's literature: Eleanor Cameron

1966

Notable book: DORP DEAD by Julia Cunningham *(Pantheon)*

Comprehensive contribution of lasting value to the field of children's literature: Carol Ryrie Brink

1967

Notable book: THE ROYAL DIRK by John and Patricia Beatty *(Morrow)*

Significant contribution in the field of illustration: FAREWELL TO SHADY GLADE by Bill Peet *(Houghton)*

Comprehensive contribution of lasting value to the field of children's literature: Margot Benary-Isbert

1968

Significant contribution to the field of illustration: SEASHORE STORY by Taro Yashima *(Viking)*

Significant contribution to the field of literature for young people: Lorenz Graham

Comprehensive contribution of lasting value in the field of literature for children and young people: Myra Cohn Livingston

Significant contribution to the field of informational books for children and young people: Charles Coombs

1969
Notable book: THE BEARS AND I by Robert Franklin Leslie *(Dutton)*
Comprehensive contribution of lasting value for children and young people: Harriet Huntingdon

1970
Notable book: THE CAY by Theodore Taylor *(Doubleday)*
Significant contribution in the field of illustration: NEW MOON COVE by Ann Atwood *(Scribner)*
Distinguished contribution to the field of folklore: Richard Chase

1971
Notable book: THE DAYBREAKERS by Jane Louise Curry *(HBJ)*
Significant contribution in the field of illustration: BOBBY SHAFTO'S GONE TO SEA by Graham Booth, ill. by Mark Taylor *(Golden Gate)*
Comprehensive contribution of lasting value to the field of children's literature: Margaret Leighton

1972
Notable book: ANOTHER PLACE, ANOTHER SPRING by Adrienne Jones *(Houghton)*
Comprehensive contribution of lasting value to the literature for children and young people: Sid Fleischman
Distinguished contribution exhibiting the fusion of poetry and photography: Ann Atwood and Mark Pines of Lyceum Productions

1973
Notable book: THE MALIBU AND OTHER POEMS by Myra Cohn Livingston *(McElderry)*
Comprehensive contribution of lasting value to the field of children's literature: Marguerite Henry

1974
Distinguished work of fiction: CHLORIS AND THE CREEPS by Kin Platt *(Chilton)*
Distinguished work of nonfiction: JUAREZ, A SON OF THE PEOPLE by Jean Rouverol *(Macmillan)*
Comprehensive contribution of lasting value to the field of children's literature: Patricia Beatty
Special contribution to children's literature: Theodor S. Geisel *(Dr. Seuss)*

1975
Distinguished work of fiction: SO, NOTHING IS FOREVER by Adrienne Jones *(Houghton)*
Distinguished work of nonfiction: BEFORE THE SUPREME COURT: THE STORY OF BELVA ANN LOCKWOOD by Terry Dunnahoo *(Houghton)*
Significant contribution to the field of illustration: SON OF THUNDER by Ethel K. McHale, ill. by Ruth Bornstein *(Children's Press)*

1976

Notable book: SHOESHINE GIRL by Clyde Robert Bulla *(Crowell)*

Significant contribution in the field of illustration for total concept and illustration: WILL'S QUILL by Don Freeman *(Viking)*

Significant contribution in the field of illustration: LITTLE PIECES OF THE WEST WIND by Christian Garrison, ill. by Diane Goode *(Bradbury);* THE SELCHIE'S SEED by Sulamith Oppenheim, ill. by Diane Goode *(Bradbury)*

Significant contribution for excellence in a series: The HENRY books by Mark Taylor *(Atheneum)*

Distinguished contribution to the field of children's literature: Helen Hinkley Jones

1977

Notable book of fiction: THE MARK OF CONTE by Sonia Levitin *(Atheneum)*

Significant contribution to the field of illustration: LITTLE GORILLA by Ruth Bornstein *(Clarion)*

Significant contribution for excellence in a series: TREEGATE CHRONICLES by Leonard Wibberley *(Farrar)*

1978

Best work of fiction: GHOST SUMMER by Eve Bunting *(Warne)*

Distinguished contribution to the field of children's literature: Theodore Taylor

1979

Distinguished work of fiction: ALONE IN WOLF HOLLOW by Dana Brookins *(Clarion)*

Significant contribution to the field of illustration: THE DREAM EATER by Christian Garrison, ill. by Diane Goode *(Bradbury)*

Significant contribution for a body of work: Jane Louise Curry

1980

Distinguished work of nonfiction: THE SNOW MONKEY AT HOME by Margaret Rau *(Knopf)*

Special recognition for a contribution of cultural significance: BEYOND THE EAST WIND; KHMERS, TIGERS AND TALISMANS; ENCIRCLED KINGDOM (Trilogy) by Jewell Rinehart Coburn and Duong Van Quyen *(Burn, Hart)*

Significant contribution for a body of work: Frank Bonham

1981

Notable work of fiction: STONE FOX by John Reynolds Gardiner *(Crowell)*

Distinguished body of work: Sonia Levitin

1982

Distinguished work of fiction: WHICH WAY COURAGE by Eiveen Weiman *(Atheneum)*

Significant contribution for excellence in a series: The JEWISH HOLIDAYS books by Malka Drucker *(Holiday House)*

Distinguished body of work: Julia Cunningham

1983
Distinguished work of fiction: JONATHAN DOWN UNDER by Patricia Beatty *(Morrow)*
Distinguished work of nonfiction: WINDOWS IN SPACE by Ann Elwood and Linda Wood *(Walker)*
Special recognition for excellence in a series: DORIS FEIN mysteries by T. Ernesto Bethancourt *(Holiday House)*
Special recognition for a contribution of cultural significance: STORY FOR A BLACK NIGHT by Clayton Bess *(Houghton)*
1984
Distinguished work of fiction: NADIA THE WILLFUL by Sue Alexander *(Pantheon)*
Recognition of merit for a first novel: ELEMENT OF TIME by Kathy Livoni *(HBJ)*
Distinguished body of work: Adrienne Jones
1985
Notable work of fiction: PRUNE by Raymond Royal Ross *(Atheneum)*
Notable work of nonfiction: TOO FAT? TOO THIN? DO YOU HAVE A CHOICE? by Caroline Arnold *(Morrow)*
Significant contribution in the field of illustration: THE NAPPING HOUSE by Audrey Wood, ill. by Don Wood *(HBJ)*
1986
Notable work of fiction: A PLACE FOR ALLIE by M. V. Carey *(Dodd)*
Notable work of nonfiction: THE COMET AND YOU by Edwin Krupp and Robin Rector Krupp *(Macmillan)*
Excellence in a series for young people with underdeveloped reading skills: LIPPINCOTT PAGE TURNERS by Eve Bunting *(Lippincott)*
1987
Distinguished work of nonfiction: I LIFT MY LAMP: EMMA LAZARUS AND THE STATUE OF LIBERTY by Nancy Smiler Levinson *(Lodestar)*
Notable achievement in photojournalism: MOTORCYCLE ON PATROL: THE STORY OF A HIGHWAY OFFICER by Joan and Richard Hewett *(Clarion)*
Outstanding contribution of lasting value in a body of work: Clyde Robert Bulla
1988
Excellence in illustration: THE FLAME OF PEACE: A TALE OF THE AZTECS by Deborah Nourse Lattimore *(Harper)*
Outstanding work of fiction for children: LILA ON THE LANDING by Sue Alexander *(Clarion)*
Outstanding work of fiction for young adults: INVINCIBLE SUMMER by Jean Ferris *(Farrar)*
1989
Outstanding literary quality in a picture book: YONDER by Tony Johnston (ill. by Lloyd Bloom) *(Dial)*

Outstanding work of fiction for children: DEAR BABY by Joanne Rocklin *(Macmillan)*

Outstanding work of fiction for young adults: A SUDDEN SILENCE by Eve Bunting *(HBJ)*

Special recognition for excellence in a poetry quartet: EARTH SONGS (1986), SEA SONGS (1986), SKY SONGS (1984), SPACE SONGS (1988) by Myra Cohn Livingston *(Holiday House)*

1990

Distinguished work of fiction for children: THE WEDNESDAY SURPRISE by Eve Bunting *(Clarion)*

Distinguished work of fiction for young adults: WRESTLING WITH HONOR by David Klass *(Lodestar)*

Distinguished work of nonfiction: ONCE UPON A HORSE by Suzanne Jurmain *(Lothrop)*

Notable book celebrating a creative life: BILL PEET: AN AUTOBIOGRAPHY by Bill Peet *(Houghton)*

1991

Distinguished work of illustrating and writing: THE DRAGON'S ROBE by Deborah Nourse Lattimore *(HarperCollins)*

Distinguished work of fiction: THE WALL by Eve Bunting *(Clarion)*

Distinguished work of fiction for young adults: DIXIE STORMS by Barbara Hall *(HBJ)*

Distinguished work of nonfiction: CHRISTOPHER COLUMBUS: VOYAGER TO THE UNKNOWN by Nancy Smiler Levinson *(Lodestar)*

1992

Notable picture book: PIGGIES by Don and Audrey Wood *(Harcourt)*

Notable work of fiction: BLUE SKYE by Lael Little *(Scholastic)*

Outstanding work of fiction for young adults: WHAT DADDY DID by Neal Shusterman *(Little, Brown)*

Significant contribution to the field of biography: NATIVE AMERICAN DOCTOR: THE STORY OF SUSAN LAFLESCHE PICOTTE by Jeri Ferris *(Carolrhoda)*

1993

Notable picture book: GOING TO SLEEP ON THE FARM by Juan Wijngaard *(Dial)*

Notable work of nonfiction: HUMMINGBIRDS: JEWELS IN THE SKY by Esther and Robert Tyrrell *(Crown)*

Notable contribution to the field of nonfiction for beginning readers: SNOWSHOE THOMPSON by Nancy Smiler Levinson *(HarperCollins)*

Distinguished body of work: Eve Bunting

1994

Excellence in illustration: EXTRA INNINGS: BASEBALL POEMS by Scott Medlock *(Harcourt)*

Outstanding work of nonfiction: LIVES OF THE MUSICIANS by Kathleen Krull *(Harcourt)*
Excellence in a picture book: STELLALUNA by Janell Cannon *(Harcourt)*
Distinguished body of work: Sonia Levitin
Captivating body of work: Caroline Arnold and Richard Hewett
1995
Distinguished picture book: SMOKY NIGHT by Eve Bunting and David Diaz *(Harcourt)*
Distinguished work of fiction: EARTHSHINE by Theresa Nelson *(Orchard)*
Distinguished adaptation and retelling of a folktale: THE TALE OF RABBIT AND COYOTE by Tony Johnston, ill. by Tomie dePaola *(Putnam)*

Southwest Book Awards ❧

"The Southwest Book Awards were instituted in 1971 to encourage the writing and publication of outstanding literature about the Southwest." In the early years of the program, books in numerous categories were honored. Currently, there are only three categories: Arts and Letters, History and Biography, and Nonfiction. Children's and young adult books are considered for honors in all three areas. "Southwest" is defined as Texas, west of the Pecos River, Northern Mexico, Southern New Mexico, and Eastern and Southern Arizona. The awards are sponsored by the Border Regional Library Association (P. O. Box 5342, El Paso, TX 79954-5342). (Certificate)

1971
THE SPIDER, THE CAVE, AND THE POTTERY BOWL by Eleanor Clymer *(Atheneum)*
1972
WHEN CLAY SINGS by Byrd Baylor, ill. by Tom Bahti *(Scribner)*
1975
THE DESERT IS THEIRS by Byrd Baylor, ill. by Peter Parnall *(Scribner)*
MANY WINTERS by Nancy Wood *(Doubleday)*
1976
HAWK, I'M YOUR BROTHER by Byrd Baylor, ill. by Peter Parnall *(Scribner)*
1979
TARANTULAS by Joan Berg Victor *(Dodd)*

1982
DESERT VOICES by Byrd Baylor, ill. by Peter Parnall *(Scribner)*
1985
GRANDMOTHER'S ADOBE DOLLHOUSE by Mary Lou M. Smith *(New Mexico Magazine)*
1986
PECOS BILL: A TALL TALE by Steven Kellogg *(Morrow)*
1987
DOCTOR COYOTE: A NATIVE AMERICAN AESOP'S FABLES by John Bierhorst, ill. by Wendy Watson *(Macmillan)*
THE PUEBLO by Charlotte and David Yue *(Houghton)*
1988
DAWN SEEKERS by Carol Hamilton, ill. by Jeremy Guitar *(Whitman)*
1989
DESERT GIANT: THE WORLD OF THE SAGUARO CACTUS by Barbara Bash *(Sierra Club/ Little, Brown)*
1990
AGAVE BLOOMS JUST ONCE by Gisela Jernigan, ill. by E. Wesley Jernigan *(Harbinger)*
1991
ROXABOXEN by Alice McLerran, ill. by Barbara Cooney *(Lothrop)*
1992
DRAGONFLY'S TALE by Kristina Roadanas *(Clarion)*
1993
A BIRTHDAY BASKET FOR TÍA by Pat Mora, ill. by Cecily Lang *(Macmillan)*
1994
IT RAINED ON THE DESERT TODAY by Ken and Debby Buchanan, ill. by Libba Tracy *(Northland)*
WATCH OUT FOR CLEVER WOMEN! by Joe Hayes, ill. by Vicki Trego Hill *(Cinco Puntos)*
BILLY by Laura Roybal *(Houghton)*
1995
No Award

State Historical Society of Wisconsin Book Awards ෴

JUVENILE BOOK CATEGORY

The State Historical Society of Wisconsin (816 State St., Madison, WI 53706) is the sponsor of an annual awards program. In years in which an award is presented for a children's book, the honored title is judged to have made a contribution to readers' knowledge of the State of Wisconsin. (Certificate)

1966
FEATHER IN THE WIND by Beverly Butler *(Dodd)*
1967
SPAN ACROSS THE RIVER by Donald Emerson *(McKay)*
1968
No Award
1969
NINE LIVES OF MOSES ON THE OREGON TRAIL by Marion Fuller Archer *(Whitman)*
1970
No Award
1971
HIGGINS OF THE RAILROAD MUSEUM by Ethelyn M. Parkinson *(Abingdon)*
1972-1974
No Awards
1975
SONGS OF THE CHIPPEWA edited by John Bierhorst *(Farrar)*
1976
No Award
1977
CUTOVER COUNTRY: JOLIE'S STORY by Jolie Paylin *(Iowa State University Press)*
1978-1982
No Awards
1983
FIRST FARM IN THE VALLEY: ANNA'S STORY by Anne Pellowski *(Philomel)*
1984
THE CHILD OF TWO MOTHERS by Malcolm and Margaret Rosholt *(Rosholt House)*
1985
No Award

1986
RAILROADS OF SOUTHERN & SOUTHWESTERN
WISCONSIN: DEVELOPMENT TO DECLINE by Daniel J.
Lanz *(Ski Printers)*

1987
No Award

1988
THE STORY OF OLD ABE by Malcolm and Margaret Rosholt
(Rosholt House)

1989-1990
No Awards

1991
ADVENTURES OF THE NORTHWOODS (series) by Lois
Walfrid Johnson *(Bethany House)*

1992-1993
No Awards

1994
OF THINGS NATURAL, WILD AND FREE: A STORY
ABOUT ALDO LEOPOLD by Marybeth Lorbiecki *(Carolrhoda)*

1995
No Award

George G. Stone Center for Children's Books Recognition of Merit Award ᨠ

Given annually since 1965 at the Claremont Reading Conference
(Claremont Graduate School, Claremont, CA 91711) to an
author or illustrator of a children's book or for a body of work
for the "power to please and to expand the awareness of
children and teachers as they have shared the book in their
classrooms." (The Center is named for a benefactor.) (Scroll)

1965
CRICKET SONGS translated by Harry Behn *(HBJ)*

1966
CALENDAR MOON by Natalia M. Belting *(Holt)*

1967
DURANGO STREET by Frank Bonham *(Dutton)*

1968
WHITE BIRD by Clyde Robert Bulla *(Crowell)*

1969
MY SIDE OF THE MOUNTAIN by Jean Craighead George *(Dutton)*
1970
CHARLOTTE'S WEB by E.B. White *(Harper)*
1971
THE PHANTOM TOLLBOOTH by Norton Juster *(Random)*
1972
BY THE GREAT HORN SPOON by Sid Fleischman *(Atlantic-Little, Brown)*
1973
THE EGYPT GAME by Zilpha Keatley Snyder *(Atheneum)*
1974
QUEENIE PEAVY by Robert Burch *(Viking)*
1975
INCIDENT AT HAWK'S HILL by Allan W. Eckert *(Little, Brown)*
1976
Body of work of Leo Lionni
1977
THE WHITE MOUNTAINS *(The Tripods Trilogy)* by John Christopher *(Macmillan)*
1978
FROG AND TOAD books by Arnold Lobel *(Harper)*
1979
Body of work of Natalie Babbitt
1980
TEETONCEY STORIES *(The Cape Hatteras Trilogy)* by Theodore Taylor *(Doubleday)*
1981
No Award
1982
Body of work of Mary Stolz
1983
Body of work of Beverly Cleary
1984
A LIGHT IN THE ATTIC by Shel Silverstein *(Harper)*
WHERE THE SIDEWALK ENDS by Shel Silverstein *(Harper)*
1985
Body of work of Bill Peet
1986
Body of work of Tana Hoban
1987
STONE FOX by John Reynolds Gardiner *(Crowell)*

1988
ALEXANDER AND THE TERRIBLE, HORRIBLE, NO
GOOD, VERY BAD DAY by Judith Viorst *(Atheneum)*
1989
THE BEARS' HOUSE by Marilyn Sachs *(Dutton)*
FRAN ELLEN'S HOUSE by Marilyn Sachs *(Dutton)*
1990
HONEY, I LOVE AND OTHER LOVE POEMS by Eloise
Greenfield *(Crowell)*
1991
LET THE CIRCLE BE UNBROKEN by Mildred D. Taylor
(Dial)
THE ROAD TO MEMPHIS by Mildred D. Taylor *(Dial)*
ROLL OF THUNDER, HEAR MY CRY by Mildred D. Taylor
(Dial)
1992
Body of work of Mitsumasa Anno
1993
BASEBALL IN APRIL AND OTHER STORIES by Gary Soto
(Harcourt)
1994
THE HOUSE ON MANGO STREET by Sandra Cisneros *(Arte
Público)*
1995
The HENRY AND MUDGE Series *(Bradbury)* and the MR.
PUTTER AND TABBY Series *(Harcourt)* by Cynthia Rylant

Flora Stieglitz Straus Award 🐾

Established in 1994 by the Child Study Children's Book
Committee at Bank Street College) 610 W. 112th St., New York,
NY 10025) this award is in memory of Flora Straus. She led the
Committee for over 75 years and stood for the values of courage,
hard work, truth, and beauty. She championed diverse opinions,
and supported humanitarian efforts. The award is presented to a
distinguished work of nonfiction which fulfills her ideals and
serves as an inspiration to young people. The year cited below is
the year of the book's publication. (Scroll and honorarium)
See also Children's Book Award.

1993
ELEANOR ROOSEVELT: A LIFE OF DISCOVERY by Russell
Freedman *(Clarion)*

1994
No Award
1995
PARALLEL JOURNEYS by Eleanor Ayer *(Atheneum)*

Joan G. Sugarman Children's Book Award ❧

This award honors excellence in writing for children by authors who are residents of Washington, DC, Virginia, or Maryland. Joan G. Sugarman, a children's book author and librarian, established the award in honor of her late husband, Norman A. Sugarman. Originally presented each year, the award is now a biennial one, administered by the Washington Independent Writers Legal and Educational Fund (220 Woodward Bldg., 733 15th St., NW, Washington, DC 20005), a nonprofit organization founded "to defend First Amendment cases and address other concerns of independent writers." ($1,000)

1987
BEETLES, LIGHTLY TOASTED by Phyllis Reynolds Naylor *(Atheneum)*
1988
TREE BY LEAF by Cynthia Voigt *(Atheneum)*
1989
SHABANU: DAUGHTER OF THE WIND by Suzanne Fisher Staples *(Knopf)*
1991
STEPPING ON THE CRACKS by Mary Downing Hahn *(Clarion)*
1993
MOONSHINER'S SON by Carolyn Reeder *(Macmillan)*
1995
WALT WHITMAN by Catherine Reef *(Clarion)*

Sydney Taylor Book Awards ❧

The Sydney Taylor Book Awards honor outstanding books of
positive Jewish content for children. They are part of the awards
program of the Association of Jewish Libraries (AJL) (15 E. 26th
St., Suite 1034, New York, NY 10010-1579). AJL first gave an
award for children's books in 1969, for a book published in
1968. Then called the Shirley Kravitz Award, this honors
program originated as an activity of AJL's School and Center
Division. In 1975 AJL integrated its award for books for young
readers into the overall Association of Jewish Libraries Awards
program, establishing a separate category for children's books.
Another distinction was added to the AJL Awards for 1978: the
Sydney Taylor Body of Work Award for an author. It honored
the memory of the creator of the warmly appreciated series of
"All-of-a-Kind Family" books about Jewish family life in New
York's Lower East Side in the early part of the 20th century. As
of the program relating to 1981 books, there were provisions for
awards for a book for older children, and also a book for
younger children. By 1985—featuring 1984 titles—the entire AJL
program, honoring children's books deemed by a committee of
professional Judaica librarians to have made outstanding
contributions to Jewish literature for young readers, was renamed
the Sydney Taylor Book Awards. In addition to honoring
published works and authors for a body of work, AJL also
sponsors an annual Sydney Taylor Manuscript Award for
unpublished authors. In the listing below, honorees are preceded
by 0 = book for older readers, Y = book for younger readers, and
B = body of work. In some years, it is apparent, awards have not
been given in all categories. (Plaque and honorarium)

1968
0: THE ENDLESS STEPPE by Esther Hautzig *(Crowell)*
1969
0: OUR EDDIE by Sulamith Ish-Kishor *(Pantheon)*
1970
0: THE YEAR by Suzanne Lange *(Phillips)*
1971
B: Isaac Bashevis Singer
1972
B: Molly Cone
1973
0: UNCLE MISHA'S PARTISANS by Yuri Suhl *(Four Winds)*
1974
No Award
1975
0: WAITING FOR MAMA by Marietta Moskin *(Coward)*

1976
0: NEVER TO FORGET: THE JEWS OF THE HOLOCAUST
by Milton Meltzer *(Harper)*

1977
0: EXIT FROM HOME by Anita Heyman *(Crown)*

1978
0: THE DEVIL IN VIENNA by Doris Orgel *(Dial)*
B: Sydney Taylor (posthumously)

1979
0: IKE AND MAMA AND THE BLOCK WEDDING by Carol
Snyder *(Coward)*
B: Marilyn Hirsch

1980
0: A RUSSIAN FAREWELL by Leonard Everett Fisher *(Four
Winds)*
B: Sadie Rose Weilerstein

1981
0: THE NIGHT JOURNEY by Kathryn Lasky *(Warne)*
Y: YUSSEL'S PRAYER: A YOM KIPPUR STORY by Barbara
Cohen *(Lothrop)*
B: Barbara Cohen

1982
0: CALL ME RUTH by Marilyn Sachs *(Doubleday)*
Y: THE CASTLE ON HESTER STREET by Linda Heller
(Jewish Publication Society)

1983
0: IN THE MOUTH OF THE WOLF by Rose Zar *(Jewish
Publication Society)*
Y: BUBBY, ME AND MEMORIES by Barbara Pomerantz
(Union of American Hebrew Congregations)

1984
0: THE ISLAND ON BIRD STREET by Uri Orlev, translated by
Hillel Halkin *(Houghton)*
Y: MRS. MOSKOWITZ AND THE SABBATH
CANDLESTICKS by Amy Schwartz *(Jewish Publication Society)*
B: Miriam Chaikin

1985
0: IKE AND MAMA AND THE SEVEN SURPRISES by Carol
Snyder *(Lothrop)*
Y: BROTHERS by Florence B. Freedman, ill. by Robert Andrew
Parker *(Harper)*
B: Carol Snyder

1986
0: BEYOND THE HIGH WHITE WALL by Nancy Pitt
(Scribner)
Y: JOSEPH WHO LOVED THE SABBATH by Marilyn Hirsh,
ill. by Devis Grebu *(Viking)*

1987
O: THE RETURN by Sonia Levitin *(Atheneum)*
Y: THE NUMBER ON MY GRANDFATHER'S ARM by David A. Adler, photog. by Rose Eichenbaum *(Union of American Hebrew Congregations)*

1988
O: THE DEVIL'S ARITHMETIC by Jane Yolen *(Viking)*
Y: THE KEEPING QUILT by Patricia Polacco *(Simon & Schuster)*

1989
O: NUMBER THE STARS by Lois Lowry *(Houghton)*
Y: BERCHICK: MY MOTHER'S HORSE by Esther Silverstein Blanc, ill. by Tennessee Dixon *(Volcano)*
B: Yaffa Ganz

1990
O: MY GRANDMOTHER'S STORIES by Adele Geras, ill. by Jael Jorden *(Knopf)*
Y: THE CHANUKKAH GUEST by Eric Kimmel, ill. by Giori Carmi *(Holiday House)*

1991
O: THE DIAMOND TREE: JEWISH TALES FROM AROUND THE WORLD by Howard Schwartz and Barbara Rush, ill. by Uri Shulevitz *(HarperCollins)*
Y: DADDY'S CHAIR by Sandy Lanton, ill. by Shelly Haas *(Kar-Ben)*
Y: CAKES AND MIRACLES: A PURIM TALE by Barbara Diamond Goldin, ill. by Erika Weihs *(Viking)*

1992
O: LETTERS FROM RIFKA by Karen Hesse *(Holt)*
Y: SOMETHING FROM NOTHING by Phoebe Gilman *(Scholastic)*

1993
O: SWORN ENEMIES by Carol Matas *(Bantam)*
Y: THE UNINVITED GUEST AND OTHER JEWISH HOLIDAY TALES by Nina Jaffe, ill. by Elivia Savadier *(Scholastic)*

1994
O: THE SHADOW CHILDREN by Steven Schnur, ill. by Herbert Tauss *(Morrow)*
Y: THE ALWAYS PRAYER SHAWL by Sheldon Oberman, ill. by Ted Lewin *(Boyds Mills Press)*

1995
O: DANCING ON THE BRIDGE AT AVIGNON by Ida Vos, translated from Dutch by Terese Edelstein and Inez Smidt *(Houghton)*
Y: STAR OF FEAR, STAR OF HOPE by Jo Hoestlandt, translated from French by Mark Polizzotti, ill. by Johanna Kang *(Walker)*

University of Southern Mississippi Medallion ❧

This award is given annually in the spring at the University of Southern Mississippi Children's Book Festival (School of Library Service, Hattiesburg, MS 39406) to a writer or illustrator who has made an outstanding contribution to the field of children's literature. The awards program is a project of the de Grummond Children's Literature Research Collection of the university's McCain Library. (Silver medallion)

1969	Lois Lenski
1970	Ernest H. Shepard
1971	Roger Duvoisin
1972	Marcia Brown
1973	Lynd Ward
1974	Taro Yashima
1975	Barbara Cooney
1976	Scott O'Dell
1977	Adrienne Adams
1978	Madeleine L'Engle
1979	Leonard Everett Fisher
1980	Ezra Jack Keats
1981	Maurice Sendak
1982	Beverly Cleary
1983	Katherine Paterson
1984	Peter Spier
1985	Arnold Lobel
1986	Jean Craighead George
1987	Paula Fox
1988	Jean Fritz
1989	Lee Bennett Hopkins
1990	Charlotte Zolotow
1991	Richard Peck
1992	James Marshall
1993	Quentin Blake
1994	Ashley Brown
1995	Tomie dePaola
1996	Patricia MacLachlan

Washington Post/Childrens' Book Guild Nonfiction Award

This awards program was initially a project of the Childrens' Book Guild, a Washington DC-area association of authors, illustrators, editors and a variety of other children's literature specialists. As of 1983, the *Washington Post* (1150 15th St., NW, Washington, DC 20071) joined with the Guild as a co-sponsor of the award, which is given to an author or illustrator for a body of work in informational books for young readers. (Inscribed paperweight and a cash award)

1977 David Macaulay
1978 Millicent Selsam
1979 Jean Fritz
1980 Shirley Glubok
1981 Milton Meltzer
1982 Tana Hoban
1983 Patricia Lauber
1984 Jill Krementz
1985 Isaac Asimov
1986 Kathryn Lasky
1987 Gail Gibbons
1988 Jim Arnosky
1989 Leonard Everett Fisher
1990 Brent Ashabranner
1991 Joanna Cole
1992 Russell Freedman
1993 Seymour Simon
1994 James Haskins
1995 Albert Marrin
1996 James Cross Giblin

Western Heritage Awards 🌢
JUVENILE BOOK CATEGORY

Given annually by the National Cowboy Hall of Fame and Western Heritage Center (1700 N.E. 63rd St., Oklahoma City, OK 73111) to a juvenile book that best portrays the authentic American West. (Bronze *Wrangler* trophy)

1962
KING OF THE MOUNTAIN by Gene Caesar *(Dutton)*
1963
THE BOOK OF THE WEST by Charles Clifton *(Bobbs)*
1964
KILLER-OF-DEATH by Betty Baker *(Harper)*
1965
THE GREATEST CATTLE DRIVE by Paul Wellman *(Houghton)*
1966
LAND RUSH by Carl C. Hodges *(Duell-Sloan)*
1967
MUSTANG by Marguerite Henry *(Rand McNally)*
1968
DOWN THE RIVERS, WESTWARD HO! by Eric Scott *(Meredith)*
1969
EDGE OF TWO WORLDS by Weyman Jones *(Dial)*
1970
AN AWFUL NAME TO LIVE UP TO by Jossie Hosford *(Meredith)*
1971
AND ONE WAS A WOODEN INDIAN by Betty Baker *(Macmillan)*
1972
THE BLACK MUSTANGER by Richard Wormser *(Morrow)*
1973
FAMOUS AMERICAN EXPLORERS by Bern Keating *(Rand McNally)*
1974
No Award
1975
SUSY'S SCOUNDREL by Harold Keith *(Crowell)*
1976
OWL IN THE CEDAR TREE by Natachee Scott Momaday *(Northland Press)*

1977-1978
No Awards
1979
THE OBSTINATE LAND by Harold Keith *(Crowell)*
1980
THE *LITTLE HOUSE* COOKBOOK by Barbara Walker
(Harper)
1981-1983
No Awards
1984
CHILDREN OF THE WILD WEST by Russell Freedman
(Clarion)
1985
No Award
1986
HAPPILY MAY I WALK: AMERICAN INDIANS AND
ALASKA NATIVES TODAY by Arlene Hirschfelder *(Scribner)*
1987
THE COVERED WAGON AND OTHER ADVENTURES by
Lynn H. Scott *(University of Nebraska)*
1988
STAY PUT, ROBBIE McAMIS by Frances G. Tunbo *(Texas
Christian University)*
1989
LETTERS TO OMA by Marj Gurasich *(Texas Christian
University)*
1990
BUNKHOUSE JOURNAL by Diane Johnston Hamm *(Scribner)*
1991
MONSTER SLAYER: A NAVAJO FOLKTALE retold by Vee
Brown, ill. by Baje Whitethorne *(Northland)*
1992
AN INDIAN WINTER by Russell Freedman *(Holiday House)*
1993
COWBOYS, INDIANS, AND GUNFIGHTERS: THE STORY
OF THE CATTLE KINGDOM by Albert Marrin *(Atheneum)*
1994
EAGLE DRUM by Robert Crum *(Simon & Schuster)*
1995
THE NIGHT THE GRANDFATHERS DANCED by Linda
Theresa Raczek, ill. by Katalin Olah Ehling *(Northland)*

Western Writers of America Spur Awards

BEST WESTERN JUVENILE CATEGORIES

The Spur Awards aim to encourage "high achievement in literature and art that portray the history and heritage of The American West." They are given to works in many categories, including novels, historical novels, nonfiction, short fiction and nonfiction, cover art, scripts for both motion pictures and television, and include awards for fiction and nonfiction books for young readers. If the quality of the entries is high for both fiction *(F)* and nonfiction *(NF)* juveniles, two awards are presented. In some years, only one award is presented to a juvenile book. In 1995, a Storyteller Award was first presented to a picture book *(PB)*. In addition to the Spur Awards, the sponsor (Western Writers of America, Inc., Attn.: James A. Crutchfield, Secretary-Treasurer, 1012 Fair St., Franklin, TN 37064) administers the Medicine Pipe Bearer's Award for a first novel, for which juveniles are eligible. The year cited is the year in which books were published. (Spurs and a plaque)

1953
SAGEBRUSH SORREL by Frank C. Robertson *(Nelson)*
1954
YOUNG HERO OF THE RANGE by Stephen Payne *(Lantern)*
1955
No Award
1956
TRAPPING THE SILVER BEAVER by Charles Niehuis *(Dodd)*
1957
WOLF BROTHER by James Kjelgaard *(Holiday House)*
1958
STEAMBOAT UP THE MISSOURI by Dale White *(Viking)*
1959
F: THEIR SHINING HOUR by Romona Maher Weeks *(John Day)*
NF: HOLD BACK THE HUNTER by Dale White *(Marion T. Place)*
1960
THE HORSE TALKER by Jeanne Williams *(Prentice-Hall)*
1961
No Award
1962
THE WESTERN HORSE by Natlee Kenoyer *(Meredith)*

1963
BY THE GREAT HORN SPOON by Sid Fleischman *(Atlantic-Little, Brown)*
THE STORY CATCHER by Mari Sandoz *(Westminster)*
1964
RIDE A NORTHBOUND HORSE by Richard Wormser *(Morrow)*
1965
THE STUBBORN ONE by Rutherford Montgomery *(Duell-Sloan)*
1966
F: THE BURNING GLASS by Annabel and Edgar Johnson *(Harper)*
NF: VALLEY OF THE SMALLEST by Aileen Fisher *(Crowell)*
1967
F: THE DUNDERHEAD WAR by Betty Baker *(Harper)*
HALF BREED by Evelyn Lampman *(Doubleday)*
NF: TO THE PACIFIC WITH LEWIS AND CLARK by Ralph Andrist and E.R. Bingham *(Harper)*
1968
F: MIDDL'UN by Elizabeth Burleson *(Follett)*
NF: RIFLES AND WARBONNETS by Marian T. Place *(Washburn)*
1969
F: THE MEEKER MASSACRE by Lewis D. Patten and Wayne D. Overholser *(Cowles)*
NF: CONQUISTADORS AND PUEBLOS by Olga Hall-Quest *(Dutton)*
1970
F: CAYUSE COURAGE by Evelyn Lampman *(HBJ)*
NF: RETREAT TO THE BEAR PAW by Marian T. Place *(Four Winds)*
SEARCH FOR SEVEN CITIES by John Upton Terrell *(HBJ)*
1971
F: THE BLACK MUSTANGER by Richard Wormser *(Morrow)*
NF: LORDS OF THE EARTH by Jules Loh *(Crowell-Collier)*
1972
F: ONLY EARTH AND SKY LAST FOREVER by Nathaniel Benchley *(Harper)*
NF: THE TIGUAS by Stan Steiner *(Crowell-Collier)*
1973
F: FREEDOM TRAIL by Jeanne Williams *(Putnam)*
NF: RED POWER ON THE RIO GRANDE by Franklin Folsom *(Follett)*
1974
SUSY'S SCOUNDREL by Harold Keith *(Crowell)*
1975
F: DUST OF THE EARTH by Vera and Bill Cleaver *(Lippincott)*

NF: LAMY OF SANTA FE by Paul Horgan *(Farrar)*
1976
ALL ABOARD by Philip H. Ault *(Dodd)*
1977
A SHEPHERD WATCHES, A SHEPHERD SINGS by Louis Irigary and Theodore Taylor *(Doubleday)*
1978
THE NO-RETURN TRAIL by Sonia Levitin *(HBJ)*
1979
No Award
1980
GETTING THERE: FRONTIER TRAVEL WITHOUT POWER by Suzanne Hilton *(Westminster)*
1981
THE LAST RUN by Mark Jonathon Harris *(Lothrop)*
1982
BEFORE THE LARK by Irene Bennett Brown *(Atheneum)*
1983
THUNDER ON THE TENNESSEE by Gary Clifton Wisler *(Lodestar)*
1984
TRAPPED IN SLICKROCK CANYON: A MOUNTAIN WEST ADVENTURE by Gloria Skurzynski *(Lothrop)*
1985
PRAIRIE SONGS by Pam Conrad *(Harper)*
1986
MAKE WAY FOR SAM HOUSTON by Jean Fritz *(Putnam)*
1987
THE ORPHAN TRAIN by Joan Lowery Nixon *(Bantam)*
1988
IN THE FACE OF DANGER by Joan Lowery Nixon *(Bantam)*
1989
MY DANIEL by Pam Conrad *(Harper)*
1990
F: HONEY GIRL by Madge Harrah *(Avon)*
NF: WOODSONG by Gary Paulsen *(Bradbury)*

1991
RESCUE JOSH McGUIRE by Ben Mikaelsen *(Hyperion)*
1992
F: THE HAYMEADOW by Gary Paulsen *(Delacorte)*
NF: CHILDREN OF THE DUSTBOWL: THE TRUE STORY OF THE SCHOOL AT WEEDPATCH CAMP by Jerry Stanley *(Crown)*
1993
F: LEAVING ELDORADO by Joann Mazzio *(Houghton)*

NF: COWBOYS, INDIANS, AND GUNFIGHTERS by Albert Marrin *(Atheneum)*
1994
THE TRAIL OF TEARS by David Fremon *(Silver Burdett)*
1995
F: INDIO by Sherry Garland *(Harcourt)*
NF: CAMELS FOR UNCLE SAM by Diane Yancy *(Hendrick-Long)*
PB: DANDELIONS by Eve Bunting *(Harcourt)*

Laura Ingalls Wilder Award ઠ

First awarded in 1954, this medal was given every five years from 1960 through 1980. As of 1983, the award has been given at three-year intervals. The award honors an author or illustrator whose books, published in the U.S., have made, over a period of years, a substantial and lasting contribution to literature for children. Administered by the Association for Library Service to Children, a division of the American Library Association (50 E. Huron St., Chicago, IL 60611). (Bronze medal)

1954   Laura Ingalls Wilder
1960   Clara Ingram Judson
1965   Ruth Sawyer
1970   E.B. White
1975   Beverly Cleary
1980   Theodor S. Geisel (Dr. Seuss)
1983   Maurice Sendak
1986   Jean Fritz
1989   Elizabeth George Speare
1992   Marcia Brown
1995   Virginia Hamilton

Carter G. Woodson Book Awards 🕭

The National Council for the Social Studies (Attn: Recognition Programs, 3501 Newark St., NW, Washington, DC 20016-3167) established this award in 1974 to recognize the most distinguished social science book appropriate for young readers which treats topics related to ethnic minorities and race relations in the United States sensitively and accurately. The awards are named for a distinguished Harvard University Professor of History. Since 1980 Outstanding Merit Books have been named (not listed here due to space limitations). Since 1989, an elementary *(E)* and a secondary *(S)* winner have been named. Books should be informational or nonfiction (not primarily a textbook), written for children or young epople, set in the U.S., and published in the U.S. in the year preceding that in which the award is given. Other specific criteria apply. (Commemorative gift, annual conference session, book-signing, national publicity, published review)

1974
ROSA PARKS by Eloise Greenfield *(Crowell)*
1975
MAKE A JOYFUL NOISE UNTO THE LORD: THE LIFE OF MAHALIA JACKSON, QUEEN OF THE GOSPEL SINGERS by Jesse Jackson *(Crowell)*
1976
DRAGONWINGS by Laurence Yep *(Harper)*
1977
THE TROUBLE THEY SEEN by Dorothy Sterling *(Doubleday)*
1978
THE BIOGRAPHY OF DANIEL INOUYE by Jane Goodsell *(Crowell)*
1979
NATIVE AMERICAN TESTIMONY: AN ANTHOLOGY OF INDIAN AND WHITE RELATIONS edited by Peter Nabokov *(Crowell)*
1980
WAR CRY ON A PRAYER FEATHER: PROSE AND POETRY OF THE UTE INDIANS by Nancy Wood *(Doubleday)*
1981
THE CHINESE AMERICANS by Milton Meltzer *(Crowell)*
1982
COMING TO NORTH AMERICA FROM MEXICO, CUBA AND PUERTO RICO by Susan Garver and Paula McGuire *(Delacorte)*

1983
MORNING STAR, BLACK SUN by Brent Ashabranner *(Dodd)*
1984
MEXICO AND THE UNITED STATES by E. B. Fincher *(Crowell)*
1985
TO LIVE IN TWO WORLDS: AMERICAN INDIAN YOUTH
TODAY by Brent Ashabranner *(Dodd)*
1986
DARK HARVEST: MIGRANT FARMWORKERS IN
AMERICA by Brent Ashabranner *(Dodd)*
1987
HAPPILY MAY I WALK: AMERICAN INDIANS AND
ALASKA NATIVES TODAY by Arlene Hirschfelder *(Scribner)*
1988
BLACK MUSIC IN AMERICA: A HISTORY THROUGH ITS
PEOPLE by James Haskins *(Harper)*
1989
E: WALKING THE ROAD TO FREEDOM by Jeri Ferris
(Carolrhoda)
S: MARIAN ANDERSON by Charles Patterson *(Watts)*
1990
E: IN TWO WORLDS: A YUP'IK ESKIMO FAMILY by Aylette
Jenness and Alice Rivers *(Houghton)*
S: PAUL ROBESON by Rebecca Larsen *(Watts)*
1991
E: SHIRLEY CHISHOLM: TEACHER AND
CONGRESSWOMAN by Catherine Scheader *(Enslow)*
S: SORROW'S KITCHEN: ZORA HURSTON by Mary E.
Lyons *(Scribner)*
1992
E: THE LAST PRINCESS: THE STORY OF PRINCESS
KÁIOLANI OF HAWAII by Fay Stanley *(Macmillan)*
S: NATIVE AMERICAN DOCTOR: THE STORY OF SUSAN
LAFLESCHE PICOTTE by Jeri Ferris *(Carolrhoda)*
1993
E: MADAM C.J. WALKER: SELF-MADE MILLIONAIRE by
Patricia C. and Fredrick L. McKissack *(Enslow)*
S: MISSISSIPPI CHALLENGE by Mildred Pitts Walter *(Bradbury)*
1994
E: STARTING HOME: THE STORY OF HORACE PIPPIN,
PAINTER by Mary E. Lyons *(Scribner)*
S: THE MARCH ON WASHINGTON by James Haskins
(HarperCollins)
1995
E: WHAT I HAD WAS SINGING: THE STORY OF MARIAN
ANDERSON by Jeri Ferris *(Carolrhoda)*
S: TILL VICTORY IS WON: BLACK SOLDIERS IN THE
CIVIL WAR by Zak Mettger *(Lodestar)*

PART II

United States Awards
Selected by Young Readers

ALABAMA
Emphasis on Reading: A Children's Choice Book Award Program ❦

The Emphasis on Reading awards aim "to insure that children get to read some of the best literature written for their age or stage before they get beyond it." The program is sponsored by the Alabama Reading Incentive Council, an umbrella organization that includes several professional associations. Representatives of at least ten of them constitute a Nominating Committee that meets annually to assemble a nominee list of eight titles in—as of 1992—three reading categories: Grades *K-2, 3-5,* and *6-8.* An attempt is made to include titles by Alabama authors, or about Alabama, when appropriate. So there is ample time for participating schools and libraries to acquire nominated titles and for children to read them, children's votes are tabulated eighteen months after the nominee list is announced. The program is managed by the Alabama State Department of Education (50 North Ripley St., Gordon Persons Bldg. #3345, Montgomery, AL 36130-3901). (Certificate)

1980-81
K-1: KATY NO-POCKET by Emmy Payne *(Houghton)*
2-3: CHARLOTTE'S WEB by E. B. White *(Harper)*
4-6: THE BEST CHRISTMAS PAGEANT EVER by Barbara Robinson *(Harper)*
7-9: THE HOBBIT by J.R.R. Tolkien *(Houghton)*
*10-12:*THE ACORN PEOPLE by Ron Jones *(Abingdon)*
1981-82
K-1: THE RUNAWAY BUNNY by Margaret Wise Brown, ill. by Clement Hurd *(Harper)*
2-3: GRANNY AND THE INDIANS by Peggy Parish, ill. by Brinton Turkle *(Macmillan)*
4-6: BUNNICULA: A RABBIT TALE OF MYSTERY by Deborah and James Howe *(Atheneum)*
7-9: MAYDAY! MAYDAY! by Hilary H. Milton *(Watts)*
10-12: CHRISTY by Catherine Marshall *(McGraw-Hill)*
1982-83
K-1: SYLVESTER AND THE MAGIC PEBBLE by William Steig *(Windmill/Simon & Schuster)*

2-3: CHOCOLATE CHIP MYSTERY by John McInnes, ill. by Paul Frame *(Garrard)*
4-6: STUART LITTLE by E. B. White *(Harper)*
7-9: KILLING MR. GRIFFIN by Lois Duncan *(Little, Brown)*
10-12: SUNSHINE by Norma Klein *(Holt)*

1983-84
K-1: THE BIG ORANGE SPLOT by Daniel Manus Pinkwater *(Hastings)*
2-3: RALPH S. MOUSE by Beverly Cleary, ill. by Paul O. Zelinsky *(Morrow)*
4-6: NOTHING'S FAIR IN FIFTH GRADE by Barthe DeClements *(Viking)*
7-9: UNICORNS IN THE RAIN by Barbara Cohen *(Atheneum)*
10-12: CAGES OF GLASS, FLOWERS OF TIME by Charlotte Culin *(Bradbury)*

1984-85
K-1: A POCKET FOR CORDUROY by Don Freeman *(Viking)*
2-3: THE GREAT GREEN TURKEY CREEK MONSTER by James Flora *(McElderry)*
4-6: THE BOXCAR CHILDREN by Gertrude Warner *(Whitman)*
7-9: A TANGLE OF ROOTS by Barbara Girion *(Scribner)*
10-12: GRENDEL by John Gardner *(Knopf)*

1985-86
K-1: THE PAIN AND THE GREAT ONE by Judy Blume, ill. by Irene Trivas *(Bradbury)*
2-3: THE ADVENTURES OF ALBERT, THE RUNNING BEAR by Barbara Isenberg and Susan Wolf, ill. by Dick Gackenbach *(Clarion)*
4-6: SUPERFUDGE by Judy Blume *(Dutton)*
7-9: DIVORCE EXPRESS by Paula Danziger *(Delacorte)*
10-12: HIM SHE LOVES? by M. E. Kerr *(Harper)*

1986-87
K-1: IF YOU GIVE A MOUSE A COOKIE by Laura Numeroff, ill. by Felicia Bond *(Harper)*
2-3: THE NEW KID ON THE BLOCK by Jack Prelutsky, ill. by James Stevenson *(Greenwillow)*
4-6: STONE FOX by John Reynolds Gardiner *(Crowell)*
7-9: YOU NEVER CAN TELL by Ellen Conford *(Little, Brown)*
10-12: YEAGER, AN AUTOBIOGRAPHY by Chuck Yeager and Leo Janos *(Bantam)*

1987-88
K-1: MY TEACHER SLEEPS IN SCHOOL by Leatie Weiss, ill. by Ellen Weiss *(Viking)*
2-3: MY MOTHER NEVER LISTENS TO ME by Marjorie Sharmat, ill. by Lynn Munsinger *(Whitman)*
4-6: THE DOLLHOUSE MURDERS by Betty Ren Wright *(Holiday House)*

7-9: REVENGE OF THE NERD by John McNamara *(Delacorte)*
10-12: WART, SON OF TOAD by Alden R. Carter *(Putnam)*
1988-89
K-2: NO JUMPING ON THE BED! by Tedd Arnold *(Dial)*
3-5: THE WAR WITH GRANDPA by Robert K. Smith *(Delacorte)*
6-8: NO SWIMMING IN THE DARK POND AND OTHER
CHILLING TALES by Judith Gorog *(Putnam)*
9-12: THE PRINCESS BRIDE by William Goldman *(Ballantine)*
1989-90
K-2: THE LITTLE OLD MAN WHO COULD NOT READ by
Irma S. Black *(Whitman)*
3-5: IN TROUBLE AGAIN, ZELDA HAMMERSMITH? by
Lynn Hall *(HBJ)*
6-8: MAD, MAD, MONDAY by Herma Silverstein *(Lodestar)*
1990-91
K-2: SOCK SNATCHERS by Lorna Balian *(Abingdon)*
3-5: MORE SCARY STORIES TO TELL IN THE DARK by
Alvin Schwartz *(Lippincott)*
6-8: THE GLORY GIRL by Betsy Byars *(Viking)*
9-12: WALKING ACROSS EGYPT by Clyde Edgerton
(Algonquin)
1991-92
K-2: JULIUS, THE BABY OF THE WORLD by Kevin Henkes
(Greenwillow)
3-5: TALES FROM GOLD MOUNTAIN: STORIES OF THE
CHINESE IN THE NEW WORLD by Paul Yee *(Macmillan)*
6-8: COUSINS by Virginia Hamilton *(Philomel)*
1992-93
K-2: MUCKY MOOSE by Jonathan Allen *(Macmillan)*
3-5: RATS ON THE ROOF AND OTHER STORIES by James
Marshall *(Dial)*
6-8: THE DAY THAT ELVIS CAME TO TOWN by Jan
Marino *(Little, Brown)*
1993-94
K-2: ZOMO THE RABBIT: A TRICKSTER TALE FROM
WEST AFRICA retold by Gerald McDermott *(Harcourt)*
3-5: AND THE GREEN GRASS GREW ALL AROUND: FOLK
POETRY FROM EVERYONE by Alvin Schwartz
(HarperCollins)
6-8: THE PIGMAN AND ME by Paul Zindel *(HarperCollins)*
1994-1995
K-2: GO AWAY, BIG GREEN MONSTER! by Ed Emberley
(Little, Brown)
3-5: POWWOW by George Ancona *(Harcourt)*
6-8: ANNE FRANK, BEYOND THE DIARY: A
PHOTOGRAPHIC REMEMBRANCE by Rian Verhoeven and
Ruud van der Rol *(Viking)*

ARIZONA
Arizona Young Reader's Award ❧

The purpose of this award "is to stimulate the interest of young readers in outstanding literature written primarily for them. The common concern of librarians, parents, administrators and teachers to assure interaction between readers and books is a major ingredient in the concept of allowing them to vote for their favorite book and identify it for others to enjoy." An additional aim of the award "is to encourage cooperation among administrators, librarians, and teachers in broadening the reading programs at all levels." Formerly held biennially, the award is now annual. Participating schools currently nominate thirty titles—ten in each of three categories: Picture books *(PB)*, Chapter Books *(CB)*, and Middle School/Young Adult Books *(MS/YA)*. Schoolchildren throughout the state may vote for one book in each category if they have read or have had read to them at least five books (three in the *MS/YA* category). The award is sponsored and administered by the Arizona State Library Association (14449 N. 73rd St., Scottsdale, AZ 85260-3133.) (Winners honored at annual conference)

1977
TALES OF A FOURTH GRADE NOTHING by Judy Blume *(Dutton)*
1979
HOW TO EAT FRIED WORMS by Thomas Rockwell *(Watts)*
1981
MISS NELSON IS MISSING! by Harry Allard, ill. by James Marshall *(Houghton)*
1983
SUPERFUDGE by Judy Blume *(Dutton)*
1985
THE STUPIDS DIE by Harry Allard, ill. by James Marshall *(Houghton)*
1987
SCARY STORIES TO TELL IN THE DARK by Alvin Schwartz *(Lippincott)*
1989
THE INDIAN IN THE CUPBOARD by Lynne Reid Banks *(Doubleday)*
1991
WHERE'S WALDO? by Martin Handford *(Little, Brown)*
THOMAS' SNOWSUIT by Robert Munsch *(Annick)*
THE JOLLY POSTMAN OR OTHER PEOPLE'S LETTERS by Janet and Allan Ahlberg *(Little, Brown)*

THERE'S A BOY IN THE GIRLS' BATHROOM by Louis
Sachar *(Knopf)*
MEANWHILE BACK AT THE RANCH by Trinka Hakes
Noble *(Dial)*

1993
PB: THE VERY QUIET CRICKET by Eric Carle *(Philomel)*
CB: WAYSIDE SCHOOL IS FALLING DOWN by Louis Sachar
(Lothrop)

1994
PB: THE THREE LITTLE JAVELINAS by Susan Lowell
(Northland)
CB: SHILOH by Phyllis Reynolds Naylor *(Atheneum)*
MS/YA: NOTHING BUT THE TRUTH: A DOCUMENTARY
NOVEL by Avi *(Orchard)*

1995
PB: THE THREE LITTLE WOLVES AND THE BIG BAD PIG
by Eugene Trivizas *(Macmillan)*
CB: TOTALLY DISGUSTING by Bill Wallace *(Holiday House)*
MS/YA: THE GIVER by Lois Lowry *(Houghton)*

ARKANSAS
Charlie May Simon Children's Book Award 🙚

Presented annually by the Arkansas Elementary School Council
(Dept. of Education, 4 State Capitol Mall, Little Rock, AR
72201), and sixteen cooperating educational agencies, the award
honors Charlie May Simon (1897-1977), Arkansas author of over
twenty-seven books that include many "children's books based on
her knowledge and love of Arkansas." Arkansas schoolchildren in
grades 4-6 vote in the spring from a master list of titles selected
by representatives from sponsoring groups. An Honor Book is
also selected. (Medallion)

1971
STRIPED ICE CREAM by Joan M. Lexau *(Lippincott)*
1972
BIG BEN by David Walker *(Houghton)*
1973
RUNAWAY RALPH by Beverly Cleary *(Morrow)*
1974
THE RUNT OF ROGERS SCHOOL by Harold Keith
(Lippincott)

1975
TALES OF A FOURTH GRADE NOTHING by Judy Blume *(Dutton)*
1976
BIGFOOT by Hal Evarts *(Scribner)*
1977
THE GHOST ON SATURDAY NIGHT by Sid Fleischman
(Atlantic-Little, Brown)
1978
SHOESHINE GIRL by Clyde Robert Bulla *(Crowell)*
1979
ALVIN'S SWAP SHOP by Clifford B. Hicks *(Scholastic)*
1980
THE PINBALLS by Betsy Byars *(Viking)*
1981
BANANA TWIST by Florence Parry Heide *(Holiday House)*
1981-82
ALL THE MONEY IN THE WORLD by Bill Brittain *(Harper)*
1982-83
DO BANANAS CHEW GUM? by Jamie Gilson *(Lothrop)*
1983-84
RAMONA QUIMBY, AGE 8 by Beverly Cleary *(Morrow)*
1984-85
BE A PERFECT PERSON IN JUST THREE DAYS! by Stephen
Manes *(Clarion)*
1985-86
MY HORRIBLE SECRET by Stephen Roos *(Delacorte)*
1986-87
THE COMPUTER NUT by Betsy Byars *(Viking)*
1987-88
SARAH, PLAIN AND TALL by Patricia MacLachlan *(Harper)*
1988-89
THE WHIPPING BOY by Sid Fleischman *(Greenwillow)*
1989-90
THERE'S A BOY IN THE GIRLS' BATHROOM by Louis
Sachar *(Knopf)*
1990-91
ALL ABOUT SAM by Lois Lowry *(Houghton)*
1991-1992
NUMBER THE STARS by Lois Lowry *(Houghton)*
1992-1993
THE GHOST INSIDE THE MONITOR by Margaret J.
Anderson *(Knopf)*
1993-94
SHILOH by Phyllis Reynolds Naylor *(Atheneum)*
1994-95
ATTABOY, SAM! by Lois Lowry *(Houghton)*

CALIFORNIA
California Young Reader Medals ❧

The purpose of this awards program is "to encourage California children to become better acquainted with good literature" and "to honor a favorite book and its author." Jointly sponsored by the California Reading Association (2790 Harbor Blvd., Suite 204, Costa Mesa, CA 92626), California Library Association (717 K St., Sacramento, CA 95814), California School Library Association (1499 Old Bayshore Hwy., Burlingame, CA 94010) and California Association of Teachers of English (Box 23833, San Diego, CA 92193-3833), participating schools and libraries submit preliminary nominations from children and young adults. A Young Reader Medal Committee determines the titles receiving the most support and prepares a list of final nominees from which young Californians vote for winners. Since 1983, each year there have been four categories: Primary *(P)*, with five final nominees; Intermediate *(I)*, three nominees; Junior High *(JH)*, three; and High School *(HS)*, three. Readers must have read *all* the nominated titles for the category in which they vote; they may vote for only one title in that category; they may vote in more than one category. In recent years, over 500,000 votes have been cast and counted annually. (Medals)

1975
I: HOW TO EAT FRIED WORMS by Thomas Rockwell *(Watts)*
1976
P: HOW DROOFUS THE DRAGON LOST HIS HEAD by Bill Peet *(Houghton)*
1977
I: FREAKY FRIDAY by Mary Rodgers *(Harper)*
HS: WATERSHIP DOWN by Richard Adams *(Macmillan)*
1978
P: LITTLE RABBIT'S LOOSE TOOTH by Lucy Bate *(Crown)*
1979
I: DANNY, THE CHAMPION OF THE WORLD by Roald Dahl *(Knopf)*
HS: THE LATE GREAT ME by Sandra Scoppettone *(Putnam)*
1980
P: BIG BAD BRUCE by Bill Peet *(Houghton)*
JH: THE PINBALLS by Betsy Byars *(Harper)*
1981
I: SUMMER OF THE MONKEYS by Wilson Rawls *(Doubleday)*
HS: A SUMMER TO DIE by Lois Lowry *(Houghton)*

1982

P: MISS NELSON IS MISSING! by Harry Allard, ill. by James Marshall *(Houghton)*

JH: HAIL, HAIL CAMP TIMBERWOOD by Ellen Conford *(Little, Brown)*

1983

P: LIZA LOU AND THE YELLER BELLY SWAMP by Mercer Mayer *(Four Winds)*

I: SUPERFUDGE by Judy Blume *(Dutton)*

JH: TIGER EYES by Judy Blume *(Bradbury)*

HS: SUMMER OF FEAR by Lois Duncan *(Little, Brown)*

1984

P: BAGDAD ATE IT by Phyllis Green, ill. by Joel Schick *(Watts)*

I: THE TROUBLE WITH TUCK by Theodore Taylor *(Doubleday)*

JH: THERE'S A BAT IN BUNK FIVE by Paula Danziger *(Delacorte)*

HS: STRANGER WITH MY FACE by Lois Duncan *(Little, Brown)*

1985

P: HERBIE'S TROUBLES by Carol Chapman, ill. by Kelly Oechsli *(Dutton)*

I: THE INDIAN IN THE CUPBOARD by Lynn Reid Banks *(Doubleday)*

JH: TAKING TERRI MUELLER by Norma Fox Mazer *(Avon)*

HS: THE TRUTH TRAP by Frances A. Miller *(Dutton)*

1986

P: SPACE CASE by Edward Marshall, ill. by James Marshall *(Dial)*

I: NOTHING'S FAIR IN FIFTH GRADE by Barthe DeClements *(Viking)*

JH: THE GIRL WITH THE SILVER EYES by Willo Davis Roberts *(Atheneum)*

HS: THE DARKANGEL by Meredith Ann Pierce *(Atlantic-Little, Brown)*

1987

P: THE NAPPING HOUSE by Audrey Wood, ill. by Don Wood *(HBJ)*

I: THE DOLLHOUSE MURDERS by Betty Ren Wright *(Holiday House)*

JH: YOU SHOULDN'T HAVE TO SAY GOOD-BYE by Patricia Hermes *(HBJ)*

HS: PURSUIT by Michael French *(Delacorte)*

1988

P: IF YOU GIVE A MOUSE A COOKIE by Laura Numeroff, ill. by Felicia Bond *(Harper)*

I: BE A PERFECT PERSON IN JUST THREE DAYS! by Stephen Manes *(Clarion)*

JH: THE ROOT CELLAR by Janet Lunn *(Scribner)*

HS: INTERSTELLAR PIG by William Sleater *(Dutton)*

1989
P: WHAT HAPPENED TO PATRICK'S DINOSAURS? by Carol Carrick, ill. by Donald Carrick *(Clarion)*
I: CASTLE IN THE ATTIC by Elizabeth Winthrop *(Holiday House)*
JH: THE STALKER by Joan Lowery Nixon *(Delacorte)*
HS: FACE AT THE EDGE OF THE WORLD by Eve Bunting *(Clarion)*

1990
P: EYES OF THE DRAGON by Margaret Leaf, ill. by Ed Young *(Lothrop)*
I: THE WAR WITH GRANDPA by Robert Kimmel Smith *(Delacorte)*
JH: THE OTHER SIDE OF DARK by Joan Lowery Nixon *(Delacorte)*
HS: IZZY, WILLY-NILLY by Cynthia Voigt *(Atheneum)*

1991
P: TACKY THE PENGUIN by Helen Lester, ill. by Lynn Munsinger *(Houghton)*
I: HARRY'S MAD by Dick King-Smith *(Crown)*
JH: DECEMBER STILLNESS by Mary Downing Hahn *(Clarion)*
HS: NIGHT KITES by M. E. Kerr *(Harper)*

1992
P: NEVER SPIT ON YOUR SHOES by Denys Cazet *(Orchard)*
I: ALL ABOUT SAM by Lois Lowry *(Houghton)*
JH: THE SNIPER by Theodore Taylor *(Harcourt)*
HS: A SUDDEN SILENCE by Eve Bunting *(Harcourt)*

1993
P: JULIUS, THE BABY OF THE WORLD by Kevin Henkes *(Greenwillow)*
I: FUDGE-A-MANIA by Judy Blume *(Dutton)*
JH: SOMETHING UPSTAIRS: A TALE OF GHOSTS by Avi *(Orchard*
HS: THE SILVER KISS by Annette Klause *(Delacorte)*

1994
P: HIGH WIRE HENRY by Mary Calhoun, ill. by Erick Ingraham *(Morrow)*
I: SCARED STIFF by Willo Davis Roberts *(Atheneum)*
JH: THERE'S A GIRL IN MY HAMMERLOCK by Jerry Spinelli *(Simon & Schuster)*
HS: WE ALL FALL DOWN by Robert Cormier *(Delacorte)*

1995
P: MARTHA SPEAKS by Susan Meddaugh *(Houghton)*
I: STONEWORDS: A GHOST STORY by Pam Conrad *(HarperCollins)*
JH: RESCUE JOSH McGUIRE by Ben Mikaelsen *(Hyperion)*
HS: DOWNRIVER by Will Hobbs *(Atheneum)*

1996
P: STELLALUNA by Janell Cannon *(Harcourt)*

I: TIME FOR ANDREW: A GHOST STORY by Mary Downing Hahn *(Clarion)*
JH: FREAK THE MIGHTY by Rodman Philbrick *(Blue Sky/Scholastic)*
HS: SHADOW OF THE DRAGON by Sherry Garland *(Harcourt)*

COLORADO

Blue Spruce Young Adult Book Award ❧

Established "to encourage young adults' active involvement with books and reading," this awards program invites cooperating schools and libraries to submit the top ten titles suggested by readers in grades 7-12 each year as the nominees for the following year's program. Voters must have read at least three titles from a list of twenty nominees before voting for their top choice. Nominated titles must be written by contemporary American authors, in print, and published within ten years of the award year. Nominees can be either fiction or nonfiction; they need not have been written exclusively for young adult readers; they must not have appeared first as a movie or a TV show. The program is co-sponsored by Colorado Council of the International Reading Association, Colorado Language Arts Society, Colorado Educational Media Association, and Colorado Library Association. (Blue Spruce Award, P.O. Box 27072, Denver, CO 80227) (Bronze medallion if author of nominated title accepts award in person; plaque if author is unable to attend annual convention of one of co-sponsors)

1985
TIGER EYES by Judy Blume *(Bradbury)*
1986
BRIDGE TO TERABITHIA by Katherine Paterson *(Crowell)*
1987
THE THIRD EYE by Lois Duncan *(Little, Brown)*
1988
THE OTHER SIDE OF DARK by Joan Lowery Nixon *(Delacorte)*
1989
THE EYES OF THE DRAGON by Stephen King *(Viking)*
1990
THE CRADLE WILL FALL by Mary Higgins Clark *(Dial)*

1991
PET SEMATARY by Stephen King *(Doubleday)*
1992
CHANGES IN LATITUDES by Will Hobbs *(Atheneum)*
1993
JURASSIC PARK by Michael Crichton *(Ballantine)*
1994
IT by Stephen King *(Signet)*
1995
THE CLIENT by John Grisham *(Dell)*

COLORADO
Colorado Children's Book Award ❦

Established "to encourage children's active involvement with books and reading," this awards program is sponsored by the Colorado Children's Book Award Committee of the Colorado Council of the International Reading Association (c/o Joan Rosenberger, 9105 W. Progress Pl., Littleton, CO 80123). The committee is composed of teachers and librarians. Young readers in participating schools and libraries throughout the state nominate titles for the award. Based entirely on a tabulation of the nominations, a list of twenty most-nominated books is compiled by the committee. Thereafter, young Colorado readers vote for their favorite book from the committee's list. Since 1992, awards have been made in two categories: Picture Book *(PB)* and Junior Novel *(JN)*. The book must be by a living American and have been published within a five-year period before the award year. (Certificate and statuette)

1976
HOW DROOFUS THE DRAGON LOST HIS HEAD by Bill Peet *(Houghton)*
1977
A DAY NO PIGS WOULD DIE by Robert Newton Peck *(Knopf)*
1978
THE SWEET TOUCH by Lorna Balian *(Abingdon)*
1979
THE GREAT GREEN TURKEY CREEK MONSTER by James Flora *(McElderry)*
1980
CLOUDY WITH A CHANCE OF MEATBALLS by Judith Barrett, ill. by Ron Barrett *(Atheneum)*

1981
CROSS-COUNTRY CAT by Mary Calhoun, ill. by Erick Ingraham *(Morrow)*
1982
SUPERFUDGE by Judy Blume *(Dutton)*
1983
SPACE CASE by Edward Marshall, ill. by James Marshall *(Dial)*
1984
THE UNICORN AND THE LAKE by Marianna Mayer, ill. by Michael Hague *(Dial)*
1985
MISS NELSON IS BACK by Harry Allard, ill. by James Marshall *(Houghton)*
1986
IN A DARK, DARK ROOM AND OTHER SCARY STORIES by Alvin Schwartz, ill. by Dirk Zimmer *(Harper)*
1987
KING BIDGOOD'S IN THE BATHTUB by Audrey Wood, ill. by Don Wood *(HBJ)*
1988
IF YOU GIVE A MOUSE A COOKIE by Laura Numeroff, ill. by Felicia Bond *(Harper)*
1989
THE MAGIC SCHOOL BUS AT THE WATERWORKS by Joanna Cole, ill. by Bruce Degen *(Scholastic)*
1990
TACKY THE PENGUIN by Helen Lester, ill. by Lynn Munsinger *(Houghton)*
1991
THE TALKING EGGS: A FOLKTALE FROM THE AMERICAN SOUTH retold by Robert D. San Souci, ill. by Jerry Pinkney *(Dial)*
1992
PB: HERSHEL AND THE HANUKKAH GOBLINS by Eric Kimmel, ill. by Trina Schart Hyman *(Holiday House)*
JN: WAYSIDE SCHOOL IS FALLING DOWN by Louis Sachar *(Avon)*
1993
PB: THE DOG WHO HAD KITTENS by Polly Robertus, ill. by Janet Stevens *(Holiday House)*
JN: SCARY STORIES 3: MORE TALES TO CHILL YOUR BONES by Alvin Schwartz *(HarperCollins)*
1994
PB: THE STINKY CHEESE MAN AND OTHER FAIRLY STUPID TALES by Jon Scieszka, ill. by Lane Smith *(Viking)*
JN: DINOTOPIA by James Gurney *(Turner)*

1995
PB: COYOTE STEALS THE BLANKET: A UTE TALE retold
& illus. by Janet Stevens *(Holiday House)*
JN: JEREMY THATCHER, DRAGON HATCHER by Bruce
Coville *(Harcourt)*

CONNECTICUT
Nutmeg Children's Book Award ❧

First awarded in 1993, this children's choice award is voted by
fourth, fifth, and sixth graders throughout the state of
Connecticut. Its purpose is to promote pleasurable reading of
high quality books. All nominated titles are fictional works
written by authors residing in the United States, and published
within five years of the award date. Nominees must be available
in paperback editions. (Contact: Catherine M. Andronik, Co-
Chair, Nutmeg Children's Book Award, c/o Seymour Middle
School, 20 Pine Street, Seymour, CT 06483.) (Stained glass
window, designed and created in Connecticut)

1993
MY TEACHER IS AN ALIEN by Bruce Coville *(Minstrel)*
1994
SHILOH by Phyllis Reynolds Naylor *(Dell)*
1995
THE BIGGEST KLUTZ IN THE FIFTH GRADE by Bill
Wallace *(Minstrel)*
1996
THE GRAND ESCAPE by Phyllis Reynolds Naylor *(Dell)*

FLORIDA
Sunshine State Young Reader's Award ❧

Co-sponsored by the School Library Media Services Office,
Florida Dept. of Education, and the Florida Association for
Media in Education (FAME), this annual award is for a work of
fiction by an author living in the U.S. and published within five
years before the award year. Students in participating schools are

welcome to suggest titles for consideration in this program through their school library media specialist. Others affiliated with the activity are also a part of the nominating process. The ultimate responsibility for selecting titles for, and handling other aspects of, the competition rests with the Young Reader's Award Selection Committee, appointed by the President of FAME and the Florida Dept. of Education. Two lists of fifteen titles each are compiled by the committee and voted on by Florida readers in grades 3-5 and 6-8. Among its several purposes, the program aims "to encourage students to read for personal satisfaction...to help students become discriminating readers in their personal selection of books...[and] to give recognition to those who write books for children and young people." (Library Media Services, Florida Dept. of Education, 522 Florida Education Center, Tallahassee FL 32399). (Glass-etched bookends featuring award logo)

1984
BUNNICULA: A RABBIT TALE OF MYSTERY by Deborah and James Howe *(Atheneum)*
1985
SUPERFUDGE by Judy Blume *(Dutton)*
1986
BE A PERFECT PERSON IN JUST THREE DAYS! by Stephen Manes *(Clarion)*
1987
THIRTEEN WAYS TO SINK A SUB by Jamie Gilson *(Lothrop)*
1988
3-5: SIXTH GRADE CAN REALLY KILL YOU by Barthe DeClements *(Viking)*
1989
3-5: SIXTH-GRADE SLEEPOVER by Eve Bunting *(HBJ)*
6-8: same title
1990
3-5: TEACHER'S PET by Johanna Hurwitz *(Morrow)*
6-8: TRAPPED IN DEATH CAVE by Bill Wallace *(Holiday House)*
1991
3-5: THERE'S A BOY IN THE GIRLS' BATHROOM by Louis Sachar *(Knopf)*
6-8: same title
1992
3-5: FUDGE by Charlotte Towner Graeber *(Lothrop)*
6-8: SOMETHING UPSTAIRS: A TALE OF GHOSTS by Avi *(Orchard)*
1993
3-5: FUDGE-A-MANIA by Judy Blume *(Dutton)*
6-8: NIGHTMARE by Willo Davis Roberts *(Atheneum)*

1994
3-5: THE SUMMER I SHRANK MY GRANDMOTHER by Elvira Woodruff *(Holiday House)*
6-8: THE TRUE CONFESSIONS OF CHARLOTTE DOYLE by Avi *(Orchard)*
1995
3-5: THE KNIGHTS OF THE KITCHEN TABLE by Jon Scieszka *(Viking)*
6-8: DEVIL'S BRIDGE by Cynthia DeFelice *(Macmillan)*

GEORGIA
Georgia Children's Book Awards ❧

This awards program has two categories. The Georgia Children's Book Award *(GCBA)* is chosen by young readers in grades 4-8; as of 1977, a second category, the Georgia Children's Picture Storybook Award *(GCPSA)*, has been chosen by children in grades K-3. In the first year of the program, approximately 5,000 children from thirty-nine schools participated; currently, approximately 185,000 children from more than 1,250 schools throughout the state participate. The award is sponsored by the university's College of Education (125 Aderhold, University of Georgia, Athens, GA 30602). For each award, a committee assembled by the sponsor selects a nominees list of twenty books by living American authors, and published within a five-year period before the award year. Children vote for books on these two lists. (Plaque)

1969
SKINNY by Robert Burch *(Viking)*
1970
RAMONA THE PEST by Beverly Cleary *(Morrow)*
1971
QUEENIE PEAVY by Robert Burch *(Viking)*
1972
J.T. by Jane Wagner *(Van Nostrand)*
1973
HEY, WHAT'S WRONG WITH THIS ONE? by Maia Wojciechowska *(Harper)*
1974
DOODLE AND THE GO-CART by Robert Burch *(Viking)*

1975
A TASTE OF BLACKBERRIES by Doris Buchanan Smith *(Crowell)*
1976
THE BEST CHRISTMAS PAGEANT EVER by Barbara Robinson *(Harper)*
1977
GCBA: TALES OF A FOURTH GRADE NOTHING by Judy Blume *(Dutton)*
GCPSA: ALEXANDER AND THE TERRIBLE, HORRIBLE, NO GOOD, VERY BAD DAY by Judith Viorst, ill. by Ray Cruz *(Atheneum)*
1978
GCBA: FREAKY FRIDAY by Mary Rodgers *(Harper)*
GCPSA: THE SWEET TOUCH by Lorna Balian *(Abingdon)*
1979
GCBA: THE PINBALLS by Betsy Byars *(Harper)*
GCPSA: BIG BAD BRUCE by Bill Peet *(Houghton)*
1980
GCBA: THE GREAT BRAIN DOES IT AGAIN by John D. Fitzgerald *(Dial)*
GCPSA: MISS NELSON IS MISSING! by Harry Allard, ill. by James Marshall *(Houghton)*
1981
GCBA: THE GREAT GILLY HOPKINS by Katherine Paterson *(Crowell)*
GCPSA: THE TAILYPO by Joanna Galdone, ill. by Paul Galdone *(Clarion)*
1982
GCBA: DON'T HURT LAURIE! by Willo Davis Roberts *(Atheneum)*
GCPSA: PINKERTON, BEHAVE! by Steven Kellogg *(Dial)*
1983
GCBA: SUPERFUDGE by Judy Blume *(Dutton)*
GCPSA: HERBIE'S TROUBLES by Carol Chapman, ill. by Kelly Oechsli *(Dutton)*
1984
GCBA: NOTHING'S FAIR IN FIFTH GRADE by Barthe DeClements *(Viking)*
GCPSA: CLOUDY WITH A CHANCE OF MEATBALLS by Judith Barrett, ill. by Ron Barrett *(Atheneum)*
1985
GCBA: SKINNYBONES by Barbara Park *(Knopf)*
GCPSA: DOCTOR DE SOTO by William Steig *(Farrar)*
1986
GCBA: THE SECRET LIFE OF THE UNDERWEAR CHAMP by Betty Miles *(Knopf)*

GCPSA: THE UNICORN AND THE LAKE by Marianna Mayer, ill. by Michael Hague *(Dial)*

1987

GCBA: BE A PERFECT PERSON IN JUST THREE DAYS! by Stephen Manes *(Clarion)*

GCPSA: MY TEACHER SLEEPS IN SCHOOL by Leatie Weiss, ill. by Ellen Weiss *(Warne)*

1988

GCBA: CHRISTINA'S GHOST by Betty Ren Wright *(Holiday House)*

GCPSA: IF YOU GIVE A MOUSE A COOKIE by Laura Numeroff, ill. by Felicia Bond *(Harper)*

1989

*GCBA:*THE WAR WITH GRANDPA by Robert Kimmel Smith *(Delacorte)*

GCPSA: MAX, THE BAD-TALKING PARROT by Patricia Demuth *(Putnam)*

1990

*GCBA:*THERE'S A BOY IN THE GIRLS' BATHROOM by Louis Sachar *(Knopf)*

GCPSA: NO JUMPING ON THE BED! by Tedd Arnold *(Dial)*

1991

GCBA: HATCHET by Gary Paulsen *(Bradbury)*

GCPSA: WE'RE BACK: A DINOSAUR'S STORY by Hudson Talbott *(Crown)*

1992

GCBA: ALL ABOUT SAM by Lois Lowry *(Houghton)*

GCPSA: TWO BAD ANTS by Chris Van Allsburg *(Houghton)*

1993

GCBA: THE DOLL IN THE GARDEN: A GHOST STORY by Mary Downing Hahn *(Clarion)*

GCPSA: THE TALKING EGGS: A FOLKTALE FROM THE AMERICAN SOUTH retold by Robert D. San Souci, ill. by Jerry Pinkney *(Dial)*

1994

GCBA: JENNIFER MURDLEY'S TOAD by Bruce Coville *(Harcourt)*

GCPSA: THE ROUGH-FACE GIRL by Rafe Martin, ill. by David Shannon *(Putnam)*

1995

GCBA: MAYFIELD CROSSING by Vaunda M. Nelson *(Putnam)*

GCPSA: HURRICANE CITY by Sarah Weeks, ill. by James Warhola *(HarperCollins)*

1996

GCBA: MARTHA SPEAKS by Susan Meddaugh *(Houghton)*

GCPSA: TIME FOR ANDREW: A GHOST STORY by Mary Downing Hahn *(Clarion)*

HAWAII
Nene Award 🌿

The purposes of this awards program, sponsored by the Hawaii Association of School Librarians, the Children's and Youth Section of the Hawaii Library Association, and the McDonalds resturaunts of Hawaii, are to help the children of Hawaii to "become acquainted with the best contemporary writers of fiction for children, become aware of the qualities that make a good book, and to choose the best rather than the mediocre." The program also honors "an author whose book has been enjoyed by the children of Hawaii." Children in grades 4-6 choose the winner, a book by a living author published within a six-year period before the award year. (The Nene, for whom the award is named, is a near-extinct native Hawaiian goose, now being bred in captivity and released into its natural Hawaiian habitat at a young age. Hawaiian children selected the name of the award, voting for Nene, the State bird, over the Hibiscus, the State flower.) (Plaque)

1964
ISLAND OF THE BLUE DOLPHINS by Scott O'Dell *(Houghton)*
1965
MARY POPPINS by Pamela L. Travers *(HBJ)*
1966
OLD YELLER by Fred Gipson *(Harper)*
1967
No Award
1968
RIBSY by Beverly Cleary *(Morrow)*
1969
THE MOUSE AND THE MOTORCYCLE by Beverly Cleary *(Morrow)*
1970
HENRY REED'S BABY-SITTING SERVICE by Keith Robertson *(Viking)*
1971
RAMONA THE PEST by Beverly Cleary *(Morrow)*
1972
RUNAWAY RALPH by Beverly Cleary *(Morrow)*
1973
SOUNDER by William H. Armstrong *(Harper)*
1974
JONATHAN LIVINGSTON SEAGULL by Richard Bach *(Macmillan)*

1975
ARE YOU THERE, GOD? IT'S ME, MARGARET by Judy Blume *(Bradbury)*
1976
HOW TO EAT FRIED WORMS by Thomas Rockwell *(Watts)*
1977
FREAKY FRIDAY by Mary Rodgers *(Harper)*
1978
CHARLIE AND THE GREAT GLASS ELEVATOR by Roald Dahl *(Knopf)*
1979
RAMONA AND HER FATHER by Beverly Cleary *(Morrow)*
1980
THE CAT ATE MY GYMSUIT by Paula Danziger *(Delacorte)*
1981
MY ROBOT BUDDY by Alfred Slote *(Lippincott)*
1982
SUPERFUDGE by Judy Blume *(Dutton)*
1983
BUNNICULA: A RABBIT TALE OF MYSTERY by Deborah and James Howe *(Atheneum)*
1984
NOTHING'S FAIR IN FIFTH GRADE by Barthe DeClements *(Viking)*
1985
JELLY BELLY by Robert Kimmel Smith *(Delacorte)*
1986
BE A PERFECT PERSON IN JUST THREE DAYS! by Stephen Manes *(Clarion)*
1987
KAREN KEPPLEWHITE IS THE WORLD'S BEST KISSER by Eve Bunting *(Clarion)*
1988
YOU SHOULDN'T HAVE TO SAY GOOD-BYE by Patricia Hermes *(HBJ)*
1989
DEAR MR. HENSHAW by Beverly Cleary *(Morrow)*
1990
FUDGE by Charlotte Towner Graeber *(Lothrop)*
1991
THERE'S A BOY IN THE GIRLS' BATHROOM by Louis Sachar *(Knopf)*
1992
THE WHIPPING BOY by Sid Fleischman *(Greenwillow)*
1993
FUDGE-A-MANIA by Judy Blume *(Dutton)*

1994
SHILOH by Phyllis Reynolds Naylor *(Atheneum)*
1995
MY TEACHER IS AN ALIEN by Bruce Coville *(Minstrel)*
1996
MANIAC MAGEE by Jerry Spinelli *(Scholastic)*

ILLINOIS
Rebecca Caudill
Young Readers' Book Award

"I was born in the Appalachian Mountains of eastern Kentucky and spent my first five years of life there. During most of my school years before college, I lived on a farm in the hill country of middle Tennessee. The rest of my life I have lived in cities, but it is Appalachia that is in my blood, and it is Appalachia that furnishes the background for most of my books," wrote Rebecca Caudill (1899-1985) for a brochure about her distributed by her publisher in the late 1960s. After extensive world travels as a young professional woman, Rebecca Caudill married, settled in Urbana, Illinois, and began to write the more than twenty books that made her famous. She wrote in a direct, unsentimental way about subjects with strong emotional appeal. Respected on account of her books, Rebecca Caudill's generous nature inspired deep bonds between herself and children's book colleagues in Illinois, and elsewhere. The children's book award in her name aims "to encourage children and young adults to read for personal satisfaction; to develop a statewide awareness of outstanding literature for children and young people and promote a desire for literacy; and to encourage cooperation among Illinois agencies providing educational and library service to young people." It is co-sponsored by the Illinois School Library Media Association, Illinois Reading Council, Illinois Association of Teachers of English, and Department of Curriculum and Instruction of Northern Illinois University. An Award Committee seeks nominations of eligible titles from a wide range of individuals, including students, statewide. A master list of twenty titles is distributed to participating institutions no later than November 30 each year; votes are tabulated by the administrator in early March, with all participants notified of the results shortly afterwards. Participating institutions pay a very modest fee to receive an Award Packet (available in late spring) that includes the essential information and forms for conducting a successful awards program. Books eligible for consideration may be fiction, nonfiction, or poetry, published within a five-year period before the master list is prepared. (Rebecca Caudill Young Readers' Book Award, P.O. Box 871, Arlington Heights, IL 60006-0871) (Plaque)

1988
THE INDIAN IN THE CUPBOARD by Lynne Reid Banks *(Doubleday)*
1989
THE DOLLHOUSE MURDERS by Betty Ren Wright *(Holiday House)*
1990
WAIT TILL HELEN COMES: A GHOST STORY by Mary Downing Hahn *(Clarion)*
1991
MATILDA by Roald Dahl *(Viking)*
1992
NUMBER THE STARS by Lois Lowry *(Houghton)*
1993
MANIAC MAGEE by Jerry Spinelli *(Little, Brown)*
1994
SHILOH by Phyllis Reynolds Naylor *(Atheneum)*
1995
FLIGHT #116 IS DOWN by Caroline B. Cooney *(Scholastic)*
1996
THE GIVER by Lois Lowry *(Houghton)*

INDIANA
Young Hoosier Book Awards

Sponsored by the Association for Indiana Media Educators (YHBA Committee, c/o AIME Administrative Office, 1908 E. 64th St., Indianapolis, IN 46220), this award program was "launched to encourage boys and girls to read and enjoy good books." Indiana schoolchildren in grades 4-8 vote for their favorite book from a list of twenty works of fiction by authors who reside in the U.S. and whose books were published in a five year period before the award year. A committee appointed by the sponsor selects the titles that appear on the nominee list. As of the 1986 award year, two awards have been chosen, one selected by readers in grades 4-6, and a second by grades 6-8. As of 1992, a Young Hoosier Picture Book Award is selected by children in grades K-3. (Plaque)

1975
THE TRUMPET OF THE SWAN by E.B. White *(Harper)*
1976
ARE YOU THERE, GOD? IT'S ME, MARGARET by Judy Blume *(Bradbury)*
1977
HOW TO EAT FRIED WORMS by Thomas Rockwell *(Watts)*
1978
THE BEST CHRISTMAS PAGEANT EVER by Barbara Robinson *(Harper)*
1979
THE GHOST ON SATURDAY NIGHT by Sid Fleischman *(Atlantic-Little, Brown)*
1980
DON'T HURT LAURIE! by Willo Davis Roberts *(Atheneum)*
1981
THE GOOF THAT WON THE PENNANT by Jonah Kalb *(Houghton)*
1982
HELP! I'M A PRISONER IN THE LIBRARY by Eth Clifford *(Houghton)*
1983
SUPERFUDGE by Judy Blume *(Dutton)*
1984
JELLY BELLY by Robert Kimmel Smith *(Delacorte)*
1985
OPERATION: DUMP THE CHUMP by Barbara Park *(Knopf)*
1986
4-6: WHEN THE BOYS RAN THE HOUSE by Joan Carris *(Lippincott)*
6-8: STRANGER WITH MY FACE by Lois Duncan *(Little, Brown)*
1987
4-6: THE WAR WITH GRANDPA by Robert Kimmel Smith *(Delacorte)*
6-8: THE THIRD EYE by Lois Duncan *(Little, Brown)*
1988
4-6: BABY-SITTING IS A DANGEROUS JOB by Willo Davis Roberts *(Atheneum)*
6-8: A DEADLY GAME OF MAGIC by Joan Lowery Nixon *(HBJ)*
1989
4-6: CHRISTINA'S GHOST by Betty Ren Wright *(Holiday House)*
6-8: WAIT TILL HELEN COMES: A GHOST STORY by Mary Downing Hahn *(Clarion)*

1990
4-6: FUDGE by Charlotte Towner Graeber *(Lothrop)*
6-8: THE DARK AND DEADLY POOL by Joan Lowery Nixon *(Delacorte)*
1991
4-6: TEN KIDS, NO PETS by Ann M. Martin *(Holiday House)*
6-8: HATCHET by Gary Paulsen *(Bradbury)*
1992
K-3: HECKEDY PEG by Don and Audrey Wood *(Harcourt)*
4-6: NIGHTMARE MOUNTAIN by Peg Kehret *(Dutton)*
6-8: DON'T LOOK BEHIND YOU by Lois Duncan *(Delacorte)*
1993
K-3: TUESDAY by David Wiesner *(Clarion)*
4-6: THE DEAD MAN IN INDIAN CREEK by Mary Downing Hahn *(Clarion)*
6-8: THE FACE ON THE MILK CARTON by Caroline B. Cooney *(Bantam)*
1994
K-3: THE DOG WHO HAD KITTENS by Polly Robertus, ill. by Janet Stevens *(Holiday House)*
4-6: SHILOH by Phyllis Reynolds Naylor *(Atheneum)*
6-8: STRIDER by Beverly Clearly *(Morrow)*
1995
K-3: THE ENCHANTED WOOD by Ruth Sanderson *(Little, Brown)*
4-6: HORROR AT THE HAUNTED HOUSE by Peg Kehret *(Clarion)*
6-8: WHISPERS FROM THE DEAD by Joan Lowery Nixon *(Dell)*

IOWA
Iowa Children's Choice Award and Iowa Teen Award ❧

The Iowa Children's Choice Award *(ICCA)* and the Iowa Teen Award *(ITA)* programs are sponsored by the Iowa Educational Media Association (Awards Committee, c/o Paula Behrendt, Executive Secretary, 2306 Sixth St., Harlan, IA 51537). Among the purposes of both awards, one is "to provide an avenue for positive dialogue between teacher, parent and children (students) about books and authors." Young readers are invited to suggest titles, fiction or nonfiction, that are appropriate for grades 3-6 *(ICCA)* and grades 6-9 *(ITA)*. In each instance, the selection of 15-25 titles as nominees for the awards is ultimately the responsibility of the members of the respective awards committees. In the case of the *ICCA*, authors must be Americans and their nominated books published within five years of the award year; for the *ITA*, the nationality of the author is not a consideration, and the nominated books must have been published within six years of the award year. (*ICCA:* engraved bronze school bell; *ITA:* engraved brass apple)

1980
ICCA: HOW TO EAT FRIED WORMS by Thomas Rockwell (*Watts*)
1981
ICCA: THE GREAT GILLY HOPKINS by Katherine Paterson (*Crowell*)
1982
ICCA: BUNNICULA: A RABBIT TALE OF MYSTERY by Deborah and James Howe (*Atheneum*)
1983
ICCA: SUPERFUDGE by Judy Blume (*Dutton*)
1984
ICCA: NOTHING'S FAIR IN FIFTH GRADE by Barthe DeClements (*Viking*)
1985
ICCA: RALPH S. MOUSE by Beverly Cleary (*Morrow*)
ITA: TIGER EYES by Judy Blume (*Bradbury*)
1986
ICCA: WHEN THE BOYS RAN THE HOUSE by Joan Carris (*Lippincott*)
ITA: WHEN WE FIRST MET by Norma Fox Mazer (*Scholastic*)
1987
ICCA: RAMONA FOREVER by Beverly Cleary (*Morrow*)
ITA: YOU SHOULDN'T HAVE TO SAY GOOD-BYE by Patricia Hermes (*HBJ*)
1988
ICCA: THE DOLLHOUSE MURDERS by Betty Ren Wright (*Holiday House*)
ITA: ABBY, MY LOVE by Hadley Irwin (*McElderry*)
1989
ICCA: NIGHT OF THE TWISTERS by Ivy Ruckman (*Crowell*)
ITA: THE OTHER SIDE OF DARK by Joan Lowery Nixon (*Delacorte*)
1990
ICCA: WAIT TILL HELEN COMES: A GHOST STORY by Mary Downing Hahn (*Clarion*)
ITA: HATCHET by Gary Paulsen (*Bradbury*)
1991
ICCA: THERE'S A BOY IN THE GIRLS' BATHROOM by Louis Sachar (*Knopf*)

ITA: SILVER by Norma Fox Mazer *(Morrow)*

1992
ICCA: FUDGE by Charlotte Towner Graeber *(Pocket)*
ITA: DON'T LOOK BEHIND YOU by Lois Duncan *(Delacorte)*

1993
ICCA: FUDGE-A-MANIA by Judy Blume *(Dell)*
ITA: THE FACE ON THE MILK CARTON by Caroline B. Cooney *(Bantam)*

1994
ICCA: NIGHTMARE MOUNTAIN by Peg Kehret *(Dutton)*
ITTA: RYAN WHITE: MY OWN STORY by Ryan White *(Dial)*

1995
ICCA: ATTABOY, SAM! by Lois Lowry *(Houghton)*
ITA: JURASSIC PARK by Michael Crichton *(Ballantine)*

KANSAS
William Allen White Children's Book Award

Named in honor of the famous Kansas newspaper editor and internationally renowned journalist William Allen White (1868-1944), this second-in-terms-of-longevity of the U.S. reader's choice awards programs was founded in 1952 by Ruth Garver Gagliardo, an eminent Kansas children's literature and reading promotion specialist. The purpose of the annual award has been to encourage "the boys and girls of Kansas to read and enjoy good books." The White Award Program is directed by Emporia State University (William Allen White Library, 1200 Commercial St., Emporia, KS 66801) and is supported in part by the Trusler Foundation. Each year a master list of books, including fiction, nonfiction and poetry titles, is compiled by the award's selection committee, representing educational and professional organizations as well as institutions in Kansas. Schoolchildren—currently more than 51,000—in grades 4-8 vote for the winner. (Bronze medal)

1953
AMOS FORTUNE, FREE MAN by Elizabeth Yates *(Dutton)*

1954
LITTLE VIC by Doris Gates *(Viking)*

1955
CHEROKEE BILL: OKLAHOMA PACER by Jean Bailey *(Abingdon)*

1956
BRIGHTY OF THE GRAND CANYON by Marguerite Henry
(Rand McNally)
1957
DANIEL 'COON by Phoebe Erickson *(Knopf)*
1958
WHITE FALCON by Elliott Arnold *(Knopf)*
1959
OLD YELLER by Fred Gipson *(Harper)*
1960
FLAMING ARROWS by William O. Steele *(HBJ)*
1961
HENRY REED, INC. by Keith Robertson *(Viking)*
1962
THE HELEN KELLER STORY by Catherine O. Peare *(Crowell)*
1963
ISLAND OF THE BLUE DOLPHINS by Scott O'Dell *(Houghton)*
1964
THE INCREDIBLE JOURNEY by Sheila Burnford *(Atlantic-Little, Brown)*
1965
BRISTLE FACE by Zachary Ball *(Holiday House)*
1966
RASCAL by Sterling North *(Dutton)*
1967
THE GRIZZLY by Annabel and Edgar Johnson *(Harper)*
1968
THE MOUSE AND THE MOTORCYCLE by Beverly Cleary
(Morrow)
1969
HENRY REED'S BABY-SITTING SERVICE by Keith Robertson
(Viking)
1970
FROM THE MIXED-UP FILES OF MRS. BASIL E.
FRANKWEILER by E. L. Konigsburg *(Atheneum)*
1971
KAVIK THE WOLF DOG by Walt Morey *(Dutton)*
1972
SASHA, MY FRIEND by Barbara Corcoran *(Atheneum)*
1973
THE TRUMPET OF THE SWAN by E. B. White *(Harper)*
1974
Posthumous citation: MRS. FRISBY AND THE RATS OF
NIMH by Robert C. O'Brien *(Atheneum)*
THE HEADLESS CUPID by Zilpha Keatley Snyder *(Atheneum)*
1975
DOMINIC by William Steig *(Ferrar)*

1976
SOCKS by Beverly Cleary *(Morrow)*

1977
HARRY CAT'S PET PUPPY by George Selden *(Farrar)*

1978
THE GREAT CHRISTMAS KIDNAPPING CAPER by Jean Van Leeuwen *(Dial)*

1979
THE SUMMER OF THE MONKEYS by Wilson Rawls *(Doubleday)*

1980
THE PINBALLS by Betsy Byars *(Harper)*

1981
THE GREAT GILLY HOPKINS by Katherine Paterson *(Crowell)*

1982
THE MAGIC OF THE GLITS by C.S. Adler *(Macmillan)*

1983
PEPPERMINTS IN THE PARLOR by Barbara Brooks Wallace *(Atheneum)*

1984
A LIGHT IN THE ATTIC by Shel Silverstein *(Harper)*

1985
THE LAND I LOST: ADVENTURES OF A BOY IN VIETNAM by Huynh Quang Nhuong *(Harper)*

1986
DAPHNE'S BOOK by Mary Downing Hahn *(Clarion)*

1987
THE WAR WITH GRANDPA by Robert Kimmel Smith *(Delacorte)*

1988
CRACKER JACKSON by Betty Byars *(Viking)*

1989
ON MY HONOR by Marion Dane Bauer *(Clarion)*

1990
HATCHET by Gary Paulsen *(Bradbury)*

1991
BEAUTY by Bill Wallace *(Holiday House)*

1992
THE DOLL IN THE GARDEN: A GHOST STORY by Mary Downing Hahn *(Clarion)*

1993
MANIAC MAGEE by Jerry Spinelli *(Little, Brown)*

1994
SHILOH by Phyllis Reynolds Naylor *(Atheneum)*

1995
THE MAN WHO LOVED CLOWNS by June Rae Wood *(Putnam)*

1996
THE GIVER by Lois Lowry *(Houghton)*

KENTUCKY
Kentucky Bluegrass Awards 🌿

This annual voluntary reading program is designed "to encourage Kentucky children to read and enjoy a variety of books and select their favorites" from two lists of recently published books. As of 1987-88, the two divisions of the awards program consisted of K-3, including picture books, beginning readers, etc., and 4-8, including "junior novels, lengthy picture books, etc." Between 15-25 titles are selected by librarians and teachers from across the state for the master reading lists for each division. The lists are distributed to participating schools and libraries in the spring, though it is not a requirement that participants have all titles on the list in order to be a part of the program. Ballots are tabulated as of early March each year, with the winning titles announced in April at the sponsoring institution (Learning Resource Center, BEP-268, Northern Kentucky University, Highland Heights, KY 41099). "Kentucky bluegrass" is a Mississippi valley grass, used for pasturage and hay. The state—known for its horse farms and horse racing—is often referred to as "the Bluegrass State." (Plaques)

1983
JUMANJI by Chris Van Allsburg *(Houghton)*
1984
MOVE OVER, TWERP by Martha Alexander *(Dial)*
1985
ANGELINA BALLERINA by Katharine Holabird, ill. by Helen Craig *(Clarkson Potter)*
1986
BADGER'S PARTING GIFTS by Susan Varley *(Lothrop)*
1987
THE POLAR EXPRESS by Chris Van Allsburg *(Houghton)*
1988
K-3: HEY, AL by Arthur Yorinks, ill. by Richard Egielski *(Farrar)*
4-8: WHO NEEDS A BRATTY BROTHER? by Linda Gondosch *(Lodestar)*
1989
K-3: THE WOLF'S CHICKEN STEW by Keiko Kasza *(Putnam)*
4-8: CLASS CLOWN by Johanna Hurwitz *(Morrow)*
1990
K-3: THE LADY WITH THE ALLIGATOR PURSE adapted and ill. by Nadine Bernard Westcott *(Joy Street/Little, Brown)*
4-8: THE STRANGER by Chris Van Allsburg *(Houghton)*

1991
K-3: CHICKA CHICKA BOOM BOOM by Bill Martin, Jr. and John Archambault, ill. by Lois Ehlert *(Simon & Schuster)*
4-8: THE BUTTERFLY JAR by Jeffrey Moss, ill. by Chris Demarest *(Bantam)*
1992
K-3: BASKET by George Ella Lyon, ill. by Mary Szilagyi *(Orchard)*
4-8: SOMETHING BIG HAS BEEN HERE by Jack Prelutsky, ill. by James Stevenson *(Greenwillow)*
1993
K-3: TUESDAY by David Wiesner *(Clarion)*
4-8: BROTHER EAGLE, SISTER SKY: A MESSAGE FROM CHIEF SEATTLE by Susan Jeffers *(Dial)*
1994
K-3: PIGS APLENTY, PIGS GALORE! by David McPhail *(Dutton)*
4-8: BOB AND JACK: A BOY AND HIS YAK by Jeffrey Moss, ill. by Chris Demarest *(Bantam)*
1995
K-3: THE COW WHO WOULDN'T COME DOWN by Paul Brett Johnson *(Orchard)*
4-8: THE HERO OF BREMEN retold by Margaret Hodges, ill. by Charles Mikolaycak *(Holiday House)*
1996
K-3: HARVEY POTTER'S BALLOON FARM by Jerdine Nolen, ill. by Mark Buehner *(Lothrop)*
4-6: THE CHRISTMAS OF THE REDDLE MOON by J. Patrick Lewis, ill. by Gary Kelley *(Dial)*

MAINE
Maine Student Book Award

Established in 1989 by Augusta school librarian Ernest Bradbury, this annual award is a joint project of the Maine Library Association, the Maine Educational Media Association, and the Maine Reading Association. It's purpose is to encourage students to become enthusiastic and discriminating readers. A committee composed of librarians and reading teachers compiles a list of approximately 30 outstanding books published for young readers in a calendar year. The list is distributed to schools and libraries across the state from which students in grades 4 to 8 read titles and vote for their favorite. In May of each year, the winner is announced and the reading list for the next school year is distributed. Since the committee membership changes regularly, a permanent source of information about the award is the School Library Consultant (Dorothy Gregory, Maine State Library, Augusta, ME 04333). (Certificate)

1991
NUMBER THE STARS by Lois Lowry *(Houghton)*
1992
FUDGE-A-MANIA by Judy Blume *(Dutton)*
1993
SHILOH by Phyllis Reynolds Naylor *(Atheneum)*
1994
THE STINKY CHEESE MAN AND OTHER FAIRLY STUPID
TALES by Jon Scieszka, ill. by Lane Smith *(Viking)*
1995
THE GIVER by Lois Lowry *(Houghton)*
1996
PINK AND SAY by Patricia Polacco *(Philomel)*

MARYLAND
Maryland Children's Book Award ❧

This award is sponsored by the State of Maryland International
Reading Association Council. Titles are nominated by teachers
and librarians for a list of about fifteen titles, selected by an
award committee annually, and voted on by young readers. The
program now comprises three categories: Primary *(P)*,
Intermediate *(I)*, and Middle School *(M)*. The State Council does
not have a permanent office to contact for information; the
award is administered by a chairperson and committee appointed
for a three year term. (Engraved plaque)

1988
CRACKER JACKSON by Betsy Byars *(Viking)*
1989
SWITCHAROUND by Lois Lowry *(Houghton)*
1990
THE HAUNTING OF CABIN 13 by Kristi D. Holl *(Atheneum)*
1991
THE DOLL IN THE GARDEN: A GHOST STORY by Mary
Downing Hahn *(Clarion)*
1992
MY TEACHER IS AN ALIEN by Bruce Coville *(Minstrel)*
1993
P: TWO BAD ANTS by Chris Van Allsburg *(Houghton)*
I: GRASSHOPPER SUMMER by Ann Turner *(Macmillan)*

1994
P: HIGH WIRE HENRY by Mary Calhoun *(Morrow)*
I: DANGER IN QUICKSAND SWAMP by Bill Wallace *(Holiday House)*
M: SNIPER by Theodore Taylor *(Harcourt)*
1995
P: HURRICANE CITY by Sarah Weeks *(HarperCollins)*
I: THE BOYS START THE WAR by Phyllis Reynolds Naylor *(Doubleday)*
M: FLIGHT #116 IS DOWN by Caroline B. Cooney *(Scholastic)*
1996
P: DOGS DON'T WEAR SNEAKERS by Laura Numeroff *(Simon & Schuster)*
I: TIME FOR ANDREW: A GHOST STORY by Mary Downing Hahn *(Clarion)*
M: RANDALL'S WALL by Carol Fenner *(McElderry)*

MASSACHUSETTS
Massachusetts Children's Book Award ❧

The impetus for establishing this award program was the observation by the award founder, Helen Constant, that, once having learned how to read, many children lose interest in books when they reach intermediate grades. Designed for schoolchildren in grades 4-6, the program also included grades 7-9 from 1978 through 1983. A committee of librarians and teachers nominates titles for the program, and considers literary quality, variety of genre, representation of diverse cultural groups, and reader appeal in selecting nominees. Originally, only books published in years immediately before the award year were considered. Between 1983 and 1995 titles published at earlier dates became eligible for the award. However, beginning with a ten-year publishing window in 1996, and decreasing one year each year until a five-year publishing window is reached, eligible books will once again be more current. To keep the cost of the books affordable, every effort will be made to include titles available in paperback editions. Sponsored by Salem State College (c/o Diane Bushner, Education Dept., Salem, MA 01970). (Certificate)

1976
HOW TO EAT FRIED WORMS by Thomas Rockwell *(Watts)*
1977
TALES OF A FOURTH GRADE NOTHING by Judy Blume *(Dutton)*
1978
4-6: MRS. FRISBY AND THE RATS OF NIMH by Robert C. O'Brien *(Atheneum)*
7-9: THAT WAS THEN, THIS IS NOW by S. E. Hinton *(Viking)*
1979
4-6: THE CRICKET IN TIMES SQUARE by George Selden *(Farrar)*
7-9: THE CAT ATE MY GYMSUIT by Paula Danziger *(Delacorte)*
1980
4-6: CHOCOLATE FEVER by Robert Kimmel Smith *(Dell)*
7-9: SUMMER OF MY GERMAN SOLDIER by Bette Greene *(Dial)*
1981
4-6: THE GREAT GILLY HOPKINS by Katherine Paterson *(Crowell)*
7-9: A SUMMER TO DIE by Lois Lowry *(Houghton)*
1982
4-6: JAMES AND THE GIANT PEACH by Roald Dahl *(Knopf)*
7-9: KILLING MR. GRIFFIN by Lois Duncan *(Little, Brown)*
1983
4-6: TALES OF A FOURTH GRADE NOTHING by Judy Blume *(Dutton)*
7-9: STRANGER WITH MY FACE by Lois Duncan *(Little, Brown)*
1984
CHARLOTTE'S WEB by E. B. White *(Harper)*
1985
NOTHING'S FAIR IN FIFTH GRADE by Barthe DeClements *(Viking)*
1986
DEAR MR. HENSHAW by Beverly Cleary *(Morrow)*
1987
WHERE THE RED FERN GROWS by Wilson Rawls *(Doubleday)*
1988
THE INDIAN IN THE CUPBOARD by Lynn Reid Banks *(Doubleday)*
1989
THE CHOCOLATE TOUCH by Patrick Catling *(Morrow)*

1990
No Award (administrator on sabbatical)

1991
THERE'S A BOY IN THE GIRLS' BATHROOM by Louis Sachar *(Knopf)*

1992
MATILDA by Roald Dahl *(Viking Kestrel)*

1993
MANIAC MAGEE by Jerry Spinelli *(Little, Brown)*

1994
SHILOH by Phyllis Reynolds Naylor *(Atheneum)*

1995
HATCHETT by Gary Paulsen *(Bradbury)*

1996
THE TRUE CONFESSIONS OF CHARLOTTE DOYLE by Avi *(Orchard)*

MINNESOTA
Maud Hart Lovelace Book Award

Named for the author of the *Betsy-Tacy* stories about growing up at the turn of the century in "Deep Valley" (Mankato), this award program is sponsored by Minnesota Youth Reading Awards, Inc. (MYRA, 4874 Adrian Ln., Hermantown, MN 55811), whose supporting members are the Minnesota Educational Media Organization, the Minnesota Library Association, and the Minnesota Reading Association, with additional financial support from various commercial book contributors. Children in grades 3-8 vote for their favorite book from a list of fifteen nominated titles, at least three of which must have been read before a participant is eligible to vote. Eligible books are fiction (not part of a formulated series), available in paperback, and appropriate for children in grades 3-8. Copyright must be within the last ten years and the author must be living in the U.S. MYRA mails an award information packet to all public libraries, school media centers, and to all participants from previous years. Anyone interested in the program may contact MYRA for a packet. The winner is announced each year on April 25, the anniversary of the birthday of Maud Hart Lovelace. (Plaque)

1980
SUMMER OF THE MONKEYS by Wilson Rawls *(Doubleday)*
1981
THE PINBALLS by Betsy Byars *(Harper)*
1982
THE BEST CHRISTMAS PAGEANT EVER by Barbara
Robinson *(Harper)*
1983
IT CAN'T HURT FOREVER by Marilyn Singer *(Harper)*
1984
NOTHING'S FAIR IN FIFTH GRADE by Barthe DeClements
(Viking)
1985
SKINNYBONES by Barbara Park *(Knopf)*
1986
ZUCCHINI by Barbara Dana *(Harper)*
1987
STONE FOX by John Reynolds Gardiner *(Crowell)*
1988
NIGHT OF THE TWISTERS by Ivy Ruckman *(Crowell)*
1989
EATING ICE CREAM WITH A WEREWOLF by Phyllis Green
(Harper)
1990
WAIT TILL HELEN COMES: A GHOST STORY by Mary
Downing Hahn *(Clarion)*
1991
HATCHET by Gary Paulsen *(Bradbury)*
1992
THIS ISLAND ISN'T BIG ENOUGH FOR THE FOUR OF US
by Gery Greer and Bob Ruddick *(HarperCollins)*
1993
THE DEAD MAN IN INDIAN CREEK by Mary Downing
Hahn *(Avon)*
1994
38 WEEKS TILL SUMMER VACATION by Mona Kerby
(Penguin)
1995
NIGHTMARE MOUNTAIN by Peg Kehret *(Pocket)*
1996
CAGES by Peg Kehret *(Minstrel)*

MISSOURI
Mark Twain Award 🐚

"The Mark Twain Award was initiated to provide children of Missouri with their very own source to enrich their lives through reading and to find the joys that lie in being able to read. Mark Twain, a native of Hannibal, Missouri, and the best-loved author the world over is the obvious Missouri author to have such an award named for him...." Sponsored by the Missouri Association of School Librarians (8049 Highway E., Bonne Terre, MO 63628), the awards program now has twelve statewide participating organizations. Twenty titles are selected for a master list by a committee representing organizations interested in children and reading. The administrators are able to supply at a modest cost many useful items to help participating institutions organize an effective program. They include a color video to introduce books on the master list, an annotated booklet of titles on the master lists from the beginning of the program through the current year, seals for winning titles and spine labels for nominees, recognition certificates for participating readers, and also posters and bookmarks for both current nominees and past winners. The voters are in grades 4-8. (Bronze bust of Mark Twain)

1972
SOUNDER by William H. Armstrong *(Harper)*
1973
MRS. FRISBY AND THE RATS OF NIMH by Robert C. O'Brien *(Atheneum)*
1974
IT'S A MILE FROM HERE TO GLORY by Robert C. Lee *(Little, Brown)*
1975
HOW TO EAT FRIED WORMS by Thomas Rockwell *(Watts)*
1976
THE HOME RUN TRICK by Scott Corbett *(Atlantic-Little, Brown)*
1977
THE GHOST ON SATURDAY NIGHT by Sid Fleischman *(Atlantic-Little, Brown)*
1978
RAMONA THE BRAVE by Beverly Cleary *(Morrow)*
1979
THE CHAMPION OF MERRIMACK COUNTY by Roger W. Drury *(Little, Brown)*

1980
THE PINBALLS by Betsy Byars *(Harper)*
1981
SOUP FOR PRESIDENT by Robert Newton Peck *(Knopf)*
1982
THE BOY WHO SAW BIGFOOT by Marian T. Place *(Dodd)*
1983
THE GIRL WITH THE SILVER EYES by Willo Davis Roberts
(Atheneum)
1984
THE SECRET LIFE OF THE UNDERWEAR CHAMP by Betty
Miles *(Knopf)*
1985
A BUNDLE OF STICKS by Pat Rhoads Mauser *(Atheneum)*
1986
THE DOLLHOUSE MURDERS by Betty Ren Wright *(Holiday
House)*
1987
THE WAR WITH GRANDPA by Robert Kimmel Smith *(Delacorte)*
1988
BABY-SITTING IS A DANGEROUS JOB by Willo Davis
Roberts *(Atheneum)*
1989
SIXTH-GRADE SLEEPOVER by Eve Bunting *(HBJ)*
1990
THERE'S A BOY IN THE GIRLS' BATHROOM by Louis
Sachar *(Knopf)*
1991
ALL ABOUT SAM by Lois Lowry *(Houghton)*
1992
THE DOLL IN THE GARDEN: A GHOST STORY by Mary
Downing Hahn *(Clarion)*
1993
MANIAC MAGEE by Jerry Spinelli *(Little, Brown)*
1994
SHILOH by Phyllis Reynolds Naylor *(Atheneum)*
1995
THE MAN WHO LOVED CLOWNS by June Rae Wood
(Putnam)

MONTANA
Treasure State Award 🐛

During the first year of this award program—1991—children in Montana were invited to select the award name; the winning suggestion came from a third-grader in Helena. The winner is selected from a list of five titles, with children in grades K-3 eligible to vote. The award is administered by the Missoula Public Library (Attn: Bette Ammon, 301 E. Main St., Missoula, MT 59802) and the Missoula County Schools (Attn: Carole Monlux, 215 S. 6th St. W., Missoula, MT 59801) with sponsorship by the Montana Library Association. This program is designed to complement the Young Reader's Choice Awards for older readers—the first children's choice award program—selected by readers in four Western States and two Canadian provinces. (Announcement)

1991
THE DRAGON NANNY by C. L. Martin, ill. by Robert Rayevsky *(Macmillan)*
1992
COCK-A-DOODLE DUDLEY by Bill Peet *(Houghton)*
1993
HIGH-WIRE HENRY by Mary Calhoun *(Morrow)*
1994
THE TROUBLE WITH TROLLS by Jan Brett *(Putnam)*
1995
COYOTE STEALS THE BLANKET: A UTE TALE retold by Janet Stevens *(Holiday House)*

NEBRASKA
Golden Sower Awards 🐛

Initiated by the Center for Curriculum and Instruction, Teachers College, University of Nebraska, this awards program is currently sponsored by the Nebraska Library Association (Reinert/Alumni Memorial Library, Creighton University, California at 24th St., Omaha, NE 68178). The administration of the award is handled by its chairperson, and that responsibility changes annually. Designed to encourage Nebraska children to read widely in several areas of picture books (grades K-3) and fiction (grades 4-6 and 6-9), two lists of fifteen titles each are compiled by a committee that considers nominations from participating institutions. The young adult category (grades 6-9) was introduced in 1993. Participants are limited to three nominations a year in each category, and are encouraged to "involve children in the nomination process as much as possible." Nominations must be of titles by people living in the U. S. at the time of nomination, and that were published in a three-year period, two years prior to the award year. The titles "should be worthy of any award from a literary and/or artistic standpoint." The administrators send a useful and informative newsletter, *The Nugget*, to participating institutions four times a year, and also offer excellent and inexpensive materials, e.g., a manual, bookmarks, stickers, to support the organization of the activity locally. The program takes its name from the monumental figure on the top of the Nebraska Capitol building in Lincoln. (Plaque)

1981
4-6: BUNNICULA: A RABBIT TALE OF MYSTERY by Deborah and James Howe *(Atheneum)*
1982
4-6: YOURS TILL NIAGARA FALLS, ABBY by Jane O'Connor *(Hastings)*
1983
K-3: CLOUDY WITH A CHANCE OF MEATBALLS by Judith Barrett, ill. by Ron Barrett *(Atheneum)*
4-6: SUPERFUDGE by Judy Blume *(Dutton)*
1984
K-3: MISS NELSON IS BACK by Harry Allard, ill. by James Marshall *(Houghton)*
4-6: NOTHING'S FAIR IN FIFTH GRADE by Barthe DeClements *(Viking)*
1985
K-3: ROUND TRIP by Ann Jonas *(Greenwillow)*
4-6: A DOG CALLED KITTY by Bill Wallace *(Holiday House)*
1986
K-3: PEABODY by Rosemary Wells *(Dial)*
4-6: NIGHT OF THE TWISTERS by Ivy Ruckman *(Crowell)*
1987
K-3: MISS NELSON HAS A FIELD DAY by Harry Allard, ill. by James Marshall *(Houghton)*
4-6: THE WAR WITH GRANDPA by Robert Kimmel Smith *(Delacorte)*
1988
K-3: DON'T TOUCH MY ROOM by Patricia Lakin, ill. by Patience Brewster *(Little, Brown)*
4-6: SIXTH GRADE CAN REALLY KILL YOU by Barthe DeClements *(Viking)*

1989
K-3: PIGGINS by Jane Yolen, ill. by Jane Dyer *(HBJ)*
4-6: FERRET IN THE BEDROOM, LIZARDS IN THE FRIDGE by Bill Wallace *(Holiday House)*

1990
K-3: THE MAGIC SCHOOL BUS AT THE WATERWORKS by Joanna Cole, ill. by Bruce Degen *(Scholastic)*
4-6: WAIT TILL HELEN COMES: A GHOST STORY by Mary Downing Hahn *(Clarion)*

1991
K-3: TACKY THE PENGUIN by Helen Lester, ill. by Lynn Munsinger *(Houghton)*
4-6: THERE'S A BOY IN THE GIRLS' BATHROOM by Louis Sachar *(Knopf)*

1992
K-3: THE TALKING EGGS: A FOLKTALE FROM THE AMERICAN SOUTH retold by Robert D. San Souci, ill. by Jerry Pinkney *(Dial)*
4-6: IS ANYBODY THERE? by Eve Bunting *(HarperCollins)*

1993
K-3: RIPTIDE by Frances Ward Weller, ill. by Robert J. Blake *(Putnam)*
4-6: NIGHTMARE MOUNTAIN by Peg Kehret *(Dutton)*
6-9: WHISPERS FROM THE DEAD by Joan Lowery Nixon *(Delacorte)*

1994
K-3: THE ROUGH-FACE GIRL by Rafe Martin, ill. by David Shannon *(Putnam)*
4-6: STEPPING ON THE CRACKS by Mary Downing Hahn *(Clarion)*
6-9: FLIGHT #116 IS DOWN by Caroline B. Cooney *(Scholastic)*

1995
K-3: MARTHA SPEAKS by Susan Meddaugh *(Houghton)*
4-6: RESCUE JOSH McGUIRE by Ben Mikaelsen *(Hyperion)*
6-9: THE GIVER by Lois Lowry *(Houghton)*

1996
K-3: SOAP! SOAP! DON'T FORGET THE SOAP! by Tom Birdseye *(Holiday House)*
4-6: THE GRAND ESCAPE by Phyllis Reynolds Naylor *(Atheneum)*
6-9: HEART OF A CHAMPION by Carl Deuker *(Little, Brown)*

NEVADA
Nevada Young Readers Awards 🙰

This awards program now includes four categories, Primary *(K-2)*, Young Reader *(3-5)*, Intermediate *(6-8)* and Young Adult *(9-12)*. Both school and public libraries throughout the state are encouraged to participate in the program, organized from the office of the Library Media/Textbook Consultant, State of Nevada Department of Education (700 E. 5th St., Capitol Complex, Carson City, NV 89710). Participants receive an array of support materials, including a Time Line for the program, a sheet detailing Selection Procedures, a Ballot, a listing of Promotional Ideas, a reproducible prototype for a Certificate of Merit for children reading all the books nominated for the awards in their categories, a Nomination Form for titles for the next year's program, and a program Evaluation Form. (Plaques)

1988
K-3: THE POLAR EXPRESS by Chris Van Allsburg *(Houghton)*
4-6: SIXTH GRADE CAN REALLY KILL YOU by Barthe DeClements *(Viking)*
1989
K-3: IF YOU GIVE A MOUSE A COOKIE by Laura Numeroff, ill. by Felicia Bond *(Harper)*
4-6: BABY-SITTING IS A DANGEROUS JOB by Willo Davis Roberts *(Macmillan)*
Y/A: LOCKED IN TIME by Lois Duncan *(Little, Brown)*
1990
K-3: HECKEDY PEG by Audrey Wood, ill. by Don Wood *(HBJ)*
4-6: THERE'S A BOY IN THE GIRLS' BATHROOM by Louis Sachar *(Knopf)*
Y/A: EXPERIMENT IN TERROR by Bernal C. Payne, Jr. *(Houghton)*
1991
K-3: WE'RE BACK: A DINOSAUR'S STORY by Hudson Talbott *(Crown)*
4-6: MY TEACHER IS AN ALIEN by Bruce Coville *(Simon & Schuster)*
Y/A: PRINCESS ASHLEY by Richard Peck *(Delacorte)*
1992
K-3: THE CALL OF THE WOLVES by Jim Murphy *(Scholastic)*
4-6: MATILDA by Roald Dahl *(Viking)*
Y/A: WHISPERS FROM THE DEAD by Joan Lowery Nixon *(Delacorte)*
1993
K-2: THE DOG WHO HAD KITTENS by Polly Robertus *(Holiday House)*

3-5: FUDGE-A-MANIA by Judy Blume *(Dutton)*
6-8: MANIAC MAGEE by Jerry Spinelli *(Little, Brown)*
9-12: JURASSIC PARK by Michael Crichton *(Knopf)*
1994
K-2: LOOK OUT, PATRICK! by Paul Geraghty *(Macmillan)*
3-5: JEREMY THATCHER, DRAGON HATCHER by Bruce Coville *(Harcourt)*
6-8: SHILOH by Phyllis Reynolds Naylor *(Atheneum)*
9-12: PLAGUE YEAR by Stephanie S. Tolan *(Morrow)*
1995
K-2: MOE THE DOG IN TROPICAL PARADISE by Diane Stanley *(Putnam)*
3-5: THE BOYS START THE WAR by Phyllis Reynolds Naylor *(Doubleday)*
6-8: FLIGHT #116 IS DOWN by Caroline B. Cooney *(Scholastic)*
9-12: THE GIVER by Lois Lowry *(Houghton)*

NEW HAMPSHIRE
Great Stone Face Award ❧

This award is named for a natural rock formation near Laconia that resembles a human face—the Great Stone Face, sometimes referred to as The-Old-Man-in-the-Mountains—closely identified with the State of New Hampshire. In the program's formative years, children in grades 4-6 were invited simply to vote for their favorite book on "I Love To Read Day," usually February 14. Currently, a nominee list of approximately twenty-five fiction and nonfiction titles is assembled, and children vote for the winner from that list. The sponsor is CHILIS, a Division of the New Hampshire Library Association-Children's Librarians (c/o Cindy O'Connor, Bedford Public Library, 3 Meeting House Rd., Bedford, NH 03110). (Crystal sculpture by Peppe Herman of Great Stone Face)

1980
ARE YOU THERE, GOD? IT'S ME, MARGARET by Judy Blume *(Bradbury)*
1981
SUPERFUDGE by Judy Blume *(Dutton)*
1982
TALES OF A FOURTH GRADE NOTHING by Judy Blume *(Dutton)*
1983
THE MOUSE AND THE MOTORCYCLE by Beverly Cleary *(Morrow)*

1984
SUPERFUDGE by Judy Blume *(Dutton)*
1985
SUPERFUDGE by Judy Blume *(Dutton)*
1986
SUPERFUDGE by Judy Blume *(Dutton)*
1987
SUPERFUDGE by Judy Blume *(Dutton)*
1988
WHERE THE RED FERN GROWS by Wilson Rawls *(Doubleday)*
1989
WHERE THE RED FERN GROWS by Wilson Rawls *(Doubleday)*
1990
MATILDA by Roald Dahl *(Viking)*
1991
THE RETURN OF THE INDIAN by Lynne Reid Banks *(Doubleday)*
1992
THE SECRET OF THE INDIAN by Lynne Reid Banks
(Doubleday)
1993
SHILOH by Phyllis Reynolds Naylor *(Atheneum)*
1994
JEREMY THATCHER, DRAGON HATCHER by Bruce Coville
(Minstrel)
1995
JUNIE B. JONES AND THE STUPID SMELLY BUS by Barbara
Park *(Random)*

NEW JERSEY
Garden State Children's Book Awards and Garden State Teen Book Awards ❧

The Garden State Children's Book Awards were established in 1977 by the Children's Services Section of the New Jersey Library Association (Attn: Garden State Book Award Committee, 4 W. Lafayette St., Trenton, NJ 08608) to recognize books of literary and artistic merit and popularity among readers in the early and middle grades (2-5). The awards are given to both authors and illustrators in three categories: Easy-to-Read *(ER)*, Younger Fiction *(Y/F)*, and Younger Nonfiction *(Y/NF)*. The Garden State Teen Book Awards were instituted in 1995 and are also given in three categories: *Fiction/Grades 6-8, Fiction/Grades*

9-12, and *Nonfiction.* For both awrds, lists of eligible titles are selected by committees of librarians and distributed to all school and public libraries in the state for voting by children and young people. Eligible books are published three years before the award date. (Certificate)

1977
ER: DINOSAUR TIME by Peggy Parish, ill. by Arnold Lobel *(Harper)*
Y/F: ENCYCLOPEDIA BROWN LENDS A HAND by Donald J. Sobol, ill. by Leonard Shortall *(Elsevier/Nelson)*
Y/NF: ON THE TRACK OF BIGFOOT by Marian T. Place *(Dodd)*
1978
ER: OWL AT HOME by Arnold Lobel *(Harper)*
Y/F: DORRIE'S BOOK by Marilyn Sachs, ill. by Anne Sachs *(Doubleday)*
Y/NF: HOW KITTENS GROW by Millicent Selsam, photos by Esther Bubley *(Four Winds)*
1979
ER: HATTIE RABBIT by Dick Gackenbach *(Harper)*
ER: HEATHER'S FEATHERS by Leatie Weiss, ill. by Ellen Weiss *(Watts)*
Y/F: NOBODY HAS TO BE A KID FOREVER by Hila Colman *(Crown)*
Y/NF: A VERY YOUNG DANCER by Jill Krementz *(Knopf)*
1980
ER: TEACH US, AMELIA BEDELIA by Peggy Parish, ill. by Lynn Sweat *(Greenwillow)*
Y/F: RAMONA AND HER FATHER by Beverly Cleary, ill. by Alan Tiegreen *(Morrow)*
Y/NF: THE QUICKSAND BOOK by Tomie dePaola *(Holiday House)*
1981
ER: GRASSHOPPER ON THE ROAD by Arnold Lobel *(Harper)*
Y/F: THE GREAT GILLY HOPKINS by Katherine Paterson *(Crowell)*
Y/NF: TYRANNOSAURUS REX by Millicent Selsam *(Harper)*
1982
ER: MRS. GADDY AND THE GHOST by Wilson Gage, ill. by Marylin Hafner *(Greenwillow)*
Y/F: RAMONA AND HER MOTHER by Beverly Cleary, ill. by Alan Tiegreen *(Morrow)*
Y/NF: MUMMIES MADE IN EGYPT by Aliki *(Crowell)*
1983
ER: CLAMS CAN'T SING by James Stevenson *(Greenwillow)*
ER: COMMANDER TOAD IN SPACE by Jane Yolen, ill. by Bruce Degen *(Coward)*
Y/F: SUPERFUDGE by Judy Blume *(Dutton)*

Y/NF: A SHOW OF HANDS: SAY IT IN SIGN LANGUAGE by Mary Beth Sullivan and Linda Bourke, ill. by Linda Bourke *(Addison)*

1984

ER: NATE THE GREAT AND THE MISSING KEY by Marjorie Sharmat, ill. by Marc Simont *(Coward)*

Y/F: RAMONA QUIMBY, AGE 8 by Beverly Cleary, ill. by Alan Tiegreen *(Morrow)*

Y/NF: A LIGHT IN THE ATTIC by Shel Silverstein *(Harper)*

1985

ER: NATE THE GREAT AND THE SNOWY TRAIL by Marjorie Sharmat, ill. by Marc Simont *(Coward)*

Y/F: RALPH S. MOUSE by Beverly Cleary, ill. by Paul O. Zelinsky *(Morrow)*

Y/NF: IT'S BASIC: THE ABC'S OF COMPUTER PROGRAMMING by Shelley Lipson, ill. by Janice Stapleton *(Holt)*

1986

ER: M & M AND THE BAD NEWS BABIES by Pat Ross, ill. by Marylin Hafner *(Knopf)*

Y/F: DEAR MR. HENSHAW by Beverly Cleary, ill. by Paul O. Zelinsky *(Morrow)*

Y/NF: DRAW 50 MONSTERS... by Lee J. Ames *(Doubleday)*

1987

ER: IN A DARK, DARK ROOM AND OTHER SCARY STORIES, ill. by Dirk Zimmer *(Harper)*

Y/F: ANASTASIA, ASK YOUR ANALYST by Lois Lowry *(Houghton)*

Y/NF: THE NEW KID ON THE BLOCK by Jack Prelutsky, ill. by James Stevenson *(Greenwillow)*

1988

ER: AMELIA BEDELIA GOES CAMPING by Peggy Parish, ill. by Lynn Sweat *(Greenwillow)*

Y/F: SARAH, PLAIN AND TALL by Patricia MacLachlan *(Harper)*

Y/NF: HOW THEY BUILT THE STATUE OF LIBERTY by Mary J. Shapiro, ill. by Huck Scarry *(Random)*

1989

ER: MERRY CHRISTMAS, AMELIA BEDELIA by Peggy Parish, ill. by Lynn Sweat *(Greenwillow)*

Y/F: ANASTASIA HAS THE ANSWERS by Lois Lowry *(Houghton)*

Y/NF: TO SPACE AND BACK by Sally Ride, with Susan Okie *(Lothrop)*

1990

ER: HENRY AND MUDGE IN PUDDLE TROUBLE by Cynthia Rylant, ill. by Suçie Stevenson *(Bradbury)*

Y/F: NIGHTY-NIGHTMARE by James Howe, ill. by Leslie Morrill *(Atheneum)*

Y/NF: KOKO'S STORY by Francine Patterson *(Scholastic)*

1991

ER: FOX ON THE JOB by James Marshall *(Dial)*

Y/F: THE BURNING QUESTIONS OF BINGO BROWN by Betsy Byars *(Viking)*
Y/F: TEACHER'S PET by Johanna Hurwitz *(Morrow)*
Y/NF: VOLCANOES by Seymour Simon *(Morrow)*
1992
ER: HENRY AND MUDGE GET THE COLD SHIVERS by Cynthia Rylant, ill. by Suçie Stevenson *(Bradbury)*
Y/F: WAYSIDE SCHOOL IS FALLING DOWN by Louis Sachar, ill. by Joel Schick *(Avon)*
Y/NF: THE MAGIC SCHOOL BUS INSIDE THE HUMAN BODY by Joanna Cole, ill. by Bruce Degen *(Scholastic)*
1993
ER: HENRY AND MUDGE AND THE HAPPY CAT by Cynthia Rylant, ill. by Suçie Stevenson *(Bradbury)*
YF: MUGGIE MAGGIE by Beverly Cleary *(Morrow)*
Y/NF: THE MAGIC SCHOOL BUS LOST IN THE SOLAR SYSTEM by Joanna Cole, ill. by Bruce Degen *(Scholastic)*
1994
ER: HENRY AND MUDGE AND THE BEDTIME THUMPS by Cynthia Rylant, ill. by Suçie Stevenson *(Bradbury)*
YF: SCHOOL'S OUT by Johanna Hurwitz, ill. by Sheila Hamanaka *(Morrow)*
Y/NF: BIG CATS by Seymour Simon *(HarperCollins)*
1995
ER: HENRY AND MUDGE AND THE LONG WEEKEND by Cynthia Rylant, ill. by Suçie Stevenson *(Bradbury)*
YF: ATTABOY, SAM! by Lois Lowry, ill, by Diane deGroat *(Houghton)*
Y/NF: THE MAGIC SCHOOL BUS ON THE OCEAN FLOOR by Joanna Cole, ill. by Bruce Degen *(Scholastic)*
Teen Book Awards:
Fiction (Gr. 6-8): NOTHING BUT THE TRUTH: A DOCUMENTARY NOVEL by Avi *(Orchard)*
Fiction (Gr. 9-12): CHILDREN OF THE NIGHT by Dan Simmons *(Putnam)*
Nonfiction: INTO THE MUMMY'S TOMB by Nicholas Reeves *(Scholastic)*
1996
ER: HENRY AND MUDGE AND THE WILD WIND by Cynthia Rylant, ill. by Suçie Stevenson *(Macmillan)*
YF: NIBBLE, NIBBLE, JENNY ARCHER by Ellen Conford, ill. by Diane Palmisciano *(Little, Brown)*
Y/NF: MY VISIT TO THE AQUARIUM by Aliki *(HarperCollins)*
Teen Book Awards:
Fiction (Gr. 6-8): THE GIVER by Lois Lowry *(Houghton)*
Fiction (Gr. 9-12): THOR by Wayne Smith *(St. Martin's)*
Nonfiction: ANNE FRANK, BEYOND THE DIARY: A PHOTOGRAPHIC REMEMBRANCE by Rian Verhoeven and Ruud van der Rol *(Viking)*

NEW JERSEY
M. Jerry Weiss Book Award 🙶

This award program was established in 1994 by the New Jersey Reading Association (50 Cubbely Rd., Trenton, NJ 08690) to honor M. Jerry Weiss, Distinguished Service Professor at Jersey City State College and nationally known advocate of children's literature. Books are nominated by school committees and then screened by a state committee. Final voting is by students. The award was originally presented in alternate years to an author and illustrator in the K-3 grade category and an author in the 4-9 grade category. It was since decided to divide the 4-9 grade category into one for grades 4-6 (1997) and another for young adult books (1998). (Glass pyramid)

1994
K-3: RIPTIDE by Frances Ward Weller, ill. by Robert J. Blake *(Philomel)*
1995
Gr. 4-9: WANTED...MUD BLOSSOM by Betsy Byars *(Dell)*
1996
K-3: THE STINKY CHEESE MAN AND OTHER FAIRLY STUPID TALES by Jon Scieszka, ill. by Lane Smith *(Viking)*

NEW MEXICO
Land of Enchantment Book Award 🙶

Co-sponsored by the New Mexico Library Association and the New Mexico State International Reading Association, this award is presented annually by the Land of Enchantment Book Award Committee (c/o Flo Starkey, Materials Center, Roswell Independent School District, 300 Kentucky St., Roswell, NM 88201). The committee compiles a list of 25-35 titles as nominees for the award. The winner is chosen from this list by students in grades 4-8. The award is for a book by a U. S. resident published during a five-year period before the award year. Originally used by the New Mexico Highway Department, the term "land of enchantment" has become a name by which the state is commonly known. (Nambé—four metals combined and polished to resemble silver, and produced only in New Mexico—medallion with reproduction of award logo)

1981
RAMONA AND HER FATHER by Beverly Cleary *(Morrow)*
1982
BUNNICULA: A RABBIT TALE OF MYSTERY by Deborah
and James Howe *(Atheneum)*
1983
SUMMER OF FEAR by Lois Duncan *(Little, Brown)*
1984
SUPERFUDGE by Judy Blume *(Dutton)*
1985
NOTHING'S FAIR IN FIFTH GRADE by Barthe DeClements
(Viking)
1986
THIRTEEN WAYS TO SINK A SUB by Jamie Gilson *(Lothrop)*
1987
ZUCCHINI by Barbara Dana *(Harper)*
1988
THE DOLLHOUSE MURDERS by Betty Ren Wright *(Holiday
House)*
1989
SIXTH GRADE CAN REALLY KILL YOU by Barthe
DeClements *(Viking)*
1990
THERE'S A BOY IN THE GIRLS' BATHROOM by Louis
Sachar *(Knopf)*
1991
PECOS BILL: A TALL TALE by Steven Kellogg *(Morrow)*
1992
WAYSIDE SCHOOL IS FALLING DOWN by Louis Sachar
(Lothrop)
1993
MANIAC MAGEE by Jerry Spinelli *(Little, Brown)*
1994
SHILOH by Phyllis Reynolds Naylor *(Atheneum)*
1995
TERROR AT THE ZOO by Peg Kehret *(Dutton)*
1996
THE KNIGHTS OF THE KITCHEN TABLE by Jon Scieszka
(Viking)

NORTH DAKOTA
Flicker Tale
Children's Book Award 🦫

Known as the Children's Choice Award through 1985, this program takes its current name from the state's nickname, the "Flickertail State"; flickertails are ground squirrels found in profusion in central regions of North Dakota. Originally, children nominated the titles for a ten-title reading list and also selected the winning title from that list. Since 1986 members of the North Dakota Library Association (515 N. 5th St., Bismark, ND 58501) Children's Roundtable have selected the ten-title nominee list in two categories, Juvenile *(J)* and Picture Book *(PB)*. Nominees—known to be titles enjoyed in libraries—must have been published within a five-year period before nomination. (Plaque)

1978
J: STAR WARS by George Lucas *(Ballantine/Del Rey)*
1979
J: ARE YOU THERE, GOD? IT'S ME, MARGARET by Judy Blume *(Bradbury)*
1980
J: TALES OF A FOURTH GRADE NOTHING by Judy Blume *(Dutton)*
1981
J: WHERE THE RED FERN GROWS by Wilson Rawls *(Doubleday)*
PB: CURIOUS GEORGE by H. A. Rey *(Houghton)*
1982
J: SUPERFUDGE by Judy Blume *(Dutton)*
PB: FOX AND HOUNDS by Walt Disney Productions *(Smith)*
1983
J: BLUBBER by Judy Blume *(Bradbury)*
PB: E. T.: THE EXTRA-TERRESTRIAL STORYBOOK by William Kotzwinkle *(Putnam)*
1984
J: RETURN OF THE JEDI STORYBOOK adapted by Joan Vinge *(Random)*
PB: A SISTER FOR SAM by Evelyn Mason, ill. by Tom Cooke *(Parker Brothers)*
1985
J: CHARLIE AND THE CHOCOLATE FACTORY by Roald Dahl *(Knopf)*
PB: MISS NELSON IS MISSING! by Harry Allard, ill. by James Marshall *(Houghton)*

1986
No Awards

1987
J: SUPERFUDGE by Judy Blume *(Dutton)*
PB: THE DAY JIMMY'S BOA ATE THE WASH by Trinka Hakes Noble, ill. by Steven Kellogg *(Dial)*

1988
J: NOTHING'S FAIR IN FIFTH GRADE by Barthe DeClements *(Viking)*
PB: MISS NELSON HAS A FIELD DAY by Harry Allard, ill. by James Marshall *(Houghton)*

1989
J: ON MY HONOR by Marion Dane Bauer *(Clarion)*
PB: LOVE YOU FOREVER by Robert Munsch, ill. by Michael Martchenko *(Firefly)*

1990
J: HATCHET by Gary Paulsen *(Bradbury)*
PB: MEANWHILE BACK AT THE RANCH by Trinka Hakes Noble, ill. by Tony Ross *(Dial)*

1991
J: HOW TO FIGHT A GIRL by Thomas Rockwell *(Watts)*
PB: NO JUMPING ON THE BED! by Tedd Arnold *(Dial)*

1992
J: MANIAC MAGEE by Jerry Spinelli *(Little, Brown)*
PB: SCARED SILLY: A HALLOWEEN TREAT by James Howe, ill. by Leslie Morrill *(Morrow)*

1993
J: FUDGE-A-MANIA by Judy Blume *(Dutton)*
PB. THE SIGNMAKER'S ASSISTANT by Tedd Arnold *(Dial)*

1994
J: SHILOH by Phyllis Reynolds Naylor *(Atheneum)*
PB: THE STINKY CHEESE MAN AND OTHER FAIRLY STUPID TALES by Jon Scieszka, ill. by Lane Smith *(Viking)*

1995
J: THE RIVER by Gary Paulsen *(Doubleday)*
PB: THE EASTER EGG GARM by Mary Jane Auch *(Holiday House)*

1996
J: THE BEST SCHOOL YEAR EVER by Barbara Robinson *(HarperCollins)*
PB: MY ROTTEN REDHEADED OLDER BROTHER by Pataricia Polacco *(Simon & Schuster)*

OHIO
Buckeye Children's Book Awards 🍂

"This award program was designed to encourage children to read literature critically, encourage teacher involvement in children's literature programs in their schools, and to commend authors...." Jointly sponsored by the International Reading Association Ohio Council, Ohio Council of Teachers of English Language Arts, Ohio Department of Education, Ohio Educational Library Media Association, Ohio Library Council and the State Library of Ohio, the administrative contact for the program is the State Library of Ohio (65 South Front St., Columbus, OH 43215). An Advisory Council currently prepares reading lists of not more than ten titles in three reading-level categories: grades *K-2, 3-5* and *6-8.* Titles selected for these lists are from nominations made by children at participating schools and libraries. Voting for the winners frequently takes place during Ohio Right to Read Week, the first full week in March. The award—now given biennially— is named for the State tree of Ohio, a state commonly referred to as "The Buckeye State." (Plaque)

1982
K-3: THE BERENSTAIN BEARS AND THE SPOOKY OLD TREE by Stan and Jan Berenstain *(Random)*
4-8: SUPERFUDGE by Judy Blume *(Dutton)*
1983
K-3: GRANDPA'S GHOST STORIES by James Flora *(McElderry/Atheneum)*
4-8: TIGER EYES by Judy Blume *(Bradbury)*
1984
K-3: E.T. THE EXTRA-TERRESTRIAL STORYBOOK by William Kotzwinkle *(Putnam)*
4-8: NOTHING'S FAIR IN FIFTH GRADE by Barthe DeClements *(Viking)*
1985
K-2: THE BERENSTAIN BEARS GET IN A FIGHT by Stan and Jan Berenstain *(Random)*
3-5: RAMONA QUIMBY, AGE 8 by Beverly Cleary *(Morrow)*
6-8: A LIGHT IN THE ATTIC by Shel Silverstein *(Harper)*
1987
K-2: IN A DARK, DARK ROOM AND OTHER SCARY STORIES by Alvin Schwartz *(Harper)*
3-5: SCARY STORIES TO TELL IN THE DARK by Alvin Schwartz *(Lippincott)*
6-8: THIRTEEN WAYS TO SINK A SUB by Jamie Gilson *(Lothrop)*

1989

K-2: IF YOU GIVE A MOUSE A COOKIE by Laura Numeroff, ill. by Felicia Bond *(Harper)*

3-5: MORE SCARY STORIES TO TELL IN THE DARK by Alvin Schwartz *(Lippincott)*

6-8: SIXTH GRADE CAN REALLY KILL YOU by Barthe DeClements *(Viking)*

1991

K-2: THE POLAR EXPRESS by Chris Van Allsburg *(Houghton)*

3-5: THERE'S A BOY IN THE GIRLS' BATHROOM by Louis Sachar *(Knopf)*

6-8: HATCHET by Gary Paulsen *(Bradbury)*

1993

K-2: THE VERY QUIET CRICKET by Eric Carle *(Philomel)*

3-5: SCARY STORIES 3: MORE TALES TO CHILL YOUR BONES by Alvin Schwartz *(HarperCollins)*

6-8: MANIAC MAGEE by Jerry Spinelli *(Little, Brown)*

1995

K-2: THE STINKY CHEESE MAN AND OTHER FAIRLY STUPID TALES by Jon Scieszka, ill. by Lane Smith *(Viking)*

3-5: SHILOH by Phyllis Reynolds Naylor *(Atheneum)*

6-8: SAY CHEESE & DIE by R.L. Stine *(Scholastic)*

OKLAHOMA
Sequoyah Children's and Young Adult Book Awards 📷

The Sequoyah Book Awards—one for children's books and, since 1988, one designated a young adult book award—honor Sequoyah (Cherokee for "lame one") for his achievement in creating the Cherokee syllabary, the 85 symbols representing the different sounds in the Cherokee language. A statue of Sequoyah is one of the two representing the State of Oklahoma in the National Hall of Fame at the Capitol in Washington, DC. Both awards programs are projects of the Oklahoma Library Association. Committees compile Masterlists of around 20 titles for the children's book award *(C)*, and around 15 titles for the young adult book award *(YA)*. Titles on the Masterlists are deemed to be of literary excellence; all are published three years prior to the award year. A wide variety of promotional materials, both free and for sale, is available for both programs. Young readers present the awards to the winners during the annual Oklahoma Library Association Spring Conference. Information about the awards is available from the Oklahoma State Department of Education (c/o Library Media/ITV, 2500 N. Lincoln Blvd., Oklahoma City, OK 73105). (Plaques)

1959
OLD YELLER by Fred Gipson *(Harper)*

1960
BLACK GOLD by Marguerite Henry *(Rand McNally)*

1961
HAVE SPACE SUIT WILL TRAVEL by Robert Heinlein *(Scribner)*

1962
THE HELEN KELLER STORY by Catherine O. Peare *(Crowell)*

1963
THE MYSTERY OF THE HAUNTED POOL by Phyllis A. Whitney *(Westminster)*

1964
WHERE THE PANTHER SCREAMS by William Powell Robinson *(World)*

1965
A WRINKLE IN TIME by Madeleine L'Engle *(Farrar)*

1966
RASCAL by Sterling North *(Dutton)*

1967
HARRIET THE SPY by Louise Fitzhugh *(Harper)*

1968
GENTLE BEN by Walt Morey *(Dutton)*

1969
BLACKBEARD'S GHOST by Ben Stahl *(Houghton)*

1970
MUSTANG by Marguerite Henry *(Rand McNally)*

1971
RAMONA THE PEST by Beverly Cleary *(Morrow)*

1972
THE MAN IN THE BOX: A STORY FROM VIETNAM by Mary Lois Dunn *(McGraw-Hill)*

1973
THE TRUMPET OF THE SWAN by E. B. White *(Harper)*

1974
FLIGHT OF THE WHITE WOLF by Mel Ellis *(Holt)*

1975
TALES OF A FOURTH GRADE NOTHING by Judy Blume *(Dutton)*

1976
HOW TO EAT FRIED WORMS by Thomas Rockwell *(Watts)*

1977
THE TOOTHPASTE MILLIONAIRE by Jean Merrill *(Houghton)*

1978
SHOESHINE GIRL by Clyde Robert Bulla *(Crowell)*

1979
SUMMER OF THE MONKEYS by Wilson Rawls *(Doubleday)*
1980
KID POWER by Susan Beth Pfeffer *(Watts)*
1981
THE GET-AWAY CAR by Eleanor Clymer *(Dutton)*
1982
BUNNICULA: A RABBIT TALE OF MYSTERY by Deborah and James Howe *(Atheneum)*
1983
A DOG CALLED KITTY by Bill Wallace *(Holiday House)*
1984
THE CYBIL WAR by Betsy Byars *(Viking)*
1985
THIRTEEN WAYS TO SINK A SUB by Jamie Gilson *(Lothrop)*
1986
DEAR MR. HENSHAW by Beverly Cleary *(Morrow)*
JUST TELL ME WHEN WE'RE DEAD! by Eth Clifford *(Houghton)*
1987
NIGHT OF THE TWISTERS by Ivy Ruckman *(Crowell)*
1988
C: CHRISTINA'S GHOST by Betty Ren Wright *(Holiday House)*
YA: ABBY, MY LOVE by Hadley Irwin *(McElderry)*
1989
C: SIXTH-GRADE SLEEPOVER by Eve Bunting *(HBJ)*
YA: THE OTHER SIDE OF DARK by Joan Lowery Nixon *(Delacorte)*
1990
C: FUDGE by Charlotte Towner Graeber *(Lothrop)*
YA: HATCHET by Gary Paulsen *(Bradbury)*
1991
C: BEAUTY by Bill Wallace *(Holiday House)*
YA: A SUDDEN SILENCE by Eve Bunting *(HBJ)*
1992
C: THE DOLL IN THE GARDEN: A GHOST STORY by Mary Downing Hahn *(Clarion)*
YA: APPOINTMENT WITH A STRANGER by Jean Thesman *(Houghton)*
1993
C: WEASEL by Cynthia DeFelice *(Macmillan)*
YA: THE SILVER KISS by Annette Curtis Klause *(Delacorte)*
1994
C: SHILOH by Phyllis Reynolds Naylor *(Atheneum)*
YA: WHAT DADDY DID by Neal Shusterman *(Little, Brown)*
1995
C: HORROR AT THE HAUNTED HOUSE by Peg Kehret *(Dutton)*

YA: FLIGHT #116 IS DOWN by Caroline B. Cooney
(*Scholastic*)
1996
C: THE GHOSTS OF MERCY MANOR by Betty Ren Wright
(*Scholastic*)
YA: THE GIVER by Lois Lowry (*Houghton*)

PACIFIC NORTHWEST
(Alaska; Alberta, Canada; British Columbia, Canada; Idaho; Montana; Oregon; Washington)
Young Reader's Choice Awards ❦

This awards program has been in existence longer than any other North American program in which children choose the winning books. For the first fifty years of the program, a single award was given to a book on a nominee list of fifteen titles assembled from suggestions by librarians, teachers, and children. These were books of appeal to readers in grades 4-8. In 1991 a second award for books published for grades 9-12 was added to the program to commemorate a notable milestone in the program's history. Currently, twelve titles are on the nominee list for grades 4-8, and five on the list for 9-12, the "Senior Division." Voting takes place throughout the region in early March, with the total number of votes for each nominated title forwarded to the administrator (Graduate School of Library & Information Science, Box 352930, University of Washington, Seattle, WA 98195-2930) for tabulation. The sponsor is the Pacific Northwest Library Association (PNLA), which offers a variety of materials at very little cost to promote the award and to help local participants administer it. It also sells a videotaped slide-cassette presentation introducing and promoting the titles nominated for the award. The award is presented to the winner during the PNLA Annual Conference. (Hand-carved medallion wrought in Idaho silver depicting the YRCA insignia)

1940
PAUL BUNYAN SWINGS HIS AXE by Dell J. McCormick
(*Caxton*)
1941
MR. POPPER'S PENGUINS by Richard and Florence Atwater
(*Little, Brown*)
1942
BY THE SHORES OF SILVER LAKE by Laura Ingalls Wilder
(*Harper*)

1943
LASSIE COME HOME by Eric Knight *(Holt)*
1944
THE BLACK STALLION by Walter Farley *(Random)*
1945
SNOW TREASURE by Marie McSwigan *(Dutton)*
1946
THE RETURN OF SILVER CHIEF by Jack O'Brien *(Holt)*
1947
HOMER PRICE by Robert McCloskey *(Viking)*
1948
THE BLACK STALLION RETURNS by Walter Farley *(Random)*
1949
COWBOY BOOTS by Shannon Garst *(Abingdon)*
1950
McELLIGOT'S POOL by Dr. Seuss *(Random)*
1951
KING OF THE WIND by Marguerite Henry *(Rand McNally)*
1952
SEA STAR by Marguerite Henry *(Rand McNally)*
1953-1955
No Awards
1956
MISS PICKERELL GOES TO MARS by Ellen MacGregor
(McGraw-Hill)
1957
HENRY AND RIBSY by Beverly Cleary *(Morrow)*
1958
GOLDEN MARE by William Corbin *(Coward)*
1959
OLD YELLER by Fred Gipson *(Harper)*
1960
HENRY AND THE PAPER ROUTE by Beverly Cleary
(Morrow)
1961
DANNY DUNN AND THE HOMEWORK MACHINE by Jay
Williams *(McGraw-Hill)*
1962
THE SWAMP FOX OF THE REVOLUTION by Stewart
Holbrook *(Random)*
1963
DANNY DUNN ON THE OCEAN FLOOR by Jay Williams
(McGraw-Hill)
1964
THE INCREDIBLE JOURNEY by Sheila Burnford *(Atlantic-Little, Brown)*

1965
JOHN F. KENNEDY AND PT-109 by Richard Tregaskis *(Random)*
1966
RASCAL by Sterling North *(Dutton)*
1967
CHITTY-CHITTY-BANG-BANG by Ian Fleming *(Random)*
1968
THE MOUSE AND THE MOTORCYCLE by Beverly Cleary *(Morrow)*
1969
HENRY REED'S BABY-SITTING SERVICE by Keith Robertson *(Viking)*
1970
SMOKE by William Corbin *(Coward)*
1971
RAMONA THE PEST by Beverly Cleary *(Morrow)*
1972
ENCYCLOPEDIA BROWN KEEPS THE PEACE by Donald J. Sobol *(Nelson)*
1973
No Award
1974
MRS. FRISBY AND THE RATS OF NIMH by Robert C. O'Brien *(Atheneum)*
1975
TALES OF A FOURTH GRADE NOTHING by Judy Blume *(Dutton)*
1976
THE GREAT BRAIN REFORMS by John D. Fitzgerald *(Dial)*
1977
BLUBBER by Judy Blume *(Bradbury)*
1978
THE GREAT BRAIN DOES IT AGAIN by John D. Fitzgerald *(Dial)*
1979
ROLL OF THUNDER, HEAR MY CRY by Mildred Taylor *(Dial)*
1980
RAMONA AND HER FATHER by Beverly Cleary *(Morrow)*
1981
HAIL, HAIL, CAMP TIMBERWOOD by Ellen Conford *(Little, Brown)*
1982
BUNNICULA: A RABBIT TALE OF MYSTERY by Deborah and James Howe *(Atheneum)*
1983
SUPERFUDGE by Judy Blume *(Dutton)*

1984
THE INDIAN IN THE CUPBOARD by Lynne Reid Banks
(Doubleday)
1985
THIRTEEN WAYS TO SINK A SUB by Jamie Gilson *(Lothrop)*
1986
THE DOLLHOUSE MURDERS by Betty Ren Wright *(Holiday House)*
1987
THE WAR WITH GRANDPA by Robert Kimmel Smith
(Delacorte)
1988
SIXTH GRADE CAN REALLY KILL YOU by Barthe
DeClements *(Viking)*
1989
WAIT TILL HELEN COMES: A GHOST STORY by Mary
Downing Hahn *(Clarion)*
1990
THERE'S A BOY IN THE GIRLS' BATHROOM by Louis
Sachar *(Knopf)*
1991
4-8: TEN KIDS, NO PETS by Ann M. Martin *(Holiday House)*
9 12: SEX EDUCATION by Jenny Davis *(Orchard)*
1992
4-8: DANGER IN QUICKSAND SWAMP by Bill Wallace
(Holiday House)
9-12: EVA by Peter Dickinson *(Delacorte)*
1993
4-8: MANIAC MAGEE by Jerry Spinelli *(Little, Brown)*
9-12: THE FACE ON THE MILK CARTON by Caroline B.
Cooney *(Bantam)*
1994
4-8: SHILOH by Phyllis Reynolds Naylor *(Atheneum)*
9-12: WOLF BY THE EARS by Ann Rinaldi *(Scholastic)*
1995
4-8: TERROR AT THE ZOO by Peg Kehret *(Cobblehill)*
9-12: WHO KILLED MY DAUGHTER? by Lois Duncan
(Delacorte)
1996
4-8: THE BOYS START THE WAR by Phyllis Reynolds Naylor
(Delacorte)
9-12: THE GIVER by Lois Lowry *(Houghton)*

PENNSYLVANIA
Pennsylvania Young Reader's Choice Award 🔔

Sponsored by the Pennsylvania School Librarians Association, this award seeks to promote reading of quality books by young people in the Commonwealth of Pennsylvania, to promote teacher and librarian involvement in children's literature, and to honor authors whose work has been recognized by the children of Pennsylvania. Eligible books are published within five years of the award presentation, written by an author currently living in North America, and appropriate for students in grades K-8, with some variation in grade categories over the years. Books must be of recognized literary quality, either fiction or nonfiction. A master list is drawn up by a committee, and children in participating public and private schools vote for their favorite title. In order to qualify to vote, students must have read or have listened to at least three books from the list. (Contact: Jeannie Bellavance, Chair, PYRCA Committee, 148 S. Bethlehem Pike, Ambler, PA 19002-9822.) (Certificate)

1992
Gr. 3-5: MY TEACHER IS AN ALIEN by Bruce Coville *(Minstrel)*
Gr. 6-8: MANIAC MAGEE by Jerry Spinelli *(Little, Brown)*
1993
Gr. 3-5: FUDGE-A-MANIA by Judy Blume *(Dutton)*
Gr. 6-8: SHILOH by Phyllis Reynolds Naylor *(Atheneum)*
1994
Gr. 3-8: THE STINKY CHEESE MAN AND OTHER FAIRLY STUPID TALES by Jon Scieszka, ill. by Lane Smith *(Viking)*
1995
K-3: MARTHA SPEAKS by Susan Meddaugh *(Houghton)*
Gr. 3-6: THE GIVER by Lois Lowry *(Houghton)*
1996
K-3: THE THREE LITTLE WOLVES AND THE BIG BAD PIG by Eugene Trivizas *(McElderry)*
3-8: THE SWEETEST FIG by Chris Van Allsburg *(Houghton)*

RHODE ISLAND
Rhode Island Children's Book Award

This award program "encourages children to read." A Book Award Committee consisting of representatives of the three sponsors—Rhode Island Library Association, Rhode Island State Council of the International Reading Association, and Rhode Island Educational Media Association—prepares a nomination list of twenty fiction and nonfiction titles appropriate for grades 3-6. Children cast their votes at participating schools and libraries on February 1 each year; the site of the fall award ceremony is a school that has participated in the program. A permanent source of information is the Dept. of State Library Services (Attn: Melody Allen, 300 Richmond St., Providence, RI 02903). (Presentation)

1991
SOMETHING UPSTAIRS: A TALE OF GHOSTS by Avi *(Orchard)*
1992
MANIAC MAGEE by Jerry Spinelli *(Little, Brown)*
1993
THE HOUDINI BOX by Brian Selznick *(Knopf)*
1994
THE STINKY CHEESE MAN AND OTHER FAIRLY STUPID TALES by Jon Scieszka, ill. by Lane Smith *(Viking)*
1995
THE SWEETEST FIG by Chris Van Allsburg *(Houghton)*
1996
JACOB AND THE STRANGER by Sally Derby *(Ticknor & Fields)*

SOUTH CAROLINA
South Carolina Children's, Junior, and Young Adult Book Awards

Sponsored by the South Carolina Association of School Librarians (P.O. Box 2442, Columbia, SC 29202) in cooperation with the State Department of Education and the College of Library and Information Science, University of South Carolina, the purposes of the awards are to encourage students to read good quality contemporary literature and to honor the authors of the books annually chosen the favorites by student vote. The Children's Book Award *(C)* is open to all students attending South Carolina public or private schools in grades 3-6, the Junior Book Award *(J)* in grades 6-9, and the Young Adult Book Award *(YA)* in grades 9-12. A list of twenty nominees for each award is selected by three award committees, made up of school librarians, students, teachers, parents, public librarians, administrators, and college professors. These lists, with review sources cited, are distributed to all public and private schools in the state. Titles must have been published within a five-year period before the award year and must appear in *Books in Print* or *Paperback Books in Print.* (Bronze medallion for each award)

1976
C: HOW TO EAT FRIED WORMS by Thomas Rockwell *(Watts)*
1977
C: TALES OF A FOURTH GRADE NOTHING by Judy Blume *(Dutton)*
1978
C: OTHERWISE KNOWN AS SHEILA THE GREAT by Judy Blume *(Dutton)*
1979
C: THE GREAT CHRISTMAS KIDNAPPING CAPER by Jean Van Leeuwen *(Dial)*
1980
C: SHOESHINE GIRL by Clyde Robert Bulla *(Crowell)*
YA: AMITYVILLE HORROR by Jay Anson *(Prentice-Hall)*
1981
C: BUNNICULA: A RABBIT TALE OF MYSTERY by Deborah and James Howe *(Atheneum)*
YA: A SHINING SEASON by William Buchanan *(Coward)*
1982
C: THE GHOST OF TILLIE CASSAWAY by Ellen Showell *(Four Winds)*
YA: THE BOY WHO DRANK TOO MUCH by Shep Greene *(Viking)*
1983
C: PRISONERS AT THE KITCHEN TABLE by Barbara Holland *(Clarion)*
YA: ABOUT DAVID by Susan Beth Pfeffer *(Delacorte)*
1984
C: JELLY BELLY by Robert Kimmel Smith *(Delacorte)*
YA: STRANGER WITH MY FACE by Lois Duncan *(Little, Brown)*
1985
C: THE MONSTER'S RING by Bruce Coville *(Pantheon)*
YA: THE DIVORCE EXPRESS by Paula Danziger *(Delacorte)*

1986
C: THE WAR WITH GRANDPA by Robert Kimmel Smith
(Delacorte)
YA: A STRING OF CHANCES by Phyllis Reynolds Naylor
(Atheneum)

1987
C: CRACKER JACKSON by Betsy Byars *(Viking)*
YA: IF THIS IS LOVE, I'LL TAKE SPAGHETTI by Ellen
Conford *(Four Winds)*

1988
C: BABY-SITTING IS A DANGEROUS JOB by Willo Davis
Roberts *(Atheneum)*
YA: LOCKED IN TIME by Lois Duncan *(Little, Brown)*

1989
C: FERRET IN THE BEDROOM, LIZARDS IN THE FRIDGE
by Bill Wallace *(Holiday House)*
YA: FACE AT THE EDGE OF THE WORLD by Eve Bunting
(Clarion)

1990
C: CLASS CLOWN by Johanna Hurwitz *(Morrow)*
YA: THE YEAR WITHOUT MICHAEL by Susan Beth Pfeffer
(Bantam)

1991
C: IS ANYBODY THERE? by Eve Bunting *(Lippincott)*
YA: FALLEN ANGELS by Walter Dean Myers *(Scholastic)*

1992
C: SNOT STEW by Bill Wallace *(Holiday House)*
YA: ON THE DEVIL'S COURT by Carl Deuker *(Little, Brown)*

1993
C: WEASEL by Cynthia DeFelice *(Macmillan)*
J: THE DEAD MAN IN INDIAN CREEK by Mary Downing
Hahn *(Clarion)*
YA: THE SILVER KISS by Annette Curtis Klause *(Delacorte)*

1994
C: THE FOURTH GRADE RATS by Jerry Spinelli *(Scholastic)*
J: STEPPING ON THE CRACKS by Mary Downing Hahn
(Clarion)
YA: JURASSIC PARK by Michael Crichton *(Ballantine)*

1995
C: SUKEY AND THE MERMAID by Robert D. San Souci
(Macmillan)
J: THE GHOST IN THE HOUSE by Betty Ren Wright
(Scholastic)
YA: WHAT YOU DON'T KNOW CAN KILL YOU by Fran
Arrick *(Bantam)*

SOUTH DAKOTA
Prairie Pasque Award ❧

The program is for children in grades 4-6 throughout the state. A committee of school and public librarians develops a reading list of twenty titles to be read through the school year. Children vote for the winners. Management of the award rotates at two-year intervals among volunteers. A permanent source of information about the program is the Director of Library Development, South Dakota State Library (800 Governor's Drive, Pierre, SD 57501). (Plaque)

1987
NIGHT OF THE TWISTERS by Ivy Ruckman *(Crowell)*
1988
SWITCHAROUND by Lois Lowry *(Houghton)*
1989
ROYAL PAIN by Ellen Conford *(Scholastic)*
1990
THIS ISLAND ISN'T BIG ENOUGH FOR THE FOUR OF US by Gery Greer and Bob Ruddick *(Crowell)*
1991
ALL ABOUT SAM by Lois Lowry *(Houghton)*
1992
THE DOLL IN THE GARDEN: A GHOST STORY by Mary Downing Hahn *(Clarion)*
1993
HUGH GLASS, MOUNTAIN MAN by Robert McClung *(Morrow)*
1994
SHILOH by Phyllis Reynolds Naylor *(Atheneum)*
1995
DEVIL'S BRIDGE by Cynthia DeFelice *(Macmillan)*

TENNESSEE
Volunteer State Book Awards ❧

Begun originally as the Tennessee Children's Choice Book Award intended for students in grades 4, 5, and 6, as of the program for 1988-89, awards have been given in four divisions: *K-3, 4-6, 7-9,* and *10-12*. In 1993, the *7-9* and *10-12* levels were combined into one *YA* division. Committees of school and public librarians and library educators select Master Lists of twenty titles for each division. Titles on the lists are read by (and to) children during the school year, with children's votes tabulated in time for formal announcements of the winners during the annual Tennessee Library Association Spring Conference, when the following year's Master Lists are also introduced. The awards program takes its name from the state's nickname: in 1847 the governor called for three regiments of soldiers to serve in the Mexican War; thirty thousand volunteered at once. The program is administered from Department of Youth Education, Middle Tennessee State University, Murfreesboro, TN 37132. (Plaques)

1979
HOW TO EAT FRIED WORMS by Thomas Rockwell *(Watts)*
1980
RAMONA AND HER FATHER by Beverly Cleary *(Morrow)*
1981
SHADOWS by Lynn Hall *(Follett)*
1982
SUPERFUDGE by Judy Blume *(Dutton)*
1983
THE CYBIL WAR by Betsy Byars *(Viking)*
1984
HOWLIDAY INN by James Howe *(Atheneum)*
1985
WHEN THE BOYS RAN THE HOUSE by Joan Carris *(Lippincott)*
1986
OPERATION: DUMP THE CHUMP by Barbara Park *(Knopf)*
1987
SKINNYBONES by Barbara Park *(Knopf)*
1988
THE WAR WITH GRANDPA by Robert Kimmel Smith *(Delacorte)*
1989
K-3: IN A DARK, DARK ROOM AND OTHER SCARY STORIES by Alvin Schwartz, ill. by Dirk Zimmer *(Harper)*
4-6: WAIT TILL HELEN COMES: A GHOST STORY by Mary Downing Hahn *(Clarion)*
7-9: DOGSONG by Gary Paulsen *(Bradbury)*
10-12: IZZY, WILLY-NILLY by Cynthia Voigt *(Atheneum)*
1990
K-3: ABIYOYO: BASED ON A SOUTH AFRICAN LULLABY AND FOLK STORY by Pete Seeger *(Macmillan)*
4-6: CHRISTINA'S GHOST by Betty Ren Wright *(Holiday House)*
7-9: PUTTING ON AN ACT by Christi Killien *(Houghton)*
10-12: LOCKED IN TIME by Lois Duncan *(Little, Brown)*

1991
K-3: THE MAGIC SCHOOL BUS AT THE WATERWORKS by Joanna Cole, ill. by Bruce Degen *(Scholastic)*
4-6: BEETLES, LIGHTLY TOASTED by Phyllis Reynolds Naylor *(Atheneum)*
7-9: THE SHADOW CLUB by Neal Shusterman *(Little, Brown)*
10-12: SAY GOODNIGHT, GRACIE by Julie Rice Deaver *(Harper)*

1992
K-3: NO JUMPING ON THE BED! by Tedd Arnold *(Dial)*
4-6: SOMETHING UPSTAIRS: A TALE OF GHOSTS by Avi *(Orchard)*
7-9: A SUDDEN SILENCE by Eve Bunting *(Harcourt)*

1993
K-3: THE VERY QUIET CRICKET by Eric Carle *(Philomel)*
4-6: THE TWENTY-FOUR HOUR LIPSTICK MYSTERY by Bonnie Pryor *(Morrow)*
YA: A KILLING FREEZE by Lynn Hall *(Morrow)*

1994
K-3: TAILYPO! by Jan Wahl, ill. by Wil Clay *(Holt)*
4-6: OUR SIXTH GRADE SUGAR BABIES by Eve Bunting *(Lippincott)*
YA: DON'T LOOK BEHIND YOU by Lois Duncan *(Delacorte)*

1995
K-3: THE LAND OF GRAY WOLF by Thomas Locker *(Dial)*
4-6: FUDGE-A-MANIA by Judy Blume *(Dutton)*
YA: THE FACE ON THE MILK CARTON by Caroline B. Cooney *(Bantam)*

1996
K-3: THE THREE LITTLE WOLVES AND THE BIG BAD PIG by Eugene Trivizas *(McElderry)*
4-6: THE GHOSTS OF MERCY MANOR by Betty Ren Wright *(Scholastic)*
YA: HEART OF A CHAMPION by Carl Deuker *(Little, Brown)*

TEXAS
The Texas Bluebonnet Award ᏓᏍ

In the words of a resolution adopted by the Texas House of Representatives, honoring this award program, the sponsors are commended for seeking "to encourage the children of Texas, through their school and public libraries, to explore and read with discrimination a variety of quality books; to recognize children's personal reading interests and selections; and to honor those who create children's books of superior quality." The award is sponsored by the Texas Association of School Librarians and the Children's Round Table, affiliates of the Texas Library Association (TLA) (3355 Bee Cave Road, Suite 401, Austin, TX 78746). The award is named for the State flower of Texas, a blue-flowered lupine. An award committee compiles a Master List of nominees after receiving suggestions from librarians, teachers and students across the state. The program is for children in grades 3-6, who must have read (or heard read aloud) at least five books on the list to be eligible to vote. Both fiction and nonfiction are represented on the Master Lists; authors must be alive, and U.S. citizens. The award is presented during the annual TLA Conference. (Medallion)

1981
RAMONA AND HER FATHER by Beverly Cleary *(Morrow)*
1982
SUPERFUDGE by Judy Blume *(Dutton)*
1983
A DOG CALLED KITTY by Bill Wallace *(Holiday House)*
1984
NOTHING'S FAIR IN FIFTH GRADE by Barthe DeClements *(Viking)*
1985
SKINNYBONES by Barbara Park *(Knopf)*
1986
THE DOLLHOUSE MURDERS by Betty Ren Wright *(Holiday House)*
1987
THE HOT AND COLD SUMMER by Johanna Hurwitz *(Morrow)*
1988
CHRISTINA'S GHOST by Betty Ren Wright *(Holiday House)*
1989
WAIT TILL HELEN COMES: A GHOST STORY by Mary Downing Hahn *(Clarion)*
1990
THERE'S A BOY IN THE GIRLS' BATHROOM by Louis Sachar *(Knopf)*
1991
ALIENS FOR BREAKFAST by Jonathan Etra and Stephanie Spinner *(Random)*
1992
SNOT STEW by Bill Wallace *(Holiday House)*
1993
THE HOUDINI BOX by Brian Selznick *(Knopf)*
1994
SHILOH by Phyllis Reynolds Naylor *(Atheneum)*

1995
THE STINKY CHEESE MAN AND OTHER FAIRLY STUPID
TALES by Jon Scieszka, ill. by Lane Smith *(Viking)*
1996
TIME FOR ANDREW: A GHOST STORY by Mary Downing
Hahn *(Clarion)*

UTAH
Utah Children's, Informational, and Young Adults' Book Awards &

Sponsored by the Children's Literature Association of Utah (209
East 500 South, Salt Lake City, UT 84111), the Children's Book
Award *(C)* was first presented in 1980, the Informational Book
Award *(I)* in 1986, and the Young Adults' Award *(Y/A)* in 1991.
The first two awards are determined by the votes of children in
grades 3-6 from, in the case of the Children's Award, a
nomination list of 10-12 titles, and, in the case of the
Informational Award, a list of 8-10 titles. The Young Adults'
Award is determined by readers in grades 7-12 from a list of
twelve titles. Titles that have won the Newbery Medal are not
eligible for any of the awards; titles that have won the Caldecott
Medal are not eligible for the Children's or Informational
Awards. Titles can be nominated for the awards one time only.
Detailed "Eligibility & Selection Criteria for Nominations"
information sheets are prepared for participating schools and
libraries. A Picture Book Award will be presented for the first
time in 1996. (Plaques)

1980
RAMONA AND HER FATHER by Beverly Cleary *(Morrow)*
1981
EDDIE'S MENAGERIE by Carolyn Haywood *(Morrow)*
THE LETTER, THE WITCH AND THE RING by John Bellairs
(Dial)
1982
SUPERFUDGE by Judy Blume *(Dutton)*
1983
THE CHOCOLATE TOUCH by Patrick Catling *(Morrow)*
1984
LOST IN THE DEVIL'S DESERT by Gloria Skurzynski
(Lothrop)

1985
STONE FOX by John Reynolds Gardiner *(Crowell)*
1986
C: ME AND THE WEIRDOS by Jane Sutton *(Houghton)*
I: GREAT PAINTERS by Piero Ventura *(Putnam)*
1987
C: SKINNYBONES by Barbara Park *(Knopf)*
I: No Award (no nominations)
1988
C: WAIT TILL HELEN COMES: A GHOST STORY by Mary Downing Hahn *(Clarion)*
I: HOW MUCH IS A MILLION? by David M. Schwartz, ill. by Steven Kellogg *(Lothrop)*
1989
C: TRAPPED IN DEATH CAVE by Bill Wallace *(Holiday House)*
I: YOUR AMAZING SENSES: THIRTY-SIX GAMES, PUZZLES, & TRICKS TO SHOW HOW YOUR SENSES WORK by Ron and Atie van der Meer *(Aladdin)*
1990
C: THIS ISLAND ISN'T BIG ENOUGH FOR THE FOUR OF US by Gery Greer and Bob Ruddick *(Crowell)*
I: HOW TO MAKE POP-UPS by Joan Irvine, ill. by Barbara Reid *(Morrow)*
1991
C: MATILDA by Roald Dahl *(Viking)*
I: BILL PEET: AN AUTOBIOGRAPHY by Bill Peet *(Houghton)*
Y/A: THE OTHER SIDE OF DARK by Joan Lowery Nixon *(Delacorte)*
1992
C: THERE'S A BOY IN THE GIRL'S BATHROOM by Louis Sachar *(Knopf)*
I: AN ANT COLONY by Heiderose and Andreas Fischer-Nagel *(Carolrhoda)*
Y/A: DON'T LOOK BEHIND YOU by Lois Duncan *(Delacorte)*
1993
C: THE DEAD MAN IN INDIAN CREEK by Mary Downing Hahn *(Clarion)*
I: DOLPHIN ADVENTURE by Wayne Grover *(Morrow)*
Y/A: SNIPER by Theodore Taylor *(Harcourt)*
1994
C: JEREMY THATCHER, DRAGON HATCHER by Bruce Coville *(Harcourt)*
I: STEPHEN BIESTY'S INCREDIBLE CROSS-SECTIONS by Richard Platt *(Knopf)*
Y/A: THE TRUE CONFESSIONS OF CHARLOTTE DOYLE by Avi *(Orchard)*

1995
C: THE GHOSTS OF MERCY MANOR by Betty Ren Wright *(Scholastic)*
I: SADAKO by Eleanor Coerr *(Putnam)*
Y/A: AMAZING GRACIE by A.E. Cannon *(Delacorte)*

VERMONT
Dorothy Canfield Fisher Children's Book Award ❧

Dorothy Canfield Fisher (1879-1958) was a long-time Vermont resident whose most notable book for young readers was *Understood Betsy* (1917), a novel first serialized in the magazine *St. Nicholas*. She was best known for her adult work as a member of the editorial selection board of Book-of-the-Month Club from its founding in 1926 until her death, and as a critic, short story writer and translator. The award established in her name was the third of its sort in this country, and modeled on the William Allen White Award program in Kansas, her birth state. At the time of its founding, literature about the program was as spirited as the writer it honored: "Parents and teachers in Vermont know that 'the only thing necessary for the complete triumph of evil is that good men do nothing,' and increasingly they are sending their children to libraries to read good books because they know that this is one of the best preventive medicines for the treatment of juvenile delinquency, as well as reading problems." This awards program is co-sponsored by the Vermont Department of Libraries and the Vermont Parent/Teacher Association, the administrator (109 State St., Montpelier, VT 05609). Children in grades 4-8 select the winner from a master list of thirty titles published two years prior to the award year and compiled by an award committee. (Illuminated scroll)

1957
OLD BONES by Mildred M. Pace *(McGraw-Hill)*
1958
FIFTEEN by Beverly Cleary *(Morrow)*
1959
COMMANCHE OF THE SEVENTH by Margaret Leighton *(Farrar)*
1960
DOUBLE OR NOTHING by Phoebe Erickson *(Harper)*
1961
CAPTAIN GHOST by Thelma Harrington Bell *(Viking)*

1962
THE CITY UNDER THE BACK STEPS by Evelyn Lampman
(Doubleday)
1963
THE INCREDIBLE JOURNEY by Sheila Burnford *(Atlantic-Little, Brown)*
1964
BRISTLE FACE by Zachary Ball *(Holiday House)*
1965
RASCAL by Sterling North *(Dutton)*
1966
RIBSY by Beverly Cleary *(Morrow)*
1967
THE SUMMER I WAS LOST by Phillip Viereck *(John Day)*
1968
THE TASTE OF SPRUCE GUM by Jacqueline Jackson *(Little, Brown)*
1969
TWO IN THE WILDERNESS by Mary W. Thompson *(McKay)*
1970
KAVIK THE WOLF DOG by Walt Morey *(Dutton)*
1971
GO TO THE ROOM OF THE EYES by Betty Erwin *(Little, Brown)*
1972
FLIGHT OF THE WHITE WOLF by Mel Ellis *(Holt)*
1973
NEVER STEAL A MAGIC CAT by Don and Joan Caulfield
(Doubleday)
1974
CATCH A KILLER by George A. Woods *(Harper)*
1975
THE EIGHTEENTH EMERGENCY by Betsy Byars *(Viking)*
1976
THE TOOTHPASTE MILLIONAIRE by Jean Merrill
(Houghton)
1977
A SMART KID LIKE YOU by Stella Pevsner *(Clarion)*
1978
SUMMER OF FEAR by Lois Duncan *(Little, Brown)*
1979
KID POWER by Susan Beth Pfeffer *(Watts)*
1980
BONES ON BLACK SPRUCE MOUNTAIN by David Budbill
(Dial)

1981
BUNNICULA: A RABBIT TALE OF MYSTERY by Deborah and James Howe *(Atheneum)*
1982
THE HAND-ME-DOWN KID by Francine Pascal *(Viking)*
1983
TIGER EYES by Judy Blume *(Bradbury)*
1984
A BUNDLE OF STICKS by Pat Rhoads Mauser *(Atheneum)*
1985
DEAR MR. HENSHAW by Beverly Cleary *(Morrow)*
1986
THE WAR WITH GRANDPA by Robert Kimmel Smith *(Delacorte)*
1987
THE CASTLE IN THE ATTIC by Elizabeth Winthrop *(Holiday House)*
1988
WAIT TILL HELEN COMES: A GHOST STORY by Mary Downing Hahn *(Clarion)*
1989
HATCHET by Gary Paulsen *(Bradbury)*
1990
WHERE IT STOPS NOBODY KNOWS by Amy Ehrlich *(Dial)*
1991
NUMBER THE STARS by Lois Lowry *(Houghton)*
1992
MANIAC MAGEE by Jerry Spinelli *(Little, Brown)*
1993
SHILOH by Phyllis Reynolds Naylor *(Atheneum)*
1994
JENNIFER MURDLEY'S TOAD by Bruce Coville *(Harcourt)*
1995
THE BOGGART by Susan Cooper *(McElderry)*

VIRGINIA
Virginia Young Readers Program ❧

This program was begun to encourage reading for pleasure at the elementary *(E)* level. For the 1984 award year, the contest was at the middle school level *(M)*, and for 1985 at the high school level *(HS)*. All three of these levels were a part of the program for 1986 and 1987. From 1988, a primary level *(P)* has been incorporated, so four awards, primary through high school, are now presented annually. One of the program's objectives is "to broaden students' awareness of literature as a life-long pleasure." The sponsor is the Virginia State Reading Association (address changes with officers), which appoints Young Readers Book Selection Committees to develop nomination lists of 10-15 titles for each level. (Pewter Virginia Cups)

1982
E: ISLAND OF THE BLUE DOLPHINS by Scott O'Dell *(Houghton)*
1983
E: BRIDGE TO TERABITHIA by Katherine Paterson *(Crowell)*
1984
M: THE WESTING GAME by Ellen Raskin *(Dutton)*
1985
HS: THE OUTSIDERS by S. E. Hinton *(Viking)*
1986
E: SUPERFUDGE by Judy Blume *(Dutton)*
M: THE CAT ATE MY GYMSUIT by Paula Danziger *(Delacorte)*
HS: THE THIRD EYE by Mollie Hunter *(Harper)*
1987
E: MY FRIEND THE VAMPIRE by Angela Sommer-Bodenburg *(Dial)*
M: THE CURSE OF THE BLUE FIGURINE by John Bellairs *(Dial)*
HS: THE MAN IN THE WOODS by Rosemary Wells *(Dial)*
1988
P: IN A DARK, DARK ROOM AND OTHER SCARY STORIES by Alvin Schwartz; ill. by Dirk Zimmer *(Harper)*
E: THE INDIAN IN THE CUPBOARD by Lynne Reid Banks *(Doubleday)*
M: THE GHOST IN MY SOUP by Judi Miller *(Bantam)*
HS: IZZY, WILLY-NILLY by Cynthia Voigt *(Atheneum)*
1989
P: HECKEDY PEG by Audrey Wood, ill. by Don Wood *(HBJ)*

E: WAIT TILL HELEN COMES: A GHOST STORY by Mary Downing Hahn *(Clarion)*

M: THE OTHER SIDE OF DARK by Joan Lowery Nixon *(Delacorte)*

HS: THE FACE AT THE EDGE OF THE WORLD by Eve Bunting *(Clarion)*

1990

P: THE MAGIC SCHOOL BUS INSIDE THE EARTH by Joanna Cole, ill. by Bruce Degen *(Scholastic)*

E: CHRISTINA'S GHOST by Betty Ren Wright *(Holiday House)*

M: HATCHET by Gary Paulsen *(Bradbury)*

HS: WOLF RIDER: A TALE OF TERROR by Avi *(Bradbury)*

1991

P: TWO BAD ANTS by Chris Van Allsburg *(Houghton)*

E: MATILDA by Roald Dahl *(Viking)*

M: GOOD NIGHT, MR. TOM by Michelle Magorian *(Harper)*

HS: SAY GOODNIGHT, GRACIE by Julie Rice Deaver *(Harper)*

1992

P: THE GREAT WHITE MAN-EATING SHARK: A CAUTIONARY TALE by Margaret Mahy, ill. by Jonathan Allen *(Dial)*

E: THE DOLL IN THE GARDEN: A GHOST STORY by Mary Downing Hahn *(Avon)*

M: A FAMILY APART by Joan Lowery Nixon *(Bantam)*

HS: DON'T LOOK BEHIND YOU by Lois Duncan *(Delacorte)*

1993

P: THE TALKING EGGS: A FOLKTALE FROM THE AMERICAN SOUTH retold by Robert D. San Souci, ill. by Jerry Pinkney *(Dial)*

E: EXPLORING THE TITANIC by Robert D. Ballard *(Scholastic)*

M: MANIAC MAGEE by Jerry Spinelli *(Little, Brown)*

HS: PLAGUE YEAR by Stephanie Tolan *(Morrow)*

1994

PL BEWARE OF BOYS by Tony Blundell *(Greenwillow)*

E: TEN KIDS, NO PETS by Ann M. Martin *(Holiday House)*

M: THE DEAD MAN IN INDIAN CREEK by Mary Downing Hahn *(Clarion)*

HS: HOW COULD YOU DO IT, DIANE? by Stella Pevsner *(Clarion)*

1995

P: THE ROUGH-FACE GIRL by Rafe Martin, ill. by David Shannon *(Putnam)*

E: GHOST CADET by Elaine Alphin *(Holt)*

M: FLIGHT #116 IS DOWN by Caroline B. Cooney *(Scholastic)*

HS: JUMPING THE NAIL by Eve Bunting *(Harcourt)*

WASHINGTON
Washington Children's Choice Picture Book Award 🐾

Sponsored by the Washington Library Media Association (c/o P.O. Box 1413, Bothell, WA 98011), this award is for a picture book—fiction or nonfiction—selected by children in grades K-3 from a ballot list of twenty titles compiled by an award committee. Titles on the ballot have been published in a 3-4-year period prior to the award year. (Engraved Wilton Armatale pewter plate)

1982
CROSS-COUNTRY CAT by Mary Calhoun, ill. by Erick Ingraham *(Morrow)*
1983
SPACE CASE by Edward Marshall, ill. by James Marshall *(Dial)*
1984
JUMANJI by Chris Van Allsburg *(Houghton)*
1985
NIMBY by Jasper Tomkins *(Green Tiger)*
1986
THE UNICORN AND THE LAKE by Marianna Mayer, ill. by Michael Hague *(Dial)*
1987
IN A DARK, DARK ROOM AND OTHER SCARY STORIES by Alvin Schwartz, ill. by Dirk Zimmer *(Harper)*
1988
KING BIDGOOD'S IN THE BATHTUB by Audrey Wood, ill. by Don Wood *(HBJ)*
1989
THE MAGIC SCHOOL BUS AT THE WATERWORKS by Joanna Cole, ill. by Bruce Degen *(Scholastic)*
1990
AMOS: THE STORY OF AN OLD DOG AND HIS COUCH by Howie Schneider and Susan Seligson, ill by Howie Schneider *(Little, Brown)*
1991
TWO BAD ANTS by Chris Van Allsburg *(Houghton)*
1992
HERSHEL AND THE HANUKKAH GOBLINS by Eric Kimmel, ill. by Trina Schart Hyman *(Holiday House)*
1993
THE GREAT WHITE MAN-EATING SHARK: A CAUTIONARY TALE by Margaret Mahy, ill. by Jonathan Allen *(Dial)*

1994
THE DOG WHO HAD KITTENS by Polly M. Robertus, ill. by Janet Stevens *(Holiday House)*
1995
TIGER by Judy Allen, ill. by Tudor Humphries *(Candlewick)*

WEST VIRGINIA
West Virginia Children's Book Award ❧

The purpose of this awards program is "to enrich the lives of children in grades 3 through 6 by encouraging the reading of books of literary quality. The award provides a personal relationship and interaction between authors and readers in order to increase children's enjoyment of books. . . [the award] is a celebration of children, books, and authors." A master list of titles — all fiction — is compiled by an award committee (WVCBA, c/o Reading Center, P.O. Box 6122, Morgantown, WV 26506) that considers "literary excellence" and "appropriateness" in assembling the list. Books are by living authors and have been published in a three-year period before the award year. Participating schools pay a modest ten dollar registration fee to help to defray postage and materials costs. (West Virginia-crafted artifact)

1985
JUMANJI by Chris Van Allsburg *(Houghton)*
1986
MUSTARD by Charlotte Towner Graeber *(Macmillan)*
1987
RALPH S. MOUSE by Beverly Cleary *(Morrow)*
1988
HERBIE JONES by Suzy Kline *(Putnam)*
1989
CLASS CLOWN by Johanna Hurwitz *(Morrow)*
1990
FUDGE by Charlotte Towner Graeber *(Lothrop)*
1991
THERE'S A BOY IN THE GIRLS' BATHROOM by Louis Sachar *(Knopf)*
1992
MATILDA by Roald Dahl *(Viking Kestrel)*

1993
MANIAC MAGEE by Jerry Spinelli *(Little, Brown)*
1994
SHILOH by Phyllis Reynolds Naylor *(Atheneum)*
1995
TAXI CAT AND HUEY by Gen LeRoy *(HarperCollins)*

WISCONSIN
Golden Archer Awards 🏹

This award program has been inactive since 1992 and is now
sponsored by the Wisconsin Educational Media Association
(1300 Industrial Dr., Fennimore, WI 35809). The Little Archer
Award *(LA)* has been discontinued but The Golden Archer
Award *(GA)* is now given at three different grade levels: Primary
(P), Intermediate *(I)*, and Middle/Junior High *(M/JH)*. Initial
nominations are made by children and submitted by their school
librarians to the Archer Awards Committee. The ten most
popular titles at each level are compiled into competitive lists
from which the winners are chosen by a vote of the children. The
competition is open to all the schools in the state who wish to
participates. The program takes its name in part from one of the
award founders, children's book writer Marian Fuller Archer,
and in part from the words of the archer in Longfellow's verse, "I
shot an arrow into the air,/It fell to earth, I know not where..."
(Brass medallion and certificate in each category)

1974
GA: Judy Blume
1975
GA: Thomas Rockwell
1976
GA: Florence Parry Heide
LA: THE FUNNY LITTLE WOMAN retold by Arlene Mosel,
ill. by Blair Lent *(Dutton)*
1977
GA: Beverly Cleary
LA: Bill Peet
1978
GA: Scott Corbett
LA: Peter Spier
1979
GA: Wilson Rawls
LA: Lorna Balian

1980
GA: Nat Hentoff
LA: CROSS-COUNTRY CAT by Mary Calhoun, ill. by Erick Ingraham *(Morrow)*
1981
GA: Betsy Byars
LA: Steven Kellogg
1982
GA: Beverly Butler
LA: Eileen Christelow
1983
GA: S. E. Hinton
LA: William Steig
1984
GA: NOTHING'S FAIR IN FIFTH GRADE by Barthe DeClements *(Viking)*
LA: THE BUTTER BATTLE BOOK by Dr. Seuss *(Random)*
1985
GA: TORNADO! by Hilary H. Milton *(Watts)*
LA: WHAT'S UNDER MY BED? by James Stevenson *(Greenwillow)*
1986
GA: WHALESONG by Robert Siegel *(Good News)*
LA: THE POLAR EXPRESS by Chris Van Allsburg *(Houghton)*
1987
GA: THE WHIPPING BOY by Sid Fleischman *(Greenwillow)*
LA: KING BIDGOOD'S IN THE BATHTUB by Audrey Wood, ill. by Don Wood *(HBJ)*
1988
GA: ON MY HONOR by Marion Dane Bauer *(Clarion)*
LA: HEY, AL by Arthur Yorinks, ill. by Richard Egielski *(Farrar)*
1989
GA: HATCHET by Gary Paulsen *(Bradbury)*
LA: UNDERWEAR! by Mary Monsell, ill. by Lynn Munsinger *(Whitman)*
1990
GA: NUMBER THE STARS by Lois Lowry *(Houghton)*
LA: THE TUB PEOPLE by Pam Conrad, ill. by Richard Egielski *(Harper)*
1991
GA: MANIAC MAGEE by Jerry Spinelli *(Little, Brown)*
LA: BORREGUITA AND THE COYOTE by Verna Aardema *(Knopf)*
1992
GA: SHILOH by Phyllis Reynolds Naylor *(Atheneum)*
LA: EASTER EGG FARM by Mary J. Auch *(Holiday House)*

1993-1995
No Awards
1996
P: JUMANJI by Chris Van Allsburg *(Houghton)*
I: WHERE THE SIDEWALK ENDS by Shel Silverstein
(HarperCollins)
M/JH: THE GIVER by Lois Lowry *(Houghton)*

WYOMING
Indian Paintbrush Book Award 🦃

Fifteen titles constitute the candidates for this award each year.
Selection of the nominees is entirely by children in grades 4-6;
the books must be fiction and have been published within a five
year period before being nominated. The sponsor is the Wyoming
Library Association (c/o Executive Secretary, P. O. Box 1387,
Cheyenne, WY 82003). (Plaque and painting)

1986
NAYA NUKI: THE GIRL WHO RAN by Kenneth Thomasma
(Baker Book House)
1987
THE HOT AND COLD SUMMER by Johanna Hurwitz
(Morrow)
1988
THE DOLLHOUSE MURDERS by Betty Ren Wright *(Holiday House)*
1989
THE RETURN OF THE INDIAN by Lynne Reid Banks
(Doubleday)
1990
THERE'S A BOY IN THE GIRLS' BATHROOM by Louis
Sachar *(Knopf)*
1991
MATILDA by Roald Dahl *(Viking)*
1992
MANIAC MAGEE by Jerry Spinelli *(Little, Brown)*
1993
PATHKI NANA: KOOTENAI GIRL by Kenneth Thomasma
(Grandview)
1994
SHILOH by Phyllis Reynolds Naylor *(Atheneum)*
1995
RESCUE JOSH McGUIRE by Ben Mikaelsen *(Hyperion)*

1996
MOHOWAT by Kenneth Thomasma *(Baker Book House)*

WYOMING
Soaring Eagle Award 🦅

Young readers suggest the nominees for this award given by
voters in grades *7-12*. (Prior to 1992, awards were given in two
grade ranges, 7-9 and 10-12.) An adult committee verifies that
the fifteen nominations have received at least two positive
reviews. The sponsors are the school section of Library Media
Personnel, a sub-division of the Wyoming Library Association
and the Wyoming Council for the International Reading
Association. Administrative responsibilities are managed by
Leanne Woodfill Dean Morgan Junior High School (1970 N.
Glenn Rd., Casper, WY 82601). (Bookends with stained glass
depiction of soaring eagle)

1989
7-9: SUPERFUDGE by Judy Blume *(Dutton)*
1990
7-9: SOMEONE IS HIDING ON ALCATRAZ ISLAND by Eve
Bunting *(Clarion)*
10-12: OF LOVE AND SHADOWS by Isabel Allende *(Knopf)*
1991
7-9: TRAPPED IN DEATH CAVE by Bill Wallace *(Holiday
House)*
10-12: PRINCESS ASHLEY by Richard Peck *(Delacorte)*
1992
DANCES WITH WOLVES by Michael Blake *(Fawcett)*
1993
HUGH GLASS, MOUNTAIN MAN by Robert McClung
(Morrow)
1994
DESPERATE PURSUIT by Gloria Miklowitz *(Starfire/Bantam)*
1995
JURASSIC PARK by Michael Crichton *(Ballantine)*
1996
WHISPERS FROM THE DEAD by Joan Lowery Nixon *(Dell)*

Australian, Canadian, New Zealand, and United Kingdom (UK) Awards

AUSTRALIA
Australian Book Publishers Association Book Design Awards ❧
SCHOLASTIC AWARD

As of 1987, the Australian Book Publishers Association (ABPA) Book Design Awards program—which had until then judged children's books annually with all other books as a group—established a series of sponsored book design awards in several categories, one of them for the "best designed illustrated children's book," sponsored by the publisher Scholastic (known as Ashton Scholastic until 1995). ABPA is at Suite 60, Level 3, 89 Jones St. Ultimo, Sydney, NSW 2007, Australia. The listing below is the publication year; the awards are decided on in the following year. (Exhibition and illustrated catalog)

1986
KOJURO AND THE BEARS by Junko Morimoto, designed by Deborah Brash *(Collins/Angus & Robertson)*

1987
DEREK THE DINOSAUR by Mary Blackwood, ill. and designed by Kerry Argent *(Omnibus)*

1988
ROSIE SIPS SPIDERS by Alison Lester, designed by Alison Lester *(Oxford)*

1989
THE STORY OF A FALLING STAR by Elsie Jones, ill. by Doug Jones, designed by Karin Donaldson and Maureen MacKenzie *(Aboriginal Studies Press)*

1990
MAGIC BEACH by Alison Lester, designed by Alison Lester and Sandra Nobes *(Allen & Unwin/Little Ark Books)*

1991
A BIT OF COMPANY by Margaret Wild, designed by Wayne Harris *(Ashton Scholastic)*

1992
SPOONER OR LATER by Paul Jennings and Ted Greenwood, designed by Cathy van Ee and Terry Denton *(Viking)*

1983
V FOR VANISHING by Patricia Mullins, designed by Patricia Mullins and Margaret Hamilton *(Margaret Hamilton Books)*
1994
POWER AND GLORY by Emily Rodda, designed by Tou-Can Design *(Allen & Unwin)*

Australian Multicultural Children's Literature Awards ❧

Inaugurated in 1991 by the Office of Multicultural Affairs (Department of the Prime Minister and Cabinet, Canberra, ACT 2600, Australia), this annual award is for books with "a multicultural theme which focuses on aspects and values of a multicultural society, for example, cultural diversity, community relations and social harmony, or social justice." Books are only eligible if they have been entered for the Children's Books of the Year Awards administered by The Children's Book Council of Australia. The Council provides titles of multicultural interest from which a short list and winners are selected. Awards are given in three categories: senior *(S)*, junior *(J)*, and picture books *(PB)*. For 1991, only a picture book was honored. ($5,000 in each category; if illustrator is not the author in the picture book category, an additional $5,000 to illustrator)

1991
PB: THE RAINBOW SERPENT by Elaine Sharpe, ill. by Jennifer Inkamala *(Yipirinya School Council)*
1992
S: THE CHINA COIN by Allan Baillie *(Penguin)*
J: DO NOT GO AROUND THE EDGES by Daisy Utemorrah *(Magabala Books)*
PB: BIG DOG by Libby Gleeson, ill. by Armin Greder *(Ashton Scholastic)*
1993
S: LOOKING FOR ALIBRANDI by Melina Marchetta *(Penguin)*
J: THE FAT AND JUICY PLACE by Diana Kidd *(Collins/Angus & Robertson)*
PB: MR. PLUNKETT'S POOL by Gillian Rubinstein, ill. by Terry Denton *(Random)*
1994
S: TOMORROW, WHEN THE WAR BEGAN by John Marsden *(Pan Macmillan)*
J: METIS, THE OCTOPUS AND THE OLIVE TREE by Jena Woodhouse *(Jam Roll Press/University of Queensland Press)*

PB: AS I GREW OLDER: THE LIFE AND TIMES OF A
NUNGA GROWING UP ALONG THE RIVER MURRAY by
Ian Abdulla *(Omnibus)*
1995
S. GRACEY by James Moloney *(University of Queensland Press)*
J: LISDALIA by Brian Caswell *(University of Queensland Press)*
PB: PRINCESS GRANDMA by Jenni Overend, ill. by Naomi C.
Lewis *(Scholastic)*

Books I Love Best
Yearly (BILBY) Awards ❧

"The aim of the BILBY Awards is to promote books for young
people to read and to give publicity to the books that appeal to
young people." The bilby is a rare species of bandicoot, a small
marsupial with long floppy ears as on a rabbit. Established by
the Queensland Branch of The Children's Book Council of
Australia (P. O. Box 484, Moorooka, Queensland 4105,
Australia), awards — chosen by children — are in categories which
vary somewhat from year to year depending on the schools which
participate. Publishers are indicated where books are Australian.
(Contace: Jenny Stubbs, 43 John St., Rosewood 4340.)
(Certificates and honoraria)

1990
Read Alone (Primary): SUPERFUDGE by Judy Blume
Read Alone (Secondary): THE SECRET DIARY OF ADRIAN
MOLE, AGED 13 3/4 by Sue Townsend
Read Aloud (P-12): MATILDA by Roald Dahl
1991
Read Alone (Primary): THE BFG by Roald Dahl
Read Alone (Secondary): THE OUTSIDERS by S. E. Hinton
Read Aloud (P-12): THE BFG by Roald Dahl
1992
Read Alone (Primary): UNREAL! EIGHT SURPRISING
STORIES by Paul Jennings *(Penguin)*
Read Alone (Secondary): WHERE'S WALLY? by Martin
Handford *(Walker)*
Read Aloud (P-12): CHARLIE AND THE CHOCOLATE
FACTORY by Roald Dahl
1993
Read Alone (Primary): THE WITCHES by Roald Dahl
Read Alone (Secondary): FLOWERS IN THE ATTIC by Virginia
Andrews

Read Aloud (P-12): BLABBER MOUTH by Morris Gleitzman *(Pan Macmillan)*
1994
Read Alone: UNDONE! MORE MAD ENDINGS by Paul Jennings *(Penguin)*
Read Aloud: FANTASTIC MR. FOX by Roald Dahl
Read Australian: MIDNITE: THE STORY OF A WILD COLONIAL BOY by Randolph Stow *(Macdonald)*
1995
Read Alone: THE LION KING by Gina Ingoglio
Read Aloud: THE PAGEMASTER by David Kirschner
Read Australian: THE WATERTOWER by Gary Crew and Steven Woolman *(Era)*
Young Adult: LOOKING FOR ALIBRANDI by Melina Marchetta *(Penguin)*

Children's Books of the Year Awards 🏵

This awards program for Australian children's books began in 1946. It was administered by a number of agencies until the Children's Book Council of Australia became responsible for it in 1959. The Council is composed of branches in Australian states and the territories, with its administrative functions handled among the states on a biennial basis. (1996 contact: Lyn Linning, 18 Emperor St., Brisbane, 4103, Australia; 1997-98 contact: Val van Putten, 104 Beulah Rd., Norwood 5067, Australia). Awards are currently given in four categories. The Eve Pownall Award for Information Books was instituted in 1993 to honor outstanding books documenting factual material with consideration to imaginative presentation, interpretation, and variation of style. All awards are for literary merit. Normally, short lists of up to six books in each category are released in April and one winner and two honour books from each short list are announced in August. (Authors and illustrators of winning books receive a medallion. There is usually $10,000 prize money per category—$6,000 for the winning book, $2,000 for each honor book. All short-listed authors and illustrators receive a certificate.)

BOOK OF THE YEAR: OLDER READERS
1946
THE STORY OF KARRAWINGI THE EMU by Leslie Rees *(Sands)*
1947
No Award

1948
SHACKLETON'S ARGONAUTS by Frank Hurley *(Angus & Robertson)*

1949
No Competition

1950
WHALERS OF THE MIDNIGHT SUN by Alan Villiers *(Angus & Robertson)*

1951
VERITY OF SYDNEY TOWN by Ruth Williams *(Angus & Robertson)*

1952
THE AUSTRALIA BOOK by Eve Pownall *(Sands)*

1953
AIRCRAFT OF TODAY & TOMORROW by J. H. and W. D. Martin *(Angus & Robertson)*
GOOD LUCK TO THE RIDER by Joan Phipson *(Angus & Robertson)*

1954
AUSTRALIAN LEGENDARY TALES by K. L. Parker *(Angus & Robertson)*

1955
THE FIRST WALKABOUT by H. A. Lindsay and N. B. Tindale *(Kestrel)*

1956
THE CROOKED SNAKE by Patricia Wrightson *(Angus & Robertson)*

1957
THE BOOMERANG BOOK OF LEGENDARY TALES by Enid Moodie-Heddle *(Kestrel)*

1958
TIGER IN THE BUSH by Nan Chauncy *(Oxford)*

1959
DEVIL'S HILL by Nan Chauncy *(Oxford)*
SEA MENACE by John Gunn *(Constable)*

1960
ALL THE PROUD TRIBESMEN by Kylie Tennant *(Macmillan)*

1961
TANGARA by Nan Chauncy *(Oxford)*

1962
THE RACKETTY STREET GANG by H. L. Evers *(Hodder & Stoughton)*
RAFFERTY RIDES A WINNER by Joan Woodbery *(Parrish)*

1963
THE FAMILY CONSPIRACY by Joan Phipson *(Angus & Robertson)*

1964
THE GREEN LAUREL by Eleanor Spence *(Oxford)*
1965
PASTURES OF THE BLUE CRANE by Hesba F. Brinsmead *(Oxford)*
1966
ASH ROAD by Ivan Southall *(Angus & Robertson)*
1967
THE MIN MIN by Mavis Thorpe Clark *(Landsdowne)*
1968
TO THE WILD SKY by Ivan Southall *(Angus & Robertson)*
1969
WHEN JAYS FLY TO BARBMO by Margaret Balderson *(Oxford)*
1970
UHU by Annette Macarthur-Onslow *(Ure Smith)*
1971
BREAD AND HONEY by Ivan Southall *(Angus & Robertson)*
1972
LONGTIME PASSING by Hesba F. Brinsmead *(Angus & Robertson)*
1973
FAMILY AT THE LOOKOUT by Noreen Shelly *(Oxford)*
1974
THE NARGUN AND THE STARS by Patricia Wrightson *(Hutchinson)*
1975
No Award
1976
FLY WEST by Ivan Southall *(Angus & Robertson)*
1977
THE OCTOBER CHILD by Eleanor Spence *(Oxford)*
1978
THE ICE IS COMING by Patricia Wrightson *(Hutchinson)*
1979
THE PLUM-RAIN SCROLL by Ruth Manley *(Hodder & Stoughton)*
1980
DISPLACED PERSON by Lee Harding *(Hyland House)*
1981
PLAYING BEATIE BOW by Ruth Park *(Nelson)*
1982
THE VALLEY BETWEEN by Colin Thiele *(Rigby)*
1983
MASTER OF THE GROVE by Victor Kelleher *(Penguin)*

1984
A LITTLE FEAR by Patricia Wrightson *(Hutchinson)*
1985
THE TRUE STORY OF LILLI STUBECK by James Aldridge *(Hyland House)*
1986
THE GREEN WIND by Thurley Fowler *(Rigby)*
1987
ALL WE KNOW by Simon French *(Angus & Robertson)*
1988
SO MUCH TO TELL YOU by John Marsden *(Walter McVitty)*
1989
BEYOND THE LABYRINTH by Gillian Rubinstein *(Hyland House)*
1990
CAME BACK TO SHOW YOU I COULD FLY by Robin Klein *(Viking Kestrel)*
1991
STRANGE OBJECTS by Gary Crew *(Heinemann)*
1992
THE HOUSE GUEST by Eleanor Nilsson *(Penguin)*
1993
LOOKING FOR ALIBRANDI by Melina Marchetta *(Penguin)*
1994
THE GATHERING by Isobelle Carmody *(Penguin)*
ANGEL'S GATE by Gary Crew *(Heinemann)*
1995
FOXSPELL by Gillian Rubinstein *(Hyland House)*

BOOK OF THE YEAR: YOUNGER READERS
1982
RUMMAGE by Christobel Mattingley, ill. by Patricia Mullins *(Angus & Robertson)*
1983
THING by Robin Klein, ill. by Alison Lester *(Oxford)*
1984
BERNICE KNOWS BEST by Max Dann, ill. by Ann James *(Oxford)*
1985
SOMETHING SPECIAL by Emily Rodda, ill. by Noela Young *(Angus & Robertson)*
1986
ARKWRIGHT by Mary Steele *(Hyland House)*
1987
PIGS MIGHT FLY by Emily Rodda, ill. by Noela Young *(Angus & Robertson)*

1988
MY PLACE by Nadia Wheatley, ill by Donna Rawlins *(Collins Dove)*
1989
THE BEST-KEPT SECRET by Emily Rodda *(Angus & Robertson)*
1990
PIGS AND HONEY by Jeanie Adams *(Omnibus)*
1991
FINDERS KEEPERS by Emily Rodda *(Omnibus)*
1992
THE MAGNIFICENT NOSE AND OTHER MARVELS by Anna Fienberg *(Allen & Unwin)*
1993
THE BAMBOO FLUTE by Garry Disher *(Collins/Angus & Robertson)*
1994
ROWAN OF RIN by Emily Rodda *(Omnibus)*
1995
ARK IN THE PARK by Wendy Orr, ill. by Kerry Millard *(HarperCollins)*

PICTURE BOOK OF THE YEAR
1956
WISH AND THE MAGIC NUT by Peggy Barnard, ill. by Sheila Hawkins *(Sands)*
1957
No Award
1958
PICCANINNY WALKABOUT by Axel Poignant *(Angus & Robertson)*
1959-1964
No Awards
1965
HUGO'S ZOO by Elisabeth MacIntyre *(Angus & Robertson)*
1966-1968
No Awards
1969
SLY OLD WARDROBE by Ivan Southall, ill. by Ted Greenwood *(Cheshire)*
1970
No Award
1971
WALTZING MATILDA by A. B. Paterson, ill. by Desmond Digby *(Collins)*

1972-1973
No Awards

1974
THE BUNYIP OF BERKELEY'S CREEK by Jenny Wagner, ill. by Ron Brooks *(Kestrel)*

1975
THE MAN FROM IRONBARK by A.B. Paterson, ill. by Quentin Hole *(Collins)*

1976
THE RAINBOW SERPENT by Dick Roughsey *(Collins)*

1977
No Award

1978
JOHN BROWN, ROSE AND THE MIDNIGHT CAT by Jenny Wagner, ill. by Ron Brooks *(Kestrel)*

1979
THE QUINKINS written and ill. by Percy Trezise and Dick Roughsey *(Collins)*

1980
ONE DRAGON'S DREAM by Peter Pavey *(Nelson)*

1981
No Award

1982
SUNSHINE by Jan Ormerod *(Kestrel)*

1983
WHO SANK THE BOAT? by Pamela Allen *(Nelson)*

1984
BERTIE AND THE BEAR by Pamela Allen *(Nelson)*

1985
No Award

1986
FELIX & ALEXANDER by Terry Denton *(Oxford)*

1987
KOJURO AND THE BEARS adapted by Helen Smith, ill. by Junko Morimoto *(Collins)*

1988
CRUSHER IS COMING by Bob Graham *(Lothian)*

1989
DRAC AND THE GREMLIN by Allan Baillie, ill by Jane Tanner *(Viking Kestrel)*
THE ELEVENTH HOUR by Graeme Base *(Viking Kestrel)*

1990
THE VERY BEST OF FRIENDS by Margaret Wild, ill. by Julie Vivas *(Margaret Hamilton)*

1991
GREETINGS FROM SANDY BEACH by Bob Graham *(Lothian)*

1992
WINDOW by Jeannie Baker *(Julia MacRae)*
1993
ROSE MEETS MR. WINTERGARTEN by Bob Graham
(Penguin)
1994
FIRST LIST by Gary Crew, ill. by Peter Gouldthorpe *(Lothian)*
1995
THE WATERTOWER by Gary Crew, ill. by Steven Woolman
(Era)

EVE POWNALL AWARD FOR INFORMATION BOOKS

1993
TJARANY ROUGHTAIL: THE DREAMING OF THE
ROUGHTAIL LIZARD AND OTHER STORIES TOLD BY
THE KUKATJA by Gracie Greene and Joe Tramacchi, ill. by
Lucille Gill *(Magabala Books)*
1994
V FOR VANISHING: AN ALPHABET OF ENDANGERED
ANIMALS by Patricia Mullins *(Margaret Hamilton Books)*
1995
NEW FACES: THE COMPLETE BOOK OF ALTERNATIVE
PETS by Robin E. Stewart *(Agmedia)*

Children's Peace Literature Award ❧

The award program is for authors who are Australian or
normally resident in Australia, and whose books considered for
the award promote the peaceful resolution of conflict. The
sponsor, Psychologists for the Prevention of War (4 Blyth St.,
Glen Osmond, South Australia 5064), a special interest group of
the Australian Psychological Society, states, "We believe that
literature has a significant influence on children's attitudes and
behaviour...we wish to support and encourage authors whose
work promotes peace and the understanding of others." The
award is given biennially; a short list of under a dozen
worthwhile titles is disseminated before a winner is selected.
($2,000)

1987
SPACE DEMONS by Gillian Rubinstein *(Omnibus)*
1989
THE MAKERS by Victor Kelleher *(Viking Kestrel)*

1991
DODGER by Libby Gleeson *(Turton & Chambers)*
1993
THE GATHERING by Isobelle Carmody *(Penguin)*
ROSE MEETS MR. WINTERGARTEN by Bob Graham
(Penguin)
1995
DEUCALION by Brian Caswell *(University of Queensland Press)*

Crichton Award

The award is for achievement in an illustrator's first major published work for children. To be eligible, the illustrator must be an Australian citizen or have resided in Australia for five yers prior to the award year. It is sponsored by the Victorian Branch of the Children's Book Council (P. O. Box 275, Carlton South 3053, Vic., Australia). (Certificate and $1,000)

1988
PHEASANT AND KINGFISHER by Catherine Berndt, ill. by Raymond Meeks *(Martin Educational)*
1989
AUSTRALIAN DINOSAURS by Marilyn Pride *(Collins)*
1990
PIGS AND HONEY by Jeanie Adams *(Omnibus)*
1991
BIP: THE SNAPPING BUNGAROO by Narelle McRobbie, ill. by Grace Fielding *(Magabala)*
1992
THE MAGNIFICENT NOSE AND OTHER MARVELS by Anna Fienberg, ill. by Kim Ganmble (Allen & Unwin)
1993
ALITJI IN DREAMLAND by Nancy Sheppard, ill. by Donna Leslie *(Simon & Schuster)*
1994
IS IT TRUE, GRANDFATHER? by Wendy Lohse, ill. by Jenny Sands
1995
I WISH I'D GONE TO THE MOON WITH NEIL ARMSTRONG by Leonie Young and Avril Janks, ill. by Astri Baker *(Weldon Kids)*
POWER AND GLORY by Emily Rodda, ill. by Geoff Kelly *(Allen & Unwin)*

Family Award ❧

The award is for a novel that contains a "realistic and balanced depiction of family life according to what are known to be the characteristics of a healthy family." "Healthy" refers to emotional and psychological health. The year in the listing is the book's publication year; the award is presented during Children's Book Week of the following year. In 1996, an additional award will be given to the best picture book entry published in 1995, the criteria for which are the same as for the novel. The awards are sponsored by the New South Wales Family Therapy Association, the Queensland Association of Family Therapists, and the Victorian Association of Family Therapists. (Contact: Julia Griffith, 142 Greville St., Chatswood, NSW 2067, Australia) ($1,000 in each category)

1987
DEEZLE BOY by Eleanor Spence *(Collins Dove)*
1988
YOU TAKE THE HIGH ROAD by Mary K. Pershall *(Penguin)*
1989
THE BLUE CHAMELEON by Katherine Scholes *(Hill of Content)*
1990
TWO WEEKS WITH THE QUEEN by Morris Gleitzman *(Pan)*
1991
CHANGE THE LOCKS by Simon French *(Ashton Scholastic)*
1992
CROSSFIRE by James Moloney *(University of Queensland Press)*
1993
DOUGY by James Moloney *(University of Queensland Press)*
1994
FRACTURE ZONE by Jonathan Harlen *(Omnibus)*

Kids Own Australian Literature Awards (KOALA) ❧

Each year children in the State of New South Wales (NSW) have the opportunity to nominate their favorite Australian books — fiction, poetry, plays, picture books, or myths and legends — for the KOALA Awards. Two shortlists of about thirty titles each in Primary *(P)* and Secondary *(S)* categories are distributed to participating institutions throughout the state, and children vote for the winners from those lists. The program is administered by an all-volunteer KOALA Council that does not have a permanent mailing address. The award was initiated as a joint undertaking of NSW branches of the Schools and Children's Sections of the Library Association, Children's Book Council, Australian Reading Association, English Teachers Association, Primary English Teachers Association, School Library Association, and Australian Book Publishers Association. (Certificate)

1987
P: POSSUM MAGIC by Mem Fox, ill. by Julie Vivas *(Omnibus)*
S: HATING ALISON ASHLEY by Robin Klein *(Puffin)*
1988
P: SISTER MADGE'S BOOK OF NUNS by Doug McLeod, ill. by Craig Smith *(Omnibus)*
S: ANIMALIA by Graeme Base *(Viking Kestrel)*
One-time only Bicentennial Award: THE COMPLETE ADVENTURES OF SNUGGLEPOT AND CUDDLEPIE by May Gibbs *(Angus & Robertson)*
1989
P: THE ELEVENTH HOUR by Graeme Base *(Viking Kestrel)*
S: SO MUCH TO TELL YOU by John Marsden *(Walter McVitty)*
1990
P: WHERE THE FOREST MEETS THE SEA by Jeannie Baker *(Julia MacRae)*
S: UNREAL! EIGHT SURPRISING STORIES by Paul Jennings *(Puffin)*
1991
P: UNBELIEVABLE! MORE SURPRISING STORIES by Paul Jennings *(Penguin)*
S: THE RED KING by Victor Kelleher *(Penguin)*
1992
P: UNMENTIONABLE! MORE AMAZING STORIES by Paul Jennings *(Penguin)*
S: PEOPLE MIGHT HEAR YOU by Robin Klein *(Penguin)*
1993
P: UNBEARABLE. MORE BIZZARE STORIES by Paul Jennings *(Penguin)*
S: LOOKING FOR ALIBRANDI by Melina Marchetta *(Penguin)*
1994
P: UNDONE! MORE MAD ENDINGS by Paul Jennings *(Penguin)*
S: THE POWER OF ONE by Bryce Courtenay *(Reed)*
1995
P: DUCK FOR COVER by Paul Jennings, Ted Greenwood, and Terry Denton *(Penguin)*
S: TOMORROW, WHEN THE WAR BEGAN by John Marsden *(Pan Macmillan)*

Kids Reading Oz Choice (KROC) Awards ଚ୍ଚ

Initially administered by the Northern Territory Library Service, this children's choice award began as one of a number of projects undertaken to celebrate the "Reading 1990" initiative. The award gives young readers the opportunity to vote for their favorite Australian book. Relevant publicity and voting cards are distributed to all public and school libraries throughout the Northern Territory. Voting cards must be signed by librarians as verification that the books have been read. All votes are then counted, and an overall winner is announced during Children's Book Week. In 1995, responsibility and funding for the program was assumed by the Darwin Public Library and Information Service (GPO Box 84, Darwin, NT 0801, Australia). Additional funding is provided by the School Libraries Association of Northern Territory (SLANT) and the Children's Book Council of Australia (NT Branch). (Certificate)

1990
UNCANNY! by Paul Jennings *(Penguin)*
1991
UNBELIEVABLE! MORE SURPRISING STORIES by Paul Jennings *(Penguin)*
1992
UNREAL! EIGHT SURPRISING STORIES by Paul Jennings *(Penguin)*
1993
UNDONE! MORE MAD ENDINGS by Paul Jennings *(Penguin)*
1994
UNDONE! MORE MAD ENDINGS by Paul Jennings *(Penguin)*
1995
THE GIZMO by Paul Jennings *(Penguin)*

National Children's Literature Award ଚ୍ଚ

The National Children's Literature Award is part of the biennial Festival Awards for Literature given since 1986 to Australian authors, or authors resident in Australia, in five categories: Fiction, Poetry, Children's Literature, Nonfiction, and Playwrighting. Independent panels of three judges select the winners, with award presentations made during Writers Week of the Adelaide Festival. The program is administered by the Awards Secretariat, Department for the Arts and Cultural Development (GPO Box 2308, Adelaide, South Australia 5001). ($12,000)

1986
THE LONG NIGHT WATCH by Ivan Southall *(Methuen)*
1988
SPACE DEMONS by Gillian Rubinstein *(Omnibus/Puffin)*
1990
BEYOND THE LABYRINTH by Gillian Rubinstein *(Hyland House)*
1992
THE HOUSE GUEST by Eleanor Nilsson *(Viking Penguin)*
1994
ANGEL'S GATE by Gary Crew *(Heinemann)*

New South Wales Premier's Literary Awards ❧
THE ETHEL TURNER PRIZE

Sponsored by The New South Wales Ministry for the Arts (GPO Box 5341, Sydney, NSW, Australia) the Premier's Literary Awards are given in several categories and also include various Prizes. The Ethel Turner Prize "is offered for a work of fiction, nonfiction, or poetry written for children. Works may be nominated by writers, their agents or publishers. In the case of books containing original illustrations, the judging committee may determine that the award be shared by the writer and illustrator." ($15,000 and medallion)

1979
JOHN BROWN, ROSE AND THE MIDNIGHT CAT by Jenny Wagner *(Kestrel)*
1980
MR. ARCHIMEDES BATH by Pamela Allen *(Collins)*
1981
WHEN THE WIND CHANGED by Ruth Park and Deborah Niland *(Collins)*
1982
WHISTLE UP THE CHIMNEY by Nan Hunt and Craig Smith *(Collins)*
1983
WHO SANK THE BOAT? by Pamela Allen *(Nelson)*

1984
POSSUM MAGIC by Mem Fox and Julie Vivas *(Omnibus)*
1985
THE HOUSE THAT WAS EUREKA by Nadia Wheatley
(Viking Kestrel)
1986
THE TRUE STORY OF SPIT MACPHEE by James Aldridge
(Viking/Penguin)
1987
A RABBIT NAMED HARRIS by Nan Hunt and Betina Ogden
(Collins)
1988
ANSWERS TO BRUT by Gillian Rubinstein *(Omnibus)*
1989
YOU TAKE THE HIGH ROAD by Mary K. Pershall *(Penguin)*
1990
THE BLUE CHAMELEON by Katherine Scholes *(Hill of Content)*
1991
STRANGE OBJECTS by Gary Crew *(Heinemann)*
1992
ALL IN THE BLUE UNCLOUDED WEATHER by Robin Klein
(Penguin)
1993
TJARANY ROUGHTAIL: THE DREAMING OF THE
ROUGHTAIL LIZARD AND OTHER STORIES TOLD BY
THE KUKATJA by Gracie Green, Lucille Gill, and Joe
Tramacchi *(Magabala)*
1994
THE WHITE GUINEA PIG by Ursula Dubosarsky *(Penguin)*
1995
MR. ENIGMATIC by Jenny Pausacker *(Reed for Kids)*

Victorian Premier's Literary Awards 🙠

THE DIABETES AUSTRALIA ALAN MARSHALL PRIZE FOR CHILDREN'S LITERATURE

The Arts Victoria (Private Bag No. 1, City Road Post Office, Victoria 3205, Australia) Literary Awards program honors Australian writers, and includes a prize for children's literature. Fiction, poetry, and nonfiction are eligible; literary merit is the most important factor in determining the winner. ($7,500)

1988
SO MUCH TO TELL YOU by John Marsden *(Walter McVitty)*
1989
THE LAKE AT THE END OF THE WORLD by Caroline McDonald *(Viking/Kestrel)*
1990
ONION TEARS by Diana Kidd *(Collins/Angus & Robertson)*
1991
STRANGE OBJECTS by Gary Crew *(Heinemann)*
1992
THE HOUSE GUEST by Eleanor Nilsson *(Penguin)*
1993
ARIEL, ZED AND THE SECRET OF LIFE by Anna Fienberg *(Little Ark)*
1994
THE WHITE GUINEA PIG by Ursula Dubosarsky *(Viking)*
1995
SONGMAN by Allan Baillie *(Penguin)*

West Australian Young Readers' Book Awards (WAYRBA) 📖

This is Australia's first statewide children's choice book award, sponsored by the School Libraries Section of the Australian Library and Information Association (P. O. Box 251, Mundaring, West Australia 6073). Its aims are to promote reading and to recognize readers and writers of children's literature. Selections from a preselected list of high quality titles nominated by young readers in two categories Primary *(P)* and Secondary *(S)* — are read by children throughout the state to choose the winners each year. In 1991, the Hoffman Award was created to honor the highest ranked Australian author in each category. In 1995, 345 schools and public libraries participated with readers recording 32,000 votes. (Publisher information prior to 1994 not available to CBC.) (Trophies made of Western Australian jarrah wood in the form of a book)

1980
P: TALES OF A FOURTH GRADE NOTHING by Judy Blume
S: MY DARLING VILLAIN by Lynne Reid Banks
1981
P: SADAKO AND THE THOUSAND PAPER CRANES by Eleanor Coerr
S: DON'T HURT LAURIE by Willow Roberts

1982
P: SUPERFUDGE by Judy Blume
S: FORBIDDEN PATHS OF THUAL by Victor Kelleher
1983
P: SAMANTHA ON STAGE by Susan Farrar
S: GOOD NIGHT, MR. TOM by Michelle Magorian
1984
P: GEORGE'S MARVELLOUS MEDICINE by Roald Dahl
S: DID YOU HEAR WHAT HAPPENED TO ANDREA? by Gloria Miklowitz
1985
P: THE BFG by Roald Dahl
S: THE SECRET DIARY OF ADRIAN MOLE, AGED 13¾ by Sue Townsend
1986
P: THE WITCHES by Roald Dahl
S: THE GROWING PAINS OF ADRIAN MOLE by Sue Townsend
1987
P: SELBY'S SECRET by Duncan Ball
S: THE EYES OF KAREN CONNORS by Lois Duncan
BACK HOME by Michelle Magorian
1988
P: GRANDMA CADBURY'S TRUCKING TALES by Dianne Bates
S: DEAD BIRDS SINGING by Marc Talbert
1989
P: MATILDA by Roald Dahl
S: WHEN THE PHONE RANG by Harry Mazer
1990
P: SELBY SPEAKS by Duncan Ball
S: REDWALL by Brian Jacques
1991
P: SELBY SCREAMS by Duncan Ball
P/Hoffman: THE PAW THING by Paul Jennings
S: MOSSFLOWER by Brian Jacques
S/Hoffman: LOCKE LEONARD HUMAN TORPEDO by Tom Winton
1992
P & P/Hoffman: UNCANNY by Paul Jennings
S: MATTIMEO by Brian Jacques
1993
P: SNOTTY BUMSTEAD by Hunter Davies
P/Hoffman: GUMBOOTS AND OTHER RISKS by Gillian Barnett
S: GUMBOOTS AND OTHER RISKS by Gillian Barnett
S/Hoffman: DEL-DEL by Victor Kelleher

1994
P & P/Hoffman: UNBEARABLE! MORE BIZARRE STORIES by Paul Jennings (Penguin)
S & S/Hoffman: LOOKING FOR ALIBRANDI by Melina Marchetta (Penguin)
1995
P & P/Hoffman: UNDONE! MORE MAD ENDINGS by Paul Jennings (Penguin)
S & S/Hoffman: TOMORROW, WHEN THE WAR BEGAN by John Marsden (Pan/Macmillan)

Whitley Awards 🐚

Named in honor of Gilbert Whitley, a prominent member of the Royal Zoological Society of New South Wales, who was an eminent ichthyologist and historian of Australia's zoology, this program presents annual awards to books in several categories in the field of Australian zoology. Children's books are honored in categories that vary from year to year. The only category on our list is Best Children's Book. The year dates are award years. The sponsor is the Royal Zoological Society (P. O. Box 20, Mosman, NSW 2088, Australia). (Certificate)

1980
THE GOULD LEAGUE BOOK OF AUSTRALIAN BIRDS by Don Goodsir, ill. by Tony Oliver (Golden)
1981
FEATHERS, FUR AND FRILLS by Kilmeny Niland (Hodder & Stoughton)
1982
THE FRIENDS OF BURRAMYS by June Epstein (Oxford)
1983
THE GOULD LEAGUE BOOK OF AUSTRALIAN MAMMALS by Don Goodsir, ill. by Tony Oliver (Golden)
1984
AUSTRALIAN ANIMALS by Peter Sloan, ill. by Ross Lathan (Methuen)
1985
AUSTRALIA'S PREHISTORIC ANIMALS by Peter Murray (Methuen)
1986
SEBASTIAN LIVES IN A HAT by Thelma Catterwall, ill. by Kerry Argent (Omnibus)
1987
THE ARROW BOOK OF BACKYARD CREATURES by Brian Macness (Ashton Scholastic)

1988
ANIMAL TRACKS by Carson Creagh, ill. by Kathie Atkinson *(Methuen)*
1989
ALDITA AND THE FOREST by Thelma Catterwall, ill. by Derek Stone *(Dent)*
1990
AUSTRALIAN JUNIOR FIELD GUIDES (entire series) by Eleanor Stodart *(Weldon)*
1991
TOM'S FRIEND by Pat Reynolds *(Allen and Unwin)*
1992
CHILDREN'S EDUCATIONAL SERIES (Set of 5 books) by Pauline Reilly, ill. by Will Roland *(Kangaroo Press)*
1993
CATCH ME IF YOU CAN by Densey Clyne *(Allen and Unwin)*
CICADA SONG BOOK by Densey Clyne *(Allen and Unwin)*
1994
AUSTRANIMALS by J.B. Bruce *(Kangaroo Press)*
1995
YAKKINN THE SWAMP TORTOISE: THE MOST DANGEROUS YEAR by G. and G. Kuchling *(Chelonia Enterprises)*

Young Australians' Best Book Awards (YABBA) ❧

This program is sponsored by the YABBA Council (P. O. Box 238, Kew 3101, Vic., Australia), an organization of volunteers from Victorian groups interested in Australian children's literature and children's reading. Young readers in the State of Victoria in grades 1-9 vote for awards for Australian fiction in three categories—Picture Story *(P)*, Junior *(J)*, and Older *(O)*. "Australian" means written in Australia, written by an Australian, or about Australia. Voting lists are compiled from children's nominations. Year dates in our listing refer to award years. (Citations)

1986
P: WHEN THE WIND CHANGED by Ruth Park, ill. by Deborah Niland *(Collins)*
J: THE TWENTY-SEVENTH ANNUAL AFRICAN HIPPOPOTAMUS RACE by Morris Lurie *(Penguin)*
0: HATING ALISON ASHLEY by Robin Klein *(Viking Kestrel)*

1987
P: ANIMALIA by Graeme Base *(Viking Kestrel)*
J: SISTER MADGE'S BOOK OF NUNS by Doug Macleod, ill. by Craig Smith *(Omnibus)*
0: UNREAL! EIGHT SURPRISING STORIES by Paul Jennings *(Penguin)*

1988
P: WHERE THE FOREST MEETS THE SEA by Jeannie Baker *(Julia MacRae)*
J: MY PLACE by Nadia Wheatley, ill. by Donna Rawlins *(Collins/Dove)*
0: UNBELIEVABLE! MORE SURPRISING STORIES by Paul Jennings *(Penguin)*

1989
P: THE ELEVENTH HOUR by Graeme Base *(Viking Kestrel)*
J: THE CABBAGE PATCH FIB by Paul Jennings *(Penguin)*
0: UNCANNY! by Paul Jennings *(Penguin)*

1990
P: THE MONSTER WHO ATE AUSTRALIA by Michael Salmon *(Lamont)*
J: PAW THING by Paul Jennings *(Penguin)*
0: SPACE DEMONS by Gillian Rubinstein *(Penguin)*

1991
P: COUNTING ON FRANK by Rod Clement *(Angus & Robertson)*
J: FINDERS KEEPERS by Emily Rodda *(Omnibus)*
0: ROUND THE TWIST by Paul Jennings *(Penguin)*

1992
P: WINDOW by Jeannie Baker *(Julia MacRae)*
J: QUIRKY TALES by Paul Jennings *(Penguin)*
0: UNMENTIONABLE: MORE AMAZING STORIES by Paul Jennings *(Penguin)*

1993
P: SIGN OF THE SEAHORSE by Graeme Base *(Viking)*
J: BLABBER MOUTH by Morris Gleitzman *(Penguin)*
0: UNBEARABLE! MORE BIZARRE STORIES by Paul Jennings *(Penguin)*

1994
P: SPOONER OR LATER by Ted Greenwood and Paul Jennings *(Penguin)*
J: UNDONE! MORE MAD ENDINGS by Paul Jennings *(Penguin)*
0: ROWAN OF RIN by Emily Rodda *(Omnibus)*

1995
P: DUCK FOR COVER by Paul Jennings and Ted Greenwood *(Penguin)*
J: THE GIZMO by Paul Jennings *(Penguin)*
0: TOMORROW, WHEN THE WAR BEGAN by John Marsden *(Penguin)*

CANADA

(Note that the Pacific Northwest Young Reader's Choice Award in Part II of this work includes the votes of young Canadian readers in the provinces of Alberta and British Columbia.)

Alcuin Society Citations ❧

The Alcuin Society (P. O. Box 3216, Vancouver, BC V6B 3X8, Canada) promotes awareness of excellence in the book arts. Its awards program honors Canadian publishers and designers of general trade books, limited editions, texts and reference works, and juveniles. We list the children's book winners, which were published in the year before being honored. (Citation)

1984
CAPTAIN CARP SAVES THE SEA by John Larsen, designed by John Larsen *(Annick)*
1985
DINNER AT AUNTIE ROSE'S by Janet Munsil, ill. by Scot Ritchie, designed by Blair Kerrigan *(Annick)*
1986
THE SORCERER'S APPRENTICE by Robin Muller, designed by Michael Solomon *(Kids Can Press)*
1987
THE SEA SERPENT OF GRENADIER POND by David Peacock, designed by David Peacock *(Hounslow)*
1988
No first prize
1989
THE WILDLIFE ABC: A NATURE ALPHABET by Jan Thornhill, designed by Wycliffe Smith *(Greey de Pencier)*
1990
THE TIME BEFORE DREAMS by Stefan Czernecki and Timothy Rhodes, ill. by Stefan Czernecki, designed by Arlene Osen *(Hyperion)*
1991
THE SIGN OF THE SCALES by Marianne Brandis, designed by Tim Inkster *(Porcupine's Quill)*
1992
THE ANNE OF GREEN GABLES TREASURY by Christina Wyss Eriksson and Carolyn Strom Collins designed by Pronk & Associates *(Penguin)*

1993
HICKORY, DICKORY, DOCK by Robin Muller, ill. by Suzanne
Duranceau, designed by Yüksel Hassan *(Scholastic)*
1994
BREWSTER ROOSTER by Russ Willms, ill. by Berny Lucas,
designed by Russ Willms *(Kids Can Press)*
1995
JOSEPHA: A PRAIRIE BOY'S STORY by Jim McGugan, ill. by
Murray Kimber, designed by Kunz & Associates Ltd. *(Red Deer)*

Prix Alvine-Bélisle

This award is for the author or illustrator of the best children's
book by a Canadian national published in French in Canada each
year. It is administered by the Association pour l'avancement des
sciences et des techniques de la documentation (A.S.T.E.D., 3414
Avenue de Parc, Bur 202, Montréal, Que. H2X 2H5, Canada).
(An art object or $500)

1975
JEANNE, FILLE DU ROY by Suzanne Martel *(Fides)*
1976
LES SAISONS DE LA MER by Monique Corriveau *(Fides)*
1977
ÉMILIE, LA BAIGNOIRE À PATTES by Bernadette Renaud
(Héritage)
1978
L'ÉVANGILE EN PAPIER by Henriette Major *(Fides)*
1979
LA PETITE FILLE AUX YEUX ROUGES by Gabrielle
Grandbois-Paquin *(Fides)*
1980
LES QUATRE SAISONS DE PIQUOT by Gilles Vigneault
(Editions de l'Arc)
1981
LE VISITEUR DU SOIR by Robert Soulières *(Fides)*
1982
LE VOYAGE À LA RECHERCHE DU TEMPS by Lucie
Ledoux, ill. by Philippe Béha *(Mondia)*
(Both author and illustrator received awards.)
1983
DORS PETIT OURS, J'AIME CLAIRE, MES CHEVEUX and
PIPI LE POT by Sylvie Assathiany and Louise Pelletier, ill. by
Philippe Béha *(Ovale)*
(Both authors and illustrator received awards.)

1984
LA SOEUR DE ROBERT by Marie-Louise Gay *(La courte échelle)*
1985
ZUNIK by Bertrand Gauthier *(La courte échelle)*
1986
LE COMPLOT by Christine Brouillet *(La courte échelle)*
1987
ALLER-RETOUR by Yves Beauchesne *(Schinkel)*
1988
VENIR AU MONDE by Marie-France Hébert, ill. by Darcia LaBrosse *(La courte échelle)*
1989
NE TOUCHES PAS A MA BABOUCHE by Gilles Gauthier *(La courte échelle)*
1990
SAUVETAGES by Sonia Sarfati *(Québec-Amérique)*
1991
LA VRAIE HISTOIRE DU CHIEN DE CLARA VIC by Christiane Duchesne *(Québec-Amérique)*
1992
PLEINE CRISE by Claudine Farch *(Héritage)*
1993
LA ROUTE DE CHLIFA by Michéle Marineau *(Québec-Amérique)*
1994
KLONK by François Gravel *(Québec-Amérique)*
1995
À PROPOS D'UN BATEAU À VAPEUR by Jean Bélisle *(Hurtubise HMH))*

Geoffrey Bilson Award for Historical Fiction for Young People 🐾

Named for a respected author and historian, whose three children's books were published by Kids Can Press. Awarded annually for an outstanding work of historical fiction for young people written by a Canadian author. Administered by the Canadian Children's Book Centre (35 Spadina Rd., Toronto, Ont. M5R 2S9, Canada). Our listing is of the year in which the award was presented; books were published the year before. ($1,000, contributed by children's book publishers and booksellers)

1988
LISA by Carol Matas *(Lester & Orpen Dennys)*
1989
MYSTERY IN THE FROZEN LANDS by Martyn Godfrey *(Lorimer)*
RACHEL'S REVOLUTION by Dorothy Perkyns *(Lancelot)*
1990
THE SKY IS FALLING by Kit Pearson *(Penguin)*
1991
THE SIGN OF THE SCALES by Marianne Brandis *(Porcupine's Quill)*
1992
No Award
1993
TICKET TO CURLEW by Celia Barker Lottridge *(Groundwood)*
1994
THE LIGHTS GO ON AGAIN by Kit Pearson *(Viking)*
1995
THE DREAM CARVERS by Joan Clark *(Viking)*

Ann Connor Brimer Award 🍂

Named for a woman who was a dedicated supporter and promoter of Canadian children's literature, and who opened Nova Scotia's first children's bookstore, this annual award for a resident of Atlantic Canada is for a book published in Canada that has made an outstanding contribution to children's literature. The sponsor is the Nova Scotia Library Association (P.O. Box 36036, Halifax, NS B3J 3S9, Canada). ($1000)

1991
PIT PONY by Joyce Barkhouse *(Gage)*
1992
EATING BETWEEN THE LINES by Kevin Major *(Doubleday Canada)*
1993
OLIVER'S WARS by Budge Wilson *(Stoddart)*
1994
GOOD IDEA GONE BAD by Lesley Choyce *(Formac)*
1995
MABEL MURPLE by Sheree Fitch *(Doubleday Canada)*

Canadian Library Association Book of the Year for Children Award ⁊

Given annually since 1947 by the Canadian Library Association (200 Elgin St., Suite 602, Ottawa, Ont. K2P lL5, Canada) to outstanding children's books, one in English, and from 1954 through 1973, one in French, published during the preceding year and written by a Canadian citizen. (Medals)

1947
STARBUCK VALLEY WINTER by Roderick Haig-Brown *(Collins)*

1948
No Award

1949
KRISTLI'S TREES by Mabel Dunham *(McClelland & Stewart)*

1950
FRANKLIN OF THE ARCTIC by Richard S. Lambert *(McClelland & Stewart)*

1951
No Award

1952
THE SUN HORSE by Catherine Anthony Clark *(Macmillan)*

1953
No Award

1954
No English Award
LE VÉNÉRABLE FRANÇOIS DE MONTMORENCY-LAVAL by Emile Gervais *(Comité des Fondateurs de l'Eglise canadienne)*

1955
No Awards

1956
TRAIN FOR TIGER LILY by Louise Riley *(Macmillan)*
No French Award

1957
GLOOSKAP'S COUNTRY by Cyrus Macmillan *(Oxford)*
No French Award

1958
LOST IN THE BARRENS by Farley Mowat *(Little, Brown)*
CHEVALIER DU ROI by Beatrice Clément *(Atelier)*

1959
THE DANGEROUS COVE by John F. Hayes *(Copp Clark)*
UN DRÔLE DE PETIT CHEVAL by Hélène Flamme *(Leméac)*

1960
THE GOLDEN PHOENIX by Marius Barbeau, retold by
Michael Hornyansky *(Oxford)*
L'ÉTÉ ENCHANTÉ by Paule Daveluy *(Atelier)*
1961
THE ST. LAWRENCE by William Toye *(Oxford)*
PLANTES VAGABONDES by Marcelle Gauvreau *(Centre de
Psychologie et de Pédagogie)*
1962
No English Award
LES ÎLES DU ROI MAHA MAHA II by Claude Aubry *(Pélican)*
1963
THE INCREDIBLE JOURNEY by Sheila Burnford *(Little,
Brown)*
DRÔLE D'AUTOMNE by Paule Daveluy *(Pélican)*
1964
THE WHALE PEOPLE by Roderick Haig-Brown *(Collins)*
FÉRIE by Cécile Chabot *(Beauchemin)*
1965
TALES OF NANABOZHO by Dorothy Reid *(Oxford)*
LE LOUP DE NÖEL by Claude Aubry *(Centre de Psychologie et
de Pédagogie)*
1966
TIKTÁ LIKTAK by James Houston *(Longmans)* (Published 1964)
THE DOUBLE KNIGHTS by James McNeil *(Oxford)* (Published
1965)
LE CHÊNE DES TEMPÊTES by Andrée Maillet-Hobden *(Fides)*
(Published 1964)
LE WAPITI by Monique Corriveau *(Jeunesse)* (Published 1965)
1967
RAVEN'S CRY by Christie Harris *(McClelland & Stewart)*
No French Award
1968
THE WHITE ARCHER by James Houston *(Academic)*
LÉGENDES INDIENNES DU CANADA by Claude Mélancon
(Editions du Jour)
1969
AND TOMORROW THE STARS by Kay Hill *(Dodd)*
No French Award
1970
SALLY GO ROUND THE SUN by Edith Fowke *(McClelland &
Stewart)*
LA MERVEILLEUSE HISTOIRE DE LA NAISSANCE by Lionel
Gendron *(Les Editions de l'Homme)*
1971
CARTIER DISCOVERS THE ST. LAWRENCE by William
Toye *(Oxford)*

LA SURPRISE DE DAME CHENILLE by Henriette Major *(Centre de Psychologie et de Pédagogie)*
1972
MARY OF MILE 18 by Ann Blades *(Tundra)*
No French Award
1973
THE MARROW OF THE WORLD by Ruth Nichols *(Macmillan)*
LA PETIT SAPIN QUI A POUSSÉ SUR UNE ÉTOILE by Simone Bussières *(Laurentiennes)*
1974
THE MIRACULOUS HIND by Elizabeth Cleaver *(Holt)*
1975
ALLIGATOR PIE by Dennis Lee *(Macmillan)*
1976
JACOB TWO-TWO MEETS THE HOODED FANG by Mordecai Richler *(McClelland & Stewart)*
1977
MOUSE WOMAN AND THE VANISHED PRINCESSES by Christie Harris *(McClelland & Stewart)*
1978
GARBAGE DELIGHT by Dennis Lee *(Macmillan)*
1979
HOLD FAST by Kevin Major *(Clarke, Irwin)*
1980
RIVER RUNNERS by James Houston *(McClelland & Stewart)*
1981
THE VIOLIN MAKER'S GIFT by Donn Kushner *(Macmillan)*
1982
THE ROOT CELLAR by Janet Lunn *(Lester & Orpen Dennys)*
1983
UP TO LOW by Brian Doyle *(Groundwood/Douglas & McIntyre)*
1984
SWEETGRASS by Jan Hudson *(Tree Frog Press)*
1985
MAMA'S GOING TO BUY YOU A MOCKINGBIRD by Jean Little *(Penguin)*
1986
JULIE by Cora Taylor *(Western Producer Prairie Books)*
1987
SHADOW IN HAWTHORN BAY by Janet Lunn *(Lester & Orpen Dennys)*
1988
A HANDFUL OF TIME by Kit Pearson *(Penguin)*

1989
EASY AVENUE by Brian Doyle *(Groundwood/Douglas & McIntyre)*
1990
THE SKY IS FALLING by Kit Pearson *(Penguin)*
1991
REDWORK by Michael Bedard *(Lester & Orpen Dennys)*
1992
EATING BETWEEN THE LINES by Kevin Major *(Doubleday Canada)*
1993
TICKET TO CURLEW by Celia Barker Lottridge *(Groundwood)*
1994
SOME OF THE KINDER PLANETS by Tim Wynne-Jones *(Groundwood)*
1995
SUMMER OF THE MAD MONK by Cora Taylor *(Douglas & McIntyre)*
1996
THE TINY KITE OF EDDIE WING by Maxine Trottier *(Stoddart)*

Children's Literature Roundtables of Canada Information Book Award ❧

"The purpose of the Roundtable Information Book Award is to recognize an outstanding information book for children (5-12 years) that captures the imagination, arouses interest, stimulates curiosity, and fosters concern for the world around us. The award's aim is to foster excellence in Canadian publishing." To be eligible, books must have been published in Canada during the previous year by a Canadian citizen or landed immigrant. Sponsored by the Children's Literature Roundtables of Canada (c/o Dept. of Language Education, University of British Columbia, Vancouver, BC V6T 1Z4, Canada), each Roundtable in Canada participates by nominating five titles submitted to an award committee, and then votes on a national list of titles compiled by that committee. (Certificate and $500 honorarium)

1987
LOOKING AT INSECTS by David Suzuki with Barbara Hehner *(Scholastic)*

1988
LET'S CELEBRATE: CANADA'S SPECIAL DAYS! by Caroline
Parry *(Kids Can Press)*
1989
EXPLORING THE SKY BY DAY by Terence Dickinson
(Camden House)
1990
WOLF ISLAND by Celia Godkin *(Fitzhenry & Whiteside)*
1991
HANDS ON, THUMBS UP by Camilla Gryski *(Kids Can Press)*
1992
A TREE IN THE FOREST by Jan Thornhill *(Greey de Pencier)*
1993
THE STORY OF CANADA by Janet Junn & Christopher
Moore *(Key Porter)*
1994
ON THE SHUTTLE: EIGHT DAYS IN SPACE by Barbara
Bondar *(Greey de Pencier)*
COWBOY: A KID'S ALBUM by Linda Granfield *(Groundwood)*
1995
A PIONEER STORY: THE DAILY LIFE OF A CANADIAN
FAMILY IN 1840 by Barbara Greenwood *(Kids Can Press)*

Sheila A. Egoff
Children's Prize

The B. C. Book Prizes (West Coast Book Prize Society, #700,
1033 Davie St., Vancouver, B.C. V6E 1M7, Canada) celebrate
the achievements of British Columbia writers in several categories
annually. The program was established in 1985, and included
children's books as of 1987. The children's book prize is named
for a distinguished former professor at the University of British
Columbia, who is also an author of works on children's literature
and a prominent critic. The prize is awarded for the best book
for children sixteen years and younger by an author and/or
illustrator who have lived in B. C. or the Yukon for three of the
most recent five years. The winner is selected from a shortlist of
books, which may have been published anywhere in the world.
(Certificate and $2000)

1987
THE BABY PROJECT by Sarah Ellis *(Groundwood/Douglas &
McIntyre)*
1988
PRIDE OF LIONS by Nicola Morgan *(Fitzhenry & Whiteside)*

1989
SUNNY by Mary-Ellen Lang Collura *(Irwin)*
1990
TALES FROM GOLD MOUNTAIN by Paul Yee
(Groundwood/Douglas & McIntyre)
1991
I HEARD MY MOTHER CALL MY NAME by Nancy Hundal
(Grounwood/Douglas & McIntyre)
1992
SIWITI: A WHALE'S STORY by Alexandra Morton *(Orca)*
1993
MY NAME IS SEEPEETZA by Shirley Sterling
(Groundwood/Douglas & McIntyre)
1994
WHITE JADE TIGER by Julie Lawson *(Beach Holme)*
1995
THE OLD BROWN SUITCASE by Lillian Boraks-Nemetz
(Ben-Simon)

Governor General's Literary Awards ❧

CHILDREN'S LITERATURE CATEGORIES

The former Canada Council Children's Literature Prizes became
Governor General's Awards as of prizes awarded for 1986 titles.
Currently, the Governor General's Awards are for the best
English-language and the best French-language work in seven
categories, including Children's Literature (text) *(T)* and
Children's Literature (illustration) *(I)*. Submissions are by
publishers only; they must be trade books written or illustrated
by Canadian citizens or permanent residents of Canada; the
books may have been published in Canada or abroad. English-
language and French-language juries review submissions
independently of each other. The administrator is the Writing
and Publishing Section of The Canada Council (350 Albert St.,
Box 1047, Ottawa, Ontario K1P 5V8, Canada). ($10,000 each)

1975
SHANTYMEN OF CACHE LAKE by Bill Freeman *(Lorimer)*
RAMINAGRADU: HISTOIRES ORDINAIRES POUR ENFANTS
EXTRAORDINAIRES by Louise Aylwin *(Editions du Jour)*
1976
THE WOODEN PEOPLE by Myra Paperny *(Little, Brown)*
ÉMILIE, LA BAIGNOIRE À PATTES by Bernadette Renaud
(Héritage)

1977
LISTEN FOR THE SINGING by Jean Little *(Clarke, Irwin)*
LUNE DE NEIGE by Denise Houle *(Maheux)*
L'ÉVANGILE EN PAPIER by Henriette Major, ill. by Claude
Lafortune *(Fides)*
1978
HOLD FAST by Kevin Major *(Clarke, Irwin)*
A SALMON FOR SIMON by Betty Waterton, ill. by Ann Blades
(Douglas & McIntyre)
LA CHICANE by Ginette Anfousse *(La courte échelle)*
LA VARICELLE by Ginette Anfousse *(La courte échelle)*
1979
T: DAYS OF TERROR by Barbara Smucker *(Clarke, Irwin)*
I: THE TWELVE DANCING PRINCESSES retold by Janet
Lunn, ill. by Laszlo Gal *(Methuen)*
T: COURTE-QUEUE by Gabrielle Roy *(Stanké)*
I: UNE FENÊTRE DANS MA TÊTE by Raymond Plante, ill. by
Roger Paré *(La courte échelle)*
1980
T: THE TROUBLE WITH PRINCESSES by Christie Harris
(McClelland & Stewart)
I: PETROUCHKA retold and ill. by Elizabeth Cleaver
(Macmillan)
T: HÉBERT LUÉE by Bertrand Gauthier *(La courte échelle)*
I: LES GENS DE MON PAYS by Gilles Vigneault, ill. by
Miyuki Tanobe *(La courte échelle)*
1981
T: THE GUARDIAN OF ISIS by Monica Hughes *(Hamish
Hamilton)*
I: YTEK AND THE ARCTIC ORCHID: AN INUIT LEGEND
by Garnet Hewitt, ill. by Heather Woodall *(Douglas &
McIntyre)*
T: NOS AMIS ROBOTS by Suzanne Martel *(Héritage)*
I: LES PAPINACHOIS by Michel Noël, ill. by Joanne Ouellet
(Hurtubise HMH)
1982
T: HUNTER IN THE DARK by Monica Hughes *(Clarke, Irwin)*
I: ABC, 123, THE CANADIAN ALPHABET AND COUNTING
BOOK by Vlasta van Kampen *(Hurtig)*
T: FABIEN 1 and FABIEN 2 by Ginette Anfousse *(Leméac)*
I: AGNÈS ET LE SINGULIER BESTIAIRE by Marie José
Théricault, ill. by Darcia LaBrosse *(Pierre Tisseyre)*
1983
T: THE GHOST HORSE OF THE MOUNTIES by Sean
Ohuigin *(Black Moss Press)*
I: THE LITTLE MERMAID retold by Margaret Crawford
Maloney, ill. by Laszlo Gal *(Methuen)*
T: HOCKE YEURS CYBERNÉTIQUES by Denis Côté
(Paulines)

I: GRAND-MAMAN, MON BÉBÉ-SOEUR, OÙ EST MA TÉTINE and QUAND ÇA VA MAL by Sylvie Assathiany and Louise Pelletier, ill. by Philippe Béha *(Ovale)*

1984
T: SWEETGRASS by Jan Hudson *(Tree Frog Press)*
I: LIZZY'S LION by Dennis Lee, ill. by Marie-Louise Gay *(Stoddart)*
T: LE CERCLE VIOLET by Daniel Sernine *(Pierre Tisseyre)*
I: DRÔLE D'ÉCOLE by Marie-Louise Gay *(Ovale)*

1985
T: JULIE by Cora Taylor *(Western Producer Prairie Books)*
I: MURDO'S STORY by Murdo Scribe, ill. by Terry Gallagher *(Pemmican)*
T: CASSE-TÊTE CHINOIS by Robert Soulières *(Pierre Tisseyre)*
I: L'ALPHABET by Roger Paré *(La courte échelle)*

1986
T: SHADOW IN HAWTHORN BAY by Janet Lunn *(Lester & Orpen Dennys)*
I: HAVE YOU SEEN BIRDS? by Joanne Oppenheim, ill. by Barbara Reid *(Scholastic-TAB)*
T: LE DERNIER DES RAISINS by Raymond Plante *(Québec-Amérique)*
I: ALBUM DE FAMILLE *(Michel Quintin)* and AS-TU VU JOSÉPHINE? *(Tundra)*, both by Stéphane Poulin

1987
T: GALAHAD SCHWARTZ AND THE COCKROACH ARMY by Morgan Nyberg *(Groundwood/Douglas & McIntyre)*
I: RAINY DAY MAGIC by Marie-Louise Gay *(Stoddart)*
T: LE DON by David Schinkel and Yves Beauchesne *(Cercle du livre de France)*
I: VENIR AU MONDE by Darcia LaBrosse *(La courte échelle)*

1988
T: THE THIRD MAGIC by Welwyn Wilton Katz *(Groundwood/Douglas & McIntyre)*
I: AMOS'S SWEATER by Janet Lunn, ill. by Kim LaFave *(Groundwood/Douglas & McIntyre)*
T: CASSIOPÉE OU L'ÉTÉ POLONAIS by Michele Marineau *(Québec-Amérique)*
I: LES JEUX DE PIC-MOTS by Marie-Antoinette Delolme, ill. by Philippe Béha *(Graficor)*

1989
T: BAD BOY by Diana Wieler *(Groundwood/Douglas & McIntyre)*
I: THE MAGIC PAINTBRUSH by Robin Muller *(Doubleday)*
T: TEMPS MORT by Charles Montpetit *(Paulines)*
I: BENJAMIN ET LE SAGA DES OREILLERS by Stéphane Poulin *(Annick)*

1990
T: REDWORK by Michael Bedard *(Lester & Orpen Dennys)*

I: THE ORPHAN BOY by Tololwa M. Mollel, ill. by Paul Morin *(Oxford)*
T: LA VRAIE HISTOIRE DU CHIEN DE CLARA VIC by Christiane Duchesne *(Québec-Amérique)*
I: LES FANTAISIES DE L'ONCLE HENRI by Bénédicte Froissart, ill. by Pierre Pratt *(Annick)*

1991
T: PICK-UP STICKS by Sarah Ellis *(Groundwood)*
I: DOCTOR KISS SAYS YES by Teddy Jam, ill. by Joanne Fitzgerald *(Groundwood)*
T: DEUX HEURES ET DEMIE AVANT JASMINE by François Gravel *(Éditions du Boréal)*
I: UN CHAMPION by Roch Carrier, ill. by Sheldon Cohen *(Tundra)*

1992
T: HERO OF LESSER CAUSES by Julie Johnston *(Lester)*
I: WAITING FOR THE WHALES by Sheryl McFarlane, ill. by Ron Lightburn *(Orca)*
T: VICTOR by Christiane Duchesne *(Québec-Amérique)*
I: SIMON ET LA VILLE DE CARTON by Gilles Tibo *(Tundra)*

1993
T: SOME OF THE KINDER PLANETS by Tim Wynne-Jones *(Groundwood)*
I: SLEEP TIGHT MRS. MING by Sharon Jennings, ill. by Mireille Levert *(Annick)*
T: LA ROUTE DE CHLIFA by Michele Marineu *(Québec-Amérique)*
I: MONDE SELON JEAN DE... by Stephane Jorisch *(Doutre et Vandal)*

1994
T: ADAM AND EVE AND PINCH-ME by Julie Johnston *(Lester)*
I: JOSEPHA: A PRAIRIE BOY'S STORY by Jim McGugan, ill. by Murray Kimber *(Red Deer College Press)*
T: UNE BELLE JOURNÉE POUR MOURIR by Suzanne Martel *(Éditions Fides)*
I: MON CHIEN EST UN ÉLÉPHANT by Rémy Simard, ill. by Pierre Pratt *(Annick)*

1995
T: THE MAESTRO by Tim Wynne-Jones *(Groundwood)*
I: THE LAST QUEST OF GILGAMESH by Ludmila Zeman *(Tundra)*
T: COMME UNE PEAU DE CHAGRIN by Sonia Sarfati *(La courte échelle)*
I: SHO ET LES DRAGONS D'EAU by Annouchka Gravel Galoucko *(Annick)*

Amelia Frances Howard-Gibbon Award for Illustration ⁊

Given annually in June since 1971 by the Canadian Library Association (200 Elgin St., Suite 602, Ottawa, Ont. K2P 1L5, Canada) for outstanding illustrations in a children's book published in Canada. Illustrator must be a native or resident of Canada. (Medal)

1971
THE WIND HAS WINGS edited by Mary Alice Downie and Barbara Robertson, ill. by Elizabeth Cleaver *(Oxford)*
1972
A CHILD IN PRISON CAMP by Shizuye Takashima *(Tundra)*
1973
AU DELA DU SOLEIL/BEYOND THE SUN by Jacques de Roussan *(Tundra)*
1974
A PRAIRIE BOY'S WINTER by William Kurelek *(Tundra)*
1975
THE SLEIGHS OF MY CHILDHOOD/LES TRAÎNEAUX DE MON ENFANCE by Carlo Italiano *(Tundra)*
1976
A PRAIRIE BOY'S SUMMER by William Kurelek *(Tundra)*
1977
DOWN BY JIM LONG'S STAGE: RHYMES FOR CHILDREN AND YOUNG FISH by Al Pittman, ill. by Pam Hall *(Breakwater)*
1978
THE LOON'S NECKLACE by William Toye, ill. by Elizabeth Cleaver *(Oxford)*
1979
A SALMON FOR SIMON by Betty Waterton, ill. by Ann Blades *(Douglas & McIntyre)*
1980
THE TWELVE DANCING PRINCESSES retold by Janet Lunn, ill. by Laszlo Gal *(Methuen)*
1981
THE TROUBLE WITH PRINCESSES by Christie Harris, ill. by Douglas Tait *(McClelland & Stewart)*
1982
YTEK AND THE ARCTIC ORCHID: AN INUIT LEGEND by Garnet Hewitt, ill. by Heather Woodall *(Douglas & McIntyre)*
1983
CHESTER'S BARN by Lindee Climo *(Tundra)*

1984
ZOOM AT SEA by Tim Wynne-Jones, ill. by Ken Nutt
(Groundwood/Douglas & McIntyre)
1985
CHIN CHIANG AND THE DRAGON'S DANCE by Ian
Wallace *(Groundwood/Douglas & McIntyre)*
1986
ZOOM AWAY by Tim Wynne-Jones, ill. by Ken Nutt
(Groundwood/Douglas & McIntyre)
1987
MOONBEAM ON A CAT'S EAR by Marie-Louise Gay
(Stoddart)
1988
RAINY DAY MAGIC by Marie-Louise Gay *(Stoddart)*
1989
AMOS'S SWEATER by Janet Lunn, ill. by Kim LaFave
(Groundwood/Douglas & McIntyre)
1990
TIL ALL THE STARS HAVE FALLEN: CANADIAN POEMS
FOR CHILDREN selected by David Booth, ill. by Kady
MacDonald Denton *(Kids Can Press)*
1991
THE ORPHAN BOY by Tololwa M. Mollel, ill. by Paul Morin
(Oxford)
1992
WAITING FOR THE WHALES by Sheryl McFarlane, ill. by
Ron Lightburn *(Orca)*
1993
THE DRAGON'S PEARL by Julie Lawson, ill. by Paul Morin
(Oxford)
1994
LAST LEAF FIRST SNOWFLAKE TO FALL by Leo Yerxa
(Groundwood)
1995
GIFTS by Barbara Reid *(North Winds)*
1996
JUST LIKE NEW by Ainslie Manson, ill. by Karen Reczuch
(Groundwood)

IODE (National Chapter of Canada) 🐑

VIOLET DOWNEY BOOK AWARD

A project of the National Chapter of Canada Imperial Order of the Daughters of the Empire (IODE) (40 Orchard View Blvd., Toronto, Ont. M4R 1B9, Canada), this award is for the best English-language book, with at least 500 words and preferably with Canadian content, for children 13 and under. The book must have been written by a Canadian citizen, and have been published in Canada in the year before receiving the award. A panel of five judges — three affiliated with IODE and two "recognized specialists in the field of children's literature" select the honorees. The award is named for a benefactor of the IODE National Chapter of Canada. (Up to $3,000)

1985
WINNERS by Mary-Ellen Lang Collura *(Western Producer Prairie Books)*
1986
THE QUARTER-PIE WINDOW by Marianne Brandis *(Porcupine's Quill)*
1987
SHADOW IN HAWTHORN BAY by Janet Lunn *(Lester & Orpen Dennys)*
1988
A BOOK DRAGON by Donn Kushner *(Macmillan)*
1989
No Award
1990
TALES FROM GOLD MOUNTAIN by Paul Yee *(Groundwood/Douglas & McIntyre)*
1991
INCREDIBLE JUMBO by Barbara Smucker *(Viking)*
REDWORK by Michael Bedard *(Lester & Orpen Dennys)*
1992
WAITING FOR THE WHALES by Sheryl McFarlane *(Orca)*
1993
HERO OF LESSER CAUSES by Julie Johnston *(Lester)*
1994
THE LIGHTS GO ON AGAIN by Kit Pearson *(Penguin)*
1995
OUT OF THE BLUE by Sarah Ellis *(Douglas & McIntyre)*

IODE (Toronto) &

BOOK AWARD

The Toronto Municipal Chapter of the Imperial Order of the Daughters of the Empire (IODE) (40 St. Clair Ave. East, Suite 205, Toronto, Ont. M4T 1M9, Canada) has given an award annually since 1975 to a Toronto-area author or illustrator of an outstanding Canadian-published book for children of 6-12 years of age. The winner must be a Canadian citizen. A committee from the Toronto Public Library Board and IODE-Toronto selects the award recipients. In our listing and in IODE's, the award year is the publication year. ($1,000)

1974
Dennis Lee, for ALLIGATOR PIE *(Macmillan)*
1975
William Kurelek, for A PRAIRIE BOY'S SUMMER *(Tundra)*
1976
Aviva Layton, for HOW THE KOOKABURRA GOT HIS LAUGH *(McClelland & Stewart)*
1977
William Toye, for THE LOON'S NECKLACE *(Oxford)*
1978
Laszlo Gal, for illustrations in MY NAME IS NOT ODESSA YARKER by Marian Engel *(Kids Can Press)*, THE SHIRT OF THE HAPPY MAN by Mariella Bertelli *(Kids Can Press)* and WHY THE MAN IN THE MOON IS HAPPY by Ronald Melzak *(McClelland & Stewart)*
1979
Janet Lunn, for THE TWELVE DANCING PRINCESSES *(Methuen)*
1980
Olena Kassian, for illustrations in AFRAID OF THE DARK by Barry Dickson *(Lorimer)* and THE HUNGRY TIME by Selwyn Dewdney *(Lorimer)*
1981
Bernice Thurman Hunter, for THAT SCATTERBRAIN BOOKY *(Scholastic-TAB)*
1982
Kathy Stinson, for RED IS BEST *(Annick)*
1983
Tim Wynne-Jones, for ZOOM AT SEA *(Groundwood/Douglas & McIntyre)*
1984
Ian Wallace, for CHIN CHIANG AND THE DRAGON'S DANCE *(Groundwood/Douglas & McIntyre)*

1985
Robin Muller, for THE SORCERER'S APPRENTICE *(Kids Can Press)*

1986
Barbara Reid, for illustrations in HAVE YOU SEEN BIRDS? by Joanne Oppenheim *(Scholastic-TAB)*

1987
Caroline Parry, for LET'S CELEBRATE! CANADA'S SPECIAL DAYS *(Kids Can Press)*

1988
Eric Beddows, for illustrations in NIGHT CARS by Teddy Jam *(Groundwood/Douglas & McIntyre)*

1989
Brenda Clark, for illustrations in LITTLE FINGERLING by Monica Hughes *(Kids Can Press)*

1990
David Booth, selector, for VOICES ON THE WIND: POEMS FOR ALL SEASONS *(Kids Can Press)*

1991
Michael Bedard, author, and Regolo Ricci, illustrator, for THE NIGHTINGALE *(Oxford University)*

1992
Janet Lunn, Christopher Moore, authors, and Alan Daniel, illustrator, for THE STORY OF CANADA *(Key Porter)*

1993
Celia Barker Lottridge, for TEN SMALL TALES *(Groundwood)*

1994
Joanne Findon, reteller, and Ted Nasmith, illustrator, for THE DREAM OF AENGUS *(Lester)*

1995
Linda Granfield, author, and Janet Wilson, illustrator, for IN FLANDERS FIELDS: THE STORY OF THE POEM BY JOHN McCRAE *(Lester)*

Vicky Metcalf Award ❧

Presented by the Canadian Authors Association (27 Doxsee Ave. North, Campbellford, Ont. K0L 1L0, Canada) to a Canadian writer—citizen or landed immigrant—who has produced a body of work with appeal for children age 7-17. (As of 1991, $10,000)

1963 Kerry Wood
1964 John F. Hayes
1965 Roderick Haig-Brown

1966   Fred Swayze
1967   John Patrick Gillese
1968   Lorrie McLaughlin
1969   Audrey McKim
1970   Farley Mowat
1971   Kay Hill
1972   William E. Toye
1973   Christie Harris
1974   Jean Little
1975   Lyn Harrington
1976   Suzanne Martel
1977   James Houston
1978   Lyn Cook
1979   Cliff Faulknor
1980   John Craig
1981   Monica Hughes
1982   Janet Lunn
1983   Claire MacKay
1984   Bill Freeman
1985   Edith Fowke
1986   Dennis Lee
1987   Robert Munsch
1988   Barbara Smucker
1989   Stéphane Poulin
1990   Bernice Thurman Hunter
1991   Brian Doyle
1992   Kevin Major
1993   Phoebe Gilman
1994   Welwyn Wilton Katz
1995   Sarah Ellis

Mr. Christie's Book Awards™ ঽ

Sponsored by Christie Brown & Co., a division of Nabisco
Brands Ltd., a manufacturer of cookies and crackers, this awards
program is designed to honor high quality in children's books
and to stimulate children to read. The Canadian Children's Book
Centre and Communication Jeunesse compile lists of eligible
titles, which must have been written or illustrated by Canadians.
During the first four years of the program, awards were given for
English Text *(ET)*, English illustration *(EI)*, French text *(FT)*,
and French illustration *(FI)*, for readers ages 12 and under. Age

categories were introduced in 1992, and in 1993 the text/ illustration distinction was eliminated. The awards are now given to the best English and best French books in each of three age categories: *7 & under, 8-11, 12 & up.* English-language and French-language panels of children's book specialists select short lists of honorees also select the winners. The program is administered by Mr. Christie's Book Awards™ Information Centre (2150 Lakeshore Blvd. West, Toronto, Ont. M8V 1A3, Canada). ($7,500 to each winner, and a seal)

1989
ET: THE SKY IS FALLING by Kit Pearson *(Penguin)*
EI: THE NAME OF THE TREE: A BANTU TALE by Celia Lottridge, ill. by Ian Wallace *(Groundwood/Douglas & McIntyre)*
FT: ROSALIE S'EN VA-T-EN GUERRE by Ginette Anfousse *(La courte échelle)*
FI: MAIS QUE FONT LES FÉES AVEC TOUTES CES DENTS? by Philippe Béha *(Raton-Laveur)*
1990
ET: COVERED BRIDGE by Brian Doyle *(Groundwood/Douglas & McIntyre)*
EI: THE STORY OF LITTLE QUACK by Kady MacDonald Denton *(Kids Can Press)*
FT: ZAMBONI by Francois Gravel *(Boréal)*
FI: LES FANTAISIES DE L'ONCLE HENRI by Bénédicte Froissart, ill. by Pierre Pratt *(Annick)*
1991
ET: THE ICE CREAM STORE by Dennis Lee *(HarperCollins)*
EI: The "ZOE" Series by Barbara Reid *(HarperCollins)*
FT: BIBITSA, OU, L'ÉTRANGE VOYAGE DE CLARA VIC by Christiane Duchesne *(Québec-Amérique)*
FI: UN VOYAGE POUR DEUX by Stéphane Poulin *(Annick)*
1992
ET (8 & under): THERE WERE MONKEYS IN MY KITCHEN by Sheree Fitch *(Doubleday Canada)*
ET (9-14): THE STORY OF CANADA by Janet Lunn & Christopher Moore *(Key Porter)*
EI: A PRAIRIE ALPHABET by Yvette Moore *(Tundra)*
FT (8 & under): LE GROS PROBLÈME DU PETIT MARCUS by Gilles Gauthier *(La courte échelle)*
FT (9-14): UN HIVER DE TOURMENTE by Dominique Demers *(La courte échelle)*
FI: C'EST PAS JUSTE! by Dominique Jolin *(Raton Laveur)*
1993
English (7 & under): BREWSTER ROOSTER by Russ Willms, ill. by Berny Lucas *(Kids Can Press)*
English (8-11): LAST LEAF FIRST SNOWFLAKE TO FALL by Leo Yerxa *(Groundwood)*

A LITTLE TIGER IN THE CHINESE NIGHT by Song Nan Zhang *(Tundra)*
English (12 & up): RAN VAN THE DEFENDER by Diana Wieler *(Groundwood)*
French (7 & under): CAILLOU-LA PETITE SOEUR & LE PETIT POT by Joceline Sanschagrin, ill. by Hélène Desputeaux *(Chouette)*
French (8-11): LA 42e SOEUR DE BÉBERT by Christiane Duchesne *(Québec-Amérique)*
French (12 & up): LES GRANDS SAPINS NE MEURENT PAS by Dominique Demers *(Québec-Amérique)*
1994
English (7 & under): THOR by W.D. Valgardson, ill. by Ange Zhang *(Groundwood)*
English (8-11): A PIONEER STORY: THE DAILY LIFE OF A CANADIAN FAMILY IN 1840 by Barbara Greenwood, ill. by Heather Collins *(Kids Can Press)*
English (12 & up): OUT OF THE BLUE by Sarah Ellis *(Douglas & McIntyre)*
French (7 & under): MON CHIEN EST UN ÉLÉPHANT by Rémy Simard, ill. by Pierre Pratt *(Annick)*
French (8-11): LE PARC AUX SORTILÈGES by Denis Côté *(La courte échelle)*
French (12 & up): L'ÉTOILE A PLEURÉ ROUGE by Raymond Plante *(Editions du Boréal)*

Elizabeth Mrazik-Cleaver Canadian Picture Book Award ❧

This award honors a Canadian illustrator whose widely praised books were published under the name Elizabeth Cleaver before her early death in 1985. It is for a Canadian illustrator's work in a distinguished children's picture book published in English or French during the previous year. The book must be a first edition and contain original illustrations. All genres are considered—fiction, non-fiction, poetry, folk, and fairy tales. The award is sponsored by the Canadian National Section of the International Board on Books for Young People (IBBY c/o Canadian Children's Book Centre, 35 Spadina Rd., Toronto, Ont. M5R 2S9, Canada). ($1,000 and certificate)

1986
BY THE SEA: AN ALPHABET BOOK by Ann Blades *(Kids Can Press)*
1987
HAVE YOU SEEN BIRDS? by Joanne Oppenheimer, ill. by Barbara Reid *(North Winds)*
1988
CAN YOU CATCH JOSEPHINE? by Stéphane Poulin *(Tundra)*
1989
NIGHT CARS by Ken Nutt (Erid Beddows, pseud.) *(Groundwood/Douglas & McIntyre)*
1990
THE NAME OF THE TREE: A BANTU TALE by Celia Barker Lottridge, ill. by Ian Wallace *(Groundwood/Douglas & McIntyre)*
1991
THE ORPHAN BOY by Tololwa M. Mollel, ill. by Paul Morin *(Oxford)*
1992
WAITING FOR THE WHALES by Sheryl McFarlane, ill. by Ron Lightburn *(Orca)*
1993
TWO BY TWO by Barbara Reid *(North Winds)*
1994
LAST LEAF FIRST SNOWFLAKE TO FALL by Leo Yerxa *(Groundwood)*
1995
JOSEPHA: A PRAIRIE BOY'S STORY by Jim McGugan, ill. by Murray Kimber *(Red Deer)*

The Ontario Silver Birch Award ❧

Developed in 1993 by the Ontario Library Association (100 Lombard St., Suite 303, Toronto, Ontario, M5C 1M3, Canada) this children's choice program seeks to encourage children to explore a variety of current books, to develop powers of discrimination, and to identify their favorite books. In addition, it provides teachers, librarians, parents, and writers with insight into young people's reading preferences and encourages and honors authors who create works with high appeal to children. Teachers and librarians in Ontario schools and public libraries enroll their institutions and each participating class or group. To be eligible to vote on a designated, province-wide voting day, children in grades 4, 5, and 6 in registered groups must have read at least five books from one or both of two official lists—

Fiction *(F)* and Non-Fiction *(N)*. Children announce the winners and honor the authors whose books were among the official selections at an annual Awards Ceremony. (Citation)

1994
DANIEL'S STORY by Carol Matas *(Scholastic)*
1995
F: THE LIGHTS GO ON AGAIN by Kit Pearson *(Penguin)*
N: POLAR, THE TITANIC BEAR by Laurie McGaw *(Madison House/Little, Brown)*

Prix Québec/Wallonie-Bruxelles du Livre de Jeunesse 🎗

This award is for a Québec or Communauté française de Belgique author or illustrator for either a body of work or a book. The award alternates between the two communities. When the award is for a book, its publisher also receives a grant to enable it to distribute the title in the other market. The award hopes to encourage the development and distribution of French-language children's books in Québec and Belgium and to make the works of each community known to the other. The Canadian sponsor and administrator is the Gouvernement du Québec, Ministère des Relations Internationales (525 Blvd. René-Lévesque Est, Québec, Québec G1R 5R9, Canada). ($3,500)

1981
Body of work of Belgian illustrator Françoise Souply-Clabots
1982
Body of work of Québec author Raymond Plante
1983
No Award
1984
ANIMAUX SAUVAGES D'EUROPE ET D'AMÉRIQUE DU NORD by René Hausman *(Éditions Jean Dupuis, Belgium)*
1985
ZUNIK by Bertrand Gauthier, ill. by Daniel Sylvestre *(La courte échelle, Québec)*
1986
No award
1987
Body of work of Belgian author Marie-Josée Sacré
1988
LES CATASTROPHES DE ROSALIE by Ginette Anfousse *(La courte échelle, Québec)*

1989
LÉONIE DÉVORE LES LIVRES by Frédéric du Bus *(Casterman, Belgium)*
1990
ALBUM DE FAMILLE by Stéphane Poulin *(Michel Quintin, Québec)*
1991
MAGRITTE by Lillo Canta *(Duculot, Belgium)*
1992
LE DOMAINE DES SANS YEUX by Jacques Lazure *(Québec-Amérique)*
1993
No Award
1994
LES GRANDS SAPINS NE MEURENT PAS by Dominique Demers *(Québec-Amérique)*
1995
No Award

Saskatchewan Book Awards

CHILDREN'S LITERATURE CATEGORY

The Saskatchewan Book Awards established a Children's Literature Award in 1995. The category includes books written for young adults. The award goes to a Saskatchewan author and is judged on the quality of writing. The Children's Literature Award is sponsored by SaskEnergy. (Contact: Joyce Wells, Executive Director, Saskatchewan Book Awards, Box 1921, Regina, SK, S4P 3E1, Canada.) ($1,000 and certificate to the author; certificate and award seals to the publisher)
1995
MISTER GOT TO GO by Lois Simmie *(Red Deer)*

Ruth Schwartz Foundation Awards for Excellence in Children's Literature

Established in 1976, the awards honor the late Ruth Schwartz, a respected Toronto bookseller committed to promoting Canadian children's literature. Originally awarded to a Picture Book *(PB)*, a Young Adult *(YA)* category was added in 1994. The authors and illustrators must be Canadian citizens or landed immigrants and the books must have been published in Canada. The program is administered jointly by the Canadian Booksellers Association, which chooses a short list of eligible books, and the Ontario Arts Council (151 Bloor St. West, Toronto, Ont. M5S 1T6, Canada), which selects the juries for each category, made up of children from a different Ontario school each year. (The author/illustrator of a picture book share a $3,000 prize; the author of a YA book is awarded $2,000.)

1976
JACOB TWO-TWO MEETS THE HOODED FANG by Mordecai Richler *(McClelland & Stewart)*
1977
THE VIOLIN by Robert Thomas Allen *(McGraw-Hill)*
1978
GARBAGE DELIGHT by Dennis Lee *(Macmillan)*
1979
HOLD FAST by Kevin Major *(Clarke, Irwin)*
1980
DAYS OF TERROR by Barbara Smucker *(Clarke, Irwin)*
1981
THE KING'S DAUGHTER by Suzanne Martel *(Douglas & McIntyre)*
1982
ONE PROUD SUMMER by Claire MacKay and Marsha Hewitt *(Women's Press)*
1983
JASMIN by Jan Truss *(Douglas & McIntyre)*
1984
ZOOM AT SEA by Tim Wynne-Jones, ill. by Ken Nutt *(Groundwood/Douglas & McIntyre)*
1985
MAMA'S GOING TO BUY YOU A MOCKINGBIRD by Jean Little *(Penguin)*
1986
THOMAS' SNOWSUIT by Robert Munsch, ill. by Michael Martchenko *(Annick)*
1987
HAVE YOU SEEN BIRDS? by Joanne Oppenheim, ill. by Barbara Reid *(Scholastic-TAB)*
1988
THE DOLL by Cora Taylor *(Western Producer Prairie Books)*
1989
AMOS'S SWEATER by Janet Lunn, ill. by Kim LaFave *(Groundwood/Douglas & McIntyre)*
1990
BAD BOY by Diana Wieler *(Groundwood/Douglas & McIntyre)*

1991
FORBIDDEN CITY by William Bell *(Doubleday)*
1992
ROSES SING ON NEW SNOW by Paul Yee, ill. by Harvey Chan *(Groundwood)*
1993
SOMETHING FROM NOTHING by Phoebe Gilman *(Doubleday)*
1994
PB: NORTHERN LIGHTS: THE SOCCER TRAILS by Michael Kusugak and Vladyana Krykorka *(Annick)*
YA: THE HUNTER'S MOON by O.R. Melling *(HarperCollins)*
1995
PB. A PIONEER STORY: THE DAILY LIFE OF A CANADIAN FAMILY IN 1840 by Barbara Greenwood, ill. by Heather Collins *(Kids Can Press)*
YA: ADAM AND EVE AND PINCH-ME by Julie Johnston *(Lester)*

Writers Guild of Alberta Awards for Excellence ❧
R. ROSS ANNETT AWARD
FOR CHILDREN'S LITERATURE

This award is for books by authors who have been recent residents of Alberta, though their works may have been published anywhere in the world. (Contact: Writers Guild of Alberta, Awards Program, 3rd floor, Percy Page Centre, 11759 Groat Rd., Edmonton, Alberta T5M 3K6, Canada) (Leather-bound copies of book, extensive promotion, i.e., bookmarks, poster, etc., and $500 honorarium)

1982
HUNTER IN THE DARK by Monica Hughes *(Clarke, Irwin)*
1983
SPACE TRAP by Monica Hughes *(Douglas & McIntyre)*
1984
IN THE CITY OF THE KING by William Pasnak *(Douglas & McIntyre)*
1985
JULIE by Cora Taylor *(Western Producer Prairie Books)*
1986
BLAINE'S WAY by Monica Hughes *(Irwin)*
1987
NOBODY SAID IT WOULD BE EASY by Marilyn Halvorson *(Irwin)*

1988
UNDER THE EAGLE'S CLAW by William Pasnak *(Douglas & McIntyre)*
1989
DOG RUNNER by Don Meredith *(Western Producer Prairie Books)*
1990
DAWN RIDER by Jan Hudson *(HarperCollins)*
1991
A CAT OF ARTIMUS PRIDE by Hazel Hutchins *(Annick)*
1992
THE CRYSTAL DROP by Monica Hughes *(HarperCollins)*
1993
THE McINTYRE LIAR by David Bly *(Tree Frog Press)*
1994
MISSION IMPOSSIBLE by Beth Goobie *(Red Deer College Press)*
1995
BIG BOY by Tololwa M. Mollel *(Stoddart)*

Young Adult Canadian Book Award ❧

Begun by the Young Adult Caucus of the Saskatchewan Library Association, as of 1989 the award sponsor became the Young Adult Services Interest Group of the Canadian Library Association (200 Elgin St., Suite 602, Ottawa, Ont. K2P 1L5, Canada). The purpose of the award was, and remains, to "recognize the author of an outstanding English-language Canadian book which appeals to young adults between the ages of 13 and 18." Designed to promote Canadian authors and publishing companies, "the title must be a Canadian publication in either hardcover or paperback, and the author must be a Canadian citizen or landed immigrant." (Seal, designed by a young adult from Regina, and leatherbound copy of book)

1981
FAR FROM SHORE by Kevin Major *(Clarke, Irwin)*
1982
SUPER BIKE! by Jamie Brown *(Clarke, Irwin)*
1983
HUNTER IN THE DARK by Monica Hughes *(Clarke, Irwin)*
1984
THE DRUID'S TUNE by O. R. Melling *(Penguin)*

1985
WINNERS by Mary-Ellen Lang Collura *(Western Producer Prairie Books)*

1986
THE QUARTER-PIE WINDOW by Marianne Brandis *(Porcupine's Quill)*

1987
SHADOW IN HAWTHORN BAY by Janet Lunn *(Lester & Orpen Dennys)*

1988
WHO IS FRANCES RAIN? by Margaret Buffie *(Kids Can Press)*

1989
JANUARY, FEBRUARY, JUNE OR JULY by Helen Fogwill Porter *(Breakwater)*

1990
BAD BOY by Diana Wieler *(Groundwood/Douglas & McIntyre)*

1991
THE LEAVING by Budge Wilson *(Anansi)*

1992
STRANDIA by Susan Lynn Reynolds *(HarperCollins)*

1993
THERE WILL BE WOLVES by Karleen Bradford *(HarperCollins)*

1994
NOBODY'S SON by Sean Stewart *(Maxwell Macmillan)*

1995
ADAM AND EVE AND PINCH-ME by Julie Johnston *(Lester)*

1996
THE MAESTRO by Tim Wynne-Jones *(Groundwood/Douglas & McIntyre)*

NEW ZEALAND
AIM Children's Book Awards 🎀

The AIM Children's Book Festival is a nationwide celebration of children's books, promoting the importance and enjoyment of books and reading and recognizing the excellent range and quality of New Zealand children's books. At the culmination of the festival each spring, the AIM Children's Book Awards are made at a ceremony in Wellington. Through 1992 awards were made in two categories: Book of the Year *(B)* and Picture Book of the Year *(P)* with a discretionary prize for a first book by a previously unpublished author or illustrator. Categories have been expanded to include: Junior Fiction *(JF)*, Senior Fiction *(SF)*, Picture Book *(P)*, and Non-Fiction *(NF)*, with the AIM Book of the Year chosen from the four category winners to honor a book of outstanding overall excellence. The principal sponsor is Lever Rexona through its AIM brand toothpaste and the program is administered by Booksellers New Zealand (P.O. Box 11-377, Wellington, New Zealand). ($5,000 prize in each category; additional $5,000 for AIM Book of the Year; $1,000 for Best First Book)

1982
P: THE KUIA AND THE SPIDER by Patricia Grace, ill. by Robyn Kahukiwa *(Longman Paul, in association with Kidarus 2, Inc.; simultaneous Maori-language edition)* (Two awards)
B: THE SILENT ONE by Joy Cowley *(Whitcoulls)*
1983
P: MR. FOX by Gavin Bishop *(Oxford)*
B: THE HALFMEN OF O by Maurice Gee *(Oxford)*
1984
P: HAIRY MACLARY FROM DONALDSON'S DAIRY by Lynley Dodd *(Mallinson Rendell)*
B: JACKY NOBODY by Anne de Roo *(Methuen)*
1985
P: THE FISH OF OUR FATHERS by Ron L. Bacon, ill. by Robert F. Jahnke *(Waiatarua)*
B: VISITORS by Caroline Macdonald *(Hodder)*
1986
P: HAIRY MACLARY SCATTERCAT by Lynley Dodd *(Mallinson Rendell)*
B: No Award
1987
P: TANIWHA by Robyn Kahukiwa *(Penguin)*
B: THE KEEPER by Barry Faville *(Oxford)*
1988
P: HAIRY MACLARY'S CATERWAUL CAPER by Lynley Dodd *(Mallinson Rendell)*
B: ALEX by Tessa Duder *(Oxford)*
1989
No Awards
1990
P: ANNIE AND MOON by Miriam Smith, ill. by Lesley Moyes *(Mallinson Rendell)*
B: ALEX IN WINTER by Tessa Duder *(Oxford)*
1991
P: MY CAT MAISIE by Pamela Allen *(Hodder)*
B: ROCCO by Sheryl Jordan *(Ashton Scholastic)*
First: WATER IN THE BLOOD by Alan Bunn *(Heinemann)*
1992
P: HAIRY MACLARY'S SHOW BUSINESS by Lynley Dodd *(Mallinson Rendel)*

B: BOW DOWN SHADRACH by Joy Cowley *(Hodder & Stoughton)*
First: OUT WALKED MEL by Paula Boock *(John McIndoe)*
1993
P: LILY AND THE PRESENT by Christine Ross *(Methuen)*
JF: UNDERRUNNERS by Margaret Mahy *(Hamish Hamilton)*
SF: SONGS FOR ALEX by Tessa Duder *(Oxford)*
First: THE OPTIMIST by Bob Kerr *(Mallinson Rendel)*
1994
P: HINEPAU by Gavin Bishop *(Ashton Scholastic)*
JF: A DOLPHIN IN THE BAY by Diana Noonan
(Omnibus/Ashton Scholastic)
SF: THE VALUE OF X by Pat Quinn *(Heinemann Educational)*
First: OLD BLUE: THE RAREST BIRD IN THE WORLD by
Mary Taylor *(Ashton Scholastic)*
1995
P: THE BEST LOVED BEAR by Diana Noonan *(Ashton Scholastic)*
JF & Book of the Year: THE FATMAN by Maurice Gee
(Viking)
SF: THE BLUE LAWN by William Taylor *(HarperCollins)*
NF: WHICH NATIVE FOREST PLANT by Andrew Crowe
(Penguin)

Russell Clark Award ❧

Established in 1976, the award was first given in 1978 by its administrator, the New Zealand Library & Information Association (P. O. Box 12-212, Wellington, New Zealand). The award is "made for the most distinguished illustrations for a children's book; the illustrator must be a citizen or resident of New Zealand." The award is named for the prominent New Zealand illustrator Russell Clark (1905-1966) whose drawings of ordinary people engaged in everyday activities have proved to be, of themselves, valuable historical records. The award "is offered annually and awarded when merited." (Medal and NZ $1000)

1978
THE HOUSE OF THE PEOPLE by Ron L. Bacon, ill. by
Robert F. Jahnke *(Collins)*
1979
KIM by Bruce Treloar *(Collins)*
1980-1981
No Awards
1982
MRS. McGINTY AND THE BIZARRE PLANT by Gavin
Bishop *(Oxford)*

1983
No Award
1984
THE TREE WITCHES by Gwenda Turner *(Penguin)*
1985
THE DUCK IN THE GUN by Joy Cowley, ill. by Robyn Belton *(Shortland Educational)*
1986
A LION IN THE NIGHT by Pamela Allen *(Hodder)*
1987
TANIWHA by Robyn Kahukiwa *(Viking Kestrel)*
1988
THE MAGPIES by Denis Glover, ill. by Dick Frizzell *(Century Hutchinson)*
1989
JOSEPH'S BOAT by Caroline Macdonald, ill. by Chris Gaskin *(Hodder)*
1990
A WALK TO THE BEACH by Chris Gaskin *(Heinemann Reed)*
1991
ARTHUR AND THE DRAGON by Pauline Cartwright, ill. by David Elliott *(Highgate)*
1992
ONE LONELY KAKAPO by Sandra Morris *(Hodder & Stoughton)*
1993
LILY AND THE PRESENT by Christine Ross *(Methuen)*
1994
THE TROLLEY by Patricia Grace, ill. by Kerry Gemmill *(Viking)*
1995
KOTUKU: THE FLIGHT OF THE WHITE HERON by Chris Gaskin *(Hodder & Stoughton)*

Esther Glen Award 🐦

Established in 1945 in honor of Esther Glen, New Zealand journalist, children's book editor and author, the award is administered by The New Zealand Library & Information Association (P. O. Box 12-212, Wellington, New Zealand). Given for the most distinguished contribution to New Zealand literature for children by an author who is a citizen or resident of New Zealand, the award "is offered annually and awarded when merited." (Medal and NZ $1000)

1945
THE BOOK OF WIREMU by Stella Morice *(Angus & Robertson)*
1946
No Award
1947
MYTHS AND LEGENDS OF MAORILAND by A. W. Reed *(Reed)*
1948-1949
No Awards
1950
THE ADVENTURES OF NIMBLE, RUMBLE AND TUMBLE by Joan Smith *(Paul's Book Arcade)*
1951-1958
No Awards
1959
FALTER TOM AND THE WATER BOY by Maurice Duggan *(Paul's Book Arcade)*
1960-1963
No Awards
1964
TURI: THE STORY OF A LITTLE BOY by Leslie C. Powell *(Paul's Book Arcade)*
1965-1969
No Awards
1970
A LION IN THE MEADOW by Margaret Mahy *(Dent)*
1971-1972
No Awards
1973
THE FIRST MARGARET MAHY STORY BOOK by Margaret Mahy *(Dent)*
1974
No Award
1975
MY CAT LIKES TO HIDE IN BOXES by Eve Sutton and Lynley Dodd *(Hamish Hamilton)*
1976-1977
No Awards
1978
THE LIGHTHOUSE KEEPER'S LUNCH by Ronda and David Armitage *(Deutsch)*
1979
TAKE THE LONG PATH by Joan de Hamel *(Lutterworth)*
1980-1981
No Awards
1982
THE YEAR OF THE YELVERTONS by Katherine O'Brien *(Oxford)*

1983
THE HAUNTING by Margaret Mahy *(Dent)*
1984
ELEPHANT ROCK by Caroline Macdonald *(Hodder)*
1985
THE CHANGEOVER: A SUPERNATURAL ROMANCE by
Margaret Mahy *(Dent)*
1986
MOTHERSTONE by Maurice Gee *(Oxford)*
1987
No Award
1988
ALEX by Tessa Duder *(Oxford)*
1989
THE MANGROVE SUMMER by Jack Lazenby *(Oxford)*
1990
ALEX IN WINTER by Tessa Duder *(Oxford)*
1991
AGNES THE SHEEP by William Taylor *(Ashton Scholastic)*
1992
ALESSANDRA: ALEX IN ROME by Tessa Duder *(Oxford)*
1993
UNDERRUNNERS by Margaret Mahy *(Hamish Hamilton)*
1994
SASSCAT TO WIN by Paula Boock *(McIndoe)*
1995
THE FATMAN by Maurice Gee *(Viking)*

New Zealand Library Association Young People's Nonfiction Award 🐚

This annual award is for the author of the book considered by
the New Zealand Library & Information Association (P. O. Box
12-212, Wellington, New Zealand) to be the most distinguished
contribution to nonfiction children's literature. (Medal and $1000)

1987
GAIJAIN: FOREIGN CHILDREN OF JAPAN by Olive Hill and
Ngaio Hill *(Longman Paul)*
1988
No Award

1989
IT'S OK TO BE YOU by Claire Patterson *(Simon & Schuster)*
1990
THE WEB by Deborah Furley *(Collins)*
1991
MODEL BOATS THAT REALLY GO by John Reid *(Random Century)*
1992
THE DAMSELFLY by Peter Garland *(Nelson, Price, Milburn)*
1993
ALBATROSS ADVENTURE by Kim Westerskov *(Nelson, Price, Milburn)*
1994
PAIKEA by Robyn Kahukiwa *(Viking)*
1995
SHADOWS ON THE WALL by Barbara Cairns and Helen Martin *(Longman)*

Te Kura Pounamu Award 🍂

Meaning 'precious greenstone,' this award will be made to the author of a book written in the Maori language which is considered to be a distinguished contribution to literature for children or young people. The author must be a citizen or resident of New Zealand. The first award will be made in late 1996 for a work published during the 1995 calendar year, and annually thereafter. The sponsor is the New Zealand Library & Information Association (P.O. Box 12-212, Wellington, New Zealand). (Greenstone taonga and $1000)

UNITED KINGDOM (UK)
Best Books for Babies Award 🍂
PARENTS MAGAZINE

Begun by the British Book Marketing Council and *Parents*, a magazine with wide readership in Britain, this program was discontinued in 1991 due to a lack of sponsorship. A panel of specialists selected a short list of books—usually ten titles—published for under-fours in the previous year. The list was widely publicized to parents throughout the country, to draw attention to the number and variety of new books published for infants and toddlers each year. *Parents* selected a "team of ten mums and dads across the country to 'test' the books" and choose the top title. (£1,000)

1985
PEEPO! by Janet and Allan Ahlberg *(Viking Kestrel)*
1986
WHERE IS BOBO? by Susan Hulme, ill. with photographs by Jan Siegieda *(Methuen)*
1987
FIVE MINUTES' PEACE by Jill Murphy *(Walker)*
1988
A DAY OF RHYMES by Sarah Pooley *(Bodley Head)*
1989
WAKE UP, DAD! by Sally Grindley, ill. by Siobhan Dodds *(Simon & Schuster)*
1990
ROSIE'S BABIES by Martin Waddell, ill. by Penny Dale *(Walker)*

British Book Awards ❧

CHILDREN'S BOOK CATEGORIES

This prize program, honoring books, publishing, bookselling, distributing and other aspects of the book trade is organized by *Publishing News* (43 Museum St., London WC1A 1LY, England). Formerly awarded in two children's book categories: Author of the Year *(A)*, and Illustrated Book of the Year *(I)*, the two awards were merged in 1995 into one Children's Book of the Year Award. Winners are selected by an 'Academy' of over 150 members of the UK book trade from publishers' nominations (Trophy)

1989
A: Roald Dahl
1990
A. Anne Fine
I: THE MOUSEHOLE CAT by Antonia Barber, ill. by Nicola Bayley *(Walker)*
1991
A: Dick King-Smith
I: FARMER DUCK by Helen Oxenbury *(Walker)*
1992
A: Raymond Briggs
I: PENGUIN SMALL by Mick Inkpen *(Hodder & Stoughton)*

1993
A: Anne Fine
I: MUMMY LAID AN EGG by Babette Cole *(Jonathan Cape)*
1994
A: Allan and Janet Ahlberg
I: THE MOST AMAZING POP-UP SCIENCE BOOK by Jay Young *(Watts)*
1995
THE HUTCHINSON TREASURY OF CHILDREN'S LITERATURE ed. by Alison Sage *(Hutchinson/Random)*

British Book Design and Production Awards ❧

Children's books have been included in this touring exhibition in recent years, and have been singled out as one of eleven categories honored as winners for the excellent quality of their production. The exhibition and prize-giving are organized and sponsored by the British Printing Industries Federation (11 Bedford Row, London WC1R 4DX, England), Publishers Association, and Book Trust. (Prize)

1987
IN GRANDPA'S HOUSE by Philip Sendak, ill. by Maurice Sendak, designed by Constance Fogler *(Bodley Head)*
1988
EACH PEACH PEAR PLUM by Janet and Allan Ahlberg, designed by Janet and Allan Ahlberg *(Penguin)*
1989
THE FOUR SEASONS OF BRAMBLY HEDGE by Jill Barklem, designed by Bob Hook and Ian Butterworth *(Collins)*
1990
ANGELINA'S BIRTHDAY by Katharine Holabird, ill. by Helen Craig, designed by Helen Craig *(Aurum)*
UNDER THE SUN AND OVER THE MOON by Kevin Crossley-Holland, ill. by Ian Penney *(Orchard)*
1991
THE MOUSEHOLE CAT by Antonia Barber, ill. by Nicola Bayley *(Walker)*
1992
POLAR BEAR SCARE by Jill Newton *(All Books for Children)*

1993
TIGERS by Roland Edwards, ill. by Judith Riches *(All Books for Children)*
1994
MAKING FRIENDS WITH FRANKENSTEIN by Colin McNaughton *(Walker)*
1995
SO MUCH by Trish Cooke, ill. by Helen Oxenbury *(Walker)*

Carnegie Medal ⁊⁊

Given annually since 1937 by the (British) Library Association (LA) (7 Ridgmount St., London WC1E 7AE, England) for a children's book of outstanding merit written in English and first published in the United Kingdom in the preceding year. As of the award for 1990—given in 1991—Peters Library Service makes a substantial annual grant, matched by the Business Sponsorship Incentive Scheme of the British government, to the LA to enable it to publicize both the Carnegie and Greenaway awards programs aggressively throughout Britain. The years cited in our listing are publication years. (Medal; in addition, as of the 1991 award year, the winner can select an organization to receive £750 worth of books)

1936
PIGEON POST by Arthur Ransome *(Cape)*
1937
THE FAMILY FROM ONE END STREET by Eve Garnett *(Muller)*
1938
THE CIRCUS IS COMING by Noel Streatfeild *(Dent)*
1939
RADIUM WOMAN by Eleanor Doorly *(Heinemann)*
1940
VISITORS FROM LONDON by Kitty Barne *(Dent)*
1941
WE COULDN'T LEAVE DINAH by Mary Treadgold *(Penguin)*
1942
THE LITTLE GREY MEN by BB *(Eyre & Spottiswoode)*
1943
No Award
1944
THE WIND ON THE MOON by Eric Linklater *(Macmillan)*
1945
No Award

1946
THE LITTLE WHITE HORSE by Elizabeth Goudge
(Brockhampton)
1947
COLLECTED STORIES FOR CHILDREN by Walter de la Mare
(Faber)
1948
SEA CHANGE by Richard Armstrong *(Dent)*
1949
THE STORY OF YOUR HOME by Agnes Allen *(Faber)*
1950
THE LARK ON THE WING by Elfrida Vipont Foulds *(Oxford)*
1951
THE WOOL-PACK by Cynthia Harnett *(Methuen)*
1952
THE BORROWERS by Mary Norton *(Dent)*
1953
A VALLEY GROWS UP by Edward Osmond *(Oxford)*
1954
KNIGHT CRUSADER by Ronald Welch *(Oxford)*
1955
THE LITTLE BOOKROOM by Eleanor Farjeon *(Oxford)*
1956
THE LAST BATTLE by C. S. Lewis *(Bodley Head)*
1957
A GRASS ROPE by William Mayne *(Oxford)*
1958
TOM'S MIDNIGHT GARDEN by Philippa Pearce *(Oxford)*
1959
THE LANTERN BEARERS by Rosemary Sutcliff *(Oxford)*
1960
THE MAKING OF MAN by I. W. Cornwall *(Phoenix)*
1961
A STRANGER AT GREEN KNOWE by Lucy Boston *(Faber)*
1962
THE TWELVE AND THE GENII by Pauline Clarke *(Faber)*
1963
TIME OF TRIAL by Hester Burton *(Oxford)*
1964
NORDY BANK by Sheena Porter *(Oxford)*
1965
THE GRANGE AT HIGH FORCE by Philip Turner *(Oxford)*
1966
No Award
1967
THE OWL SERVICE by Alan Garner *(Collins)*

1968
THE MOON IN THE CLOUD by Rosemary Harris *(Faber)*
1969
THE EDGE OF THE CLOUD by K. M. Peyton *(Oxford)*
1970
THE GOD BENEATH THE SEA by Leon Garfield and Edward
Blishen *(Longman)*
1971
JOSH by Ivan Southall *(Angus & Robertson)*
1972
WATERSHIP DOWN by Richard Adams *(Rex Collings)*
1973
THE GHOST OF THOMAS KEMPE by Penelope Lively
(Heinemann)
1974
THE STRONGHOLD by Mollie Hunter *(Hamish Hamilton)*
1975
THE MACHINE-GUNNERS by Robert Westall *(Macmillan)*
1976
THUNDER AND LIGHTNINGS by Jan Mark *(Kestrel)*
1977
THE TURBULENT TERM OF TYKE TILER by Gene Kemp
(Faber)
1978
THE EXETER BLITZ by David Rees *(Hamish Hamilton)*
1979
TULKU by Peter Dickinson *(Gollancz)*
1980
CITY OF GOLD AND OTHER STORIES FROM THE OLD
TESTAMENT by Peter Dickinson *(Gollancz)*
1981
THE SCARECROWS by Robert Westall *(Chatto)*
1982
THE HAUNTING by Margaret Mahy *(Dent)*
1983
HANDLES by Jan Mark *(Kestrel)*
1984
THE CHANGEOVER: A SUPERNATURAL ROMANCE by
Margaret Mahy *(Dent)*
1985
STORM by Kevin Crossley-Holland *(Heinemann)*
1986
GRANNY WAS A BUFFER GIRL by Berlie Doherty *(Methuen)*
1987
THE GHOST DRUM by Susan Price *(Faber)*

1988
A PACK OF LIES by Geraldine McCaughrean *(Oxford)*
1989
GOGGLE-EYES by Anne Fine *(Hamish Hamilton)*
1990
WOLF by Gillian Cross *(Oxford)*
1991
DEAR NOBODY by Berlie Doherty *(Orchard)*
1992
FLOUR BABIES by Anne Fine *(Hamish Hamilton)*
1993
STONE COLD by Robert Swindells *(Hamish Hamilton)*
1994
WHISPERS IN THE GRAVEYARD by Theresa Bresling *(Methuen)*

Children's Book Award ❧

Organized by the Federation of Children's Book Groups (Award Coordinator: Jenny Blanch, 30 Senneleys Park Rd., Northfield, Birmingham B31 1AL, England) and sponsored by Save & Prosper Educational Foundation, this program currently involves more than 60,000 children nationally in selecting the winners now in three categories: Longer Novel *(LN)*, Shorter Novel *(SN)*, and Picture Book *(PB)*, one of which is also voted the overall winner. Children's involvement begins when regional Federation (adult) members, reflecting children's ratings, select fifty titles as "Pick of the Year." The top ten are re-tested; ten titles make up a shortlist that is ranked by children in order of preference to select the overall winner. Authors and illustrators sometimes share the award. (Portfolios prepared by children for all honorees on shortlist; overall winner receives a glass bowl, specially commissioned from a leading British craftworker and engraved with a theme from the book.)

1981
MR. MAGNOLIA by Quentin Blake *(Cape)*
1982
FAIR'S FAIR by Leon Garfield *(Macdonald)*
1983
THE BFG by Roald Dahl *(Cape)*
1984
THE SAGA OF ERIK THE VIKING by Terry Jones, ill. by Michael Foreman *(Pavilion)*

1985
BROTHER IN THE LAND by Robert Swindells *(Oxford)*
1986
ARTHUR by Amanda Graham, ill. by Donna Gynell
(Spindlewood)
1987
THE JOLLY POSTMAN OR OTHER PEOPLE'S LETTERS by
Janet and Allan Ahlberg *(Heinemann)*
1988
WINNIE THE WITCH by Valerie Thomas, ill. by Korky Paul
(Oxford)
1989
MATILDA by Roald Dahl *(Cape)*
1990
ROOM 13 by Robert Swindells *(Doubleday)*
1991
THREADBEAR by Mick Inkpen *(Hodder & Stoughton)*
1992
Overall & LN: KISS THE DUST by Elizabeth Laird *(Methuen)*
SN: FIND THE WHITE HORSE by Dick King-Smith *(Viking)*
PB: SHHH! by Sally Grindley, ill. by Peter Uttop *(ABC)*
1993
Overall & SN: THE SUITCASE KID by Jacqueline Wilson
(Doubleday)
LN: GULF by Robert Westall *(Methuen)*
PB: SNOWY by Berlie Doherty and Keith Bowen *(Collins)*
1994
Overall & LN: THE BOY IN THE BUBBLE by Ian Strachan
(Methuen)
SN: THE FINDERS by Nigel Hinton *(Viking)*
PB: AMAZING ANTHONY ANT by Lorna and Grahamn
Philpot *(Orion)*
1995
Overall & SN: HARRIET'S HARE by Dick King-Smith
(Doubleday)
LN: WALK TWO MOONS by Sharon Creech *(Macmillan)*
PB: THE RASCALLY CAKE by Jeanne Willis, ill. by Korky Paul
(Andersen)

Children's Book of the Year ❧

Organized by the Lancashire County Library (143 Corporation
St., Preston PRl 2UQ, Lancashire, England) and sponsored by
National Westminster Bank, this program honors original fiction
for readers 11-14 years old. All secondary schools in Lancashire

County are invited to participate; one school in each of the fourteen districts of the county is chosen as the participant each year. Pupils 13-14 years old participate in the voting, with student representatives attending meetings to discuss the entries, which are made by publishers. One reader from each school is on the final judging panel, which selects a shortlist and then a winner. (Engraved glass decanter and honorarium)

1987
RUBY IN THE SMOKE by Philip Pullman *(Oxford)*
1988
REDWALL by Brian Jacques *(Century Hutchinson)*
1989
GROOSHAM GRANGE by Anthony Horowitz *(Methuen)*
1990
PLAGUE '99' by Jean Ure *(Methuen)*
1991
MATTIMEO by Brian Jacques *(Random Century)*
1992
WHITBY WITCHES by Robin Jarvis *(Simon & Schuster)*
1993
GULF by Robert Westall *(Methuen)*
SALAMANDASTRON by Brian Jacques *(Hutchinson)*
1994
THE BOY IN THE BUBBLE by Ian Strachan *(Methuen)*
1995
THE ELECTRIC KID by Garry Kilworth *(Bantam)*

Earthworm Award 🐛

This awards program has as its motto: The Prize for books that help children to enjoy and care for the Earth. It is designed "to promote and reward environmental awareness and sensitivity in literature for children of all ages..." and honors "books which not only highlight the threats to our natural world, but also explore and celebrate its richness, variety and beauty." It is an activity of The Arts for the Earth, Friends of the Earth (26-28 Underwood St., London N1 7JQ, England), sponsored by the investment house Save & Prosper. (£2,000 to winner; £250 for up to three other titles)

1987
THE BOY AND THE SWAN by Catherine Storr *(Deutsch)*
1988
WHERE THE FOREST MEETS THE SEA by Jeannie Baker *(Julia MacRae)*

1989
AWAITING DEVELOPMENTS by Judy Allen *(Julia MacRae)*
1990
THE YOUNG GREEN CONSUMER GUIDE by John Elkington and Julia Hailes *(Gollancz)*
1991
THE LAST RABBIT edited by Jennifer Curry *(Methuen))*
1992
CAPTAIN ECO AND THE FATE OF THE EARTH by Jonathan Porritt *(Dorling Kindersley)*
1993
STRANGE ORBIT by Margaret Simpson *(Scholastic)*
1994
PROJECT KITE by Sian Lewis *(Andersen)*
1995
THE LIVING FORESTS, Kaleidoscopes Series *(Kingfisher)*

Kathleen Fidler Award 🐌

Suggested by the Edinburgh Children's Book Group, this award is a memorial to the author of over eighty books for children. It is a manuscript competition for novels for children ages 8-12; entrants have not previously had a novel published for this age group. The winning entry each year is published. While a panel of children's book professionals selects the winners, children in two schools read shortlisted entries and their views are considered when final selections are made. The program is administered by Book Trust Scotland (The Scottish Book Centre, 137 Dundee St., Edinburgh EH11 1BG, Scotland). (£1,000 cash prize; publication by Blackie Children's Books, now known as Dutton, an imprint of Penguin Children's Books; rosewood and silver trophy held for one year)

1983
ADRIFT by Allan Baillie *(Blackie)*
1984
NO SHELTER by Elizabeth Lutzeier *(Blackie)*
1985
BARTY by Janet Collins *(Blackie)*
1986
DIAMOND by Caroline Pitcher *(Blackie)*
1987
SIMON'S CHALLENGE by Theresa Breslin *(Blackie)*
1988
FLIGHT OF THE SOLAR DUCKS by Charles Morgan *(Blackie)*

1989
MIGHTIER THAN THE SWORD by Clara Bevan *(Blackie)*
1990
MAGIC WITH EVERYTHING by Roger Burt *(Blackie))*
1991
GREG'S REVENGE by George Hendry *(Blackie)*
1992
RICHARD'S CASTLE by Susan Coon *(Blackie)*
1993
48 HOURS WITH FRANKLIN by Mij Kelly *(Blackie)*
1994
RUN, ZAN, RUN by Catherine MacPhail *(Blackie)*
1995
EDGE OF DANGER by Clare Dudman *(Dutton)*

Kate Greenaway Medal ৯

Given annually by the (British) Library Association (LA) (7
Ridgmount St., London WC1E 7AE, England) to the most
distinguished work in the illustration of children's books first
published in the United Kingdom in the preceding year. As of the
award for 1990—given in 1991—Peters Library Service makes a
substantial annual grant, matched by the Business Sponsorship
Incentive Scheme of the British government, to the LA to enable
it to publicize both the Greenaway and Carnegie awards
programs aggressively throughout Britain. The years cited in our
listing are publication years. (Medal; in addition, as of the 1991
award year, the winner can select an organization to receive £750
worth of books)

1955
No Award
1956
TIM ALL ALONE by Edward Ardizzone *(Oxford)*
1957
MRS. EASTER AND THE STORKS by V. H. Drummond
(Faber)
1958
No Award
1959
KASHTANKA AND A BUNDLE OF BALLADS by William
Stobbs *(Oxford)*
1960
OLD WINKLE AND THE SEAGULLS by Elizabeth Rose, ill. by
Gerald Rose *(Faber)*

1961
MRS. COCKLE'S CAT by Philippa Pearce, ill. by Antony Maitland *(Longman)*

1962
BRIAN WILDSMITH'S A B C by Brian Wildsmith *(Oxford)*

1963
BORKA by John Burningham *(Cape)*

1964
SHAKESPEARE'S THEATRE by C. W. Hodges *(Oxford)*

1965
THREE POOR TAILORS by Victor Ambrus *(Hamish Hamilton)*

1966
MOTHER GOOSE TREASURY by Raymond Briggs *(Hamish Hamilton)*

1967
CHARLIE, CHARLOTTE & THE GOLDEN CANARY by Charles Keeping *(Oxford)*

1968
DICTIONARY OF CHIVALRY by Grant Uden, ill. by Pauline Baynes *(Longman)*

1969
THE QUANGLE-WANGLE'S HAT by Edward Lear, ill. by Helen Oxenbury *(Heinemann)*
DRAGON OF AN ORDINARY FAMILY by Margaret Mahy, ill. by Helen Oxenbury *(Heinemann)*

1970
MR. GUMPY'S OUTING by John Burningham *(Cape)*

1971
THE KINGDOM UNDER THE SEA by Jan Pieńkowski *(Cape)*

1972
THE WOODCUTTER'S DUCK by Krystyna Turska *(Hamish Hamilton)*

1973
FATHER CHRISTMAS by Raymond Briggs *(Hamish Hamilton)*

1974
THE WIND BLEW by Pat Hutchins *(Bodley Head)*

1975
HORSES IN BATTLE by Victor Ambrus *(Oxford)*
MISHKA by Victor Ambrus *(Oxford)*

1976
THE POST OFFICE CAT by Gail E. Haley *(Bodley Head)*

1977
DOGGER by Shirley Hughes *(Bodley Head)*

1978
EACH PEACH PEAR PLUM by Allan Ahlberg, ill. by Janet Ahlberg *(Kestrel)*

1979
THE HAUNTED HOUSE by Jan Pieńkowski *(Heinemann)*
1980
MR. MAGNOLIA by Quentin Blake *(Cape)*
1981
THE HIGHWAYMAN by Alfred Noyes, ill. by Charles Keeping
(Oxford)
1982
LONG NECK AND THUNDER FOOT by Helen Piers, ill. by
Michael Foreman *(Kestrel)*
SLEEPING BEAUTY & OTHER FAVOURITE FAIRY TALES
chosen by Angela Carter, ill. by Michael Foreman *(Gollancz)*
1983
GORILLA by Anthony Browne *(Julia MacRae)*
1984
HIAWATHA'S CHILDHOOD by Errol Le Cain *(Faber)*
1985
SIR GAWAIN AND THE LOATHLY LADY by Selina Hastings,
ill. by Juan Wijngaard *(Walker)*
1986
SNOW WHITE IN NEW YORK by Fiona French *(Oxford)*
1987
CRAFTY CHAMELEON by Mwenye Hadithi, ill. by Adrienne
Kennaway *(Hodder & Stoughton)*
1988
CAN'T YOU SLEEP, LITTLE BEAR? by Martin Waddell, ill. by
Barbara Firth *(Walker)*
1989
WAR BOY: A COUNTRY CHILDHOOD by Michael Foreman
(Pavilion)
1990
THE WHALE'S SONG by Dyan Sheldon, ill. by Gary Blythe
(Hutchinson)
1991
THE JOLLY CHRISTMAS POSTMAN by Janet & Allan
Ahlberg *(Heinemann)*
1992
ZOO by Anthony Browne *(Julia MacRae)*
1993
BLACK SHIPS BEFORE TROY by Rosemary Sutcliff, ill. by
Alan Lee *(Frances Lincoln)*
1994
WAY HOME by Libby Hawthorne, ill. by Gregory Rogers
(Andersen)

Guardian Award for Children's Fiction ❧

Given annually by *The Guardian* (119 Farringdon Road, London EC1R 3ER, England), for an outstanding work of fiction for children by a British or Commonwealth author, which was first published in the United Kingdom during the preceding year. The award is chosen by a panel of authors and *The Guardian*'s children's books review editor. Picture books and previous winners are excluded from consideration. In the listing below, the year cited is the year in which the award was made. (£1000)

1967
DEVIL-IN-THE-FOG by Leon Garfield *(Longman)*
1968
THE OWL SERVICE by Alan Garner *(Collins)*
1969
THE WHISPERING MOUNTAIN by Joan Aiken *(Cape)*
1970
FLAMBARDS (The Trilogy) by K. M. Peyton *(Oxford)*
1971
THE GUARDIANS by John Christopher *(Hamish Hamilton)*
1972
A LIKELY LAD by Gillian Avery *(Collins)*
1973
WATERSHIP DOWN by Richard Adams *(Rex Collings)*
1974
THE IRON LILY by Barbara Willard *(Longman)*
1975
GRAN AT COALGATE by Winifred Cawley *(Oxford)*
1976
THE PEPPERMINT PIG by Nina Bawden *(Gollancz)*
1977
THE BLUE HAWK by Peter Dickinson *(Gollancz)*
1978
A CHARMED LIFE by Diana Wynne Jones *(Macmillan)*
1979
CONRAD'S WAR by Andrew Davies *(Blackie)*
1980
THE VANDAL by Ann Schlee *(Macmillan)*
1981
THE SENTINELS by Peter Carter *(Oxford)*
1982
GOODNIGHT, MISTER TOM by Michelle Magorian *(Kestrel)*

1983
THE VILLAGE BY THE SEA by Anita Desai *(Heinemann)*
1984
THE SHEEP-PIG by Dick King-Smith *(Gollancz)*
1985
WHAT IS THE TRUTH? by Ted Hughes *(Faber)*
1986
HENRY'S LEG by Ann Pilling *(Viking Kestrel)*
1987
THE TRUE STORY OF SPIT MACPHEE by James Aldridge
(Viking Kestrel)
1988
THE RUNAWAYS by Ruth Thomas *(Hutchinson)*
1989
A PACK OF LIES by Geraldine McCaughrean *(Oxford)*
1990
GOGGLE-EYES by Anne Fine *(Hamish Hamilton)*
1991
THE KINGDOM BY THE SEA by Robert Westall *(Methuen)*
1992
THE EXILES by Hilary McKay *(Gollancz)*
PAPER FACES by Rachel Anderson *(Oxford)*
1993
LOW TIDE by William Mayne *(Jonathan Cape)*
1994
THE MENNYMS by Sylvia Waugh *(Julia MacRae)*
1995
MAPHEAD by Lesley Howarth *(Walker)*

Mary Vaughan Jones Award 🙶

Mary Vaughan Jones was an outstanding contributor to Welsh
children's literature, and the author of nearly forty books. In
addition, her Welsh-language reading textbook *Sali Mali*
introduced the language to thousands of very young children,
selling nearly 40,000 copies in the last twenty years, a record for
a minority language book. She also translated English-language
books into Welsh, such as Tamasin Cole's *Fourteen Rats and a
Rat Catcher* and Pat Hutchins' *Rosie's Walk*. The award
honoring her is presented every three years to "a person who has
made an outstanding contribution to children's literature in the
Welsh language over a considerable period of time." The sponsor
is the Welsh National Centre for Children's Literature (Castell
Brychan, Heol y Bryn, Aberystwyth, Dyfed, SY23 2JB, Wales).
(Silver trophy depicting characters from Mary Vaughan Jones' books)

1985   Ifor Owen
1988   Emily Huws
1991   T. Llew Jones
1994   W.J. Jones

Macmillan Prize
for a Children's Picture Book

The object of this competition, sponsored by Macmillan
Children's Books (25 Eccleston Pl., London SW1W 9NF,
England) is "to stimulate new work from young illustrators in art
schools and to help them start their professional lives." Working
to a length of 24 or 32 pages, art students in higher education
establishments in the UK submit portfolios that are judged by a
distinguished panel of authors, illustrators, and the Publisher of
Macmillan Children's Books. Cash prizes for the winner and
those placing second and third in the competition are made;
Macmillan Children's Books has an option—not always
exercised—to publish any of the prize winners. (£1000 for the
first-place winner; lesser amounts to other winners)

1986
SHH! IT'S THE SECRET CLUB by John Watson *(Macmillan)*
1987
BUSH VARK'S FIRST DAY OUT by Charles Fuge *(Macmillan)*
1988
ALPHABET CITY by Mark Hudson *(Macmillan)*
1989
A CLOSE CALL by Amanda Harvey *(Macmillan)*
1990
No first-place winner
1991
MY GRANDPA HAS BIG POCKETS by Selina Young
(Macmillan, 1993)
1992
BUTTON by Sara Fanelli *(ABC Books)*
1993
WHEN THE MOON COMES OUT by Joanne Kouyoumdjian
(Macmillan, 1966)
1994
THE SEA HOLE by Ross Collins
1995
No first-place winner

Kurt Maschler Award ঞ

The award is for "a work of imagination in the children's field in which text and illustration are of excellence and so presented that each enhances yet balances the other." The award was established by the founder of Atrium Press in Zurich, which published banned German writers in the 1930s. Formerly known as the 'Emil' Award, it honors Erich Kästner's *Emil und die Detektive*, illustrated by Walter Trier, and is administered by Book Trust (Book House, 45 East Hill, London SW18 2QZ, England). (£1,000 and bronze statuette of 'Emil')

1982
SLEEPING BEAUTY & OTHER FAVOURITE FAIRY TALES chosen by Angela Carter, ill. by Michael Foreman *(Gollancz)*
1983
GORILLA by Anthony Browne *(Julia MacRae)*
1984
GRANPA by John Burningham *(Cape)*
1985
THE IRON MAN by Ted Hughes, ill. by Andrew Davidson *(Faber)*
1986
THE JOLLY POSTMAN OR OTHER PEOPLE'S LETTERS by Janet and Allan Ahlberg *(Heinemann)*
1987
JACK THE TREACLE EATER by Charles Causley, ill. by Charles Keeping *(Macmillan)*
1988
ALICE'S ADVENTURES IN WONDERLAND by Lewis Carroll, ill. by Anthony Browne *(Julia MacRae)*
1989
THE PARK IN THE DARK by Martin Waddell, ill. by Barbara Firth *(Walker)*
1990
ALL JOIN IN by Quentin Blake *(Cape)*
1991
HAVE YOU SEEN WHO'S JUST MOVED IN NEXT DOOR TO US? by Colin McNaughton *(Walker)*
1992
THE MAN by Raymond Briggs *(Julia MacRae)*
1993
THINK OF AN EEL by Karen Wallace, ill. by Mike Bostock *(Walker)*
1994
SO MUCH by Trish Cooke, ill. by Helen Oxenbury *(Walker)*
1995
THE LITTLE BOAT by Kathy Henderson, ill. by Patrick Benson *(Walker)*

Mind Boggling Books Award 🐛

Sponsored and administered by W. H. Smith (Books Dept., Greenbridge Rd., Swindon SN3 3LD, England), this award was established in 1993 with the aim of promoting children's books which are accessible to children in content and price. Entries must be in paperback and must offer a gripping read—there are no further criteria. Children aged 9 to 12 are invited to enter a book reviewing competition via *Bookcase,* W. H. Smith's free magazine, and other national media. Six winners are selected who then choose the winning book from a shortlist of six titles previously selected by the W. H. Smith children's book department. (£5,000)

1993
KRINDLEKRAX by Philip Ridley *(Red Fox)*
1994
HACKER by Malorie Blackman *(Transworld)*
1995
MEMOIRS OF A DANGEROUS ALIEN by Maggie Prince *(Orion)*

Mother Goose Award 🐛

Established in 1979 by bookseller Clodagh Corcoran, this award is presented in the spring to "the most exciting newcomer to British children's book illustration." Its sponsor and administrator is Books for Children Book Club (4 Furzeground Way, Stockley Park, Uxbridge, Middlesex UB11 1DP, England). Recipients are selected by a panel of illustrators and children's book specialists. (£1,000 and bronzed, engraved, real goose egg)

1979
PIPPIN AND POD by Michelle Cartlidge *(Heinemann)*
1980
MR. POTTER'S PIGEON by Patrick Kinmouth, ill. by Reg Cartwright *(Hutchinson)*
1981
GREEN FINGER HOUSE by Rosemary Harris, ill. by Juan Wijngaard *(Eel Pie)*
1982
SUNSHINE by Jan Ormerod *(Kestrel)*
1983
ANGRY ARTHUR by Satoshi Kitamura *(Andersen)*

1984
THE HOB STORIES by William Mayne, ill. by Patrick Benson *(Walker)*

1985
BADGER'S PARTING GIFTS by Susan Varley *(Andersen)*

1986
No Award

1987
A BAG OF MOONSHINE selected by Alan Garner, ill. by Patrick James Lynch *(Collins)*

1988
LISTEN TO THIS compiled by Laura Cecil, ill. by Emma Chichester-Clark *(Bodley Head)*

1989
BUSH VARK'S FIRST DAY OUT by Charles Fuge *(Macmillan)*

1990
STRAT AND CHATTO by Jan Mark, ill. by David Hughes *(Walker)*

1991
A CLOSE CALL by Amanda Harvey *(Macmillan)*

1992
INSIDE THE WHALE AND OTHER ANIMALS by Steve Parker, ill. by Ted Dewan *(Dorling Kindersley)*

1993
THE SEASHELL SONG by Susie Jenkins-Pearce, ill. by Claire Fletcher *(Bodley Head)*

1994
WHERE THE GREAT BEAR WATCHES by Lisa Flather *(ABC)*

1995
I LOVE ANIMALS by Flora McDonnell *(Walker)*

Nottinghamshire Children's Book Awards 🦢

Organized by the Nottingham County Library Service (Education Library South, Glaisdale Parkway, Nottingham NG8 4GP, England) and the Dillons Bookstores, these awards aim to promote the enjoyment of reading. A shortlist of eight titles is selected by the County Children's Librarians; the list is widely publicized and voted on by "children, parents, teachers, librarians—in fact anyone who has an interest in children's books." Titles may be borrowed from libraries throughout the county, or purchased at Dillons. The Acorn Award *(A)* is for books for children up to 7; the Oak Tree Award *(O)* is for titles for readers 8-12. (£250 for each award, shared between the author and illustrator if they are not the same person)

1989
A: SIDNEY THE MONSTER by David Wood, ill. by Clive Scruton *(Walker)*
0: MATILDA by Roald Dahl *(Cape)*

1990
A: KNICKERLESS NICOLA by Kara May, ill. by Duffy Weir *(Macmillan)*
0: BILL'S NEW FROCK by Anne Fine *(Methuen)*

1991
A: THREADBEAR by Mick Inkpen *(Hodder & Stoughton)*
0: THE AFTERDARK PRINCESS by Annie Dalton *(Methuen)*

1992
A: KIPPER by Mick Inkpen *(Hodder)*
0: THE STORY OF TRACY BEAKER by Jacqueline Wilson *(Doubleday)*

1993
A: JONPANDA by Gwen Grant *(Heinemann)*
0: PONGWIFFY AND THE SPELL OF THE YEAR by Kaye Umansky *(Viking)*

1994
A: BLOOMING CATS by David Morgan *(Deutsch)*
0: THE WATCHERS by Helen Cresswell *(Viking)*

1995
A: SUDDENLY by Colin McNaughton *(Andersen)*
0: THE DIARY OF A KILLER CAT by Anne Fine *(Hamish Hamilton)*

Quest for a Kelpie Competition 🦎

This biennial manuscript competition which aimed to encourage new children's writers living in Scotland or those of Scottish birth residing elsewhere, has been discontinued due to editorial changes at Canongate Press. Texts for readers 8-12 years of age were eligible and the winner was published by Canongate and serialized by BBC Radio Scotland. Co-sponsored by BBC Scotland, the Scotish Library Association, and Canongate Press (14 High Street, Edinburgh EH1 1TE, Scotland), the award also paid a £1,000 advance against royalties on a paperback edition of the winning book.

1987
QUEST FOR A KELPIE by Frances Mary Hendry *(Canongate)*

1989
THE DARK SHADOW by Mary Rhind *(Canongate)*
1991
THE BAILIE'S DAUGHTER by Donald Lightwood *(Canongate)*

Science Book Prizes 🔊

This program honors authors of popular nonfiction science and technology books written in English and first published in the United Kingdom "which are judged to contribute most to the public understanding of science." It is a joint project of the (British) Science Museum (The National Museum of Science & Industry) and the Committee on the Public Understanding of Science (COPUS), which administers the prize from The Royal Society (6 Carlton House Terrace, London SW1Y 5AG, England). One prize is for a book for a general reading audience; another prize—listed below—is for "books aimed primarily at young people, i.e., under-14 year olds" (under-16 in 1989); (£10,000 for each prize as of 1991, with the sponsorship of the chemical company Rhône-Poulenc)

1989
THE WAY THINGS WORK by David Macaulay *(Dorling Kindersley)*
1990
THE STARTING POINT Series (WHAT MAKES A FLOWER GROW?, WHAT MAKES IT RAIN?, WHAT'S UNDER THE GROUND?, and WHERE DOES ELECTRICITY COME FROM?) by Susan Mayes *(Usborne)*
DP: THE GIANT BOOK OF SPACE by Ian Ridpath *(Hamlyn)*
1991
CELLS ARE US and CELL WARS by Fran Balkwill and Mic Rolph *(HarperCollins)*
1992
THE AMAZING VOYAGE OF THE CUCUMBER SANDWICH by Peter Rowan *(Cape)*
HOW NATURE WORKS by David Burnie *(Dorling Kindersley)*
1993
MIGHTY MICROBES by Thompson Yardley *(Cassell)*
1994
EYEWITNESS GUIDE: EVOLUTION by Linda Gamlin *(Dorling Kindersley)*
SCIENCE WITH WEATHER by Rebecca Heddle and Paul Shipton *(Usborne)*
THE ULTIMATE DINOSAUR BOOK by David Lambert *(Dorling Kindersley)*

1995
THE MOST AMAZING POP-UP SCIENCE BOOK by Jay
Young *(Watts)*

Signal Poetry Award 🙶

Intended to honor excellence in a variety of areas associated with
poetry for children, the award has been presented to single-poet
collections published for children, and to poetry anthologies
published for children. The award is given for work published in
the preceding year in Britain, regardless of the original country of
publication. The sponsor is the journal *Signal: Approaches to
Children's Books* (The Thimble Press, Lockwood, Station Road,
South Woodchester, Stroud, Glos. GL5 5EQ, England). In its
May issue each year, *Signal* includes lively reports from its
award's judges; the pieces—even in a year when the award is not
given—constitute a first-class critical retrospective of the year in
poetry for children in Britain. (£100 and Certificate)

1979
MOON-BELLS AND OTHER POEMS by Ted Hughes *(Chatto)*
1980-1991
No Awards
1982
YOU CAN'T CATCH ME! by Michael Rosen, ill. by Quentin
Blake *(Deutsch)*
(Poet and illustrator shared the award.)
1983
THE RATTLE BAG edited by Seamus Heaney and Ted Hughes
(Faber)
1984
SKY IN THE PIE by Roger McGough *(Kestrel)*
1985
WHAT IS THE TRUTH? by Ted Hughes *(Faber)*
1986
SONG OF THE CITY by Gareth Owen *(Fontana)*
1987
EARLY IN THE MORNING by Charles Causley *(Viking Kestrel)*
1988
BOO TO A GOOSE by John Mole *(Peterloo Poets)*
1989
WHEN I DANCE by James Berry *(Hamish Hamilton)*
1990
HEARD IT IN THE PLAYGROUND by Allan Ahlberg *(Viking
Kestrel)*

1991
THIS POEM DOESN'T RHYME edited by Gerald Benson *(Viking)*
1992
SHADES OF GREEN edited by Anne Harvey *(Julia MacRae)*
1993
TWO'S COMPANY by Jackie Kay *(Blackie)*
1994
THE ALL NITE CAFÉ by Philip Gross *(Faber)*
1995
SECRETS by Helen Dunmore *(Bodley Head)*
1996
BUNS FOR THE ELEPHANTS by Mike Harding *(Viking)*

Smarties Book Prize 🍬

The Smarties Book Prize is designed to encourage high standards and stimulate interest in children's books. Prizes are currently given in three age categories; one of the three category winners receives a Grand Prize. Winners are selected from a shortlist of 15 titles, 5 in each category. Eligible books are published during the preceding year, written in English by a citizen or resident of the UK, living at the time of publication. In 1994 for the first time, the overall winner was chosen by a panel of children from the shortlist drawn up by adult judges. The prize is administered by Book Trust (Book House, 45 East Hill, London SW18 2QZ, England) and sponsored by Rowntree Mackintosh Confectionery Ltd., manufacturers of numerous taste treats for children, including "Smarties," multicolored chocolate beans that are described as the "number one confectionery line in the UK." (£2,000 to each cagetgory winner; additional £8,000 to grand prize winner)

1985
Grand Prize + over 7: GAFFER SAMSON'S LUCK by Jill Paton Walsh *(Viking Kestrel)*
7 & under: IT'S YOUR TURN, ROGER! by Susanna Gretz *(Bodley Head)*
Innovation: WATCH IT WORK! THE PLANE by Ray Marshall and John Bradley *(Viking Kestrel)*
1986
Grand Prize + 7-11: THE SNOW SPIDER by Jenny Nimmo *(Methuen)*
6 & under: THE GOOSE THAT LAID THE GOLDEN EGG retold and ill. by Geoffrey Patterson *(Deutsch)*
Innovation (joint winner): THE MIRRORSTONE by Michael Palin, Alan Lee and Richard Seymour *(Cape)*

Innovation (joint winner): VILLAGE HERITAGE by Miss Pinnell and the Children of Sapperton School *(Alan Sutton)*

1987

Grand Prize + 9-11: A THIEF IN THE VILLAGE by James Berry *(Hamish Hamilton)*

5 & under: THE ANGEL AND THE SOLDIER BOY by Peter Collington *(Methuen)*

6-8: TANGLE AND THE FIRESTICKS by Benedict Blathwayt *(Julia MacRae)*

1988

Grand Prize + 5 & under: CAN'T YOU SLEEP LITTLE BEAR? by Martin Waddell, ill. by Barbara Firth *(Walker)*

6-8: CAN IT BE TRUE? by Susan Hill, ill. by Angela Barrett *(Hamish Hamilton)*

9-11: RUSHAVENN TIME by Theresa Whistler *(Brixworth Primary School)*

1989

Grand Prize + 5 & under: WE'RE GOING ON A BEAR HUNT by Michael Rosen, ill. by Helen Oxenbury *(Walker)*

6-8: BILL'S NEW FROCK by Anne Fine *(Methuen)*

9-11: BLITZCAT by Robert Westall *(Macmillan)*

1990

Grand Prize + 9-11: MIDNIGHT BLUE by Pauline Fisk *(Lion)*

5 & under: SIX DINNER SID by Inga Moore *(Simon & Schuster)*

6-8: ESIO TROT by Roald Dahl, ill. by Quentin Blake *(Cape)*

1991

Grand Prize + 5 & under: FARMER DUCK by Martin Waddell, ill. by Helen Oxenbury *(Walker)*

6-8: JOSIE SMITH by Magdalen Nabb, ill. by Pirkko Vainio *(HarperCollins)*

9-11: KRINDLEKRAX by Philip Ridley *(Cape)*

1992

Grand Prize + 9-11: THE GREAT ELEPHANT CHASE by Gillian Cross *(Oxford)*

5 & under: NICE WORK, LITTLE WOLF by Hilda Offen *(Hamish Hamilton)*

6-8: THE STORY OF THE CREATION by Jane Ray *(Orchard)*

1993

Grand Prize + 6-8: WAR GAME by Michael Foreman *(Pavilion)*

5 & under: HUE BOY by Rita Phillips Mitchell, ill. by Caroline Binch *(Gollancz)*

9-11: LISTEN TO THE DARK by Maeve Henry *(Heinemann)*

1994

Grand Prize + 9-11: THE EXILES AT HOME by Hilary McKay *(Gollancz)*

5 & under: SO MUCH by Trish Cooke, ill. by Helen Oxenbury *(Walker)*

6-8: DIMANCHE DILLER by Henrietta Branford, ill. by Lesley Harker *(Young Lions)*
1995
Grand Prize + 9-11: DOUBLE ACT by Jacqueline Wilson *(Doubleday)*
Joint 9-11 Winner: WEATHER EYE by Elizabeth Howarth *(Walker)*
5 & under: THE LAST NOO-NOO by Jill Murphy *(Walker)*
6-8: THOMAS AND THE TINNERS by Jill Paton Walsh *(Macdonald)*

W. H. Smith Illustration Awards

This program which continued the Francis Williams Illustration Awards designed to "encourage and advance the art of book illustration" has been discontinued. The award was given at five-year intervals and then annually, with a Premier Prize for either book or magazine work, and two Second Prizes. The award submissions formed the basis of an annual exhibition at the Victoria and Albert Museum. The award sponsor, W. H. Smith, is a prominent book and magazine retail chain in the UK. In the listing below, winners of the Premier Prize, only, are cited, and then only if the work honored was a children's book. (£3,000 to winner; £1,000 to Second Prize winners)

1968-1972
Michael Foreman, for THE GREAT SLEIGH ROBBERY *(Hamish Hamilton, 1968)* and HORATIO *(Hamish Hamilton, 1969)*
1972-1977
John Laurence, for RABBIT AND PORK *(Hamish Hamilton, 1975)*
1977-1982
Raymond Briggs, for THE SNOWMAN *(Hamish Hamilton, 1978)*
1982-1987
(Premier Prize for adult book)
1988
Charles Keeping, for CHARLES KEEPING'S CLASSIC TALES OF THE MACABRE *(Blackie)*
1989
(Premier Prize for magazine cover)
1990
John Vernon Lord, for AESOP'S FABLES retold by James Michie *(Cape)*
1991
Angela Barrett, for THE HIDDEN HOUSE by Martin Waddell *(Walker)*

Times Educational Supplement Information Book Awards ❧

Established in 1972 by the *Times Educational Supplement* (Priory House, St. John's Lane, London EC1, England), this award is given for distinction in content and presentation in informational (nonfiction) trade books originated in the United Kingdom or Commonwealth countries. Two panels of three judges each select the winners. Awards are offered for books in both Junior (up to age 10), *J* in the listing below, and Senior (ages 11-16), *S* in the listing below, categories. Although no awards were made in 1994 and 1995, the program continues in 1996. (£500 to the winner in each category)

1972
INTRODUCING ARCHAEOLOGY by Magnus Magnusson *(Bodley Head)*

1973
J: No Award
S: HUMAN POPULATIONS by David Hay *(Penguin)*

1974
J: FROGS, TOADS AND NEWTS by F. D. Ommaney *(Bodley Head)*
S: UNDERSTANDING ART by Betty Churcher *(Holmes McDougall)*

1975
J: SPIDERS by Ralph Whitlock *(Priory)*
S: WINDOW INTO A NEST by Geraldine Lux-Flanagan and Sean Morris *(Kestrel)*

1976
J: WASH AND BRUSH UP by Eleanor Allen *(A. & C. Black)*
S: MACDONALD'S ENCYCLOPEDIA OF AFRICA *(Macdonald Educ.)*

1977
J: STREET FLOWERS by Richard Mabey *(Kestrel)*
S: MEN AND MACHINES. THE MITCHELL BEAZLEY JOY OF KNOWLEDGE LIBRARY *(Mitchell Beazley)*

1978
J: TOURNAMENTS by Richard Barber *(Kestrel)*
S: BUTTERFLIES ON MY MIND by Dulcie Gray *(Angus & Robertson)*

1979
J: THE COMMON FROG by George Bernard *(Oxford Scientific Films/Whizzard/Deutsch)*
S: MAKE IT HAPPY: WHAT SEX IS ALL ABOUT by Jane Cousins *(Virago)*

1980
J: EARTHQUAKES AND VOLCANOES by Imelda and Robert
Updegraff *(Methuen)*
S: OXFORD JUNIOR ENCYCLOPEDIA OF MUSIC by Michael
Hurd *(Oxford)*

1981
J: No Award
S: SKULLS by Richard Steel *(Heinemann)*

1982
J: A DAY WITH A MINER by Phillippa Aston *(Wayland)*
S: THE EASY WAY TO BIRD RECOGNITION by John
Kilbracken *(Kingfisher)*

1983
J: MUM—I FEEL FUNNY by Ann McPherson and Aidan
Macfarlane *(Chatto)*
S: DEFENCE by Charles Freeman *(Batsford)*
JUST IMAGINE by Robert Cumming *(Kestrel)*

1984
J: No Award
S: IN DEUTSCHLAND by Rod Nash *(Nelson)*

1985
J: KWAZULU SOUTH AFRICA by Nancy Durrell McKenna *(A.
& C. Black)*
S (joint winner): GROWING UP, ADOLESCENCE BODY
CHANGES AND SEX by Susan Meredith *(Usborne)*
S (joint winner): THE SUNDAY TIMES COUNTRYSIDE
COMPANION by Geoffrey Young *(Country Life)*

1986
J: THE YOUNG GEOGRAPHER INVESTIGATES POLAR
REGIONS by Terry Jennings *(Oxford)*
S: THE LEGEND OF ODYSSEUS by Peter Connolly *(Oxford)*

1987
J: BEING BORN by Sheila Kitzinger, ill. with photographs by
Lennart Nilsson *(Dorling Kindersley)*
S (joint winner): GALAXIES AND QUASARS by Heather ·
Couper and Nigel Henbest *(Watts)*
S (joint winner): THE ULTIMATE ALPHABET by Mike Wilks
(Pavilion)

1988
J (joint winner): CONKER by Barrie Watts *(A. & C. Black)*
J (joint winner): MAKING A BOOK by Ruth Thomson *(Watts)*
S: MARTIN LUTHER KING by Pam Brown and Valerie Scheldt
(Exley)

1989
J: WHY DO PEOPLE SMOKE? by Pete Sanders *(Watts)*
S: THE WAY THINGS WORK by David Macaulay *(Dorling
Kindersley)*

1990
J: THE TREE by Judy Hindley, ill. by Alison Wisenfeld *(ABC)*
S: THE NEW OXFORD SCHOOL ATLAS edited by Patrick Wiegand *(Oxford)*
1991
J: IAN AND FRED'S BIG GREEN BOOK by Fred Pearce and Ian Winton *(Kingfisher/Bennett)*
S: AN EGYPTIAN PYRAMID by Jacqueline Morley *(Simon & Schuster)*
1992
J: MY FIRST BOOK OF TIME by Claire Llewellyn *(Dorling Kindersley)*
S: BLACK AND BRITISH by David Bygott *(Oxford)*
1993
J: THINK OF AN EEL by Karen Wallace *(Walker)*
S: GETTING PHYSICAL by Aric Sigman *(BBC)*
1994-1995
No Awards

Tir na n-Og Awards 🐚

Sponsored by the Welsh Books Council (Castell Brychan, Aberystwyth, Dyfed, SY23 2JB, Wales), the "purpose of the Tir na n-Og Awards is to acknowledge the work of authors and illustrators; to raise the standard of writing for children and young people; and to encourage book buying and reading...." Currently, there are awards in three categories: for Fiction *(F)*, original Welsh-language novels, stories, and picture books; for Other *(0)* outstanding Welsh-language books of the year, but not translations produced overseas; and for the best English-language *(E)* book with an authentic Welsh background. (£1,000 in each category; prizes donated by Welsh Arts Council and the Welsh Library Association)

1976
F: TÂN AR Y COMIN by T. Llew Jones *(Gomer)*
E: THE GREY KING by Susan Cooper *(Chatto)*
1977
F: TRYSOR BRYNIAU CASPAR by J. Selwyn Lloyd *(Gomer)*
E: A STRING IN THE HARP by Nancy Bond *(McElderry)*
1978
F: MIRIAM by Jane Edwards *(Gomer)*
E: SILVER ON THE TREE by Susan Cooper *(Chatto)*
1979
F: Y FLWYDDYN HONNO by Dyddgu Owen *(Christopher Davies)*

E: TIME CIRCLES by Bette Meyrick *(Abelard)*

1980
F: Y LLONG by Irma Chilton *(Gomer)*
E: No Award

1981
F: Y DRUDWY DEWR by Gweneth Lilly *(Gomer)*
E: THE BLINDFOLD TRACK by Frances Thomas *(Macmillan)*

1982
F: GAEAF Y CERRIG by Gweneth Lilly *(Gomer)*
E: No Award

1983
F: CROES BREN YN NORWY by J. Selwyn Lloyd *(Gomer)*
E: BLUESTONES by Mary John *(Barn Owl Press)*

1984
F (joint winner): Y LLINYN ARIAN by Mair Wynn Hughes *(Gomer)*
F (joint winner): HERIO'R CERTYLL by Malcolm M. Jones, Cyril Jones, and Gwen Redvers Jones *(Gwasg Prifysgol Cymru)*
E: THE PRIZE by Irma Chilton *(Barn Owl Press)*

1985
No Awards

1986
F: Y LLIPRYN LLWYD by Angharad Tomos *(Y Lolfa)*
E: THE REGION OF THE SUMMER STARS by Frances Thomas *(Barn Owl Press)*

1987
F: JABAS by Penri Jones *(Dwyfor)*
0: GARDD O GERDDI by Alun Jones and J. Pinion Jones *(Gomer)*
E: THE SNOW SPIDER by Jenny Nimmo *(Methuen)*

1988
F: TYDI BYWYD YN BOEN! by Gwenno Hywyn *(Gwynedd)*
0: YR ATLAS CYMRAEG (no editor/compiler attribution; translates as *The Welsh Atlas*) *(George Philip)*
E: STEEL TOWN CATS by Celia Lucas *(Tabb House)*

1989
F (joint winner): LIW by Irma Chilton *(Gomer)*
F (joint winner, for illustration): BEN Y GARDDWR A STORIAU ERAILL by Mary Vaughan Jones, ill. by Jac Jones *(Cymdeithas Lyfrau Ceredigion)*
0: CULHWCH AC OLWEN by Gwyn Thomas and Margaret Jones *(Gwasg Prifysgol Cymru)*
E: No Award

1990
F: LLYGEDYN O HEULWEN by Mair Wynn Hughes *(Gomer)*
0: LLEUAD YN OLAU by T. Llew Jones, ill. by Jac Jones *(Gomer)*
E: No Award

1991
F: O DDAWNS I DDAWNS by Gareth F. Williams *(Lolfa)*
0: CYMRU, DDOE A HEDDIW by Geraint H. Jenkins
(Prifysgol)
E: No Award
1992
F (joint winner): WMFFRA by Emily Huws *(Gomer)*
F (joint winner: BROC MÔR by Gwen Redvers Jones *(Gomer)*
0: YN Y DECHREUAD by Robert M. Morris and Catrin
Stevens *(Gwasg Prifysgol Rhydychen/CBAC)*
E: WHO STOLE A BLOATER? by Frances Thomas *(Seren)*
1993
F: 'TISIO TSHIPSAN? by Emily Huws *(Gomer)*
0: CHWEDL TALIESIN by Gwyn Thomas and Margaret Jones
(Gwasg Prifysgol Cymru)
E: No Award
1994
F: SOTHACH A SGLYFATH by Angharad Tomos *(Y Lolfa)*
0: CRISTION YDW I by Huw John Hughes and Rheinallt
Thomas *(Canolfan Genedlaethol Addysg)*
E: DENNY AND THE MAGIC POOL by Pamela Purnell
(Gomer)
1995
F: PAM FI, DUW, PAM FI? by John Owen *(Y Lolfa)*
0: GEIRIADUR GOMER I'R IFANC by D. Geraint Lewis
(Gomer)
E: THE CANDLE MAN by Catherine Fisher *(Bodley Head)*

Whitbread Books of the Year ❧
CHILDREN'S BOOK CATEGORY

Initiated in 1971, a children's book category became part of this
program in 1972. It was the intention of the founders of the
award "to acknowledge outstanding books in particular categories
of literature not only for the qualities accorded to them by the
critics of the day, but for popular qualities which in the opinion
of the judges make them readable on a wide scale." Currently,
the categories are Novel, First Novel, Poetry, Biography/
Autobiography, and Children's Novel. Whitbread, sponsor of the
award, is a prominent brewery in the UK; the administrator of
the program is The Booksellers Association of Great Britain and
Ireland (272 Vauxhall Bridge Road, London SW1V 1BA,
England). Panels of knowledgeable judges pick shortlists and
winners for each category. Judges representing each of the
categories are joined by some others prominent in the arts to
select the winning title from the top titles in each catetory. The

listing below includes only winners in the children's book category. (£3,000 to winner in each category; Book of the Year receives total of £21,000)

1972
THE DIDDAKOI by Rumer Godden *(Macmillan)*

1973
THE BUTTERFLY BALL AND THE GRASSHOPPER'S FEAST by Alan Aldridge and William Plomer *(Cape)*

1974 (joint winners)
HOW TOM BEAT CAPTAIN NAJORK AND HIS HIRED SPORTSMEN by Russell Hoban, ill. by Quentin Blake *(Cape)*
THE EMPEROR'S WINDING SHEET by Jill Paton Walsh *(Macmillan)*

1975
Category not included in program

1976
A STITCH IN TIME by Penelope Lively *(Heinemann)*

1977
NO END TO YESTERDAY by Shelagh Macdonald *(Deutsch)*

1978
THE BATTLE OF BUBBLE AND SQUEAK by Philippa Pearce, ill. by Alan Baker *(Deutsch)*

1979
TULKU by Peter Dickinson *(Gollancz)*

1980
JOHN DIAMOND by Leon Garfield *(Kestrel)*

1981
THE HOLLOW LAND by Jane Gardam *(Julia MacRae)*

1982
THE SONG OF PENTECOST by W. J. Corbett *(Methuen)*

1983
THE WITCHES by Roald Dahl *(Cape)*

1984
THE QUEEN OF THE PHARISEES' CHILDREN by Barbara Willard *(Julia MacRae)*

1985
THE NATURE OF THE BEAST by Janni Howker *(Julia MacRae)*

1986
THE COAL HOUSE by Andrew Taylor *(Collins)*

1987
A LITTLE LOWER THAN THE ANGELS by Geraldine McCaughrean *(Oxford)*

1988
AWAITING DEVELOPMENTS by Judy Allen *(Julia MacRae)*

1989
WHY WEEPS THE BROGAN? by Hugh Scott *(Walker)*
1990
AK by Peter Dickinson *(Gollancz)*
1991
HARVEY ANGELL by Diana Hendry *(Julia MacRae)*
1992
THE GREAT ELEPHANT CHASE by Gillian Cross *(Oxford)*
1993
FLOUR BABIES by Anne Fine *(Hamish Hamilton)*
1994
GOLD DUST by Geraldine McCaughrean *(Oxford)*
1995
THE WRECK OF THE ZANZIBAR by Michael Morpurgo
(Methuen)

PART IV ❧

Selected International and Multinational Awards

Hans Christian Andersen Awards ❧

Given biennially since 1956 by the International Board on Books for Young People (Nonnenweg 12, Postfach, CH-4003, Basel, Switzerland) to one author and one illustrator (since 1966) in recognition of his or her entire body of work. (Medals)

See also International Board on Books for Young People (IBBY) Honor List.

1956
Eleanor Farjeon *(Great Britain)*

1958
Astrid Lindgren *(Sweden)*

1960
Erich Kästner *(Germany: Federal Republic)*

1962
Meindert DeJong *(USA)*

1964
René Guillot *(France)*

1966
Author: Tove Jansson *(Finland)*
Illustrator: Alois Carigiet *(Switzerland)*

1968
Authors: James Krüss *(Germany: Federal Republic)*
José Maria Sanchez-Silva *(Spain)*
Illustrator: Jiří Trnka *(Czechoslovakia)*

1970
Author: Gianni Rodari *(Italy)*
Illustrator: Maurice Sendak *(USA)*

1972
Author: Scott O'Dell *(USA)*
Illustrator: Ib Spang Olsen *(Denmark)*

1974
Author: Maria Gripe *(Sweden)*
Illustrator: Farshid Mesghali *(Iran)*

1976
Author: Cecil Bødker *(Denmark)*
Illustrator: Tatjana Mawrina *(USSR)*

1978
Author: Paula Fox *(USA)*
Illustrator: Svend Otto S. *(Denmark)*

1980
Author: Bohumil Ríha *(Czechoslovakia)*
Illustrator: Suekichi Akaba *(Japan)*

1982
Author: Lygia Bojunga Nunes *(Brazil)*
Illustrator: Zbigniew Rychlicki *(Poland)*

1984
Author: Christine Nöstlinger *(Austria)*
Illustrator: Mitsumasa Anno *(Japan)*

1986
Author: Patricia Wrightson *(Australia)*
Illustrator: Robert Ingpen *(Australia)*

1988
Author: Annie M. G. Schmidt *(Holland)*
Illustrator: Dǔsan Kállay *(Czechoslovakia)*

1990
Author: Tormod Haugen *(Norway)*
Illustrator: Lisbeth Zwerger *(Austria)*

1992
Author: Virginia Hamilton *(USA)*
Illustrator: Kvéta Pacovská *(Czechoslovakia)*

1994
Author: Michio Mado *(Japan)*
Illustrator: Jörg Müller *(Switzerland)*

1996
Author: Uri Orlev *(Israel)*
Illustrator: Klaus Ensikat *(Germany)*

Award for Writing Children's Books in German ❦

Formerly sponsored by the Austrian Ministry for Education, Art, and Sports, this biennial awards program honoring the most outstanding books for children *(C)* and young adults *(Y/A)* originally written in German has been discontinued. The International Board on Books for Young People (IBBY) National Sections in Austria, Germany, and Switzerland could enter up to five candidates for each award. A jury comprised of experts from the participating IBBY sections selected the winners, and also an Honor List.

1985
C: LIPPELS TRAUM (Lipple's Dream) by Paul Maar *(Oetinger, Germany: Federal Republic)*

Y/A: WIE IN FREMDEN SCHUHEN (Like Being in Someone Else's Shoes) by Renate Welsh *(Jungbrunnen, Austria)*
1987
C: DER HUND KOMMT! (Here Comes the Dog!) by Christine Nöstlinger *(Beltz & Gelberg, Germany: Federal Republic, and Switzerland; N. B. author is Austrian)*
Y/A:
WIE EIN ROSTIGER NAGEL IM BRETT ODER: DIE ZWEITE FLUCHT (Like a Rusty Nail in a Board or: The Second Escape) by Hanna Lehnert *(Anrich, Germany: Federal Republic)*
1989
C: DRACHENFLÜGEL (Dragon's Wings) by Renate Welsh *(Obelisk, Austria)*
Y/A: PLASCHA ODER: VON KLEINEN LEUTEN UND GROSSEN TRÄUMEN (Plascha or: Of Little People and Big Dreams) by Inge Meyer-Dietrich *(Anrich, Germany: Federal Republic)*

Biennale of Illustrations Bratislava 🐌

The Biennale of Illustrations Bratislava is an international competition and exposition of original children's book illustrations that have been published in book format. It takes place in September-October of odd-numbered years in the Slovak city of Bratislava, and typically includes around 3,000 illustrations from over fifty countries worldwide; it is probably the best single-site source available for studying trends in children's book illustration internationally. BIB is organized and administered from Bibiana (BIB Secretariat, International House of Art for Children, Panská 41, 814 99 Bratislava, Slovakia), itself a study center and museum gallery devoted to children's book illustration. Our listing includes only the recipients of the Grand Prix. (One Grand Prix, five Golden Apples, ten Plaques, Honorable Mentions, and other honors; many winners also receive stipends of various amounts)

1967
TARO AND A BAMBOO SHOOT by Masaku Matsuno, ill. by Yasuo Segawa *(Fukuinkan Shoten, Tokyo, Japan)*
1969
CHINESISCHE VOLKSMARCHEN by Eva Bednářová *(Artia, Prague, Czechoslovakia)*

1971
NARZECOZONY Z MORZA by Robert Stieler, ill. by Ardrezej
Strumitto *(Nasza Ksiegarnia, Warsaw, Poland)*
1973
DER TRAUMMACHER by Leiselotte Schwarz *(Verlag Heinrich
Ellermann, Munich, Germany: Federal Republic)*
1975
ROBINSON CRUSOE by Daniel Defoe, ill. by Nikolaj Popov
(Chudozestvenaja Literatura, Moscow, USSR)
1977
HARLEKIN by Ulf Löfgren *(Awe/Gebbers, Stockholm, Sweden)*
1979
DER KLEINE DÄUMLING by Klaus Ensikat *(Der
Kinderbuchverlag, Berlin, Germany: Democratic Republic)*
TAIPI by Klaus Ensikat *(Verlag Neues Leben, Berlin, Germany:
Democratic Republic)*
1981
KRISTOFFERS REJSE by Roald Als *(Borgen, Copenhagen,
Denmark)*
1983
ALICA V KRAJINE ZÁZRAKOV by Dŭsan Kállay *(Mladé leta,
Bratislava, Czechoslovakia)*
1985
BESTIARE FABLEUX by C. Meral, ill. by Frédéric Clément
(Editions Magnard, Paris, France)
1987
HERRA KUNINGAS by Raija Siekkinen, ill. by Hannu Taina
(Otava, Helsinki, Finland)
1989
KSIEGA BAJEK POLSKICH by Marian Murawski *(Ludowa
Spóldzielnia Wydawnicza, Warsaw, Poland)*
1991
DER GESTIEFELTE KATER by Stasys Eidrigevicious *(Nord-
Süd, Gossau, Switzerland; N. B. illustrator is Polish)*
1993
EUGENIO by M. Cockenpot, ill. by Lorenzo Mattotti, Italy
(Seuil Jeunesse, Paris, France)
1995
DIE ENTSTEHUNG DER GÜRTELTIERE by Rudyard Kipling,
ill. by John Rowe, Great Britain *(Neugebauer Verlag, Gossau,
Switzerland)*

Bologna Children's Book Fair Prizes ❧

Given annually in the spring at the Bologna Children's Book Fair (Piazza Costituzione 6, 40128 Bologna, Italy) by the Bologna Fair Organization in three categories through 1994: "Fiera di Bologna" Graphic Prize for Children *(C)*, Graphic Prize for Youth *(Y)* and "Critici in Erba" prize *(C/E)*. Beginning in 1995, the traditional prizes were replaced by a new Book Fair award called "BolognaRagazzi" awarded in the following categories: Children's Fiction *(C/F)* and children's Nonfiction *(C/N)* for children 8 and younger; Young Adult Fiction *(YA/F)* and Young Adult Nonfiction *(YA/N)* for ages 9-15. At the jury's discretion, a "Novelty" *(N)* prize may be awarded to an especially innovative work. Selection criteria include graphic design, educational, artistic, and technical qualities, with special emphasis on the overall publishing project. Participation in the competition is open to all Italian and foreign publishers displaying their books, individually or collectively, at the Bologna Children's Book Fair. As the prizes we list in this edition are actually awarded to the publisher of the winning work, only publishers' names are listed after the titles below. (Trophy)

1966
C: GESU OGGI *(Rizzoli, Italy)*
C/E: L'ALBUM DE BAMBI *(Bias, France)*
1967
C: DREI VÖGEL *(Otto Maier, Germany: Federal Republic)*
Y: DIE ALTE LINDE GONDULA *(Sigbert Mohn, Germany: Federal Republic)*
C/E: ICH SCHENK DIR EINEN PAPAGEI *(Diogenes, Switzerland)*
1968
C: DIE WICHTELMÄNNER *(Atlantis, Switzerland)*
Y: PRIBEHY *(Albatros, Czechoslovakia)*
C/E: ALLA SCOPERTA DELL 'AFRICA *(Vallecchi, Italy)*
1969
C: THE LITTLE BLACK FISH *(Institute for the Intellectual Development of Children and Young Adults, Iran)*
Y: LA CITÉ DE L'AN 2000 *(Casterman, France)*
C/E: POCAHONTAS IN LONDON *(Seymour Lawrence, USA)*
1970
C: 1, 2, 3, EIN ZUG ZUM ZOO *(Stalling, Germany: Federal Republic)*
Y: VERTEL HET UW KINDEREN *(Nederlandsche Zondacs-School Vereniging, Holland)*

C/E: LA STORIA DAI FRANCESCO E CHIARA
"RACCONTATA DAI BIMBI DE CROCE" *(Stadiv l'Aquila, Italy)*
1971
C: ARM IN ARM *(Parents, USA)*
Y: TUTTO SU GERUSALEMME BIBLICA *(C.E. Giunti-Bemporad Marzocco, Italy)*
C/E: ALLE MEINE BLÄTTER...*(Gertraud Middlehauve, Germany: Federal Republic)*
1972
C: STADTMAUS UND LANDMAUS *(Atlantis, Switzerland)*
Y: SLAVISCHE MÄRCHEN *(Artia, Czechoslovakia)*
C/E: WALTZING MATILDA *(Collins, Great Britain)*
1973
C: KOPFBLUMEN *(Der Kinderbuchverlag, Germany: Democratic Republic)*
Y: HODINA NACHOVE RUZE *(Albatros, Czechoslovakia)*
C/E: SNOW-WHITE AND THE SEVEN DWARFS *(Farrar, USA)*
1974
C: ROTKÄPPCHEN *(Diogenes, Switzerland)*
Y: THE LAST OF THE MOHICANS *(Felix Gluck, England)*
C/E: A YEAR IN THE WOODS *(Detskaya Literatura, USSR)*
1975
C: TROIS PETITS FLOCONS *(Grasset, France)*
Y: DAS SPRACHBASTELBUCH *(Jugend und Volk Verlagsges, Austria)*
C/E: IL PRINCIPE FELICE *(Paoline, Italy)*
1976
C: MAGIC FOR SALE *(Kaisei-Sha, Japan)*
Y: THE BRONZE HORSEMAN *(Detskaya Literatura, USSR)*
C/E: DAS GELBE HAUS *(Carlsen, Germany: Federal Republic)*
1977
C: SCHORSCHI SCHRUMPFT *(Diogenes, Switzerland)*
Y: TAKERU *(Kaisei-Sha, Japan)*
C/E: DIE GESCHICHTE VON BABAR DEM KLEINEN ELEFANTEN *(Diogenes, Switzerland)*
1978
C: GRABIANSKIS STADTMUSIKANTEN *(Carl Ueberreuter, Austria)*
Y: ANNO'S UNIQUE WORLD *(Kodansha, Japan)*
C/E: NICHOLAS AND THE MOON EGGS *(Collins, Australia)*
1979
C: HISTOIRE DU PETIT STEPHAN GIRARD *(Gallimard, France)*
Y: AURORA *(Dalla Parte delle Bambine, Italy)*
C/E: EIN TAG IM LEBEN DER DOROTHEA WUTZ *(Diogenes, Switzerland)*

1980
C: ANNO'S SONG BOOK *(Kodansha, Japan)*
Y: HIMMELSZELT UND SCHNECKENHAUS *(Sauerländer, Switzerland)*
C/E: DAS BUCH VOM DORF *(Fabula, Germany: Federal Republic)*
1981
C: YOK-YOK *(Gallimard, France)*
Y: L'UNIVERS A DEUX VOIX: INSECTE *(La Noria, France)*
C/E: MR. SQUINT *(World's Work, Great Britain)*
1982
C: LES SECRETS DE L'IMAGE *(Gallimard, France)*
Y: CITY OF GOLD AND OTHER STORIES FROM THE OLD TESTAMENT *(Gollancz, Great Britain)*
C/E: THE PIXIES' INVITATION *(Kaisei-Sha, Japan)*
1983
C: THE FAVERSHAMS *(Gollancz, Great Britain)*
Y: IL ÉTAIT UNE FOIS LES MOTS *(La Farandole/Messidor, France)*
C/E: OUR CHANGING WORLD *(Collins, Great Britain)*
1984
C: LE PETIT CHAPERON ROUGE *(Grasset, France, and Creative, USA)*
Y: ALENKA KRAJI DIVU *(Albatros, Czechoslovakia)*
C/E: MAME'S CATS, 1, 2, 3 *(Kaisei-Sha, Japan)*
1985
C: LEAVES *(Institute for the Intellectual Development of Children and Young Adults, Iran)*
Y: UNTITLED CHILDREN'S STORY (N.B. This is the title of a book by Kit Williams) *(Cape, Great Britain)*
C/E: SOL SOLET *(Edicions de l'Eixample, Spain)*
1986
C: ONE MORNING *(G. C. Press, Japan)*
Y: DER HUT DES KAMINFEGERS *(Basilius, Switzerland)*
C/E: PETER UND DER WOLF *(Sauerlander, Switzerland)*
1987
C: THE GREAT GAMES BOOK *(Black, Great Britain)*
Y: DÉCOUVERTES GALLIMARD *(Gallimard, France)*
C/E: THAT'S MY DAD *(Andersen, Great Britain)*
1988
C: ANIMAL NUMBERS *(Lutterworth, Great Britain)*
Y: LE LIVRE DE LA CRÉATION *(Centurion, France)*
C/E: DIE BLUMENSTADT *(Bohem, Switzerland)*
1989
C: A LONG LONG SONG *(Farrar, USA)*
Y: LES YEUX DE LA DÉCOUVERTE *(Gallimard, France)*
C/E: DEAR MILI *(Farrar, USA)*

1990
C: MIJN HELD *(Querido, Holland)*
Y: DIE GESCHICHTE VON DER KLEINEN GANS, DIE
NICHT SCHNELL GENUG WAR *(Nagel & Kimche,
Switzerland)*
C/E: A FROG PRINCE *(Holt, USA)*
1991
C: AN ALPHABET OF ANIMALS *(HarperCollins, Great Britain)*
Y: RUE DE LA MÉDITERRANEE *(Hatier/Ragéot, France)*
C/E: KLEINER EISBÄR NIMM MICH MIT! *(Nord-Süd,
Switzerland)*
1992
C: OH! *(Rainbow Graphics International/Baronian Books,
Belgium)*
Y: "JEDER NACH SEINER ART": KINDERLIEDER VON
HOFFMANN VON FALLERSIEBEN *(Beltz & Gelberg, Germany)*
C/E: IRIS *(Aura Comunicación, Spain)*
1993
C: DICTIONNAIRE DU PÈRE NOËL *(Gallimard, France)*
Y: ESCALES-CARNET DE CROQUIS *(Pastel/L'Ecole des
Loisirs, Belgium)*
C/E: DER REGENBOGENFISCH *(Nord-Süd, Switzerland)*
1994
C: THE RAINBABIES *(Lothrop, USA)*
Y: LA GRANDE PEUR SOUS LES ÉTOILES *(Syros, France)*
C/E: I AM A LITTLE PANDA *(Barron's, USA)*
1995
C/F: WAS MACHEN DIE MÄDCHEN? *(Beltz & Gelberg,
Germany)*
C/N: INCOMMODITÉS *(Editions Syros, France)*
YA/F: GROWING UP AND OTHER VICES *(Jonathan Cape,
UK)*
YA/N: ENFANTS PROSTITUÉS EN AISE *(Syros, France)*
Novelty: LES RACINES DU SAVOIR *(Gallimard, France)*
1996
C/F: CLOWN *(Jonathan Cape, UK)*
C/N: VIVE LA MUSIQUE *(Seuil, France)*
YA/F: MAGASIN ZIN ZIN *(Albin Michel, France)*
YA/N: CAUGHT IN THE CROSSFIRE *(Walker, USA)*
Novelty: LE SOURIRE QUI MORD *(Gallimard, France)*

Premi Catalònia d'Il·lustracio' ❧

The Catalonian Prize for Illustration is awarded at a biennial exhibit and competition of original art from published children's books. The event takes place in Barcelona, Spain, and is cosponsored by the Departament de Cultura de la Generalitat de Catalunya, the Consell Català del Libre per a Infants, and by the Fundació de l'Enciclopèdia Catalana, in cooperation with l'Associació d'Editors en Llengua Catalana and l'Associació Professional d'Il·lustradors. The prize is designed to honor "the best illustrations for children's books published anywhere in the world...." In addition to a Grand Prize, the international jury also selects three Plaque and five Diploma recipients. (Sculpture and stipend)

1984
LA LLUNA D'EN JOAN (Joan's Moon) by Carmen Solé i Vendrell *(Spain)*
1986
Z PROWROTEM (The Shelter) by Stasys Eidrigevičius *(Poland)*
1988
THREE CATS by Kvéta Pacovská *(Czechoslovakia)*
1990
EL GUARDIÁN DEL OLVIDO (Olvido's Keeper) by Alfonso Ruano *(Spain)*
1992
THE MOUSE BRIDE by Lesley Liu *(Taiwan)*
1994
KASHTANKA by Gennady Spirin *(Russia)*

European Award of Literature for Children and Young Adults ❧

Four European publishers—Ediciones B of Spain, Arena Verlag of Germany, Éditions L'Amitié of France, and HarperCollins of the UK—projected this annual competition "aimed at promoting excellence in writing for young readers between the ages of 8-16 within the EEC." The program no longer exists and the CBC was unable to accertain whether the prize was ever awarded.

European Prize for Children's Literature "Pier Paolo Vergerio" ૨ઌ

The Premio Europeo di Letteratura Giovanile is designed to honor the best works of European literature that help "to evaluate our culture and civilization...to point out a true humanistic way of development for new generations." In addition to singling out the winner of the European Prize, this program — judged by a European-wide jury — gives prizes for "illustrated albums," poetry, "school literature," and historical fiction, and also includes an Honor List of titles recommended for translation into all European languages. The administrator is Settore Letteratura Giovanile, Dipartimento Scienze Educazione, Università di Padova (via Marsala 59, 35122, Padova, Italia). (3,000,000 lira)

1962
LES ENFANTS DE LA TERRE *(The Children of the Earth)* by Père Castor *(Paul Faucher) (France)*
STORIE MERAVIGLIOSE DEGLI ANIMALI IN PARADISO *(Wonderful Stories of Animals In Paradise)* by Aldo Alberti *(Italy)*
1964
THE PUFFIN BOOK OF NURSERY RHYMES by Iona and Peter Opie *(Great Britain)*
MISTER MASTER by Donatella Ziliotto *(Italy)*
1966
LES CANONS DE VALMY *(The Cannons of Valmy)* by Léonce Bourliaguet *(France)*
1968
CARLA DEGLI SCAVI *(Carla of the Rocks)* by Renée Reggiani *(Italy)*
1973
KRABAT (published in English with same title) by Otfried Preussler *(Germany: Federal Republic)*
1976
LE COEUR SOUS LA CENDRE *(The Heart Under the Ashes)* by Pierre Pelot *(France)*
1978
PIERRE EST VIVANT *(Pierre Is Alive)* by Jean Coué *(France)*
1980
DIE UNENDLICHE GESCHICHTE *(The Neverending Story)* by Michael Ende *(Germany: Federal Republic)*
EL LOCO *(The Fool)* by Alberto Manzi *(Italy)*

1982
VIVA BABYMOON *(Long Live Babymoon)* by G. L. Picciolli *(Italy)*

1985
DIE PERLE *(The Pearl)* by Helme Heine *(Germany: Federal Republic)*

1987
HOE SCHILDER, HOE WILDER *(Great Painters, Great Slaughterer)* by Miep Diekmann and Marlleke van Wersch *(Holland)*

1989
LO STRALISCO *(The Crippled Boy)* by Roberto Piumini *(Italy)*

1992
LA FORCE DU BERGER by Azouz Begag and Catherine Louis *(Svizzera)*

International Board on Books for Young People (IBBY) Honor List ❧

Every two years since 1956, on the occasion of the Congresses of the International Board on Books for Young People, an IBBY Honor List is announced. In its early days, books selected for the Honor List were identified by the same jury that selects the recipient of the Hans Christian Andersen Awards. At the present time, each National Section of IBBY selects two books (one for the *text* and one for *illustration*), published in a given period before the year in which they are selected, for an IBBY biennial Congress. Those titles are the Honor Books on the List. Important considerations in selecting the Honor List titles are that the books chosen be representative of the best in children's literature from each country, and that the books are recommended as suitable for publication throughout the world, thus furthering the IBBY objective of encouraging world understanding through children's literature. In 1978 a third category was added to the IBBY Honor List, which now includes a *translator*, with at least one notable book of that translator cited as an example of his or her work. The listing below includes only Honor List titles from IBBY National Sections whose main language is English. The United Kingdom was not a member of IBBY from 1992-1994 but rejoined in 1995. New Zealand is not a member of IBBY. In 1986, Nigeria selected an Honor List title for *Text*: WITHOUT A SILVER SPOON by Eddie Iroh *(Spectrum)*. (Certificates)
   See also Hans Christian Andersen Award.

<u>UNITED STATES</u>
1956
CARRY ON, MR. BOWDITCH by Jean Lee Latham
(Houghton)
MEN, MICROSCOPES AND LIVING THINGS by Katherine
Shippen *(Viking)*
PLAY WITH ME by Marie Hall Ets *(Viking)*
1958
THE HOUSE OF SIXTY FATHERS by Meindert DeJong
(Harper)
1960
ALONG CAME A DOG by Meindert DeJong *(Harper)*
THE WITCH OF BLACKBIRD POND by Elizabeth George
Speare *(Houghton)*
1962
ISLAND OF THE BLUE DOLPHINS by Scott O'Dell
(Houghton)
1964
THE BRONZE BOW by Elizabeth George Speare *(Houghton)*
1966
WHERE THE WILD THINGS ARE by Maurice Sendak
(Harper)
1968
VALLEY OF THE SMALLEST by Aileen Fisher *(Crowell)*
1970
UP A ROAD SLOWLY by Irene Hunt *(Follett)*
1972
THE TRUMPET OF THE SWAN by E. B. White *(Harper)*
1974
Text: THE HEADLESS CUPID by Zilpha Keatley Snyder
(Atheneum)
Illustration: THE FUNNY LITTLE WOMAN retold by Arlene
Mosel, ill. by Blair Lent *(Dutton)*
1976
Text: M. C. HIGGINS, THE GREAT by Virginia Hamilton
(Macmillan)
Illustration: DAWN by Uri Shulevitz *(Farrar)*
1978
Text: TUCK EVERLASTING by Natalie Babbitt *(Farrar)*
Illustration: HUSH LITTLE BABY ill. by Margot Zemach
(Dutton)
Translation: Sheila La Farge, translator of GLASSBLOWER'S
CHILDREN by Maria Gripe *(Delacorte/Lawrence)*
1980
Text: RAMONA AND HER FATHER by Beverly Cleary
(Morrow)
Illustration: NOAH'S ARK by Peter Spier *(Doubleday)*

Translation: Richard and Clara Winston, translators of THE MAGIC STONE by Leonie Kooiker *(Morrow)*

1982

Text: AUTUMN STREET by Lois Lowry *(Houghton)*

Illustration: THE GARDEN OF ABDUL GASAZI by Chris Van Allsburg *(Houghton)*

Translation: Elizabeth Shub for her translations of books by Isaac Bashevis Singer, especially ZLATEH THE GOAT AND OTHER STORIES *(Harper)*

1984

Text: SWEET WHISPERS, BROTHER RUSH by Virginia Hamilton *(Philomel)*

Illustration: DOCTOR DE SOTO by William Steig *(Farrar)*

Translation: George Blecher and Lone Thygesen-Blecher, translators of THE BATTLE HORSE by Harry Kullman *(Bradbury)*

1986

Text: ONE-EYED CAT by Paula Fox *(Bradbury)*

Illustration: THE PEOPLE COULD FLY: AMERICAN BLACK FOLKTALES by Virginia Hamilton, ill. by Leo and Diane Dillon *(Knopf)*

Translation: Edward Fenton for his translations from Greek of books by Alki Zei, such as PETROS' WAR *(Dutton)*

1988

Text: SARAH, PLAIN AND TALL by Patricia MacLachlan *(Harper)*

Illustration: THE PAPER CRANE by Molly Bang *(Greenwillow)*

Translation: Elizabeth D. Crawford, translator of DON'T SAY A WORD by Barbara Gehrts *(McElderry)*

1990

Text: LINCOLN: A PHOTOBIOGRAPHY by Russell Freedman *(Clarion)*

Illustration: OWL MOON by Jane Yolen, ill. by John Schoenherr *(Philomel)*

Translation: Elizabeth D. Crawford, translator of CRUTCHES by Peter Härtling *(Lothrop)*

1992

Text: SHABANU: DAUGHTER OF THE WIND by Suzanne Fisher Staples *(Knopf)*

Illustration: LITTLE TRICKER THE SQUIRREL MEETS BIG TROUBLE THE BEAR by Ken Kesey, ill. by Barry Moser *(Viking)*

Translation: Antonia W. Bouis, translator of WE WERE NOT LIKE OTHER PEOPLE by Ephraim Sevela *(HarperCollins)*

1994

Text: LYDDIE by Katherine Paterson *(Lodestar)*

Illustration: EMILY by Michael Bedard, ill. by Barbara Cooney *(Doubleday)*

Translation: Hillel Halkin, translator of THE MAN FROM THE OTHER SIDE by Uri Orlev *(Houghton)*

1996
Text: CATHERINE, CALLED BIRDY by Karen Cushman *(Clarion)*
Illustration: THE CREATION by James Weldon Johnson, ill. by James E. Ransome *(Holiday House)*
Translation: Myra Cohn Livingston and Joseph F. Dominguez, translators of PLATERO Y YO by Juan Ramón Jimenez *(Clarion)*

<u>AUSTRALIA</u>
1970
I OWN THE RACECOURSE by Patricia Wrightson *(Hutchinson)*

1972
BLUE FIN by Colin Thiele *(Rigby)*

1974
Text: JOSH by Ivan Southall *(Angus & Robertson)*
Illustration: JOSEPH AND LULU AND THE PRINDIVILLE HOUSE PIGEONS by Ted Greenwood *(Angus & Robertson)*

1976
Text: THE NARGUN AND THE STARS by Patricia Wrightson *(Hutchinson)*
Illustration: MULGA BILL'S BICYCLE by R. A. Pattersonn, ill. by Kilmany and Deborah Niland *(Collins)*

1978
Text: THE OCTOBER CHILD by Eleanor Spence *(Oxford)*
Illustration: THE RUNAWAY PUNT by Robert Ingpen *(Rigby)*

1980
Text: A DREAM OF SEAS by Lilith Norman *(Collins)*
Illustration: THE QUINKINS by Jercy Treazuse *(Collins)*

1982
Text: PLAYING BEATIE BOW by Ruth Park *(Nelson)*
Illustration: THE RAINFOREST CHILDREN by Margaret Pittaway, ill. by Heather Philpott *(Oxford)*

1984
Text: THE WATCHER IN THE GARDEN by Joan Phipson *(Methuen)*
Illustration: WHO SANK THE BOAT? by Pamela Allen *(Nelson)*

1986
Text: DANCING IN THE ANZAC DELI by Nadia Wheatley *(Oxford)*
Illustration: POSSUM MAGIC by Mem Fox, ill. by Julie Vivas *(Omnibus)*

1988
Text: RIVERMAN by Allan Baillie *(Nelson)*
Illustration: FIRST THERE WAS FRANCES by Bob Graham *(Lothian)*

1990
Text: MY PLACE by Nadia Wheatley and Donna Rawlins
(Collins/Dove)
Illustration: WHERE THE FOREST MEETS THE SEA by
Jeannie Baker *(Julia MacRae))*
1992
Text: DODGER by Libby Gleeson *(Turton & Chambers)*
Illustration: AESOP'S FABLES by Rodney McCrae *(Margaret Hamilton)*
1994
Text: THE BAMBOO FLUTE by Garry Disher *(Angus & Robertson)*
Illustration: DO NOT GO AROUND THE EDGES by Daisy
Utemorrah, ill. by Patricia Torres *(Magabala)*

CANADA
1958
LOST IN THE BARRENS by Farley Mowat *(Little, Brown)*
1960
NKWALA by Edith Lambert Sharp *(Little, Brown)*
1962
THE SUNKEN CITY by James McNeill *(Oxford)*
1964
THE INCREDIBLE JOURNEY by Sheila Burnford *(Little, Brown)*
1976
Text: ALLIGATOR PIE by Dennis Lee *(Macmillan)*
Illustration: LES TRAINAUX DE MON ENFANCE by Carlo
Italiano *(Tundra)*
1978
Text (English): THE MOUSE WOMAN AND THE VANISHED
PRINCESSES by Christie Norris *(McClelland & Stewart)*
GARBAGE DELIGHT by Dennis Lee (Macmillan)
Text (French): LES SAISONS DE LA MER by Monique
Corriveau *(Fides)*
Illustration: LA CACHETTE by Ginette Anfousse *(Le Tamanoir)*
1980
Text: HOLD FAST by Kevin Major *(Clarke-Irwin)*
Illustration: LA CHICANE by Ginette Anfousse *(La courte échelle)*
Translation: Paule Daveluy, translator of LES CHEMINS
SECRETS DE LA LIBERTÉ *(Pierre Tisseyre)*
1982
Text: THE KEEPER OF THE ISIS LIGHT by Monica Hughes
(Hamish Hamilton)
Illustration: PETROUCHKA by Elizabeth Cleaver *(Macmillan)*
Translation: David Toby Homel and Margaret Rose, translators
of THE KING'S DAUGHTER by Suzanne Martel *(Douglas & McIntyre)*

1984
Text (English): THE ROOT CELLAR by Janet Lunn *(Lester &*
Orpen Dennys)
Text (French): L'HOMME AUX OISEAUX by Robert Soulières
Québec-Amérique)
Illustration: A NORTHERN ALPHABET by Ted Harrison *(Tundra)*
Translation: Claude Aubry, translator of JE T'ATTENDS À
PEGGY'S COVE by Brian Doyle *(Pierre Tisseyre)*
1986
Text (English): SWEETGRASS by Jan Hudson *(Tree Frog Press)*
Text (French): L'ENFANT DE LUMIÈRE by Suzanne Martel
(Méridien)
Illustration: CHIN CHIANG AND THE DRAGON'S DANCE
by Ian Wallace *(Groundwood/Douglas & McIntyre)*
Translation: Paule Daveluy, translator of EMILIE DE LA
NOUVELLE LUNE by Lucy Maud Montgomery *(Pierre
Tisseyre)*
1988
Text (English): SHADOW IN HAWTHORN BAY by Janet Lunn
(Lester & Orpen Dennys)
Text (French): LE DERNIER DES RAISINS by Raymond Plante
(Québec-Amérique)
Illustration: THE EMPEROR'S PANDA by David Day, ill. by
Eric Beddows *(McClelland & Stewart)*
Translation: Marie-Andrée Clermont, translator of JASMIN by
Jan Truss *(Pierre Tisseyre)*
1990
Text (English): BAD BOY by Diana Wieler
(Groundwood/Douglas & McIntyre)
Text (French): LE DON by David Schinkel and Yves Beauchesne
(Pierre Tisseyre)
Illustration: COULD YOU STOP JOSEPHINE? by Stéphane
Poulin *(Tundra)*
Translation: Paule Daveluy, translator of EMILIE DE LA
NOUVELLE LUNE 2 by Lucy Maud Montgomery *(Pierre
Tisseyre)*
1992
Text (English): REDWORK by Michael Bedard *(Lester & Orpen*
Dennys)
Text (French): BIBITSA OU L'ETRANGE VOYAGE DE
CLARA VIC by Christiane Duchesne *(Québec-Amérique)*
Illustration: THE ORPHAN BOY by Tololwa M. Mollel, ill. by
Paul Morin *(Oxford)*
1994
Text (English): TICKET TO CURLEW by Celia Barker
Lottridge *(Groundwood/Douglas & McIntyre)*
Text (French): LE GROS PROBLÈME DU PETIT MARCUS by
Gilles Gauthier *(La Courte Échelle)*

Illustration: UN VOYAGE POUR DEUX by Stéphane Poulin *(Annick)*

1996
Text (English): TRAVELING INTO THE LIGHT AND OTHER STORIES by Martha Brooks *(Groundwood)*
Text (French): LES GRANDS SAPINS NE MEURENT PAS by Dominique Demers *(Québec-Amérique)*
Illustration: GIFTS by Jo Ellen Bogart, ill. by Barbara Reid *(North Winds)*
Translation: Susan Ouriou, translator of LA ROUTE DE CHLIFA by Michele Marineau *(Québec-Amérique)*

UNITED KINGDOM

1956
LAVENDER'S BLUE by Kathleen Lines *(Oxford)*
MINNOW ON THE SAY by Philippa Pearce *(Oxford)*
1958
THE FAIRY DOLL by Rumer Godden *(Macmillan)*
1960
TOM'S MIDNIGHT GARDEN by Philippa Pearce *(Oxford)*
WARRIOR SCARLET by Rosemary Sutcliff *(Oxford)*
1962
TANGARA by Nan Chauncy *(Oxford)*
THE BORROWERS AFLOAT by Mary Norton *(Dent)*
1964
THE TWELVE AND THE GENII by Pauline Clarke *(Faber)*
1966
THE NAMESAKE by Walter Hodges *(Bell)*
1968
LOUIE'S LOT by E. W. Hildick *(Faber)*
1974
Text: WHAT THE NEIGHBOURS DID by Philippa Pearce *(Longmans)*
Illustration: TICH by Pat Hutchins *(Bodley Head)*
1976
Text: THE GHOST OF THOMAS KEMPE by Penelope Lively *(Heinemann)*
Illustration: HOW TOM BEAT CAPTAIN NAJORK AND HIS HIRED SPORTSMEN by Russell Hoban, ill. by Quentin Blake *(Cape)*
1978
Text: A YEAR AND A DAY by William Mayne *(Hamish Hamilton)*
Illustration: THORN ROSE by Errol Le Cain *(Faber)*
Translation: Anthea Bell, translator of THE CUCUMBER KING by Christine Nöstlinger *(Andersen)*

1980
Text: THE GODS IN WINTER by Patricia Miles *(Hamish Hamilton)*
Illustration: EACH PEACH PEAR PLUM by Janet and Allan Ahlberg *(Kestrel)*
Translation: Patricia Crampton, translator of THE SEA LORD by Alet Schouten *(Methuen)*

1982
Text: TULKU by Peter Dickinson *(Gollancz)*
Illustration: MISTER MAGNOLIA by Quentin Blake *(Cape)*
Translation: Anthea Bell, translator of THE BIG JANOSCH BOOK OF FUN by Janosch *(Andersen)*

1984
Text: ALL THE KING'S MEN by William Mayne *(Cape)*
Illustration: HANSEL AND GRETEL by the Brothers Grimm, ill. by Anthony Browne *(Julia MacRae)*
Translation: Elizabeth Watson Taylor, translator of THE MAGIC INKSTAND AND OTHER STORIES by Heinrich Seidel *(Cape)*

1986
Text (English): THE CHANGEOVER: A SUPERNATURAL ROMANCE by Margaret Mahy *(Dent)*
Text (Welsh): Y MABINOGI by Gwyn Thomas *(University of Wales Press)*
Illustration: HIAWATHA'S CHILDHOOD by Henry Wadsworth Longfellow, ill. by Errol Le Cain *(Faber)*
Translation: Patricia Crampton, translator of THE FIFTH CORNER by Kristina Ehrenstråle *(Methuen)*

1988
Text: WOOF! by Allan Ahlberg *(Viking Kestrel)*
Illustration: THE JOLLY POSTMAN OR OTHER PEOPLE'S LETTERS by Janet and Allan Ahlberg *(Heinemann)*

1990
Text (English): SLAMBASH WANGS OF A COMPO GORMER by Robert Leeson *(Collins)*
Text (Welsh): BEN Y GARDDWR A STORIAU ERAILL by Mary Vaughan Jones *(Cymdeithas Lyfrau Ceredigion)*
Illustration: EASTER by Jan Pieńkowski *(Heinemann)*

1992-1994
No Awards

1996
Text: SOMEONE CAME KNOCKING by Anne Merrick *(Spindlewood)*
Illustration: WAR GAME by Michael Foreman *(Pavilion)*
Translation: Isabel Quigly, translator of MATTIE AND GRANDPA by Roberto Piumini *(Penguin)*

International Reading Association Children's Book Awards ❧

This prize program honors new talents in children's literature. Publishers worldwide are invited to submit candidates for the awards, which are designed to single out writers whose early work suggests unusual promise for a successful career in creating books for children. As of the 1987 awards, one prize is for people writing for older readers *(0)*, a second is for creators of books for younger readers *(Y)* and, beginning in 1995, a third prize is given to the author of an information book *(I)*. Administered by the International Reading Association (800 Barksdale Rd., P.O. Box 8139, Newark, DE 19714-8139). ($500 to each)

1975
TRANSPORT 7-41-R by T. Degens *(Viking, USA)*
1976
DRAGONWINGS by Laurence Yep *(Harper, USA)*
1977
A STRING IN THE HARP by Nancy Bond *(McElderry, USA)*
1978
A SUMMER TO DIE by Lois Lowry *(Houghton, USA)*
1979
RESERVED FOR MARK ANTHONY CROWDER by Alison Smith *(Dutton, USA)*
1980
WORDS BY HEART by Ouida Sebestyen *(Atlantic-Little, Brown, USA)*
1981
MY OWN PRIVATE SKY by Delores Beckman *(Dutton, USA)*
1982
GOODNIGHT, MISTER TOM by Michelle Magorian *(Kestrel, Great Britain)*
1983
THE DARKANGEL by Meredith Ann Pierce *(Atlantic-Little, Brown, USA)*
1984
RATHA'S CREATURE by Clare Bell *(McElderry, USA)*
1985
BADGER ON THE BARGE by Janni Howker *(Julia MacRae, Great Britain)*
1986
PRAIRIE SONGS by Pam Conrad *(Harper, USA)*

1987
0: AFTER THE DANCING DAYS by Margaret I. Rostkowski *(Harper, USA)*
Y: THE LINE-UP BOOK by Marisabina Russo *(Greenwillow, USA)*

1988
0: THE RUBY IN THE SMOKE *and* SHADOW IN THE NORTH by Philip Pullman *(Oxford, Great Britain)*
Y: THE THIRD-STORY CAT by Leslie Baker *(Little, Brown, USA)*

1989
0: PROBABLY STILL NICK SWANSEN by Virginia Euwer Wolff *(Holt, USA)*
Y: RECHENKA'S EGGS by Patricia Polacco *(Philomel, USA)*

1990
0: CHILDREN OF THE RIVER by Linda Crew *(Delacorte, USA)*
Y: NO STAR NIGHTS by Anna Egan Smucker, ill. by Steve Johnson *(Knopf, USA)*

1991
0: UNDER THE HAWTHORN TREE by Marita Conlon-McKenna *(O'Brien Press, Ireland)*
Y: IS THIS A HOUSE FOR HERMIT CRAB? by Megan McDonald, ill. by S. D. Schindler *(Orchard, USA)*

1992
0: RESCUE JOSH McGUIRE by Ben Mikaelsen *(Hyperion, USA)*
Y: TEN LITTLE RABBITS by Virginia Grossman, ill. by Sylvia Long *(Chronicle, USA)*

1993
0: LETTERS FROM RIFKA by Karen Hesse *(Holt, USA)*
Y: OLD TURTLE by Douglas Wood, ill. by Cheng-Khee Chee *(Pfeifer-Hamilton, USA)*

1994
0: BEHIND THE SECRET WINDOW: A MEMOIR OF A HIDDEN CHILDHOOD by Nelly S. Toll *(Dutton, USA)*
Y: SWEET CLARA AND THE FREEDOM QUILT by Deborah Hopkinson, ill. by James E. Ransome *(Knopf, USA)*

1995
0: SPITE FENCES by Trudy Krisher *(Bantam, USA)*
Y: THE LEDGERBOOK OF THOMAS BLUE EAGLE by Gay Matthaei & Jewel Grutman, ill. by Adam Cvijanovic *(Thomasson-Grant, USA)*
I: STRANDED AT PLIMOTH PLANTATION 1626 by Gary Bowen *(HarperCollins, USA)*

1996
0: THE KING'S SHADOW by Elizabeth Adler *(Farrar, USA)*

Y: MORE THAN ANYTHING ELSE by Marie Bradby and Chris K. Soentpiet *(Orchard, USA)*
I: THE CASE OF THE MUMMIFIED PIGS AND OTHER MYSTERIES IN NATURE by Susan E. Quinlan *(Boyds Mills, USA)*

International Reading Association Lee Bennett Hopkins Promising Poet Award ❧

The goal of this award is to recognize and promote promising new poets who write for children and young adults up to grade 12. It is given every three years to a poet who has published no more than two books of children's poetry. A book-length single poem is eligible, as is poetry in any language. (Non-English poetry must be accompanied by an English translation.) The award is for published works only, copyrighted during the three years prior to the award year. Defined as "poetry rather than light verse," the work is judged on literary merit, appeal to children, and evidence of a fresh, insightful voice. Entries for the 1998 award may be submitted beginning in May 1997. The committee chair's name and address will be available from the Executive Office of the International Reading Association (800 Barksdale Rd., Newark, DE 19714-8139) in March 1997. ($500 donated by Mr. Hopkins)

1995
Deborah Chandra for BALLOONS AND OTHER POEMS and RICH LIZARD AND OTHER POEMS *(both Farrar, USA)*

Janusz Korczak Literary Awards ❧
(ANTI-DEFAMATION LEAGUE OF B'NAI B'RITH)

This awards program is named for the Polish pediatrician, child welfare pioneer and founder and administrator for two Warsaw orphanages, one housing Jewish children and the other Catholic. In 1942 he refused to abandon his wards, an option available to him, and went with them to his death in gas chambers at Treblinka. This competition is for books exemplifying the principles of selflessness and human dignity characteristic of Janusz Korczak. Prizes are given in two categories: a book for young readers, fiction or nonfiction, and suitable for use at either the elementary or secondary school level; and a book about the welfare and nurturing of children, directed to parents and educators, as well as to the helping professions. Books published in any language, anywhere in the world are eligible. The program was temporarily suspended for reorganization from 1989-1991. The administrator is the Braun Center for Holocaust Studies (Anti-Defamation League of B'nai B'rith, 823 United Nations Plaza, New York, NY 10017). This listing includes only the winning titles published *for* children. ($1,000 and plaque)

1981
BLACK AS I AM by Zindzi Mandela *(Guild of Tudors Press, South Africa)*

1982
UPON THE HEAD OF THE GOAT: A CHILDHOOD IN HUNGARY 1939-1944 by Aranka Siegal *(Farrar, USA)*

1984
SEAWARD by Susan Cooper *(McElderry, USA)*

1986
DAYS OF HONEY by Irene Awret *(Schocken, USA)*

1988
ELIEZER BEN-YEHUDA: THE FATHER OF MODERN HEBREW by Malka Drucker *(Lodestar, USA)*

1990
No Award

1992
SHADOW OF THE WALL by Christa Laird *(Greenwillow, USA)*

1995
THE FROZEN WATERFALL by Gaye Hicyilmaz *(Farrar)*

Janusz Korczak Literary Prize ෨

(POLISH NATIONAL SECTION OF IBBY)

The Polish National Section of the International Board on Books for Young People (IBBY) (Ul. Nowy Swiat 69, Pok. 314, IBIN UW, PL-00-46 Warsaw, Poland) sponsors a literary competition honoring the memory of a renowned Polish physician and Holocaust victim. (See the previous entry for a brief biographical note about Janusz Korczak.) IBBY National Sections worldwide are invited to submit titles that "promote understanding and friendship among children all over the world." There are two winning titles; one is a book *for* children (the titles on our list), and the other a book *about* children. Three additional titles are awarded Janusz Korczak Medals, and three others are designated Honor List titles. (Medal and cash prize)

1979
BRÖDERNA LEJONHJÄRTA (The Brothers Lionheart) by Astrid Lindgren *(Sweden)*
NOVÝ GULIWER *(New Gulliver)* by Bohumil Ŕiuha *(Czechoslovakia)*
1981
DIE UNENDLICHE GESCHICHTE (The Neverending Story) by Michael Ende *(Germany: Federal Republic)*
LAMPAS MALEHO PLAVCIKA (The Ship Boy's Lamp) by Jana Navratila *(Czechoslovakia)*
1983
DZIEŃ, NOC I PORA NICZYJA (Day, Night and Nobody's Time) by Ewa Nowacka *(Poland)*
1985
POGRESZNA STYPKA (The Wrong Step) by Latchesar Stantchev *(Bulgaria)*
1987
DOKAD WRACAJA LATAWCE (Whence Do the Dragons Return?) by Maria Borowa *(Poland)*
1990
HA-I BI-REHOV HA-TSIPORIM (The Island on Bird Street) by Uri Orlev *(Israel)*
1992
THE YEAR OF THE DRAGON by Joanna Rudniańska *(Poland)*
1994
THE INVISIBLE WALLS by Ofra Geibart-Avni *(Israel)*

Astrid Lindgren Translation Prize ❧

Sponsored by the International Federation of Translators (Heiveldstraat 245, B-9040 Sint-Amandsberg/Gent, Belgium), this prize is named for the Swedish author and Hans Christian Andersen Medalist whose books have appeared worldwide. Its object is to promote the translation of works written for children and to draw attention to the role of the translator in bringing together people of the world and enriching their cultural and literary lives. The prize is given at three or four year intervals at conventions of the Fédération Internationale des Traducteurs for either a single translation of outstanding quality or for a translator's body of work. (Diploma and/or sum of money)

1981
Åke Holmberg *(Sweden)* for his children's book translations into Swedish
1984
Patricia Crampton *(Great Britain)* for her translations into English of children's books in German, Dutch and the Scandanavian languages
1987
Liselotte Remané *(Germany: Democratic Republic)* for her translations into German of children's books in English and Russian
1990
Anthea Bell *(Great Britain)* for her translations into English of children's books in German, French, and Danish
Lyudmila Braude *(USSR)* for her translations into Russian of classic Scandanavian children's literature and of German fairy tales and legends
1993
Jo Tenfjord *(Norway)*, translator of Astrid Lindgren into Norwegian

Noma Concours for Children's Picture Book Illustrations ❧

Named after its founder, the distinguished Japanese publisher and recipient of the 1974 International Book Award, Shoichi Noma, this awards program is sponsored by the Asia/Pacific Cultural Centre for UNESCO (No. 6, Fukuromachi, Shinjuku-ku, Tokyo, 162, Japan). Organized biennially, the program gives prizes for excellent and original illustrations for picture books by artists in Asia, the Pacific, Africa, the Arab States, Latin America and the Caribbean. Entries include both published and unpublished works. Its purpose is to continue the improvement of the quality of children's book illustrations in developing countries. The listing below includes only the recipients of the Grand Prix. (Grand Prix: $3,000, a special medal and an invitation to the award ceremony in Tokyo; two second prizes: $1000 and a medal; ten runners up: $300 and a medal; twenty encouragement prizes: a medal)

1978
THE HERO CHAMPIONS by Ali-Akbar Sadeghi *(Iran)*
IF THE ANIMALS HAD COLORED FACES by Nikzad
Nojoumi *(Iran)*
1980
ANCIENT CHINESE FABLES by Zhang Shi-ming *(China)*
1982
A PLANE AND A VIOLA by Gian Calvi *(Brazil)*
1984
MR. FOX by Gavin Bishop *(New Zealand)*
1986
THE DINOSAUR OF THE DESERT by Kang Woo-hyung
(Republic of Korea)
1988
NAZHA CREATED TREMENDOUS UPROAR IN THE SEA
by Yu Dawu *(China)*
1990
ANIMALS HAVE MANY FACES by Enrique Martinez Blanco
(Cuba)
1992
THE UGLY DUCKLING by Park Sung-Woan *(Republic of
Korea)*
1994
HOW ANIMALS CHOOSE THEIR COLOURS by Seif Edeen
L'owta *(Sudan)*

Nordic Children's Book Prize ❧

This award is for outstanding achievement in children's literature
in Denmark, Finland, Iceland, Norway, and Sweden. It is an
activity of the Nordic School Librarians' Association (Nordisk
Skolebibliotekarforening, Rønnevej 7, DK 6880 Tarm,
Denmark). (Glass vase and certificate)

1985
Maria Gripe *(Sweden)* for AGNES CECILIA, HVEM ER DU?
(Agnes Cecilia, Who Are You?) and other books
1986
Tormod Haugen *(Norway)* for DAGEN, DER FORSVANDT
(The Lost Day) and VINTERSTEDET (The Winter Residence)
1987
Kaarina Helakisa *(Finland)* for LILLE JONAS (Little Jonas)
1988
Mette Newth *(Norway)* for BORTFØRELSEN (Forced Away)

1989
Svend Otto S. *(Denmark)* for STORMFLODEN (The Flood)
1990
Mats Wahl *(Sweden)* for MAJ DARLIN (May Darlin)
1991
Olavur Michelsen (author, *Faroe Islands*) and Erik Nielsen (ill.,
Denmark) for ROSSINI À SKORADALI (The Horse from Skoradali)
1992
Gudrún Halgadóttir *(Iceland)* for UNDAN ILLGRESINU
(Hidden from the Daylight)
1993
Bjarne Reuter *(Denmark)* for his authorship
1994
Torill Thorstad Hauger *(Norway)* for her authorship
1995
Torun Lian *(Norway)* for BARE SKYER BEVEGER
STJERNERNE and Viveca Lärn Sundvall *(Sweden)* for
EDDIEBO/GERNE (The books about Eddie)

UNESCO *Prize for Children's and Young People's Literature in the Service of Tolerance* 🦢

On the occasion of the United Nations Year for Tolerance
(1995), the United Nations Educational, Scientific and Cultural
Organization (UNESCO, Book and Copyright Division, Attn:
Ms. Maha Bulos, 1, rue Miollis, 75732 Paris Cedex 15, France)
established this prize with the sponsorship of Santamería/
Ediciones S.M. of Spain. It will recognize works for children and
young people that best embody the concepts and ideals of
tolerance and peace and promote mutual understanding based on
respect for other peoples and cultures. To be awarded biennially
beginning in 1997, entries must be published during the two-year
period preceding the closing date for nominations (April 30, 1996
for the first prize). Novels, short stories, picture books, comics,
and works of nonfiction may be submitted by publishers in two
categories: books for children up to age 12, and books for young
people aged 13 to 18 (one work per category). Submissions
written in languages other than Arabic, Chinese, English, French,
Russian, or Spanish should be accompanied by a summary in
English or French. Winners will be chosen by UNESCO's Director-
General on the recommendation of an international jury. An
awards ceremony will be held every two years at the Bologna
Children's Book Fair. ($8,000 in each category)

UNICEF-Ezra Jack Keats International Award for Excellence in Children's Book Illustration ❧

This biennial awards program was designed to encourage illustrators new to children's books (no more than five published books). It is funded by the Ezra Jack Keats Foundation, and named in honor of Mr. Keats (1916-1983), the well-known U. S. illustrator and Caldecott Medal recipient who was also a contributing artist to the UNICEF greeting card program. This program is currently in abeyance for re-design. Administered by UNICEF (United Nations Children's Fund) Greeting Card Operation (Information: UNICEF House, 3 United Nations Plaza, New York, NY 10017, USA). ($5,000 and silver medal)

1986
Felipe Dávalos for LAS TORTUGAS DE MAR (Turtles of the Sea) *(Consejo Nacional de Fomento Educativo) and* UN ASALTO MAYUSCULO (A Capital Assault) *(Tomas Meyer Brom), Mexico*

1988
Barbara Reid for HAVE YOU SEEN BIRDS? by Joanne Oppenheim *(Scholastic-TAB), Canada*

1990
Jan Thornhill for THE WILDLIFE 1-2-3 *(Greey de Pencier), Canada*

1992
Arone Raymond Meeds for ENORA AND THE BLACK CRANE *(Ashton Scholastic), Australia*

1994
Takehide Harada for FRANCESCO *(Suemori Books), Japan)*

1996
No Award

PART V 🐦

Publications and Lists for Selecting U. S. Children's and Young Adult Books

NOTE: This section is a partial listing of the many publications and (usually) annual lists that evaluate books for young readers, recommending titles considered especially meritorious. Extensive examination of the books in these selection aids would be far more rewarding to a children's literature specialist than an examination of award-winning titles that — by definition — do not represent the variety and scope of books available for young readers.

AMERICAN BOOKSELLERS ASSOCIATION
(828 S. Broadway, Tarrytown, NY 10591)

The monthly magazine *American Bookseller* includes semi-annual "Pick of the Lists" of forthcoming children's books, titles booksellers predict will have a vigorous sales life in bookstores.

AMERICAN LIBRARY ASSOCIATION
(50 East Huron St., Chicago, IL 60611)

Booklist. Published twice a month, this periodical reviews children's and young adult books, and prints special-interest lists regularly. It stars especially noteworthy titles. Also runs "Editors' Choices" of the most outstanding books of the year annually.

The Association for Library Service to Children (ALSC) sponsors "Notable Children's Books," an annual list of children's books compiled by a national committee of librarians; available in pamphlet format.

The Young Adult Library Services Association (YALSA) publishes two important lists annually, "Best Books for Young Adults" and "Recommended Books for the Reluctant Young Reader," both available in pamphlet format.

Book Links. Published bimonthly, this journal is designed to help teachers make effective use of literature across the curriculum; includes articles and special-interest booklists.

THE BOOK REPORT
(Linworth Publishing, Inc., 480 East Wilson Bridge Rd., Suite L, Worthington, OH 43085-2372)

Regularly reviews children's and young adult books; emphasis is on curriculum uses, though not exclusively.

BULLETIN OF THE CENTER FOR CHILDREN'S BOOKS
(Children's Research Center, 51 Gerty Dr., Champaign, IL 61820)

This monthly (except for summer) book review publication was affiliated with the University of Chicago for many years, and is now published by the Graduate School of Library and Information Science, University of Illinois at Urbana-Champaign. It uses a symbols rating scheme—"R" for recommended through "NR" for not recommended—in addition to providing critical reviews; some of the "R" books are asterisked to indicate that titles are highly recommended; curriculum and developmental uses are indicated at the end of each review. The journal also includes interesting editorials from time to time—when there is something one of its editors feels is worth writing about.

CHILD STUDY ASSOCIATION
(Bank Street College of Education, 610 West 112th St., New York, NY 10025)

"Books of the Year" is a booklet listing a generous sampling of outstanding titles that reinforce the Child Study Children's Book Committee's conviction that good books deal honestly and courageously with the great and small problems of the world.

CHILDREN'S LITERATURE CENTER, LIBRARY OF CONGRESS
(Library of Congress, Washington, DC 20540)

"Children's Books of the Year" is an annual booklet listing recommended titles evaluated by a committee of Washington, D.C.-area children's literature specialists under the chairmanship of the Library's Children's Literature Specialist.

THE FIVE OWLS
(Hamline University Graduate School, Crossroads Center, MS-C 1924, 1536 Hewitt Ave., St. Paul, MN 55104)

An attractive newsletter-format publication with accessible articles, occasional booklists-in-depth, and reviews that are longer than most.

THE HORN BOOK MAGAZINE
(11 Beacon St., Boston, MA 02108)

This venerable publication is published six times a year; includes reviews of (mainly) recommended children's and young adult titles, and stars some of them; also publishes "Fanfare," a highly selective annual list of recommended books that appears in an issue of the magazine.

The Horn Book Guide is a semi-annual work that evaluates as many current books as possible, both those the reviewers like and do not like.

INTERNATIONAL READING ASSOCIATION (IRA)
(800 Barksdale Rd., P. O. Box 8139, Newark, DE 19714)

The journals Reading Teacher (elementary-middle school) and Journal of Reading (middle-high school, and advanced) review books in each school-year issue. "Children's Choices," a project of the IRA-CBC Joint Committee, is an annual listing of about 100 titles that 10,000 young readers on five teams across the country have voted their "best reads." It is published in October issues of Reading Teacher; reprints (s-3 oz.-s/a/e-6 x 9 min.) are available free from IRA, which sells the list in bulk as well.

"Young Adult Choices" and "Teachers Choices" first appear in IRA journals and are offered on the same terms as "Children's Choices."

KIRKUS REVIEWS
(200 Park Ave. So., New York, NY 10003)

This pre-publication review service uses "pointers" to single out children's and young adult titles of special merit.

NATIONAL COUNCIL OF TEACHERS OF ENGLISH (NCTE)
(1111 Kenyon Rd., Urbana, IL 61801)

The journals Language Arts (elementary-middle school) and English Journal (secondary) review books in each school-year issue.

NCTE'S publications program includes booklists for children's through young adult books, including "Adventuring with Books," "Your Reading," and "High Interest-Easy Reading for Junior and Senior High School Students."

NEW YORK PUBLIC LIBRARY
(455 Fifth Ave., New York, NY 10016)

Children's Books: 100 Titles for Reading and Sharing and *Books for the Teen Age* appear in booklet formats annually. They are listed here as they are well-established and prestigious; many fine library systems throughout the U. S. publish similar listings.

NEW YORK TIMES BOOK REVIEW
(229 West 43rd St., New York, NY 10036)

The "national newspaper of record" reviews children's books regularly, and also publishes special Spring and Fall children's book issues. In addition, it makes selective choices of outstanding children's books.

PARENTS' CHOICE
(P. O. Box 185, Newton, MA 02168)

Since its founding in 1978, this newspaper-format publication has served as a consumer guide for parents who wish to expose children to high-quality materials. It has grown to include books, videos, toys, audiotapes, computer software, television programs, magazines, and popular music. Each year a special awards issue honors "the best of the best" in these categories and the Parents' Choice seal on a product has become a bellwether of quality children's media.

PUBLISHERS WEEKLY
(249 West 17th St., New York, NY 10011)

This magazine reviews forthcoming titles weekly. It also carries a "Children's Book Scene" feature weekly, and publishes an interesting "Children's Booksellers" list each month, based on reports from stores and other vendors.

SCHOOL LIBRARY JOURNAL
(249 West 17th St., New York, NY 10011)

Published monthly, this journal reviews nearly all new children's and young adult books, stars those of special merit, and also includes a "Best Books" feature (available in reprint format in bulk) each year in its December issue; the magazine also includes articles and news about the library world, not just school libraries as its name might suggest.

VOICE OF YOUTH ADVOCATES (VOYA)
(Scarecrow Press, Dept. VOYA,
4720 Boston Way, Lanham, MD 20706)

This publication reviews books intended for a young adult
readership; it uses a dual rating code in evaluating titles, one
relating to the quality of the writing and presentation, and the
second relating to the likely appeal of a book to adolescents.
VOYA also reviews other media and publishes articles, as well as
lively editorials. To rectify the absence of nonfiction on most
selected lists, VOYA will also publish a Nonfiction Honor List
for middle school or junior high school readers beginning in
1996. Nominations made by publishers must satisfy a personal
information or general curriculum need, have a format attractive
to the intended audience and appropriate for the subject matter,
and have a distinctive author voice.

Special-Interest Lists, Publications, Etc.

AMERICAN INSTITUTE OF GRAPHIC ARTS (AIGA)
(1059 Third Ave., New York, NY 10021)

Sponsors The Book Show annually, a big selection of titles—
including many children's books—chosen for excellence in design
and manufacturing. Criteria for inclusion have varied from year
to year. The annual *AIGA Graphic Design USA* (Watson-Guptil)
includes The Book Show.

APPRAISAL
(605 Commonwealth Ave., Boston, MA 02215)

Science books evaluated by subject specialists and librarians.

HUNGRY MIND REVIEW
(1648 Grand Ave., St. Paul, MN 55105)

This theme-based, quarterly book review magazine features book
reviews and essays by notable contemporary writers and has
sponsored the Children's Books of Distinction Awards since 1992
to honor books of lasting quality, with special appeal to readers
building a home library. Criteria for the awards require that the
books be compelling to children and adults, that they offer bold
and fresh perspectives, and that they be sensitive to issues of culture
and gender. Awards are given for fiction, nonfiction, and poetry.

KLIATT YOUNG ADULT PAPERBACK BOOK GUIDE
(425 Watertown St., Newton, MA 02158)

Major issues in winter, spring and fall, and five newsletter issues.

THE KOBRIN LETTER
(732 N. Greer Rd., Palo Alto, CA 94303)

Nonfiction for young readers.

"NOTABLE CHILDREN'S TRADE BOOKS IN THE FIELD OF SOCIAL STUDIES"
[Reprint available from CBC, 568 Broadway, Suite 404, New York, NY 10012 (Single copy: $2.00—please send #10 envelope with 3 oz. first class postage affixed. Contact CBC for multiple-copy rates.)

An annual listing sponsored by The National Council for the Social Studies (NCSS)- CBC Joint Committee that first appears in NCSS's journal *Social Studies*.

"OUTSTANDING SCIENCE TRADE BOOKS FOR CHILDREN"
[Reprint available from CBC, 568 Broadway, Suite 404, New York, NY 10012 (Single copy: $2.00—please send #10 envelope with 2 oz. first class postage affixed. Contact CBC for multiple-copy rates.)

An annual listing sponsored by The National Science Teachers Association (NSTA)-CBC Joint Committee that first appears in NSTA's journal *Science and Children*.

Academic Journals Reviewing Children's Books

CHILDREN'S LITERATURE
(University of Connecticut, Dept. of English, U-25, 337 Mansfield Rd., Room 442, Storrs, CT 06269-1025)

THE LION AND THE UNICORN
(The Johns Hopkins University Press, Journals Division, 701 West 40th St., Suite 275, Baltimore, MD 21211)

THE NEW ADVOCATE
(Christopher-Gordon Publishers, Inc., 480 Washington St., Norwood, MA 02062)

Title Index 🌿

Person Index ❧

Please note that our Person Index does not include authors who were not a party to the creation of the particular edition of a book that has been cited for honors in this volume. Thus, while their names appear in the awards listings themselves, Andersen, the Brothers Grimm, Charles Perrault, and others are not included in this index.